Aspects of Teaching Secondary Geography

The Open University *Flexible*
Postgraduate Certificate of Education

The readers and the companion volumes in the *flexible* PGCE series are:

Aspects of Teaching and Learning in Secondary Schools: Perspectives on practice

Teaching, Learning and the Curriculum in Secondary Schools: A reader

Aspects of Teaching Secondary Mathematics: Perspectives on practice

Teaching Mathematics in Secondary Schools: A reader

Aspects of Teaching Secondary Science: Perspectives on practice

Teaching Science in Secondary Schools: A reader

Aspects of Teaching Secondary Modern Foreign Languages: Perspectives on practice

Teaching Modern Foreign Languages in Secondary Schools: A reader

Aspects of Teaching Secondary Geography: Perspectives on practice

Teaching Geography in Secondary Schools: A reader

Aspects of Teaching Secondary Design and Technology: Perspectives on practice

Teaching Design and Technology in Secondary Schools: A reader

Aspects of Teaching Secondary Music: Perspectives on practice

Teaching Music in Secondary Schools: A reader

All of these subjects are part of the Open University's initial teacher education course, the *flexible* PGCE, and constitute part of an integrated course designed to develop critical understanding. The set books, reflecting a wide range of perspectives, and discussing the complex issues that surround teaching and learning in the twenty-first century, will appeal to both beginning and experienced teachers, to mentors, tutors, advisers and other teacher educators.

If you would like to receive a *flexible* PGCE prospectus please write to the Course Reservations Centre at The Call Centre, The Open University, Milton Keynes MK7 6ZS. Other information about programmes of professional development in education is available from the same address.

Aspects of Teaching Secondary Geography

Perspectives on practice

Edited by Maggie Smith

The Open University

London and New York

First published 2002
by RoutledgeFalmer
11 New Fetter Lane, London EC4P 4EE

Simultaneously published in the USA and Canada
by RoutledgeFalmer
29 West 35th Street, New York, NY 10001

RoutledgeFalmer is an imprint of the Taylor & Francis Group

Typeset in Bembo by Bookcraft Ltd, Stroud, Gloucestershire
Printed and bound in Great Britain by Bell & Bain Ltd, Glasgow

British Library Cataloguing in Publication Data
A catalogue record for this book is available from the British Library

Library of Congress Cataloging in Publication Data
A catalog record has been requested

ISBN 0–415–26086–8

Contents

SECTION 3 Geography for the twenty-first century

SECTION 4 Research geography and professional development

Figures

Tables

Abbreviations

AT	Attainment Target
AVCE	Advanced Vocational Certificate of Education
CASE	Cognitive Acceleration in Science Education
CoRT	Cognitive Research Trust
DEC	Development Education Centre
DES	Department of Education and Science
DfEE	Department for Education and Employment
EDC	Economically Developing Country
EP	Exceptional Performance
GA	Geographical Association
GCSE	General Certificate of Secondary Education
GIS	Geographical Information Systems
GNC	Geography National Curriculum
GNP	Gross National Product
GYSL	Geography for the Young School Leaver
HMI	Her Majesty's Inspector(ate)
ICT	Information and Communication Technology
IT	Information Technology
KS	Key Stage
LEA	Local Education Authority
PGCE	Postgraduate Certificate of Education
PoS	Programme of Study
QCA	Qualifications and Curriculum Authority
ROSLA	Raising of the school leaving age
SATs	Standard Assessment Tasks
SCAA	School Curriculum and Assessment Authority
SOA	Statement of Attainment
SPaG	Spelling, punctuation and grammar
TGAT	Task Group on Attainment and Testing
TTG	Thinking Through Geography
VGCSE	Vocational GCSE

Note
In the chapters which have previously been published elsewhere an ellipsis denotes omitted material, while an ellipsis in square brackets […] indicates that a paragraph or more has been omitted.

Sources

Where a chapter in this book is based on or is a reprint or revision of material previously published elsewhere, details are given below, with grateful acknowledgements to the original publishers.

Chapter 5 This is based upon Marsden, B. 'Continuity after the National Curriculum' originally published in *Teaching Geography* 22(2), The Geographical Association, Sheffield (1997); and Jones, B. 'Continuity in the Key Stage 2–3 geography curriculum' originally published in *Teaching Geography* 24(1), The Geographical Association, Sheffield (1999).

Chapter 7 This is an edited version of Chapter 3.2 in Boardman, D. (ed.) (1986) *Handbook for Geography Teachers*, The Geographical Association, Sheffield.

Chapter 8 This chapter was originally published in Tilbury, D. and Williams, M. (eds) (1997) *Teaching and Learning Geography*, Routledge, London.

Chapter 9 This is based on Tilbury, D. and Williams, M. (eds) (1997) *Teaching and Learning Geography*, Routledge, London.

Chapter 11 This is based upon Norton, A. 'Differentiation in practice' originally published in *Teaching Geography* 24(3), The Geographical Association, Sheffield (1999); and Kitchin, R. 'Investigating disability and inclusive landscapes' originally published in *Teaching Geography* 26(2), The Geographical Association, Sheffield (2001).

Chapter 12 This is based upon Howes, N. and Hopkin, J. 'Improving formative assessment in geography' originally published in *Teaching Geography* 25(3), The Geographical Association, Sheffield (2000); Leat, D. and McGrane, J. 'Diagnostic and formative assessment of students' thinking' originally published in *Teaching Geography* 25(1), The Geographical Association, Sheffield (2000); and Balderstone, D. and Lambert, D. 'Sunday evening at the kitchen table' originally published in *Teaching Geography* 24(2), The Geographical Association, Sheffield (1999).

Chapter 13 This is an edited version of a chapter originally published in Bailey, P. and Fox, P. (eds) (1996) *Geography Teachers' Handbook*, The Geographical Association, Sheffield.

Chapter 14 This is an edited version of a chapter originally published in Bailey, P. and Fox, P. (eds) (1996) *Geography Teachers' Handbook*, The Geographical Association, Sheffield.

Chapter 15 This is based upon Martin, F. 'Using ICT to raise achievement' originally published in *Teaching Geography* 26(3), The Geographical Association, Sheffield (2001); Williams, A. 'Teaching and learning with geographical information systems' originally published in *Teaching Geography* 25(1), The Geographical Association Sheffield (2000); and Taylor, L. (2001) 'Using presentation packages for collaborative work' originally published in *Teaching Geography* 26(1), The Geographical Association, Sheffield.

Chapter 18 This is based on a chapter originally published in Fisher, C. and Binns, T. (eds) (2000) *Issues in Teaching Geography*, Routledge, London.

Chapter 19 This was originally published as Hicks, D. 'Envisioning a better world' in *Teaching Geography* 26(2), The Geographical Association, Sheffield (2001).

Chapter 20 This was originally published as Thompson, L. 'Young people's geovisions' in *Teaching Geography* 25(2), The Geographical Association, Sheffield (2000).

Chapter 21 This is an edited version of Kent, A. Guest Editorial originally published in *International Research in Geographical and Environmental Education* 8(2), Multilingual Matters, Clevedon (1999).

Chapter 23 This chapter was originally published in Kent, A. (ed.) (2000) *Reflective Practice in Geography Teaching*, Paul Chapman Publishing, London.

Chapter 24 This is an edited version of Holloway, S. and Valentine, G. 'Corked hats and Coronation Street' originally published in *Childhood* 7(3), Sage, London (2000).

Chapter 25 This is an edited version of Wridt, P. 'The worlds of girls and boys: Geographic experience and informal learning opportunities' originally published in *Journal of Geography* 98(6), National Council for Geographic Education, Indiana (1999).

Chapter 26 This chapter was originally published in Williams, M. (ed.) (1996) *Understanding Geography and Environmental Education*, Cassell, London.

Acknowledgements

Many people contributed to the production of this book and grateful thanks are extended to all of them. The comments of the advisory group at the Open University were particularly valuable, especially the advice of Mark Thomas, Lliswerry School, Newport, and Gill Davidson, Oxford Brookes University. John Morgan, University of Bristol and also a member of the advisory group, provided much of the inspiration for Section 4. The authors of the commissioned chapters coped magnificently with deadlines and word limits; and many other colleagues in geography education and on the PGCE course team at the Open University provided advice and support that was most welcome.

Foreword

The nature and form of initial teacher education and training are issues that lie at the heart of the teaching profession. They are inextricably linked to the standing and identity that society attributes to teachers and are seen as being one of the main planks in the push to raise standards in schools and to improve the quality of education in them. The initial teacher education curriculum therefore requires careful definition. How can it best contribute to the development of the range of skills, knowledge and understanding that makes up the complex, multi-faceted, multi-skilled and people-centred process of teaching?

There are, of course, external, government-defined requirements for initial teacher training courses. These specify, amongst other things, the length of time a student spends in school, the subject knowledge requirements beginning teachers are expected to demonstrate or the ICT skills that are needed. These requirements, however, do not in themselves constitute the initial training curriculum. They are only one of the many, if sometimes competing, components that make up the broad spectrum of a teacher's professional knowledge that underpin initial teacher education courses.

Certainly today's teachers need to be highly skilled in literacy, numeracy and ICT, in classroom methods and management. In addition, however, they also need to be well grounded in the critical dialogue of teaching. They need to be encouraged to be creative and innovative and to appreciate that teaching is a complex and problematic activity. This is a view of teaching that is shared with partner schools within the Open University Training Schools Network. As such it has informed the planning and development of the Open University's initial teacher training programme and the *flexible* PGCE.

All of the *flexible* PGCE courses have a series of connected and complementary readers. The *Teaching in Secondary Schools* series pulls together a range of new thinking about teaching and learning in particular subjects. Key debates and differing perspectives are presented, and evidence from research and practice is explored, inviting the reader to question the accepted orthodoxy, suggesting ways of enriching the present curriculum and offering new thoughts on classroom learning. These readers are accompanied by the series *Perspectives on practice*. Here, the focus is on the application of these developments to educational/subject policy and the classroom, and on the illustration of teaching skills, knowledge and understanding in a variety of school contexts. Both series include newly commissioned work.

This series from RoutledgeFalmer, in supporting the Open University's *flexible* PGCE, also includes two key texts that explore the wider educational background.

These companion publications, *Teaching and Learning and the Curriculum in Secondary Schools* and *Aspects of Teaching and Learning in Secondary Schools: Perspectives on practice,* explore a contemporary view of developments in secondary education with the aim of providing analysis and insights for those participating in initial teacher training education courses.

Hilary Bourdillon – Director ITT Strategy
Steven Hutchinson – Director ITT Secondary
The Open University
September 2001

Preface

This book, together with the other geography text and two generic texts, provide in-depth discussion to the subject matter covered in the online modules which are the 'teaching blocks' of the Open University *flexible* PGCE course. The emphasis in this book is excellent practice in teaching Geography and it will be an invaluable guide to students during blocks of practical teaching whether they are working with the OU course or another Geography PGCE.

Readings have been selected from a wide range of articles and books, and some have been specially commissioned. In selecting work from the UK's leading geography educators the editor has brought together a unique and useful collection of work which will inform, support and challenge its readers.

Sheila King
Director of Training Partnerships and
Lecturer in Geography Education
Institute of Education, University of London

Introduction

The aim of this book is to provide both practical support and inspiration for trainee teachers as they undertake their various periods of school experience as part of an initial teacher training course. In particular the book is designed to complement its companion, *Teaching Geography in Secondary Schools: A reader*, by providing classroom illustrations of the issues that face geography teachers today. Together with *Teaching Geography in Secondary Schools: A reader*, it provides expanded discussion linked to the subject matter covered in the Open University's *flexible* PGCE course material for initial teacher training in secondary level Geography. It is hoped, however, that more experienced teachers too may find some ideas here that challenge their thinking and encourage them to reflect on the ways in which they plan for the teaching of Geography in schools and colleges.

There is an extensive collection of excellent material already in print to support the teaching of the subject and this book draws widely (and gratefully) from that pool. The material that has been selected for inclusion in the book is varied – it provides questions to think about, it shares good practice, it offers guidelines and it suggests areas of geography education that need further developing. In addition the book also draws on the experience of practising geography teachers, examiners, geography consultants and other geography experts who have written material specially for this publication and bring to it their insights and wisdom.

The book is divided into four sections which mirror those of its companion reader. The first, Geography in the school curriculum, sets out the formal curriculum context within which trainee teachers will find themselves working. It explores the National Curriculum for Geography at Key Stage 3, and the main options for Geography post-14 including GCSE, AS, A2 and the vocational pathways.

Section 2, Geography in (and out of) the classroom, is the largest section and could easily have filled a volume in its own right. Tight word limits meant that difficult choices had to be made; the material included supplements or expands on the particular aspects of the course materials and the set books, and is a mixture of both new ideas and established ideas that have been tried and tested over the years.

The final two sections look towards the future. Section 3 focuses on Geography for the twenty-first century with discussions of themes that are relevant to the immediate future, such as citizenship, and the image of Geography. Section 4 looks at research into geography teaching and at professional development for geography teachers. It aims to give a flavour of some of the research that is currently underway and to encourage geography teachers to participate in pushing forward the frontiers of geography education.

1 Geography in the school curriculum

This section explores the complexities of the frameworks within which geography teachers work in the school or college setting. The four authors look at the constraints and opportunities provided by Geography as set out currently in the National Curriculum at Key Stage 3, at GCSE, in the new specifications for AS and A2, and in the vocational pathway. The background to each of these developments is explained so that each can be set in context – as one author stated, it is important to understand the past history of curriculum developments in order to appreciate fully the impacts that the past has had on the current state and status of Geography in the 11–18 sector of education. The authors in this section are all experienced teachers who, from being 'at the chalk face', are familiar with the practicalities of implementing the curriculum requirements at a period of time in which the goalposts are frequently changing.

1 Working with the National Curriculum

Mark Jones

Key Stage 3 (KS3) is an important period in the development of young geographers. It builds on their varied experience at primary school and encourages a broader and more in-depth understanding of the subject. For some pupils who choose not to continue with Geography at GCSE, KS3 may provide their last formal geographical experience. It is important for trainee teachers to understand the impact that the Geography National Curriculum (GNC) had at KS3 and how the GNC has evolved since its introduction in 1991.

Pre-National Curriculum teaching of Geography in secondary schools (pre-1991)

Prior to the Education Reform Act 1988 there was no requirement to follow a nationally agreed syllabus at KS3. Geography departments were free to decide on content, method of delivery and the nature of assessment that fitted their localities and needs. Much of the innovative curriculum development of the 1970s and 1980s had led departments to develop a humanities course at KS3. This topic-, theme- or issues-based style of delivery involved elements of History, Geography and Religious Studies either being taught together or as separate units. A variety of approaches existed, with teachers of Geography delivering a range of subjects at KS3. Figure 1.1 shows Humanities being delivered in Years 7 and 8, with core Geography, History and Religious Education courses taught in Year 9 by subject specialists. Ofsted reported that such an approach was the case in a quarter of the schools it visited in 1991 to 1992 (Ofsted 1993). This allowed for greater flexibility but often led to Geography being taught by non-specialists and a danger that instead of it being a discrete subject it would be lost within broader-based humanities teaching.

In the 1980s geographers had to defend their subject as the Department of Education and Science (DES) suggested a more peripheral role for the subject in the curriculum (DES 1980). The Geographical Association was proactive in leading the campaign to keep Geography firmly on the school curriculum agenda. Having invited the then Education Secretary, Sir Keith Joseph, to address the Association, they published 'A Case for Geography' (1987), which promoted the essential skills, attitudes and values that Geography contributes to the curriculum. This emphasized the importance for Geography at a time when the government was reviewing the school curriculum as part of education reform. Continuing discussion then revolved around the final content and assessment of Geography, and by 1991 the place of Geography had been secured in the National Curriculum.

	First (11–12yrs)	Second (12–13yrs)	Third (13–14yrs)
Autumn	Where we live Past and present	Beliefs Farming	What is geography?
Spring	Story of the earth The solar system	Trade Colonization	Earth processes
Summer	Early people Hunter-gatherers to farmers	Industry Power and politics	Rich world Poor world

Figure 1.1 *Example of a geography department KS3 curriculum plan (1980s)*

First version (1991–5)

The Education Reform Act 1988 required that all state schools in England and Wales were to provide a broad and balanced curriculum for pupils aged 5–16. This new National Curriculum introduced a framework for the teaching of three core and seven foundation subjects.

The individual subject documents contained the Attainment Targets, Programmes of Study and assessment arrangements for the four Key Stages. This first version of the National Curriculum for Geography (DES 1991) consisted of five Attainment Targets, made up of 17 strands (Figure 1.2). Within each Attainment Target (AT) were the Statements of Attainment (SOAs), 183 in total. The SOAs represented the knowledge, skills and understanding that pupils were expected to have acquired by the end of each Key Stage. Pupils were to be assessed against these SOAs through ongoing teacher assessment and externally marked tests – Standard Assessment Tasks or SATs. The expected range of levels of attainment within the ten-level scale that pupils should be working within were specified as follows:

- Key Stage 1: levels 1–3
- Key Stage 2: levels 2–5
- Key Stage 3: levels 3–7
- Key Stage 4: levels 4–10

The separate Programme of Study (PoS; see Figure 1.3) represented the matters, skills and processes which had to be taught during the different Key Stages. The arrival of this document in school had a number of positive impacts. Geography clearly had to be taught to all pupils aged 5 to 16; this was particularly important in terms of its status in primary schools. The content also encouraged a balance between skills, the study of place, environmental issues and human and physical geography. In response departments reviewed their existing KS3 courses. At this time the key issues faced in geography departments were:

1   Content changes – what topics to lose, adapt or add to existing schemes of work?
2   Teaching and learning styles – what impact would the GNC have on the way Geography was taught?

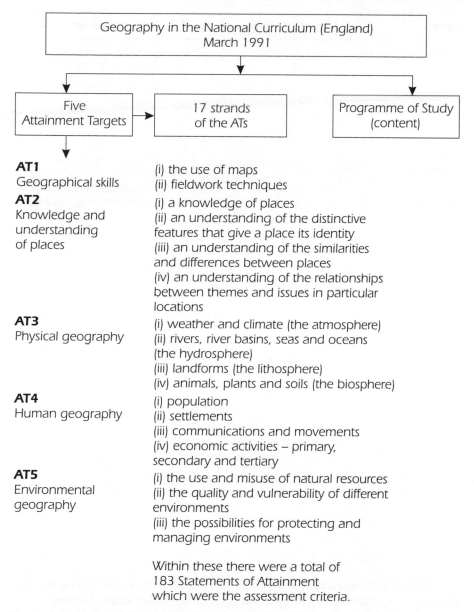

Geography in the National Curriculum (England)
March 1991

Five
Attainment Targets

17 strands
of the ATs

Programme of Study
(content)

AT1
Geographical skills

(i) the use of maps
(ii) fieldwork techniques

AT2
Knowledge and
understanding
of places

(i) a knowledge of places
(ii) an understanding of the distinctive
features that give a place its identity
(iii) an understanding of the similarities
and differences between places
(iv) an understanding of the relationships
between themes and issues in particular
locations

AT3
Physical geography

(i) weather and climate (the atmosphere)
(ii) rivers, river basins, seas and oceans
(the hydrosphere)
(iii) landforms (the lithosphere)
(iv) animals, plants and soils (the biosphere)

AT4
Human geography

(i) population
(ii) settlements
(iii) communications and movements
(iv) economic activities – primary,
secondary and tertiary

AT5
Environmental
geography

(i) the use and misuse of natural resources
(ii) the quality and vulnerability of different
environments
(iii) the possibilities for protecting and
managing environments

Within these there were a total of
183 Statements of Attainment
which were the assessment criteria.

Figure 1.2 National Curriculum for Geography 1991

3   Assessment strategies – how was assessment of the 183 SOAs to be achieved?
What methods would be used? How much and when?
4   Recording and reporting – how was student progress to be monitored and
the teacher assessment recorded and reported?

One outcome of this self-review was that some departments decided, in order to
deliver the History and Geography National Curriculums, that these should be
taught separately (see Figure 1.4). While some opted out of the humanities approach,

1991	1995 (England)	2000 (England)
Geographical skills	1 Enquiry Skills	Knowledge, skills and understanding
1 Enquiry		Geographical enquiry and skills
2 Measure, select information, identify/describe patterns	2 Identify questions, collect, record, present, analyse and evaluate evidence	1 Enquiry (a–f)
3 Maps, photographs, cross-sections, field sketches	3 Vocabulary, fieldwork, maps (D to F), globes, atlases, photographs and IT	2 Skills (a–g) vocabulary, fieldwork, atlases, maps, photographs, ICT, decision-making
4 Working towards L7 skills		
Places and themes	Places	Knowledge and understanding of places
5 Rationale	4 Two countries other than UK from specified lists	3 Places (a–e)
6 Identify points of reference on six maps	5 Aspects to teach on each country	Knowledge and understanding of patterns and processes
7 Seven place studies	Thematic studies (9)	
8 Local area & home region	6 Rationale for study	4 Physical and human features (a–b)
9 Working towards L7 home region	7 Tectonic processes (volcanoes or earthquakes)	Knowledge and understanding of environmental change and sustainable development
10 EU country	8 Geomorphological processes (coasts or rivers)	
11 Working towards L7 – EU theme	9 Weather and climate	
12 Economically Developing Country (EDC)	10 Ecosystems	5 Environmental issues (a–b)
13 Working towards L7 EDC	11 Population	Breadth of study
14 USA, Japan & USSR	12 Settlement	6 (a) Countries
15 Working towards L7	13 Economic activities	Themes
16 International trade	14 Development	(b) Tectonic processes
Physical geography	15 Environmental issues (energy or fresh water provision)	(c) Geomorphological processes
17 Topics of study		(d) Weather & climate
18 Working towards L7		(e) Ecosystems
Human geography		(f) Population
19 Topics of study		(g) Settlements
20 Working towards L7		(h) Economic activity
Environmental geography		(i) Development
21 Topics of study		(j) Environmental issues
22 Working towards L7		(k) Resource issues
		7 In study of above (a–d)

Figure 1.3 Comparison of the Programmes of Study for Geography

others continued with it. In making these decisions, departments were working with a document that was content-heavy and it soon became clear that to cover all the PoS in detail was simply not possible (the recommendation was for between 7.5 and 10 per cent of curriculum time). Successful units of work that had been developed before the National Curriculum now had to be omitted or justified in relation to the

	Year 7 (11–12yrs)	Year 8 (12–13yrs)	Year 9 (13–14yrs)
Autumn	Map skills	Earth processes	Development (Brazil/Kenya)
Spring	The home region Transport and communications	Europe (France/Germany)	Weather and water
Summer	Environment	Economic activities	Superpowers (USA, Japan, USSR)

Figure 1.4 Example of a geography department curriculum plan (1991–5)

PoS. This was a period of trying to avoid overloading pupils with content whilst still developing their skills, understanding, values and attitudes. The latter was a particular strength of the previous 'humanities-style' curriculum.

Restructuring of the curriculum plan and the more detailed planning of schemes of work (see Figure 1.5) brought productive discussion about the subject at KS3 but increased the workload of teachers in terms of curriculum review and development. Updated schemes of work, primarily a teacher resource, were also available to outside visitors – particularly LEA advisors, HMIs and Ofsted inspectors – as one source of evidence that the statutory requirements of the National Curriculum were being met.

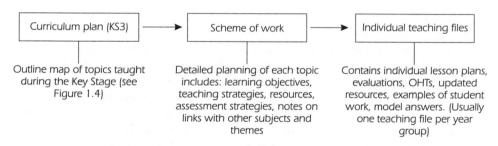

Figure 1.5 Levels of department and teacher planning

While curriculum plans had been drawn up by schools there was little detailed planning beyond Year 7 as departments devised new schemes of work and sequences of lessons. Variation between schools in terms of extra funding meant that some departments faced resources problems, reverting to a reliance on the in-house production of worksheets. Where funding allowed, key texts were purchased and became the basis for the three-year course. One series in particular tended to dominate the market in those early stages of the GNC.

There were issues with the content. Problems encountered included how the Programme of Study and the Statements of Attainment fitted together, as there seemed to be overlap:

Example

PoS: To investigate and compare the colour, texture and organic content of different types of soil (DES 1991:45)

AT3 Statement of Attainment level 4e: Compare characteristics of different types of soil

---

This was a level 4 statement but there were no other levelled statements relating to this aspect of the curriculum, apart from one relating to a different aspect of pedology.

AT3 level 4e: Compare characteristics of different types of soil

AT3 level 7d: Explain the causes and effects of soil erosion, and explain why some places are especially vulnerable

---

So once they had written an enquiry comparing soils around the school site – how did one assess a mixed-ability class of 30 Year 9 students? Clearly there would be a wide range of abilities and variation in the projects produced. This became frustrating for teachers as it became clear that the assessment aspect of the geography order was in need of urgent revision.

There was a danger that departments would become assessment led. With the prospect of Standard Assessment Tasks (SATs) in the summer of 1994, there was a concern that teachers would succumb to teaching to these tests, as schools and departments would be judged on their results – i.e. the number of students achieving the nationally expected standards by the end of Key Stage 3. Geography departments were left to work with a content-heavy curriculum that had a confusing and disjointed assessment element. The 183 Statements of Attainment meant that some departments developed tick-box recording systems to show individual pupil achievement against every Statement of Attainment. The School Curriculum and Assessment Authority (SCAA) emphasized that there was no requirement for such elaborate tick-lists as a basis for assessment. The curriculum was becoming assessment-driven. Assessment was a problem because some of the strands in the Attainment Targets lacked clear progression (SCAA 1993). Missing levelled Statements of Attainment made the notion of progression difficult. Here is an example.

Taking the theme of earth processes from the Programme of Study levels 3–7 (DES 1991: 44):

---

17   Pupils should be taught:

The nature and effects of earthquakes and volcanic eruptions, and how the latter produce craters, cones and lava flows; and to investigate the global distribution of earthquakes and volcanoes and how this relates to the boundaries of the crustal plates.

Level	Statement
3	
4	4d Describe how some earth movements are violent, and explain, in simple terms, how volcanic craters, cones and lava flows are formed
5	5e Relate the distribution of earthquakes and volcanoes to the boundaries of the plates in the earth's crust
6	6g Describe some of the physical processes which can give rise to one type of natural hazard and how people respond to that hazard
7	

Figure 1.6 AT3 – The levelled statements that relate to physical geography

Departments planned their delivery of the unit incorporating an end-of-unit test or activity that could then be assessed against the assessment criteria – the Statements of Attainment (see Figure 1.6). In this example pupils could achieve levels 4 to 6 only and these were content-tied. There were no SOAs relating to this topic at other levels. In a mixed-ability class there will be a wide variation in the quality of responses. Departments were faced with the challenge of how to show attainment of pupils who did not achieve level 4 but had demonstrated a basic understanding of volcanoes and their formation. Similarly, what of the more able pupils who were able to explain volcanic eruptions at a higher level of response? How were they to be credited?

Useful comment at the time on what teacher assessment is for came from Daugherty (1992: 115). There was a concern that some departments would go down the summative assessment route and neglect the formative aspects that helped to guide students' learning.

Lambert and Daugherty (1993: 113–15) researched teachers' reactions to the GNC at the time. Positive aspects were that it gave departments clear areas to be studied which could then be incorporated into an individual school's schemes of work. However, there were many concerns at this time:

- It was a content-heavy curriculum – too much in too little time
- There were too many Statements of Attainment
- There was no clear distinction between the Attainment Targets and the Programme of Study
- Issues of how to apply the ten-level scale of assessment needed to be addressed
- The need for reporting attainment led to more formal methods of assessment – more testing
- Many departments devised bureaucratic strategies of administrating and monitoring assessment – tick boxes, individual student portfolios, complex databases
- Stimulating topics not strictly covered in the National Curriculum became marginalized and disappeared from some schemes of work altogether

During this first version there was still the prospect of SATs for Geography. It was intended that Year 9 students would sit two one-hour tests in the summer of 1994. Although piloted, these never found their way into schools and the assessment of Geography remained based on Teacher Assessment (TA) alone.

To support teachers, excellent materials were produced by the Geographical Association (see *Assessment Matters* (Balderstone and Lambert 1992), for example). The fact that it was not necessary to keep records relating to individual pupils' achievement at the SOA level was emphasized. More importantly the Task Group on Assessment and Testing (TGAT) report (1988) had emphasized assessment in its broadest terms, that the purpose of assessment was formative as well as summative, the former being in danger of neglect in the climate of curriculum change at this time.

In terms of evidence-keeping, recording and reporting there was huge variation between schools. The minimalist approach was adopted by some while others developed individual student portfolios of evidence. These contained a variety of assessed material including tests, investigations, homework and IT projects and were added to each year, ready for the awarding of the TA at the end of the Key Stage. However, the reporting of TA was put on hold. The 1991 version will at best be remembered by practising teachers for its overloaded content and unworkable assessment. An overhaul of the order was essential. Even with such a review, the impact of the 1991 order would have lasting consequences for geography departments because of the large amount of time, resourcing and developmental work that had been necessary.

First review 1995

Concerns expressed over the 1991 order had already set in motion discussion regarding a review. During 1993 Sir Ron Dearing, at the request of the Secretary for State for Education, reviewed the National Curriculum as a whole. The Dearing Review 1993–5 brought about changes to the content of the curriculum but also to the status of Geography: it became an optional subject at KS4.

> History and geography are absorbing and valuable subjects. But I cannot see a reason, either nationally or in terms of the individual student, why these subjects should, as a matter of law, be given priority in this Key Stage over others, such as the creative arts, a second foreign language, home economics, the classics, religious studies, business studies or economics. I recommend therefore, that they be optional in Key Stage 4.
>
> (Dearing 1993: 46)

While this decision freed up the curriculum at KS4 for other subjects, it meant that Year 9 became an option battlezone in many schools, with subjects vying for adequate numbers for multiple GCSE groups. Where schools offered a range of GNVQ courses, the choice post-14 for pupils was increased and Geography had to be promoted strongly by departments. He also suggested that SCAA develop tests in Geography and other non-core subjects after 1996, with SATs limited to the three core subjects only. The outcome of the Dearing Review meant that the new orders (DFE 1995) arrived in schools in January 1995 for implementation from the following September. This short timescale further increased the workload of geog-

	Year 7 (11–12yrs)	Year 8 (12–13yrs)	Year 9 (13–14yrs)
Autumn	Map skills including home region	Earth processes	Development
Spring	Settlements and transport	Europe – Italian tourism	Brazil
Summer	Environment issues	Economic activity	Weather and water

Figure 1.7 Example of a geography department curriculum plan (1995–9)

raphy teams in schools. It should be remembered that throughout these changes there were also fundamental changes occurring at KS4 and post-16, which also required planning, developmental work, Inset activity and meeting time. Also, it was felt that KS3 had had a greater proportion of curriculum development time compared to other Key Stages and there was a reluctance to give yet more, particularly based on the experiences of the first order and its imperfections.

The 1995 order saw a reduction in the amount of content that had to be covered. Also, the content was no longer tied to specific Statements of Attainment. This meant that there was more flexibility as to which topics came where in the overall KS3 curriculum plan, although many departments made minimal changes to their curriculum plans (Figure 1.7). Place studies were cut from seven to two (see Figure 1.8) and themes from eleven to nine (see Figure 1.3). Geography teams welcomed this reduction in content but faced decisions regarding units of work written for the previous order, such as the superpowers, transport and communications, and the home region. There were many excellent examples of enquiry-based lessons yet these topics could be dropped.

With regard to assessment, new level descriptions were introduced to replace the SOAs. There were now 8 level descriptions, levels 9 and 10 being replaced by an 'Exceptional Performance' criterion to differentiate those students achieving above level 8. These could be related to the now single Attainment Target called 'Geography'.

Although they represented a clear step forward from the original Statements of Attainment there were still concerns regarding their application (Marsden 1995: 178–80). With no SATs, Teacher Assessment was to be the only source of summative assessment information on pupils at KS3. During this period advice from SCAA was made available to schools via its exemplification material (SCAA 1996a). This very useful booklet helped teachers to explore standards and arrive at judgements regarding the overall 'level' of pupil work. Departments created portfolios which contained assessed pupil work from across the Key Stage with examples of each level. Such portfolios have been termed 'standards portfolios' by Lambert and Balderstone (2000: 348). They are a valuable tool in the moderation process, helping non-specialist, newly qualified and trainee teachers to become confident in 'levelling' pupil work. They should be added to as assessments are revised and new ones written.

The publication of non-statutory materials 'Optional tests and tasks' (SCAA 1996b) and the Welsh equivalent (ACAC 1997) proved of great value to teachers at this time in helping to further develop assessment material. Both SCAA and ACAC

1991   Number of place studies = seven

- local area
- home region
- a locality in an EDC
- a locality in an EU country
- an EU country
- an EDC
- USA, Japan & USSR

EU scale choice of one from: France, Germany, Italy or Spain

Economically Developing Country choice of one from: Bangladesh, Brazil, China, Egypt, Ghana, India, Kenya, Mexico, Nigeria, Pakistan, Peru or Venezuela

Maps A to F with specified points of reference that pupils had to be able to identify on globes or maps

1995   Number of place studies = two

Two countries other than those in the United Kingdom should be studied. One country should be selected from the areas in List A and one from those in List B

List A	List B
Australia & New Zealand	Africa
Europe	Asia (excluding Japan)
Japan	South and Central America (including the Caribbean)
North America	
Russian Federation	

Maps D to F emphasized at KS3 as before

2000   Two countries in significantly different states of economic development (PoS 6a)

'Pupils should be taught the location of places and environments studied … in the news and other significant places and environments. Examples of significant places and environments are included in the document and exemplar maps are available on the website (www.nc.uk.net)'

Greater flexibility for geography departments to choose the areas of study

Figure 1.8   Changing emphasis on the study of place in the National Curriculum (England)

emphasized that level descriptions are not designed to *level* individual pieces of work. The tests and tasks could help departments to show attainment that was indicative of certain levels. SCAA (1996a: 4) suggested that one way of exploring the level descriptions was to consider four aspects of performance. These were:

- Knowledge and understanding of places
- Knowledge and understanding of patterns and processes

- Knowledge and understanding of environmental relationships and issues
- Ability to undertake geographical enquiry and use skills.

It was suggested that broad lines of progression could be identified in each of these aspects from level 1 to Exceptional Performance (EP) and these were summarized in tabular form for ease of reference (SCAA 1996b: 6–13). In the same booklet, examples of pupil work were provided to exemplify broad bands of performance. These broad bands of levels were:

- Levels 1 to 3
- Levels 4 to 5
- Levels 6 to 8
- Exceptional Performance.

The SCAA booklet's second section demonstrated how the level descriptions could be used in making judgements about a pupil's work to arrive at the end of the Key Stage TA level. All of this activity on assessment was occurring as statutory teacher assessment in Geography at Key Stage 3 was due to be reported for the first time in the summer of 1997, three years later than originally planned. Dearing had emphasized that teachers were in the best position to provide professional judgements about which level best described the overall performance of a pupil, and that one could not expect an exact fit on all parts of the level description paragraph, hence the phrase 'best fit'. He also re-emphasized the fact that there was no statutory requirement to keep detailed records or evidence on every pupil (SCAA 1996b).

During 1997 schools reported levels for the first time and individual school data had to be submitted for all Year 9 pupils, showing the percentage of pupils achieving at the different levels in each subject. Figure 1.9 shows how a geography department's results could look. Level 5/6 is the expected attainment for the majority of pupils at the end of Key Stage 3. Advice is given annually regarding this process in the 'KS3 Assessment and Reporting Arrangements' booklet. This was a time when LEAs, some more successfully than others, were running Inset on TA and encouraging judgements to be shared between schools. There was limited moderation between schools, however, as the absence of funding meant that it relied on twilight meetings. Even within schools Inset time related to this issue had to be justified alongside other areas of curriculum development.

Schools were now becoming data-rich environments and, alongside the levels awarded, it was possible to show the 'value added': in other words, how much progress pupils had made in their three years. Departments that assessed the geographical knowledge and understanding through a 'baseline assessment' were able to be very specific. An assessment that had been developed through consultation with partner primary schools was particularly useful. Primary–secondary liaison at the subject level is very important, particularly with Year 6 teachers and the geography co-ordinator in the primary school.

Based on Key Stage 2 results, schools can produce individual pupil-indicative Key Stage 3 levels: the expected average level for a pupil at the end of Year 9. It is possible to monitor progress yearly and some departments produce an end-of-year level in Years 7 and 8. This requires in-built time for moderation so that consistency occurs

W	1	2	3	4	5	6	7	8	EP
0	0	2	9	21	33	29	5	1	0

These show approximately 68 per cent of pupils at or above the expected level.

Figure 1.9 Key Stage 3 National Curriculum results 1997 (percentage at each level)

between teachers and from year to year. Otherwise, inflated levels in Years 7 and 8 could make it appear that a pupil made no progress in Year 9 – where pupil progress is being linked to performance management and threshold applications this could have implications.

The 1995 order was seen as successful in terms of getting rid of the content-loaded Statements of Attainment, restructuring the PoS and introducing the new level descriptions. With support materials departments refined their assessment processes as geography teams became more confident in the awarding of levels. Classroom experience tended to revolve around key textbooks purchased after the 1991 order was introduced and in some departments there has been minimal change to the curriculum content as a result of the 1995 order.

Second review 2000

Following the five-year moratorium on curriculum changes laid down as part of the Dearing Review, the revised orders 'Curriculum 2000' (DfEE/QCA 1999) were produced in December 1999. Whereas previous English and Welsh orders had been very similar, the revised Welsh order, 'Cwricwlwm Cymru 2000' now had significant differences to the English order. In England Geography was now one of twelve statutory subjects to be studied at Key Stage 3 with Citizenship being introduced from September 2002. An important change was that a common structure and design had been agreed for all subjects in terms of the booklet and Programme of Study layout. For Geography, whereas the previous revision had concentrated on reducing content and reworking the Statements of Attainment the focus of the 2000 review was to reduce prescription and increase flexibility. This minimal change was welcomed by teachers, as was the new format, which includes a number of important and helpful sections. It has many positive aspects compared to the original order 1991 and the first review 1995 (see Figure 1.10).

Firstly, the layout is more informative with regard to the structure of the National Curriculum, the Programmes of Study, Attainment Targets and level descriptions, and assessing attainment at the end of a Key Stage. For trainee, newly qualified and non-specialist teachers having to deliver the GNC it provides a clear rationale, with aims set out at the start of each Key Stage (for Key Stage 3, see DfEE/QCA 1999: 22). The GA 'Geography in the curriculum position statement' (GA 2000) outlines the purpose of the subject and its distinctive and wider contribution to the curriculum, and now provides the Foreword to the Curriculum 2000 document. Specific mention is made early on that schemes of work should be planned around the Programme of Study, something that had always been the case but never stated. Teachers are already familiar with its terminology and structure, making it a more teacher-friendly document (see Figure 1.11).

Key Stage 3	1991 Order	1995 Review	Curriculum 2000
Attainment Targets (AT) These set out the expected standards of pupils' performance	Five Attainment Targets: • ATl Skills • AT2 Places • AT3 Physical • AT4 Human • AT5 Environmental 17 strands were identified	One AT called 'Geography' replaced the five previous ones, with emphasis on the integration of skills, places and themes within Geography	One AT called 'Geography' – which sets out the knowledge, understanding and skills that pupils should have by the end of Year 9 (at age 14)
Programme of Study (PoS) – general This sets out what pupils should be taught	Very prescriptive and content-heavy Programme of Study with separate emphasis on aspects to be taught for those pupils working towards level 7	15 aspects to be covered including skills, places, and thematic study (human, physical and environmental) Non-statutory examples were given as possible areas/topics to study	Four key aspects emphasized: 1/2 Enquiry and skills 3 Places 4 Patterns and processes 5 Environmental change and sustainable development
PoS – themes	11 of the 17 strands identified at start of Attainment Targets related to the areas to be studied: e.g. AT3 iii) landforms (the lithosphere)	Reduction from 11 to 9	Part of the breadth of study. Through the 10 themes pupils should be taught the knowledge, skills and understanding relating to the four aspects of geographical study
Teacher guidance	Circular No. 5/91 provided general guidance only	Foreword and common requirements – brief statements to access, use of language, IT, referencing and use of examples	Clearer layout and presentation. Statutory requirements supported by marginal notes providing help with planning (including ICT opportunities, cross-curricular links with core & ICT and technical advice). Detailed notes regarding 'Learning across the National Curriculum'

(continued on next page)

(cont.)

Key Stage 3	1991 Order	1995 Review	Curriculum 2000
Teaching and learning strategies	Little reference to the approaches that teachers should use except for the statement that 'an enquiry approach should be adopted for classroom activities' (DES 1991: 41)	PoS brief reference to enquiry approach (1b) and skills (2), the use of language and information technology	Detailed emphasis on enquiry approach – makes clearer links to skills and integrated with subject content Support from QCA schemes of work
Assessment	Within each Attainment Target there were Statements of Attainment (183 in total) against which pupils were to be assessed. These statements were arranged to show progression from level 1 through to level 10	Eight level descriptions of increasing difficulty with an additional level above L8 for 'exceptional performance (EP)' (DFE 1995: 18–20) – summative judgements made based on 'bestfits': a pupil's performance at end of the Key Stage	Eight level descriptions and EP. Reference to critical evaluation at levels 7 and above. Also explicit reference to sustainability and values and attitudes across levels
Recording for reporting	Teachers were 'expected to keep a record of pupils' progress in relation to each Attainment Target' (DES 1989: 6.9) Summer 1995 – first reported assessment	At the end of KS3 a level must be awarded for each student and this is reported to parents. The percentage of pupils at each level is sent off to the DFE each year	At the end of KS3 a level must be awarded for each student based on teacher assessment. This is reported to parents. The percentages of pupils achieving each level is sent off to the DFE each year

Figure 1.10 Comparison of the Geography Orders (England) 1991, 1995 and Curriculum 2000

The four aspects of Geography, suggested by SCAA (1996a: 4), are identified as the areas in which pupils make progress. These appear in the PoS and are developed through the study of places and themes, set out in the breadth of study (see Figure 1.3). With regard to content, it is the breadth of study (6 and 7) that clarifies what has to be studied, whereas the knowledge, skills and understanding (1 to 5) represent what pupils should develop and make progress in as they study the countries and themes outlined in the breadth of study. Certainly the freeing up of place study (see Figure 1.8) has allowed departments to widen the choice of country used for an in-depth study. However, a reliance on previously purchased texts and supporting

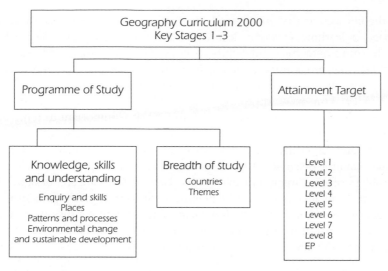

Figure 1.11 Curriculum 2000

video programmes means that certain countries continue to dominate the curriculum: France, Italy, Brazil, USA and Japan, for example. There was also greater flexibility in the themes: no longer just coasts or rivers.

Within the Programme of Study there are marginal notes to aid teacher planning.
These notes contain four types of non-statutory information:

- Key information to take into account when delivering a topic
- Definitions of terms used in the PoS
- ICT opportunities
- Links with other subjects.

They are useful and departments could add their own marginal notes to supplement
the examples given. Learning across the curriculum shows how Geography can
contribute to a range of areas including Personal, Moral, Social and Cultural development (PMSC), Citizenship, Key Skills, work-related learning, thinking skills and
sustainable development. These naturally occur in the planning of dynamic geography lessons and it is possible for departments simply to map where they occur in
their schemes of work rather than have to rewrite lessons to promote these aspects of
cross-curricular learning.

In terms of assessment there were minor changes to the level descriptions. Some
wording was altered so that they became clearer, and references throughout to environmental issues and sustainable development appear more prominently. How
these descriptions were to be used throughout the Key Stage was not expanded on,
but their summative function is emphasized, meaning that their value and use as part
of informative assessment remain issues.

Alongside Curriculum 2000 the DfEE/QCA scheme of work (2000) provided
guidance and a set of 24 geography units, 16 of which formed a complete scheme of
work. The material is useful, not only in terms of the ideas it generates, but also in
providing clear formats for the teaching of topics. Each unit has information about

the unit, the key aspects that are covered, expectations, reference to prior learning and language for learning. Layout is clear, with learning objectives, possible teaching activities, learning outcomes and points to note. There are suggested resources which include video programmes, teaching packs, internet sites and a variety of texts.

Some clearly help to raise the profile of Geography and make the subject relevant to pupils (such as Unit 6: World sport; Unit 18: The global fashion industry; and Unit 21: Virtual volcanoes and internet earthquakes). It is important to remember that Curriculum 2000 arrived at the same time as the post-16 changes with the introduction of AS and A2 levels; in some departments these support materials for Key Stage 3 have had little discussion because of curriculum development elsewhere.

The problem of assessment remains that level descriptions are still designed for the purpose of summative assessment, representing the overall level of attainment a student has reached at the end of the Key Stage. There is still confusion about the distinction between summative and formative assessment (Rawling 2000). In schools, alongside the development of levelled assessments, there is some evidence of levelled marking of pupil work, although some geographers question the latter's use (see Lambert and Balderstone 2000). While any individual piece of work cannot possibly satisfy the range or variety of scale indicated in the complete level description, some departments mark work as indicative of working around a particular level.

Some schools are now internally awarding levels at the end of each year and reporting these to pupils and parents. This has built-in problems, most notably with consistency. Where the KS3 team is large and non-specialist teachers deliver the subject there is a need for shared understanding of what typifies performance at the various levels. This can be achieved through regular sharing of work and moderation of assessments at departmental meetings. For useful discussion and Inset activities regarding assembling and moderating standards portfolios, see Lambert and Balderstone (2000: 351–60).

Working with Curriculum 2000

Bailey, nearly 30 years ago, wrote that 'of all subjects, geography needs to take note of a changing world' (Bailey 1974: 7). The content of the 2000 review has not moved on in ten years and, with falling numbers at GCSE between 1996 and 2000, there is an urgent need to examine what type of Geography is being taught at Key Stage 3. Ofsted (1999) has highlighted Key Stage 3 as an area of concern regarding the quality of teaching and learning, compared to other subjects. All geographers would agree with the comments made by Westaway and Rawling (2001: 110) regarding Key Stage 3: that it should be a positive experience which builds on KS1 and KS2, and that there should be high-quality schemes of work supported by varied and challenging resources and a full programme of fieldwork. The critical issue for geography teams remains that of time. In 2000 schools were planning for the new specifications to be introduced post-16. Much of 2001 was spent on implementing AS, planning for A2 and the new GCSE specifications, again diverting energy and planning away from KS3. In 2001–2 GCSE and A2 are departmental priorities. What is important is that KS3 is given adequate time and resourcing alongside other courses. The 2000 GNC allows increased flexibility for departments to provide a stimulating, relevant and challenging experience for pupils (Figure 1.12).

	Year 7 (11–12yrs)	Year 8 (12–13yrs)	Year 9 (13–14yrs)
Autumn	Everyone needs geography	The active earth: a risky business	What's it like living in a LEDC today?
Spring	Where we live: 'global villages'	The EU – what's that all about?	Tourism: our holidays, their lives
Summer	Planet earth: is our future sustainable?	Working now and in the future	Wild weather and climate change

Figure 1.12 Example of a geography department's developing curriculum plan (2000 onwards)

School-based curriculum development requires funding and time, and the issue for many geography departments remains one of wanting to develop their KS3 curriculum, but limited funding, time and human resources mean that this is taking place only very slowly. To some extent there is a polarization of geography departments occurring. Those with teams that are responsibility-heavy, and who have not had recent appointments of newly qualified teachers, find it difficult to move forward due to the burden of bureaucracy and other demands relating to responsibility points outside of Geography. In those teams where responsibility points have been created within the department, and which have large classes at GCSE and AS/A2, further appointments can be made for geography teachers. Both departmental types have equally committed teachers. However, the problem remains as to when and how geography teams will find the time to reshape their KS3 schemes of work in order to deliver a dynamic, stimulating and relevant curriculum. This is vitally important if the image of our subject and numbers following KS3 are to be raised.

Appendix 1.1   Table of documentation 1986–2001

Date	Document	Publisher
1986	HM Inspectorate series: Curriculum Matters – Geography from 5 to 16	HMSO
1989	The Education Reform Act 1988: The School Curriculum and Assessment	DES Circular 5/89
1989	National Curriculum: From Policy to Practice	DES HMSO
March 1991	Geography in the National Curriculum (England)	DES HMSO
July 1991	Geography in the National Curriculum: Non-Statutory Guidance for Teachers	CCW
October 1991	Teacher Assessment at KS3 (leaflet)	SEAC

(continued on next page)

Date	Document	Publisher
November 1991	Teacher Assessment in Practice (leaflet)	SEAC
March 1992	Teacher Assessment in KS3: Geography (leaflet)	SEAC
July 1992	CCW Teacher Support Programme. Inset Activities for National Curriculum Geography	CCW
February 1993	KS3 Pupils' Work Assessed: Geography	SEAC
1993	Geography: Key stages 1, 2 and 3. First Year, 1991–1992	Ofsted HMSO
December 1993	Final Report. The National Curriculum and its Assessment. Ron Dearing	SCAA ref: COM/94/039
May 1994	Geography in the National Curriculum: Draft Proposals	SCAA ref: COM/94/054
1995	Geography: A review of inspection findings 1993/94	Ofsted HMSO
January 1995	Geography in the National Curriculum	DfE HMSO
1995	An introduction to the revised National Curriculum	SCAA ref: COM/95/159
1996	Optional tests and tasks for Geography	SCAA ref: KS3/96/513
1996	Geography. Consistency in Teacher Assessment. Exemplification of Standards	SCAA ref: Gg/96/472
1996	Subjects and standards: Issues for school development arising from Ofsted inspection finding 1994–1995 (KS3, KS4 & Post-16)	Ofsted HMSO
1996	Consistency in teacher assessment. Exemplification of Standards Key Stage 3 Geography	ACAC
1997	Geography optional tests and tasks	ACAC
1997	Geography and the use of language: Key Stage 3	SCAA
1998	Geographical enquiry at Key Stages 1–3. Discussion paper No. 3	QCA
1999	Geography. The National Curriculum for England Key Stages 1–3	DfEE QCA

Date	Document	Publisher
2000	Geography. A Scheme of Work for Key Stage 3. Teacher's guide	QCA
2000	Cwricwlwm Cymru 2000	ACCAC
2000	KS3 Assessment and reporting arrangements 2001 (annual booklet)	DfEE QCA QCA/oo/612
2001	Standards and Quality in Secondary Schools: Good Practice in Geography	Estyn (HMI for education and training in Wales)

Appendix 1.2 Summary of the content of geography curriculum at Key Stage 3 in the National Curriculum in Wales 2000

Geographical enquiry and skills

Including identifying questions, collecting, recording, presenting, analysing and evaluating evidence, vocabulary, fieldwork, using and making maps, using photographs, using ICT, problem-solving and decision-making.

Places

Study of three places:

- Wales
- An EU country (other than those of UK)
- A less economically developed country.

Themes

- Earthquakes and volcanoes
- Rivers or coasts
- Weather and climate
- Ecosystems
- Population
- Settlement
- Economic activity
- Environmental issues
- Resource issues
- Global environmental change.

Appendix 1.3   Summary of the Programme of Study for Geography at Key Stage 3 in the Northern Ireland Curriculum (1996)

Geographical skills

- OS mapwork skills
- Fieldwork skills
- Research, data handling and presentation skills.

Geographical themes

Physical environments

- Rocks and the process of landscape development
- Weather and climate
- Ecosystems.

Human environments

- Population
- Settlement
- Economic activities.

Places and locational knowledge

- No prescribed countries – but the development of a sense of place through a range of case studies at different scales
- Locational knowledge of a prescribed set of places and features.

Issues

- An environmental issue
- An issue related to an aspect of world development.

The geography curriculum also contributes to the following educational (cross-curricular) themes:

- Education for mutual understanding
- Cultural heritage
- Health education
- Economic awareness
- Information technology
- Careers education.

References

ACAC (1997) *Geography: Optional Tests and Tasks*, Cardiff: ACAC.

Bailey, P. (1974) *Teaching Geography*, Newton Abbot: David & Charles.

Balderstone, D. and Lambert, D. (1992) *Assessment Matters*, Sheffield: Geographical Association.

Daugherty, R. (1992) 'Teacher assessment at Key Stage 3: a ten point guide', *Teaching Geography*, 17(3): 112–15.

Dearing, R. (1993) *The National Curriculum and its Assessment: Final Report*, London: SCAA.

Department for Education (DfE) (1995) *Geography in the National Curriculum (England)*, London: HMSO.

Department for Education and Employment (DfEE) and Qualifications and Curriculum Authority (QCA) (1999) *Geography. The National Curriculum for England, Key Stages 1–3*, London: HMSO.

—— (2000) *Geography: A Scheme of Work for Key Stage 3*, London: HMSO.

Department of Education and Science (DES) (1980) *A Framework for the School Curriculum*, London: HMSO.

—— (1989) *DES Circular 5/89 The Education Reform Act 1988. The School Curriculum and Assessment*. London: HMSO.

—— (1991) *Geography in the National Curriculum (England)*, London: HMSO.

Geographical Association (GA) (2000) *Geography in the Curriculum: A Position Statement*, Sheffield: Geographical Association.

Lambert, D. and Balderstone, D. (2000) *Learning to Teach Geography in the Secondary School: A Companion to School Experience*, London: RoutledgeFalmer.

Lambert, D. and Daugherty, R. (1993) 'Teacher assessment in Key Stage 3: a snapshot of practice', *Teaching Geography* 18(3): 113–15.

Marsden, B. (1995) *Geography 11–16: Rekindling Good Practice*, London: David Fullerton Publishers.

Ofsted (1993), *Geography, Key Stages 1, 2 and 3; The First Year, 1991–92*, London: HMSO.

—— (1995) *Geography, a Review of Inspection Findings, 1993/94*, London: The Stationery Office.

—— (1999) *Standards in the Secondary School Curriculum, 1997–1998*, London: HMSO.

Rawling, E. (2000) 'National Curriculum geography: new opportunities for curriculum development', in A. Kent (ed.) *Reflective Practice in Geography Teaching*, London: Paul Chapman Publishing.

School Curriculum and Assessment Authority (SCAA) (1993) *KS3 Geography: Pupils' Work Assessed*, London: SCAA.

School Curriculum and Assessment Authority (SCAA) (1996a) *Exemplification of Standards*, London: SCAA.

School Curriculum and Assessment Authority (SCAA) (1996b) *Consistency in Teacher Assessment, Key Stage 3 Geography Optional Tests and Tasks*, London: SCAA.

TGAT (1988) *Task Group on Assessment and Testing*, London: HMSO.

Westaway, J. and Rawling, E. (2001) 'The rise and falls of Geography', *Teaching Geography* 26(3): 108–10.

2 Geography at GCSE level

Nick Rowles

The General Certificate of Secondary Education (GCSE) was first examined in 1988. During the previous few years, there were an increasing number of Joint O-level/CSE examinations developed which aimed to cover the whole ability-range. Ordinary level (O level) was introduced in the early 1960s and was the only leaving examination at 16+. However, it was geared only towards the higher-ability school pupil: until the raising of the school leaving age in the early 1970s it was felt that there was no need for an external examination for children who left school at 15. After ROSLA (the raising of the school leaving age) there was an increasing need for some kind of leaving examination for the lower 70 per cent of children for whom the O-level examination was not considered suitable. Therefore, in 1965, the Certificate of Secondary Education (CSE) was introduced. From then, until the mid-1980s, the two examinations ran side by side. CSE never gained the educational kudos enjoyed by the O-level examination. It was possible to double-enter, but teachers always had the problem of which was the best examination for a particular candidate; although a grade 1 at CSE was considered the equivalent of a pass at Ordinary level, there was always the suggestion that one was an easier route than the other. For this reason Joint O-level/CSE examinations were introduced by some examination boards. There was also the fact that schools had a choice of which of the examination boards, all of which with the exception of the Associated Examining Board (AEB) were controlled by the universities, they could choose to enter. The CSE examinations were run by regional examination boards, which meant that schools had no choice for their CSE candidates.

With the introduction of the GCSE, the O-level and CSE examination boards merged to form six examining groups, namely the Southern Examining Group (SEG), the Midland Examining Group (NEG), the Northern Examination and Assessment Board (NEAB), the London and East Anglia Examining Group (LEAG), the Welsh Joint Education Committee (WJEC) and the Northern Ireland Secondary Examination and Assessment Council (NISEAC). Schools were given the right to choose any of the examinations offered by these boards. All geography examinations had to satisfy both the general and subject criteria as well as being accepted by the government quango responsible for examinations and assessment. This has had several changes of form and title, namely SEAC, SCAA and, most recently, QCA, the Qualifications and Curriculum Authority.

The Geography Subject Specific Criteria were sufficiently broad to allow a number of different interpretations. The examining groups therefore developed a number of different syllabuses, reflecting the different paradigms influencing school Geography. There were those which were largely thematic in nature, those where place was the main emphasis and those adopting an issue-based approach. The last of these had developed out of the curriculum development by the Schools Council in the 1960s and 1970s. This had resulted in the Geography 14–18 project aimed at the most able pupils, commonly known as the 'Bristol project' as its development had taken place at the University of Bristol. The raising of the school leaving age meant that there was a need for a development of an appropriate geography curriculum for those pupils required to stay on an extra year until the new leaving age of 16. The Geography for the Young School Leaver (GYSL) was developed at the former Avery Hill College of Education, now part of Brunel University; it is therefore sometimes known as the 'Avery Hill Project'. It was developed around three themes: 'Man, Land and Leisure', 'People, Place and Work' and 'Cities and People'. It developed a wider range of geographical skills than was seen in some of the more traditional sylla-buses. These were mostly based on memorizing a large number of geographical facts, largely related to regional geography. The two projects were very popular and, with the introduction of the GCSE, all examining groups wished to offer examina-tions reflecting the philosophy of these important curriculum developments. The government regulating authority would allow only one official examination syllabus based on each of the projects, so MEG and WJEC jointly ran the official Bristol project examination, and MEG was also responsible for running the official Avery Hill Project examination. However, all the other examining groups offered sylla-buses that reflected the ideas of the projects, but they were not allowed to use the names of the projects in their titles.

The other main difference between the different syllabuses was the amount of coursework allowed as a component in the final examination. Examining groups could allocate anything between 5 and 40 per cent of the final marks to coursework. This work is completed by the candidate and marked internally by the candidate's teacher; a sample is then sent to the examining group to be moderated in order to maintain a consistency of standards. While there were some examples of syllabuses with 40 per cent coursework, by far the most common allocation was 25 per cent. The coursework could consist of several pieces of work or just one piece, but it had to include a fieldwork enquiry (where there was evidence of the candidate having collected some primary or new data as part of fieldwork). Between 1988 and 1998, the fieldwork often had to show evidence of people's attitudes and values and so it was difficult to produce a purely physical geographical enquiry.

Following the Dearing Report on the National Curriculum, Ron Dearing turned his attention to foundation subjects, such as Geography, at Key Stage 4. This revision came into force with the 1998 examination. There were a number of changes in the Geography Subject Specific Criteria and in the General Criteria for the GCSE; the maximum amount of coursework allowed was reduced to 25 per cent. Values and attitudes were no longer a compulsory assessment objective, thereby making purely physical geographical topics acceptable.

Between 1988 and 1998, some examining groups had tiered papers while others went for a single tier. WJEC had a common paper for the middle tiers and two sepa-rate papers, one geared towards the lower abilities and the other for candidates aiming for the highest grades. NEG had three separate tiers, namely Higher, Intermediate and Foundation. NISEAC had a common paper with an extension paper for candidates aiming for grades A or B. The major change in 1998 was the introduction of compulsory tiering. All examinations were to be tiered, with a Higher Tier with allowed grades of A* to D and a Foundation Tier covering grades C to G. Any candidate not achieving a grade D on the Higher Tier would be Unclassified (U). The government was concerned that many candidates would be entered for the wrong tier, which would result in a large number of candidates being unclassified. At the last moment, they therefore added an allowed grade E on the Higher Tier for those candidates who fell half a grade below a D. This allowed grade E was originally only to be for one year, but it has now been allowed up to and beyond the 2003 examinations.

A further development in the later part of the 1990s was the introduction of short-course GCSEs. These were of the same difficulty as the long-course equivalents, and were to be tiered and so cover the whole ability-range, but were to cover only half the content. It was intended that they could be taught in half the time and therefore could be combined with a short-course GCSE in another subject. The take-up for these courses has been relatively small. With increasing congestion on the Key Stage 4 curriculum, with the introduction of new subjects and the requirement for Citizenship to be delivered in some form from 2002, it is possible that they will become more popular. There is no requirement for pupils to study a humanities subject in Years 10 and 11, apart from Religious Education, and so some schools may see a short course in Geography and/or History as a way of maintaining a balance in the pupils' curriculum at this level.

With the introduction of the GCSE in 1988, it was the intention that it would cater for candidates of all abilities. However, it became clear that there would still be a sizeable number of pupils at the lowest end of the ability-range in mainstream schools who would not be able to cope with the demands of these courses. This continued after 1998, even with the introduction of Foundation Tier examination papers. This group is likely to increase, as the policy of inclusion develops and more and more pupils who previously would have been educated in special schools because of their learning difficulties are now in mainstream schools. To cater for these pupils, several examining groups began offering examination papers targeted at lower levels than the grades F and G achievable on Foundation Tier papers. These are Certificates of Achievement and they test parts of a GCSE syllabus. These continued, but from 2001 their name changed to Entry Level Certificates.

The last years of the twentieth century saw a greater emphasis on literacy and numeracy, with the introduction of the Literacy Hour and the National Numeracy Strategy in primary schools. At the same time, examining groups were required to assess the quality of candidates' written work in subjects such as Geography. In the GCSE examination, extra marks worth up to 5 per cent would be available for spelling, punctuation and grammar, and the use of specialist terms (SPaG). This would be assessed in both the coursework (marks awarded by the candidates' own teachers) and the written papers (marks awarded by the examiners appointed by the examining group).

The emphasis on GCSE from 1988 was on positive achievement: marks were awarded for 'what the candidates know, understand and can do'. The O-level examinations were testing geographical knowledge, along with a few tests of skills largely concerned with the reading and interpretation of Ordnance Survey maps. Skills were given greater emphasis in the GCSE, where up to 40 per cent of the marks could be available for testing skills. These covered a wide range of geographical sources such as photographs, including aerial photographs and satellite images, and pictorial sources such as cartoons. The introduction of coursework based on fieldwork meant that candidates were required to show their ability both to represent data graphically and to interpret numerical data presented both statistically and in the form of graphs. There was a greater emphasis on the understanding of process at the expense of mere knowledge of geographical facts and figures. An example was the requirement for detailed understanding of the geomorphological processes involved in land formation. Physical geography was a requirement of all GCSE geography syllabuses, but the Geography Subject Specific Criteria required that physical geography should be studied in a human context with an emphasis on a people–environment theme. This was one way in which pupils were required to show evidence of their own values on environmental matters as well as other people's attitudes. There was greater emphasis on values and attitudes in the study of human geographical topics such as settlement, agriculture, industry and development. The new GCSE syllabuses moved from a predominantly regional approach to one that reflected the developments resulting from the quantitative revolution of the 1960s. Apart from some more radical A-level examination courses these had been largely confined to Geography in Higher Education.

Curriculum 2000 saw modifications to the Geography National Curriculum covering the first three years of the secondary phase. This gave greater emphasis to environmental concerns and, in particular, the concept of sustainability and sustainable development. It was logical to review the Geography Subject Specific Criteria and hence the content of the Geography GCSE examination courses on offer. The government, in the form of the QCA, was concerned at the large number of different GCSE syllabuses on offer. Fourteen syllabuses were available and this did raise the question of comparability. This was despite the fact that, from 1998 onwards, inter-board comparability studies had taken place in all subjects, including Geography. In addition to the multiplicity of examination courses there were also a large number of organizations responsible for external examinations. In addition to GCSE and GCE A-level examinations there had been a great growth in GNVQ (General National Vocational Qualifications), which developed more vocationally based examination courses. These had their own organizations responsible for their delivery. For their Year 11 pupils, schools had to deal with a large number of different examination groups, which had evolved their own ways of working and awarding, and whose administration took very different forms. The government was also concerned that, like the CSE examinations in the 1960s and 1970s, the GNVQ was not achieving the public recognition and acceptance of the more academic GCSE and GCE examinations. There was a requirement, therefore, for a reduction in the number of examining groups, with new groups offering the full range of academic and vocational examinations. The organizations in Wales and Northern Ireland remained much the same, although NISEAC changed its title to the Northern Ireland Council for the Curriculum, Examinations and Assessment (CCCEA). The situation in England, however, was more radical with a reduction to only three examining groups. The Oxford, Oxford and Cambridge, and Cambridge GCE boards joined with the MEG GCSE board and the RSA Vocational examination to become OCR. The AEB GCE

Board and the SEG and NEAB GCSE Boards bought some GNVQ examinations from City and Guilds to form the Assessment and Qualifications Alliance (AQA). The University of London GCE Board, the LEAG GCSE Board and the BTec vocational examination board became Edexcel. QCA imposed a code of practice on all examining, in order to ensure greater consistency and comparability.

Each of these new examining groups could only offer a limited range of geography syllabuses. QCA accepted more than one specification from a particular examining group only if there were significant differences between them in their approach or assessment. All had to comply with a new set of geography subject-specific criteria, but these still allowed differing interpretations. What this has meant is that in addition to the official 'Bristol' and 'Avery Hill' project syllabuses, the groups are offering specifications based on either a thematic or an issue-based approach. In addition, there is one place-based specification where there are specified regions of the world to be studied, albeit in a thematic context.

QCA have approved the specifications shown in Figure 2.1, and these will be first examined in 2003. In the main, the approved specifications replaced existing syllabuses that were last examined in 2002. In some cases, where boards have joined and they previously offered syllabuses reflecting the same approach, a new specification had to be written that would try to satisfy the schools that had been following the discontinued examination syllabuses. For example, the issue-based AQA C specification reflects the previous NEAB B and SEG B courses.

There are, however, some changes from the 1998–2002 syllabuses that all courses will have to show because of the changes in the geography subject-specific criteria. In line with the changes in the National Curriculum in Key Stages 1–3, there will be the same greater emphasis given to sustainability and the environment. This has the effect of reinforcing the people–environment theme, and further emphasizing the effect of physical geographical change and the impact these changes have on the human geographical environment. Candidates are required to study the management of these changes and the extent to which the strategies employed are sustainable. An example of this would be the impact of different coastal defence systems on the environment.

The government is very keen that all pupils, whatever subjects they study at Key Stage 4, should be exposed to Information and Communication Technology (ICT).

All the GCSE specifications that are to be first examined in 2003 have to emphasize where ICT is used in delivering the syllabus. Geography and Business Studies are the only subjects where candidates have to be assessed in their use of ICT. It is obviously not possible to examine a candidate's ICT expertise in the written examination, so each geography specification has to show how ICT is to be examined in the coursework component. ICT is interpreted very widely; Information Technology covers use of computers, which gives the candidate the opportunity to make use of word processors, and to use programs such as Excel to produce computer-generated graphs. The increasing availability of software packages opens up more and more possibilities. One of the main problems geography teachers now face is to test the candidates' geographical performance rather than their expertise on the computer. However, the Communication technology will give opportunities to those candidates without the high computer skills perhaps due to the lack of the appropriate hardware at home or school. Communication technological skills

Course	Group	Specification
GCSE	AQA	Geography A
		Geography B
		Geography C
	Edexcel	Geography A
		Geography B
	OCR	Geography A
		Geography B (Avery Hill)*
		Geography C (Bristol Project)
	WJEC	Geography A
		Geography B (Avery Hill)*
	CCEA	Geography
GCSE (short course)	AQA	Geography A
		Geography B
		Geography C
	Edexcel	Geography
	OCR	Geography

Figure 2.1 QCA-approved GCSE specifications

Note
* Run jointly by WJEC and OCR.

include the use of photographs and satellite images or the extraction of information from video or TV programmes. This has an impact on the coursework, which can make up between 20 and 25 per cent of the total marks.

In order to give greater consistency with National Curriculum Geography at Key Stage 3, there has been a requirement from 2003 to add problem-solving and decision-making to all geography GCSE specifications. Some examining groups have satisfied this requirement by a having a decision-making paper as one of the written papers; others have indicated that these strategies should be used to deliver some of the content.

All geography GCSE specifications have to give pupils opportunities to:

I   acquire knowledge and understanding of a range of places, environments and geographical patterns at a range of scales from local to global, as well as an understanding of the physical and human processes, including decision-making, which affect their development;

II develop a sense of place and an appreciation of the environment, as well as an awareness of the ways in which people and environments interact, and of the opportunities, challenges and constraints that face people in different places;

III appreciate that the study of geography is dynamic, not only because places, geographical features, patterns and issues change but also because new ideas and methods lead to new interpretations;

IV acquire and apply the skills and techniques – including those of mapwork, fieldwork and ICT – needed to conduct geographical study and enquiry.

(GCSE Criteria for Geography)

Like the Curriculum 2000 version of the Geography Orders the specifications emphasize the importance of enquiry-based learning in the delivery of the geographical content. This is made much more explicit than in earlier syllabuses: there has to be a balanced coverage of the physical, human and environmental aspects of geography. The study of the themes must be at different (local, regional, national, international and global) scales; the international scale is additional to those required in the examinations before 2003. The thematic studies have to be studied in the context of the UK, the European Union and countries in various states of development. The interdependence of places and environments is emphasized, as is the study of how physical and human processes contribute to geographical patterns.

All specifications have to allocate 20–30 per cent of the marks for knowledge, 20–30 per cent for understanding, 15–25 per cent for applied understanding and 30–40 per cent for skills. An important development in 2003 was the addition to a requirement of an understanding of the geographical content specified: pupils have to show they can apply their knowledge and understanding in a variety of physical and human contexts. This reinforces the importance in geographical education of the study of place, which, since the decline of regional geography in the 1970s and 1980s, has played a decreasingly important part in external examinations in Geography. Geographical theory, while still important, has to be studied in a real-world context. This means that case studies from both LEDCs and MEDCs are very important. Another area where pupils are required to show this applied understanding is in their coursework. Their small-scale fieldwork investigation in a particular locality has to be underpinned by sufficient geographical theory to allow them to suggest explanations for their findings.

The development and assessment of Key Skills were very important aspects of the developments in post-16 secondary education from 2000. The 2003 examinations gave opportunities for Key Stage 4 pupils to access these Key Skills at levels 1 and 2. Geography GCSE specifications gave the opportunities for teaching, developing and providing opportunities for generating evidence of attainment in aspects of Communication, Application of Number, Information Technology, and the wider key skills of Improving own Learning and Performance, Working with Others and Problem Solving.

Geography GCSEs are also able to contribute to the wider curriculum, which the government has been encouraging. An important aspect of this is the opportunity the subject gives to heighten pupils' awareness of spiritual, moral/ethical, social and cultural issues. This can help clarify and develop a pupil's own values and attitudes in relation to both physical and human issues. This can be illustrated by examples from one specification (Figure 2.2).

	Study of glacial landscapes	Managing resources
Spiritual	The wonder and power of natural forces and the beauty of the landscape	The wealth of the resources on the planet
Moral/ethical	Economic and environmental arguments in glaciated areas	Competing attitudes to changes and developments in farming, e.g. organic farming
Social	Attitudes and perceptions to conflicting land issues	Social influences in resource development and different values about recycling, renewable power
Cultural	Different attitudes and values of interest groups – farmers, locals and tourists	Cultural issues and global concerns about the environment and cultural dangers by western tourists to LEDCs

Figure 2.2 Geography's contribution to the wider curriculum

Source: AQA Specification A, pp. 43–4.

From 2002, all state schools have to offer Citizenship as part of their Key Stage 4 curriculum. There have been National Curriculum regulations for Citizenship issued which indicate the content, but the government has left schools to make their own decision on how it is to be taught. It can be taught as a separate discrete subject or delivered as a cross-curricular subject. If this is the case, then schools will have to undertake an audit and show how the existing subjects in the curriculum can contribute to the delivery of Citizenship. Geography is well placed to deliver much of the required content, covering knowledge, understanding and skills. The study of Citizenship embraces the development of social and moral rights and responsibilities, legal and democratic institutions and processes, issues of diversity, economic development and environmental issues, and participation in community activity. Geography GCSE gives considerable opportunity to develop these themes. For example, there can be the consideration of the different roles and opinions of interest groups in conflict resolution such as the siting of a new quarry or a bypass; the roles and responsibilities that people have in relief efforts to deal with the consequences of natural disasters can be studied; thought can be given to the quality of life in inner cities, shantytowns and between LEDCs and MEDCs. Sustainable development and the responsibilities of people to the environment figure very largely in the specifications offered from 2003. The study of global citizenship includes the use of resources and environments for activities such as farming and industry as well as tourism and settlement. Geography gives many opportunities for the development of the skills of debate and discussion and the development of empathy with other opinions and situations in topical political and other issues.

The introduction of the GCSE in 1988 changed the form of assessment from one that is norm-referenced to one that is based on criteria. In a norm-referenced examination such as O level, a certain percentage passed each year. In a criteria-referenced examination there are grade descriptions against which a candidate's work is judged. If the quality of the work reaches that described in the criteria, the candidate will achieve that grade. This means that there is not a laid-down percentage of candidates that will achieve a particular grade. In practice, in a large-entry subject such as Geography the percentage achieving each grade does not vary greatly from year to year because the pattern of entry is normally distributed. Grades A, C and F are judgemental boundaries for which there are grade descriptions. The grade description for a grade A candidate is as follows.

> Candidates recall accurately detailed information about places, environments and themes, across all scales, as required by the specification, and show detailed knowledge of location and geographical terminology.

> Candidates understand thoroughly ideas from the specification content, and apply their understanding to analyses of unfamiliar contexts. They understand thoroughly the way in which a wide range of physical processes interact to influence the development of geographical patterns, their geographical characteristics of particular places and environments, and the interdependence between them. They understand complex relationships between people and the environment and understand how considerations of sustainable development affect the planning and management of environments and resources. They evaluate the significance and effects of attitudes and values of those involved, in geographical issues and in decision-making about the uses and management of resources.

> Candidates undertake geographical enquiry, identifying relevant geographical questions, implementing effective sequences of enquiry, collecting a range of appropriate evidence from a variety of primary and secondary sources, using effectively appropriate techniques, drawing selectively on geographical ideas to interpret evidence, reaching substantiated conclusions, communicating clearly and effectively outcomes, and evaluating the validity and limitation of evidence and conclusions.

A candidate would achieve a grade F if there were evidence of the following.

> Candidates recall basic information about places, environments and themes, at more than one scale as required by the specification, and show an elementary knowledge of location and geographical terminology.

> Candidates understand some simple geographical from the specification content in a particular context. They understand some simple physical and human processes and recognize that they contribute to the development of geographical patterns and the geographical characteristics of places and environments. They understand some simple interrelationships between peoples and the environment and the idea of sustainable development. They show some awareness of the attitudes and values of people involved in geographical issues and in decision-making about the use and management of environments.

Candidates undertake geographical enquiry, collecting and recording geographical evidence from primary and secondary sources, drawing simple maps and diagrams, communicating information by brief statements, and recognizing some of the limitations of the evidence.

Once the A, C and F grade boundaries have been established by judging the quality of the work against the grade descriptions, all other boundaries are established by arithmetic calculations. This includes the A★ boundary set up by the government in 1994 to award the very highest-ability candidates.

All GCSEs are positively marked, and the written examination questions are marked in two ways. Sections of questions with three or fewer marks are likely to be point-marked, where there will be one mark for each correct, relevant point. In most cases, the wording of the question will indicate whether a question is point-marked. If there are three marks for a question asking for three features of an Equatorial ecosystem, the allocation of those marks is obvious. Level-marked questions are those sections with higher mark allocations. On Foundation Tier papers, targeted at grades C to G, there are usually two levels; on Higher Tier papers, three levels are more common. The question is marked as a whole, and it is not necessary for the answer to go through all levels. If the first part is of level 3 standard then the minimum score will be at the bottom end of the level 3 range of marks. A typical mark scheme may be divided as follows: level 1, 1–3 marks; level 2, 4–6 marks; and level 3, 7–9 marks. The quality of the whole answer has to be considered in awarding marks and, unlike a point-marked answer, there are not particular points where the marks are gained. If the overall quality of the answer is detailed, often with plenty of case-study exemplification, then the answer could gain between 7 and 9 marks. A clear answer would be at level 2 whereas a basic answer, irrespective of the number of points, could only achieve a maximum of three marks.

The quality of the written work in both the examination and the coursework components of the GCSE examination is assessed. Up to 2003, this was done with the addition of a mark for SPaG, as explained on p. 26. The use of technical terms is now considered under the assessment objective of applied understanding. A candidate's spelling, punctuation and grammar are now assessed under the general title of the quality of the written communication. Candidates are required to present information in a form that suits its purpose and to ensure that the text is legible and that spelling, punctuation and grammar are accurate so that the meaning is clear. The candidates' teachers will be required to assess the written communication in the coursework. In the written examination it will be one of the criteria that the marker will have to consider when deciding which level to award in a level-marked answer.

3 The new AS and A2 specifications for Geography

Sheila Morris

The summer of 2001 saw the first in the new system of Advanced-level (A-level) examinations. These have been the culmination of developments in national examinations that followed the Dearing Review 1996, which recommended a broadening of the curriculum for 16–19-year-olds with the inclusion of vocational courses alongside the traditional A levels for those students who stayed on in schools and colleges at the end of Key Stage 4. Vocational courses, including BTec and RSA, had been on offer in many institutions. However, recognition of vocational qualifications for higher education was slow, and as a result two-year A-level courses still remained the goal for the majority of students. These offered the opportunity for entry to most higher-education courses.

The last 20 years of the twentieth century saw considerable change in the content and teaching of A levels. These have meant that a concentration on academic content and the assessment of a student's ability to absorb and describe facts have to some extent been discarded. There is a new appreciation of the importance of different teaching methodologies as well as learning outcomes and a far greater acknowledgement of student-centred learning.

During the 1960s the raising of the school leaving age to 16 years led to a rethink in methods of teaching and indeed of occupying and involving young people who were forced to stay on in school. Many were youngsters who did not have the background or training to attempt the more academic O levels or even CSEs. The establishment of the Schools Council in 1964 led to the development of projects such as GYSL (Geography for the Young School Leaver) and the Bristol Project (1970) – the latter for more able students. It became obvious that there was a need for a broader range of courses for 16–19-year-olds, as the sixth form was no longer the home of a restricted number of able students. The Crowther report had called for education in depth at this level, whilst recognizing the need to broaden the curriculum.

Geography at university level had driven the examination boards to set up syllabuses which were largely regional or systematically based. Students needed to know vast amounts of facts and figures about areas, usually continental land masses such as North America and Africa. Mapwork, often purely descriptive, statistical work associated with the early quantitative revolution of the 1960s and separate human and physical geography were the norm. Students had to prepare themselves to write essays which mainly regurgitated facts and paid little or no heed to values and attitudes.

There were moves in the early 1970s towards curriculum change. The conceptual revolution of the 1960s period through the work of Chorley and Haggett had developed a more scientific approach, with explanations involving hypothesis testing and the use of models and statistics. The London Board (ULEAC) and Joint Matriculation Board (JMB) produced two A-level syllabuses which involved papers reflecting the changes in the subject.

In 1976 the Schools Council Geography 16–19 Project was set up at the University of London Institute of Education (ULIE), directed by Michael Naish. This was in response to the changing nature of the intake of sixth forms and colleges. The educational needs of the age-group were carefully researched and this work underpinned much highly successful development. Throughout its life (1976–85) the project consulted educators, including teachers, and set up a series of regional consultations linking groups of schools. This was to be highly significant in the production of materials at sixth-form level involving exam boards and teachers in developing a previously untried school-based approach. The changing nature of Geography was linked to a new approach and a curriculum framework that involved people and environment as well as a basic enquiry approach to all topics (Figure 3.1). Teaching materials were prepared and tested in schools and colleges, resulting in the successful launch of the ULEAC (London) A219 syllabus in 1981. As with the other Schools Council Projects, support for schools included a team of regional moderators, usually practising teachers, who helped with the moderation and assessment of school-based coursework together with regular Inset courses.

The 16–19 A level had a distinctive content and approach which made it attractive to those involved with students who were not necessarily highly academic. It was a modular course divided into four main themes, each divided into core and option modules allowing considerable choice for individual institutions (Figure 3.2).

The amount of choice available for teachers was welcome, allowing them greater opportunity to develop their own schemes of work within the broad framework. It was also possible for students to contribute to the choice of option modules. The introduction of the individual study gave freedom for young people to think about their own research and to work out a careful programme based on the route to enquiry. Some teachers considered that workloads were heavy as the amount of internal assessment of coursework and the individual study was 35 per cent of the total. Modules could be taken twice a year although in practice relatively few students were entered for examination in the January of their first year. The examination was modular and allowed choice of timing for most of the topics, although the individual study was frequently tackled in the second year of the course when students were more mature. The decision-making exercise, which involved skills developed through all the modules, was also usually taken at the end of the second year.

Within the modules teachers were encouraged to develop their own schemes of work based upon the enquiry route of key questions, issues and problems and encouraging students to develop their own values and attitudes to a particular issue. There were many instances of groups of teachers from different institutions working together, sometimes with their regional co-ordinator, to develop detailed schemes which were often highly successful. It was important for teachers to produce a course of which they were confident in delivery and which was balanced and interesting for the students, and which satisfied the demands of an A-level course. In the classroom the students became involved in discussions, group work and problem-solving, which resulted in positive development of their geographical understanding as well

Framework	Syllabus structure	Degree of direction within the syllabus	Assessment	Assessment weighting
Four environmental themes and principles provide the framework for the syllabus throughout	Core syllabus 6 × 6-week modules (36 weeks)	Full direction for teachers	Terminal examination Paper 1: Decision-making exercise (2.5 hours) (22%)	Core and option (external) (22%) Core (external) (43%)
	Option modules 3 × 6-week modules (18 weeks) or	Increasing freedom of choice	Paper 2: Four resource-based questions (3 hours) (43%) Coursework assessment	Option modules (internal) (24%)
	2 × 6-week modules and 1 special option module 1 × 6 weeks (18 weeks)	Greater freedom in choice and planning	Coursework including: • Two timed essays (8%) • A techniques application unit (8%) • An extended essay (8%)	
	Individual study 2–6 weeks guidance		• Individual study report (11%)	Individual study (internal) (11%)

Figure 3.1 Summary diagram of original geography 16–19 A-level course (University of London Examination Board Syllabus Regulations, June 1986)

Source: Naish et al. 1987.

as in their personal skills. Between 1986 and 1994 numbers entered for the ULSEB 16–19 course increased dramatically to 13,000.

Changes to Advanced levels and Advanced Subsidiary (AS) levels came during the 1990s following a series of government initiatives. The National Curriculum Council's *Analysis of Core Skills* in 1990 suggested that all students should have a knowledge of problem-solving, communication, personal skills, numeracy, Information Technology and a modern foreign language. Wherever possible these should be delivered through their subjects. In this respect, Geography was well placed, especially for students following the 16–19 course.

In 1992 the government through SEAC issued a set of general A and AS principles to be followed by the examination boards. This was done in order to maintain standards of A levels. It reduced the amount of school-based assessment to 20 per cent

Theme 1
The challenge of natural environments
Core modules:

- Managing landform systems
- Ecosystems and human activity

Option modules:

- Climatic change and uncertainty
- Response to difficult environments
- Natural hazards
- Pollution of natural environments
- The geological challenge

Theme 2
Use and misuse of natural resources
Core module:

- The energy question

Option modules:

- Water resource management
- Minerals as a resource
- Land as a resource
- Soils and the future
- Managing woodland and forest
- Potential of oceans and seas

Theme 3
Issues of global concern
Core module:

- The challenge of urbanization

Option modules:

- Global limits to growth
- Feeding the world's population
- Environments and political systems
- Migrations of people
- Alternative approaches to development
- The communications revolution

Theme 4
Managing Human Environments
Core modules:

- Impact of the manufacturing industry
- Changing agricultural systems

Option modules:

- Changing tertiary activities
- Demand for recreation and leisure
- Regional disparities
- Changing urban environments
- Rural management
- Mobility and the environment
- Policy, planning and the environment

Figure 3.2 Core and option modules

Source: Naish et al. 1987.

and forced ULEAC to reduce the proportion of coursework undertaken by those following the 16–19 syllabus.

Then in 1993 came a move which required all examination boards to include a subject core for Geography in all A- and AS-level syllabuses by September 1996. It is interesting to note that the subject core required:

- Studies of people and environment themes at different scales to include systems and processes, changes over time, issues, responses and strategies.
- A chosen physical environment to include physical processes (terrestrial atmospheric, biotic and human), interactions of these processes and changes over time.
- A chosen human environment, its cultural, economic, social, political characteristics, interaction and changes over time.

And for A-level candidates only:

- An investigative study based on first-hand and secondary data.

The importance of knowledge, understanding and skills was stressed, together with values and perceptions which should be developed through the wider use of analytical work and decision-making. Many teachers saw the influence of the 16–19 project in this core proposal to the extent that it allowed greater continuity than had been expected. Those involved in teaching the traditional A levels found it more challenging.

The greatest change came following the 1996 SCAA *Review of the Qualifications for 16–19-year-olds* by Sir Ron Dearing. This set out to give 'structure and coherence' to the plethora of 16–19-year-old qualifications and attempted to align some A levels and GNVQs. The review stated that achievement at all ability levels needed to be recognized and that there should be national targets to raise levels of achievement. It was also a recognition of the aim to broaden the studies of students in the 16–19 age-range. The old AS level – consisting of half the former A level, assessed at the A-level standard and taken after either a one-year or two-year course – was replaced by Advanced Subsidiary (AS).

All students would take four subjects at AS level at the end of their first year and could receive a qualification, which was an opportunity for those who did not wish to do a full A-level course. Those wishing to stay on for a further year could then choose three subjects for their final year which would be at the Advanced-level standard. In addition, the Advanced-level courses would offer opportunities for students to develop and generate evidence of attainment in a number of Key Skills.

Having established new syllabuses for September 1996 the examination boards had to revise their subject cores by December 1996. These had to incorporate many of the ideas and developments referred to above. Syllabuses, now called *specifications*, were approved by mid-2000 to allow new teaching programmes to begin for the first examination of the AS level in summer 2001. The AS- and A-level subject criteria published by QCA in 1999 are similar to the 1993 subject core.

AS- and A-level specifications in Geography should require study of physical, human and environmental aspects of the subject, and their interactions at a variety of scales and in different contexts including the UK and regions at varying levels of development.

Students should undertake investigative work, based on evidence from primary sources, including fieldwork, and secondary sources. An important change is the increase in the maximum internal assessment to 30 per cent.

The specifications accredited by QCA (Figure 3.3) introduced a three-unit AS level to be taken at the end of the first year. There is opportunity for staged or end-of-course assessment, which allows institutions to enter students at the end of their second year as in the former traditional A-level courses. Key Skills must include communication, number and IT skills.

All the A levels must have a synoptic paper at the end of the course, which is allocated 20 per cent of the final assessment. Assessment of these modular courses takes place in January and June. Students may retake an assessment once only and count the better mark towards their final result. It is now possible to retake the whole specification more than once.

The published specifications have some difference in emphasis. AQA and Edexcel include the aims published by QCA in the subject criteria, whilst OCR add aims on Key Skills and changes in geographical methodology as well as spiritual,

Board specification	AS Modules			A2 Modules		
	1	**2**	**3**	**4**	**5**	**6**
AQA A	Core concepts in physical geography Water on land Climatic hazards and change Energy and life Written exam 17.5%	Core concepts in human geography Population dynamics Settlement patterns and process Economic activity Written exam 17.5%	Geographical skills Content from 1 and 2 Investigation to show evidence of fieldwork Written exam 15%	Challenge and change in natural environments Coasts, process and problems Geomorphologic process and hazards Cold environments and human activities Written exam 15%	Challenge and change in human environments Population pressure and resource management Managing cities Recreation and tourism Written exam 15%	6 Personal study Externally assessed coursework 20% or: 7 Investigative skills Written unit 20%
AQA B	Dynamics of change Short-term and long-term change Atmospheric, geomorphologic change and human process affecting drainage basin hydrology in UK Written exam 20%	Physical options for change One from: ▪ Glacial environments ▪ Coastal environments ▪ Urban physical environments Written exam 15%	Human options for change Either: Urban change in UK and wider world over last 30 years or: Historic rural and urban landscapes in England and Wales Written exam 15%	Global change Physical geography Plate tectonics Seasonal atmospheric change in tropical Africa Change in UK vegetation and soils Environmental hazards Conflict over resource use Written exam 15%	Synoptic unit Decision-making exercise with advance information Written exam 20%	6 Practical paper Investigative paper based on aspects of modules 1 and 4 Written exam 15% or: 7 Geographic investigation Coursework, centre assessed and Board moderated 15%
Edexcel A	Physical environments Earth systems Fluvial environments Coastal environments Written exam 15%	Human environments Population characteristics Settlement patterns Population movements Written exam 15%	Personal enquiry Coursework, internally assessed 20% or: Applied geographical skills Written exam 20%	Physical systems, process and patterns Atmospheric systems Glacial systems Ecosystems Written exam 15%	Human systems, process and patterns Economic systems Rural–urban relations Development problems Written exam 15%	Synoptic paper Based on 1, 2, 4 and 5 Written exam 20%

(continued on next page)

Board specification	AS Modules			A2 Modules		
	1	2	3	4	5	6
Edexcel B	Changing landforms and management — Riverine environments, Coastal environments — Written exam 16.7%	Managing human environments — Urban, rural and urban–rural inter-relationships — Written exam 16.7%	Environmental investigation — Group or individual fieldwork investigation — Coursework, internal assessment, Board moderation 16.7%	Global challenge — Broad global issues and management challenges — Written exam 15%	Researching global futures — In-depth study of one natural environmental theme and one human development theme — Research essay as written exam 15%	Synoptic paper — Decision-making paper with advance information based on 1,2 and 4 — Written exam 20%
OCR A	Physical systems and management — Hydrological systems, Ecosystems, Atmospheric systems, Lithosphere — Written exam 20%	Human environments — Population, pattern, process and change. Rural/urban settlement. Pattern, process and change — Written exam 15%	Geographical investigation — Environmental investigation and written paper, Board assessed 15%	Options in physical and human geography — Choice of one from: Coastal environments, Fluvial environments, Glacial and periglacial, Hot arid and semi-arid, Applied climatology and one from: Agriculture and food, Manufacturing, Industry, location and change, Service activities, Tourism and recreation — Written exam 15%	Synoptic paper — Choice of two from: Geography of EU, Managing urban environments, Managing rural environments, Hazardous environments — Written exam 20%	Personal study — Research based on primary data — Coursework 15% or: Investigation skills Fieldwork report and written exam 15%, Board assessed

Board specification	AS Modules			A2 Modules		
	1	2	3	4	5	6
OCR B	Physical systems and management — Atmospheric systems and people; Landforms and people; Coastal systems and people. Written paper 15%	Human systems and management — Economic activity and change; Settlement dynamics; Population and development. Written paper 15%	Geographical investigation — Investigative skills. Written exam 20%	Geographical investigation — Coursework, internally assessed, Board moderated 15%	Issues in the environment — Physical option. One from: Hazards and responses; Climate and society; Cold environments and human response; Tropical environments and people. Human option. One from: Changing urban places; Leisure and tourism; Global issues in economic activity. Written exam 15%	Issues in sustainable development — Resource and land use management – widening the examples in previous models. Pre-released material for written exam 20%
WJEC	Process and issues in physical geography — Global processes – earthquakes, vulcanicity; Drainage basins; Small-scale ecosystems. Written exam 16.7%	Processes and issues in the human environment — Population; Rural changes; Growth and decline in urbanization. Written exam 16.7%	Investigative Geography — Written paper to assess the skills derived from 1 and 2 16.7%	Geographical processes and their management — Two out of four options: Landforms process and management or: Climatic hazards, causes and management and either: Inequalities in development or: Changing geographies of economic activities. Written exam 15%	Sustainable development — Food supply; Water Supply; Natural environments; Urban environments. Synoptic paper to include essay and DME 20%	Personal Enquiry — Either: Individual investigation Internally assessed coursework 15% or: Geographical assignment External assessment 15%

Figure 3.3 Assessment objective weighting

Table 3.1 Assessment objective weighting

Specification	Knowledge	Critical understanding	Application of knowledge and understanding	Skills and techniques
AS level only				
AQA A	22	23	22	33
AQA B	25	25	20	30
Edexcel A	20	26	20	34
Edexcel B	24	30	16	30
OCR A	26	26	21	27
OCR B	25	20	20	35
WJEC	30	26	19	25
A level as a whole				
AQA A	20.6	27.9	22	29.5
AQA B	24.5	25.5	21	29
Edexcel A	22	29	23	26
Edexcel B	23	30	21	26
OCR A	21.5	25.5	25	28
OCR B	25	20	20	35
WJEC	27.5	25.5	17	30

moral and cultural issues. In the other specifications guidance is given on these in varying degrees (Table 3.1).

Bradford (2001) provides a critical view of the new specifications, commenting that the change has been limited and lacks the development of AS courses which might have broadened the viewpoints of students involved in subjects such as the pure sciences or even some arts and other humanities. It is also significant that none of the specifications provides equal weighting for the 3 AS and 3 A2 modules. This is complicated by the assessment limits imposed of 30 per cent coursework and 20 per cent for the synoptic element. Two specifications (Edexcel B and OCR B) have 16.7 per cent for equal units at AS level. Skills assessment is strongest at AS with critical understanding (now emphasized in the assessment objectives) much stronger at A2 level.

A synoptic paper might be considered superfluous for geography students because of the content of the subject, which traditionally uses interactions and interconnections. Investigative skills are assessed by written examination and coursework with elements at AS and A2, although AQA B does not require coursework at AS level, considering that students are not sufficiently mature until their A2 year to deal with this element successfully.

September 2000 saw the introduction of Curriculum 2000. It brought significant changes to organization and teaching at the 16–19 level. The delay in accreditation had given some teachers little time to prepare new detailed schemes of work and the amount of information available varied between the examining boards. All the specifications were available on the examining boards' websites, as were teachers' guides and examination questions. The last did provide some guidance as to the level of the AS. There were more data response questions than with previous examinations, and short, structured questions indicated the need to have tight, precise answers. It was also apparent that clear definitions needed to be provided for all topics (lists are provided in some teachers' guides). The timescale for units of work was suggested to be six weeks, which gave relatively little grace for upgrading the factual knowledge and the skills and understanding of those students who had not taken the subject to KS4. The range of abilities within an AS group provided a challenge for many tutors who had perhaps been used to a more homogenous intake for the first year of an A-level course. Study skills training needs to be intense. Tutors have found that many students have little knowledge of basic techniques such as notetaking, and that essay-writing skills need careful nurturing. There was less time for more advanced skills training, or for the in-depth discussion of topics, or for meaningful group work.

Assessing the level of an AS was one of the most difficult tasks even for an experienced tutor, even though the boards had given guidance to a limited extent. It was hard to reduce the amount of material to be included in a topic so that it would be satisfactory to those who had little background and yet provide a challenge to the more able or those who had more experience of the subject. Textbooks were rushed out to meet the September deadline but many teachers and students were left with the books they had found most useful for the former A-level courses. Finance for new or adapted texts was difficult, and indeed it was obvious that some authors were still catering for the former courses.

The time element with the pressures of four AS subjects and Key Skills was critical. Some institutions devised full courses of Key Skills demanding inclusion of topics with relatively little reference to subject areas including Geography. Careful study of the skills requirements would show that many Key Skills can be delivered through Geography, but there was insufficient recognition of this fact in many institutions. The impact of Key Skills has been a major criticism of Curriculum 2000.

The workload of teachers and students has increased significantly. The position of an environmental investigation as a third module of the AS means that fieldwork must be done early in the course. It is possible that students have not gained sufficient maturity to benefit at this time. Alternatively, it can be said that residential fieldwork early in a two-year course is highly beneficial for group ethos.

Major criticisms also include the tight timescale, with practical examinations in other subject areas beginning before the end of April, reducing the time for meaningful revision. This has also had an impact on the timing of fieldwork and the consequent production of coursework especially where it has to be assessed internally. The demands of other subjects for coursework, are high and students have found great difficulty in coping with this and with their revision. The examination timetable was crowded, with too many students finding themselves taking more than two subjects on one day and with unnecessary timetable clashes where subjects were set by different boards.

A further serious criticism has been that the increased number of subjects being taken has had a detrimental effect on the enrichment activities of many 16–19-year-olds. This is directly contrary to the spirit of the Dearing Review, which sought to widen the interest and understanding of young people.

After broad and rapid consultation in early July 2001 a preliminary report on the examinations was made by QCA to the Secretary of State. This conceded that, whilst the Curriculum 2000 reforms are welcome and supported, there are serious issues to be addressed. These include

- The standards expected at AS level
- The excessive content of many AS levels
- The reduction in effective teaching time to just over two terms in many cases
- Students' comments on the excessive assessment demand of four AS and Key Skills plus three A2 subjects, meaning 20 written examinations totalling 30 hours, plus coursework/practicals/portfolio.

It was announced on 12 September 2001 that new arrangements to reduce timetabling clashes at AS level are to be made for summer 2002. This is to reduce the burden of assessment for 95 per cent of AS candidates. In many subjects, students will take their AS written papers in a single half-day session of up to three hours. The exams timetable will be extended from two and a half weeks to three weeks. It has to be recorded that these arrangements do not apply to Geography for 2002.

QCA have published a full set of guidelines entitled *Managing Curriculum 2000* which are available from their website. The full review of the consultations and possible changes are to be published in early December when it is confidently expected that changes will be made to the issue of Key Skills assessment.

The geography tutor has to be constantly aware of the changing nature of the subject and willing to incorporate this into his or her teaching. Some background in and ability to use Information Technology is important at this time, although it is recognized that some find this a burden. Interest and enthusiasm for one's subject are essential but these must be tempered by an ability to relate to the level of work required by one's students. The burden of assessment is high but one recognizes that there is a need for the students to see progression. This is not done by marking/assessing once a term. Production of detailed schemes of work, as opposed to using the specifications on their own, is not only useful for the department handbook but is a genuine help in timing and coverage of the course. These do not have to be set in stone but should be regularly revised to cover new issues. There are great challenges in the teaching of AS and A levels but there is also a great degree of satisfaction to be had.

References

Bradford, M. (2001) 'The New AS/A Framework', *Teaching Geography* 26(1).

Butt, G. and Weedon, P. (1999) 'Arrangements for the new A and AS levels in geography', *Assessment Matters Teaching Geography*.

Naish, M. (1997) 'Curriculum developments in A level courses', in *Handbook of Post 16 Geography*, Sheffield: Geographical Association.

Naish, M. *et al.* (1987) *The Contribution of a Curriculum Project to 16–19 Education*, London: Longman.

Palot, I. (2000) 'AS and A2 specifications', *Teaching Geography* 25(4).

QCA (1999) *Subject Criteria for Geography*, London: QCA (see website for more details).

—— (2001) *Managing Curriculum 2000*, London: QCA (see website for more details).

Further resources

Specifications

AQA (1999) *Advanced Subsidiary and A level – Geography A and B 2001/2002*, London: AQA.
Edexcel (2000) *AS/A GCE in Geography A and B,* London: Edexcel.
OCR (2000) *Advanced Subsidiary and Advanced GCE in Geography A and B*, Cambridge: OCR.
WJEC (2000) *GCE Advanced Subsidiary and Advanced Geography*, Cardiff: WJEC.

Useful websites

AQA: www.aqa.org.uk
Edexcel: www.edexcel.org.uk
OCR: www.ocr.org.uk
WJEC: www.wjec.co.uk
QCA: www.qca.org.uk
Geographical Association: www.geography.org.uk
RGS/IBG: www.rgs.org

4 The contribution of Geography to vocational courses post-16

Alan Marvell

GNVQs, General National Vocational Qualifications, were first announced in the White Paper *Education and Training for the 21st Century* (DES/DOE/WO 1991) as a clear qualification pathway for schools and colleges in the 1990s. The aim was to extend appropriate learning opportunities to a wider range of young people and to increase the all-round levels of attainment (Rawling 1997: 168). They were first piloted in September 1992 at Intermediate and Advanced levels. The Advanced level was designed to be an alternative to GCE A-level qualifications whilst the Intermediate level, equivalent to four GCSEs, also suited the qualification to post-16. Part One GNVQs were piloted from September 1995, equivalent to two GCSEs, and appeared mainly at Key Stage 4.

The implementation of the Dearing report (1993) dramatically reduced the status of Geography to being 'optional' for students over the age of 14, along with other foundation subjects. The emphasis on compulsory subjects and the publicity surrounding the new vocational qualifications resulted in a fear that smaller numbers of students would opt for Geography. As a consequence, departments in schools and colleges considered their position regarding vocational qualifications. Vocational education has been a contentious issue with some purists viewing developments as a threat whilst others are embracing the changes as a sign of new opportunity.

In order to place the developments that have occurred into context, it is useful to refer to Dearing's National Qualification Framework (see Figure 4.1). Dearing's National Qualification Framework clearly defines three columns – GCSE/GCE, GNVQ and NVQ – with progression from Entry level to Advanced level. Within this framework a commonality exists between GNVQs and NVQs, National Vocational Qualifications, which share competence-based assessment arrangements, while GCE A-level and GCSE qualifications maintain a distinctive 'academic' focus. Three educational pathways are visible: the 'academic route' traditionally occupied by GCE A levels and GCSEs, the 'vocational route' of NVQs linked to qualifications achieved in the workplace, and a 'general vocational study route', GNVQs, which applies the focus of work-based practice and theory in the classroom.

Since September 2000 the structure of Advanced GNVQs has been revised to give them a higher degree of equivalence to that of GCE A-level qualifications. GNVQs at Advanced level have been replaced with Advanced Vocational Certificates of Education (AVCEs) commonly referred to as 'Vocational A levels'. A Vocational A level is of the same standard as a traditional A level but with a vocational focus. The

National Award: Advanced level

Advanced Subsidiary GCE	Advanced Subsidiary VCE	NVQ Level 3
Advanced GCE	Advanced VCE	
	Advanced VCE (double award)	

National Award: Intermediate level

GCSE (including short courses) grades A*–C	GNVQ 6-unit and Part One 3-unit awards	NVQ Level 2

National Award: Foundation level

GCSE (including short courses) grades D–G	GNVQ 6-unit and Part One 3-unit awards	NVQ Level 1

National Award: Entry level

E.g. Certificate of Achievement – common to all pathways

Key Skills levels 1, 2, 3, 4

Common to all pathways

Figure 4.1   Dearing's National Qualification Framework

Source: Dearing 1996: 8.

qualification relates to the world of work and employment in contrast to GCSEs and A levels which are based on knowledge and understanding of academic subjects. Vocational A levels are based on developing an understanding of the ways in which people earn their living in travel and tourism, in leisure and recreation, in hospitality and catering and in many other areas.

At Key Stage 4 vocational education has been largely delivered through GNVQ Part One at Foundation and Intermediate levels. From September 2002 the GNVQ Part One qualification is set to be replaced by Vocational GCSEs. The Vocational GCSE, or VGCSE as it will be known, will be based on the existing GNVQ Part One award. It is to be available in eight subject areas in the first instance – those for which Part One GNVQs are now available, plus Science – and includes Business, Health and Social Care, and Leisure and Tourism.

The GNVQ six-unit award is equivalent to four GCSEs and is available at Foundation and Intermediate levels. It is mainly delivered at post-16 level, although is due to be replaced by the VGCSE qualification. At the time of writing its future is uncertain as there is a lot of pressure from school sixth forms and colleges of Further Education that the qualification is maintained to meet the needs of students who have achieved at GCSE but not sufficiently to allow them to progress to Advanced-level study (see Figure 4.2).

The vocational awards that are currently available include a diverse range of GNVQs and AVCEs. Apart from courses based around travel, tourism and leisure, many other titles exist within the current arrangements, although few have a geographical component (see Figure 4.3).

Qualification title	Comparability	Achievement
GNVQ Part One (3-unit award)	Equals 2 GCSEs	Pass, Merit, Distinction
▪ Foundation	▪ grades D–G	
▪ Intermediate	▪ grades A–C	
GNVQ (6-unit award)	Equals 4 GCSEs	Pass, Merit, Distinction
▪ Foundation	▪ grades D–G	
▪ Intermediate	▪ grades A–C	
Advanced Subsidiary VCE (3 units)	AS A–E	E–A
Advanced VCE (6 units)	A2 A–E	E–A
Advanced VCE (Double award) (12 units)	A2 A–E + A2 A–E	E–A

Figure 4.2 Vocational qualifications and comparability

Subject	GNVQ		AVCE
	Foundation	Intermediate	
Art and Design	✓	✓	✓
Business	✓	✓	✓
Construction and the Built Environment	✓	✓	✓
Engineering	✓	✓	✓
Health and Social Care	✓	✓	✓
Hospitality and Catering	✓	✓	✓
Communication Technology	✓	✓	✓
Leisure and Recreation			✓
Leisure and Tourism	✓	✓	
Manufacturing	✓		✓
Media: Communication and Production		✓	✓
Performing Arts	✓	✓	✓
Science	✓	✓	✓
Travel and Tourism			✓

Figure 4.3 GNVQ and AVCE subject areas

Many of the GNVQ courses were heavily biased towards Business Studies in terms of their curriculum and approach. Although the geographical content of vocational courses can be limited, the main focus of interest for geographers has been towards courses based on travel, tourism and leisure. Geographers have a lot to offer to these courses. As Rawling (1997: 167) comments:

> *Scale of operation* is fundamental to an appreciation of the difference between leisure activities (predominantly local scale) and travel and tourism (typically national, international and global scale). Geography can also add the necessary spatial dimension to studies of the location of leisure facilities and tourist attractions and help students to understand the mix of *physical and human factors* which give tourist places their distinctive characteristics. Finally the wider *social, economic and environmental impacts* of leisure and tourism comprise an area which can be addressed effectively through Geography.

It is perhaps misleading to suggest that all GCSE and A-level qualifications are purely 'academic' as some of these qualifications already have a strong vocational theme, such as GCSE Travel and Tourism. Some departments have adopted this qualification to augment the number of subjects or to offer a vocationally based course without delivering a GNVQ qualification (Marvell and Smyth 1996). The aims of GCSE Travel and Tourism reflect a vocational mix of Geography and Business Studies (see Figure 4.4).

A direct comparison is problematic as VGCSE and GNVQ at Intermediate and Foundation levels study Leisure and Tourism rather than Travel and Tourism. At Advanced level the qualifications have been separated to form AVCE Travel and Tourism and AVCE Leisure and Recreation. The vocational awards place a focus on the individual based on industrial need in terms of skills, both practical and cognitive, and their application:

> The fundamental philosophy of this specification is that, in order to understand the nature of the travel and tourism, students must actively experience the working environment. This can be achieved through a variety of approaches including work experience, links with local employers, case studies and research.
>
> (AQA 2000b)

Figure 4.4 demonstrates how the approaches at both qualification title and level are distinct. GCSE Travel and Tourism is an academic qualification with a work-related focus: it offers students the opportunity to learn about key travel and tourism characteristics, assess the impacts of tourism, demonstrate knowledge of how the industry is structured, how the business is run, and demonstrate a range of skills. In contrast, the Intermediate GNVQ places more of an emphasis on vocational skills and as such focuses on a knowledge of the industry and how it operates, the importance of the industry in terms of economic growth, as well as an awareness of leisure and sport. The AVCE retains a vocational focus but also addresses a wider range of skills including critical thinking as well as knowledge. The business-orientated approach is reflected more clearly in the range of unit titles (see Figure 4.5).

GCSE Travel and Tourism	GNVQ Intermediate Leisure and Tourism	AVCE Travel and Tourism
To be able to define the nature and character-istics of travel and tourism and identify the factors which have contributed to its growth; To be able to assess the social, cultural, econo-mic and environmental impact of travel and tourism; To demonstrate knowledge and under-standing of the structure of the travel and tourism industry, and of the roles of the private, public and voluntary sectors in its development; To demonstrate knowledge and under-standing of business practices in the travel and tourism industry, highlighting approaches to promotion of products and services, customer care, personnel and training, information handling and business evaluation; To demonstrate skills in research information handling, evaluation and presentation related to travel and tourism.	Develop a knowledge of the key components and functions of the leisure and recreation and the travel and tourism industries and their products and processes; Develop an awareness of how leisure and tourism organizations operate as businesses, through exploration of such concepts as marketing, promotion and customer service; Study the growth of tourism, its importance to the UK economy and the positive and negative impacts of tourism; Develop an under-standing of the importance of health and fitness, exercise and sport and fitness provision.	Stimulate and sustain students' interest in, and enjoyment of, the travel and tourism industry; Enable students to gain a knowledge and understanding of travel and tourism appropriate to level 3 of the national qualification framework; Develop students' practical skills and enable them to carry these out with due regard for health and safety; Develop students' ability to acquire knowledge by means of practical work; Foster imaginative and critical thinking as well as the acquisition of knowledge; Develop students' understanding of the travel and tourism industry and recognize the value of the industry to local and national economy; Provide appropriate courses for those who will progress into employment at the end of their study of the subject, as well as laying a secure foundation for those who will continue their studies in this or related subjects.
AQA 2000a	OCR 2000	Edexcel 2000

Figure 4.4 Aims of vocational courses

Vocational courses are also distinct in the way that they are assessed. Each of the units has one form of assessment, either portfolio evidence or an external assessment which is set and marked by the awarding body. Internal assessment accounts for two-thirds of the weighting and external assessment one-third. External assessments fall into three models, taken under controlled conditions:

Title	Compulsory units	Optional units		
		Edexcel	AQA	OCR
Vocational GCSE in Leisure and Tourism[a] (3 compulsory units with 1 unit externally assessed)	Unit 1 Investigating Leisure and Tourism[b] Unit 2 Marketing in Leisure and Tourism Unit 3 Customer Service in Leisure and Tourism			
Foundation GNVQ in Leisure and Tourism (3+3 model: 3 compulsory units and 3 optional units with 2 units externally assessed)	Unit 1 Investigating Leisure and Tourism Unit 2 Promotion in Leisure and Tourism[b] Unit 3 Customer Service in Leisure and Tourism	Unit 4 Running an Event Unit 5 Sport and Activity Leadership Unit 6 European Travel Destinations	Unit 4 Working as Part of a Team Unit 5 Using Displays in Leisure and Tourism Unit 6 Travel Planning Unit 7 UK Leisure and Tourism Destinations[b] Unit 8 People and Leisure[b] Unit 9 Preparing for Employment Unit 10 Receiving and Making Payments	
Intermediate GNVQ in Leisure and Tourism (3+3 model: 3 compulsory units and 3 optional units with 2 units externally assessed)	Unit 1 Investigating Leisure and Tourism Unit 2 Marketing in Leisure and Tourism[b] Unit 3 Customer Service	Unit 7 Leisure, Sport and Recreational Facilities[b] Unit 8 Travel and Tourism Organizations[b] Unit 9 The Changing Face of Leisure Unit 10 Health, Fitness and Lifestyle Unit 11 Outdoor Adventure Unit 12 Travel and Tourism Information Unit 13 Impacts of Leisure and Tourism	Unit 4 Impacts of Tourism Unit 5 UK Tourist Destinations Unit 6 Major Short-Haul Destinations[b] Unit 7 Relating Exercise to Health and Fitness Unit 8 Sport and Fitness Provision[b] Unit 9 Running a Group Activity Session	

(continued on next page)

Title	Compulsory units	Optional units		
		Edexcel	**AQA**	**OCR**
Advanced Vocational Certificate of Education in Travel and Tourism (6+6 model: 6 compulsory units + 6 optional units with a minimum of 4 units externally assessed)	Unit 1 Investigating Travel and Tourism	Unit 7 UK Travel Destinations[b]	Unit 7 Business Systems in Travel and Tourism[b]	Unit 7 Tourism Information Services
	Unit 2 Tourism Development[b]	Unit 8 Travel Agency Operations	Unit 8 Human Resources in Travel and Tourism	Unit 8 Travel Service Providers[b]
	Unit 3 World-wide Travel Destinations	Unit 9 Business Travel	Unit 9 Financial Planning in Travel and Tourism	Unit 9 UK Tour Operators
	Unit 4 Marketing Travel and Tourism[b]	Unit 10 Tour Operations	Unit 10 Overseas Tourism Markets	Unit 10 Travel Agency Operations
	Unit 5 Customer Service in Travel and Tourism	Unit 11 Passenger Transport	Unit 11 Tourism Geography[b]	Unit 11 Tourist and Visitor Attractions[b]
	Unit 6 Travel and Tourism in Action	Unit 12 Working as an Overseas Representative	Unit 12 Health, Safety and Security[b]	Unit 12 Hospitality in Travel and Tourism
		Unit 13 Staging Conferences and Related Events	Unit 13 Investigating Heritage Tourism in the UK	Unit 13 Business and Executive Travel
		Unit 14 Visitor Attractions	Unit 14 Sports Tourism[b]	Unit 14 Conference and Events Organization
		Unit 15 Hospitality in Travel and Tourism	Unit 15 Countryside Recreation	Unit 15 UK Passenger Transport
		Unit 16 UK Public Sector Tourism	Unit 16 Resort Representatives	Unit 16 Human Resources in Travel and Tourism
		Unit 17 Responding to Other Cultures	Unit 17 Conference and Event Planning	Unit 17 Business Systems in Travel and Tourism
		Unit 18 Financial Planning and Control	Unit 18 The UK Retail Travel Industry	Unit 18 Financial Management
		Unit 19 Business Systems in Travel and Tourism[b]	Unit 19 UK Tour Operations	Unit 19 Working Overseas
		Unit 20 Human Resources in Travel and Tourism[b]	(Language units also available)	Unit 20 Legal Aspects of Travel and Tourism
		Unit 21 Arts, Museums and Cultural Heritage		Unit 21 Countryside Tourism
		Unit 22 Countryside Recreation		Unit 22 Adventure Tourism Activities
		(Language units also available)		(Language units also available)

Figure 4.5 Unit titles

Notes
Unit numbers may differ between awarding bodies
a   Proposed unit titles
b   Externally assessed unit

- an unseen examination paper between 1.5 and 2.5 hours;
- pre-release material 2–4 weeks in advance, followed by a 1.5–2.5-hour examination (at least 50 per cent of which is targeted at grade E responses); and
- task-orientated assessment following a visit to a facility or attraction. Students will be expected to produce plans, letters, posters and other related materials within 10 to 15 hours.

The external assessment concentrates on skills, knowledge and understanding associated with the content of the specified unit. Sample examination papers are available from each of the three awarding bodies.

The total mark or grade awarded for the assessment determines the candidate's grade for that unit. There are two opportunities (January and June) for the student to take the external assessments, but the student may take the external assessment only twice. At Advanced level the outcomes from each unit are expressed in grades E–A. There are assessment evidence descriptors at grades E, C and A (formerly GNVQ equivalents of Pass, Merit and Distinction) (see Figure 4.2). Each grade is allocated a number of points, with a final grade being calculated on the basis of aggregation. Students who study the twelve-unit or double award receive a double grade: A/A, B/A, B/B, C/B, C/C, D/C, D/D, E/D, E/E. In order to maintain national standards, internal assessment portfolios are checked through standards moderation. The process can involve a combination of postal sampling, meetings of standards moderators and centre representatives, and centre visits. The process is carried out at unit level: where grades are found to vary from national standards they may be altered (Marvell *et al.* 2000).

Early indications reveal that the AVCE external examinations make a different set of demands on both teachers and students. A survey by the *Times Educational Supplement* revealed that students who sat the first set of examinations did not perform as well as expected. Approximately one-half to a third of the 100,000 AVCE students sat the examinations in January 2001 and more than three-quarters of these failed to achieve a pass at grade E. 'Schools and colleges … reported that pass rates have plummeted in business and leisure to as low as 10 per cent in some cases' (Henry 2001: 3). It should be noted that this was the first occasion that the qualification had been examined and that students were assessed at A2 level after studying the qualification for five months. Under the regulations students will have a chance of re-sitting at a later date. The survey suggested reasons why students had a negative experience: 'it is thought that attempts to put vocational A-levels on a par with traditional A-levels may have pitched the new qualifications too high. Headteachers also blamed the rushed introduction of the new qualification, which caused confusion about what should be taught' (Henry 2001: 3). Vocational qualifications (NVQs and GNVQs) are often criticized for lacking rigour. The sheer volume of work required by the qualifications tended to be overlooked by critics, as students built up portfolios of evidence as the result of active investigations, but the academic comparability was often cited as being an issue. It could be argued that the pendulum has begun to swing the other way towards rigour and comparability.

The rise in popularity of vocational courses has caused some teachers to blame their introduction for a decline in traditional subject areas. GCSE Geography

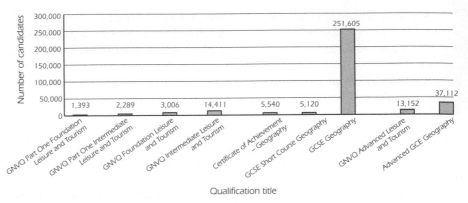

Figure 4.6 Candidate entries June 2000

Source: QCA 2001a, b.

numbers declined from 302,000 entries in 1996 to 252,000 entries in 2000, a fall of almost 17 per cent. A-level Geography numbers have also been in decline: 6 per cent in 1999, 12 per cent in 2000. In 2000 nearly 8,000 fewer students sat A-level Geography than in 1998 (Westaway and Rawling 2001: 108–9).

The introduction of Part One GNVQs might have had an impact in reducing geography numbers in schools; the inclusion of 'Leisure and Tourism', which is closely associated with Geography, may well also have reduced numbers. In 2000 Part One Leisure and Tourism GNVQ entry at Intermediate level was 2,300 (compared to 1,500 in 1999). Figure 4.6 compares numbers of students taking geography qualifications with leisure and tourism qualifications. Clearly Geography remains a well-established subject in spite of growth in travel-, tourism- and leisure-based vocational qualifications. Advanced GNVQ may be a factor in reducing the number of students taking A-level Geography, but the diversification of A-level subjects is likely to be more important (Westaway and Rawling 2001: 110).

GNVQs are often criticized for having low pass rates. For GNVQ Advanced Leisure and Tourism, the figure for June 2000 was 60.1 per cent. This compares with a pass rate of 53.5 per cent for GNVQ Intermediate Leisure and Tourism and 37.2 per cent for GNVQ Foundation Leisure and Tourism. At Part One GNVQ, Intermediate level achievement in Leisure and Tourism was recorded at 40.2 per cent whilst at Part One GNVQ Foundation Leisure and Tourism the figure was as low as 29.4 per cent (QCA 2001a).

On the surface the results of vocational qualifications appear to compare less well to the pass rates of their academic equivalents. However, by extracting the provisional GCSE Geography results for 2000 and dividing them between grades A–C and D–G, the pass rate within each category is not dissimilar. The pass rate for GCSE Geography A–C was 58.2 per cent (53.5 per cent Intermediate GNVQ) whilst the pass rate D–G was 39.5 per cent (37.2 per cent Foundation GNVQ) (QCA 2001b). For A-level Geography A–E grades are recorded at 92.5 per cent (QCA 2001b) which is significantly greater than the Advanced GNVQ pass rate of 60.1 per cent.

It was originally stressed that GNVQs, and vocational qualifications in general, should not be offered solely to students with low academic achievement. Students have to 'assume the responsibility for many aspects of their learning and must plan, organize, administer and research as part of their … courses' (Butt 1996: 185). For the academically less able more suitable qualifications exist, including the Certificate of Achievement, Certificate for Work-Related Learning and other Entry-level awards.

Lower-than-expected pass rates and recruitment helped to prompt the revision to the qualification along with a polarized view in some schools that vocational qualifications were only for the 'less able'. Some schools offered GNVQ Foundation-level subjects targeting students likely not to achieve GCSEs. It was made worse by some centres who entered this cohort of students for GNVQ Intermediate-level qualifications which were clearly beyond the achievement of many students in that group. A minority of schools saw GNVQ as a way of increasing the ratio of GCSEs or equivalent qualifications per student to aid them in gaining a more favourable position in school league tables.

Vocational qualifications are not 'easier' than their academic counterparts; they demand a different set of skills from the more traditional GCSEs and A-level qualifications – a reinforcement of the claim that vocational qualifications are aimed at a different type of learner, not a less able learner. Non-completion rates may be high but often mask the numbers of students who have been offered employment with training while part of the way through their courses. If the purpose of these qualifications is to prepare students for the workplace, then leaving to take up a position of employment should be regarded as a positive statement of ability and achievement rather than as a non-achievement or the student categorized as a 'drop-out'.

Advanced GNVQs have not deterred candidates from entering higher education. Early cynicism led to headlines such as 'University tutors slate GNVQs' (Nash and Blackburne 1995) and to positive statements regarding an expansion of opportunity, such as 'Vocational exams open doors: more than 90 per cent of GNVQ applicants win their university place' (Nash 1996). In 2000 9.2 per cent of applicants to higher education were students with GNVQ qualifications: 35,708 out of a total of 389,091 applicants. In 1999 33,693 GNVQ students applied to higher education out of total of 388,691: 8.7 per cent (UCAS 2001). When considering vocational education as a whole other qualifications such as BTec and SCOTVEC should be taken into account. Nearly 20 per cent (18.75 per cent) of students who entered higher education in 2000 studied a vocational qualification (see Table 4.1).

Vocational qualifications have had a direct impact on teaching and learning styles. Students are encouraged to take more responsibility for their own learning. The GNVQ teacher often becomes a facilitator of learning, taking more time to interact with individuals and groups rather than with the class as a whole. Although the 'underpinning knowledge' has to be taught to the class, very often this is achieved through a mixture of traditional methods and student-centred learning. There is a large emphasis on coursework, as two-thirds of the assessment is based on the production of assignments and reports which are marked internally.

Teachers not only have to be aware of the differences between 'traditional' and vocational courses but also be able to express those differences in approach through

Table 4.1 Applicants to higher education with vocational qualifications

	2000
Applicants with GNVQ	35,708
Applicants with BTec/SCOTVEC	37,250
Total number of applicants (A level, GNVQ, BTec, etc.)	389,091
Percentage of total applicants with GNVQ qualifications	9.2%
Percentage of total applicants with vocational qualifications (GNVQ + BTec/SCOTVEC)	18.8%

Source: UCAS 2001.

their teaching and contact with students. A study by Newcastle University identified a set of characteristics that vocational teachers should possess:

- Good academic qualifications
- Good recent knowledge and experience of the vocational area
- Empathy with/interest in young people
- A willingness to work harder and handle a heavy assessment workload
- Willingness to train and develop new skills
- Resourcefulness: the ability to find equipment, work placements and generally 'make things happen'
- Flexibility: the ability to manage change
- The ability to work in teams to deliver the courses.

(Meagher 1997: 77)

There is no reason why existing staff, especially those with A-level teaching experience, will necessarily have these characteristics. A programme of appraisal and Inset should be available to support those teaching on vocational courses. Work placements should also be considered to provide teachers with the opportunity to experience the working environment related to the area that they are teaching. This allows not only greater empathy between educational and work-related environments but also greater knowledge of examples and working practices that can be passed on to students.

Students studying for a vocational qualification will tend to take a greater responsibility for their own learning, for planning and research, for making their own investigations often in conjunction with assignments set by the tutor. Investigations may involve drawing upon several sources of information. In the introduction to the Collins *Advanced Vocational Travel and Tourism*, several ways in which a student may carry out investigations are suggested:

- Do research in libraries and resource centres
- Visit workplaces and talk to people currently working in the travel and tourism industry

- Learn from visits by local employers and business people
- Carry out surveys of people's activities, preferences and opinions
- Study company brochures and gather information from press and television reports
- Study particular examples of people, places and firms that relate to your work
- Learn from work experience with a local employer (if this can be arranged).

(Outhart *et al*. 2000: v)

These help to encourage students to develop a range of skills that are essential in the workplace and link with Key Skills qualifications. The process of acquiring Key Skills and the method of investigative learning through research is not dissimilar to that of fieldwork, as geography fieldwork provides a real-world context for much Key Skills work (Nowicki 1999: 121). The benefits to students include increasing independent learning, and developing and applying a range of transferable skills.

Key Skills form an integral part of vocational courses. They are:

- Communication
- Application of Number
- Information Technology
- Working With Others
- Improving Own Learning and Performance
- Problem Solving.

Where they used to form part of the qualification, they are now recorded and certificated separately. Schools and colleges will continue to encourage students to achieve Key Skills qualifications. Different Key Skills can be certificated at different levels (see Figure 4.1): Communication level 3, Application of Number level 2 and Information Technology level 4, for example. Opportunities for Key Skills are identified and written at the end of each unit within the specification:

Keys to Attainment are identified Key Skills which are central to vocational achievement. Where a student has met the indicated vocational requirements of the unit, the Keys to Attainment show the relevant aspect of Key Skills that have been achieved.

Signposting indicates naturally occurring opportunities for the development of Key Skills during teaching, learning and assessment. Students will not necessarily achieve the signposted Key Skill through the related vocational evidence.

In general, the amount of geographical content can be limited in vocational courses, although many geography teachers see vocational courses as important opportunities to develop some geographical input into the vocational area and indeed strengthen the role of the geography department, particularly in schools which are offering these courses. Some staff may be divided on this issue but in the main geographers have contributed to the development of vocational and cross-curricular courses such as Citizenship, Environmental Education, and Economic and Industrial Understanding.

As Grimwade comments, vocational courses are not a substitute for Geography, 'but [it] will be taught more effectively if a geography teacher is involved. There is scope for enriching the students' experience by developing geographical themes. These might include the impact of tourism on the environment, or the factors underlying the origin, destination and modes of transport of different groups of tourists' (Grimwade 1997: 140).

Teacher expertise may be an issue, as will be finding room on the timetable to accommodate the growing range of courses.

> Many schools already find it difficult to put on GCSEs in German, Spanish and Drama. Any school looking to offer extra qualifications will probably have to drop something else. The courses they offer will depend on the pupils they have and the skills of their teachers. There is likely to be an increase in the number of courses linked with further education colleges.
>
> (John Dunford, Secondary Heads Association, cited in Slater 2001: 23)

For vocational courses to be accepted as 'different but equal' qualifications to A levels they must confront what is a deep-seated reluctance to achieve a parity of esteem to practical knowledge and vocational qualifications in comparison with the higher-order skills and understanding associated with academic study. As Meagher comments,

> Without this parity of esteem it is unlikely that any vocational course will be accepted as equivalent to academic study, even when it manifestly produces students capable of working at advanced levels and competing for academic honours. But to see GNVQ courses only in terms of their comparability to A-levels is to miss the point.
>
> (1997: 81)

During the next few years it will become apparent if the development of AVCEs and VGCSEs have brought about a positive improvement to the range and delivery of vocational education.

Over the next few years key issues and questions will need to be addressed: will vocational qualifications find their place along GCSE and A levels and will they achieve parity of esteem? How well will the new vocational alternatives be accepted by schools and colleges, students and parents? What will be the perceived value of vocational qualifications to higher education and potential employers? Will the distinctive teaching style of GNVQ be replaced by more traditional methods? What combinations of vocational and traditional subjects will be popular? What are the opportunities for Key Skills? What resources and opportunities are required to ensure that students receive a quality learning experience? In terms of a subject point of view, how will these new courses impact on the provision of traditional subject areas including Geography? GNVQs have placed vocational education at the forefront of mainstream education. It is up to the teachers of AVCEs and VGCSEs to deliver a vocational curriculum that meets the needs of students, employers and higher education.

References

AQA (2000a) *General Certificate of Secondary Education Travel and Tourism for 2003*, Guildford: Assessment and Qualifications Alliance.

—— (2000b) *Advanced Vocational Certificate of Education: Travel and Tourism Advanced*, Guildford: Assessment and Qualifications Alliance.

Butt, G. (1996) 'Developments in 14–19: a changing system', in E.M. Rawling and R.A. Daugherty (eds) *Geography into the Twenty-First Century*, Chichester: Wiley.

Dearing, R. (1993) *The National Curriculum and its Assessment (Final Report)*, London: School Curriculum and Assessment Authority.

—— (1996) *Review of Qualifications for 16–19 Year Olds (Full Report)*, London: School Curriculum and Assessment Authority.

Department of Education and Science (DES)/Department of Employment (DOE)/Welsh Office (WO) (1991) *Education and Training for the 21st Century*, London: HMSO.

Edexcel (2000) *Advanced Vocational Certificate of Education in Travel and Tourism*, London: Edexcel Foundation.

Grimwade, K. (1997) 'Part 1 GNVQs: what implications do they have for Geography?', *Teaching Geography* 22(3): 140–2.

Henry, J. (2001) 'Students fail to make grade in new A levels', *Times Educational Supplement*, 30 March 2001, p. 3.

Marvell, A. and Smyth, T. (1996) 'Should you consider GCSE Travel and Tourism?', *Teaching Geography* 21(2): 92–4.

Marvell, A., Smith, J. and Shuff, K. (2000) 'Opportunities of a changing curriculum', *Teaching Geography* 25(4): 170–4.

Meagher, N. (1997) *Methods and Effectiveness in Advanced GNVQ Teaching and Learning*, Newcastle: Newcastle University.

Nash, I. (1996) 'Vocational exams open doors', *Times Educational Supplement*, 23 August 1996, p. 1.

Nash, I. and Blackburne, L. (1995) 'University tutors slate GNVQs', *Times Educational Supplement*, 13 January 1995, p. 6.

Nowicki, M. (1999) 'Developing Key Skills through geography fieldwork', *Teaching Geography* 24(3): 116–21.

OCR (2000) *Intermediate General National Vocational Qualification in Leisure and Tourism*, Cambridge: OCR.

Outhart, T., Taylor, L., Barker, R. and Marvell, A. (2000) *Advanced Vocational Travel and Tourism*, London: Collins.

QCA (2001a) 'Research and statistical information', site accessed 27 June 2001.

—— (2001b) 'Geography 4–19', *Geographical Association Conference*, University of Sussex, 9–11 April 2001.

Rawling, E. (1997) 'Geography and vocationalism – opportunity or threat?', *Geography* 82(2): 163–78.

Slater, J. (2001) 'A very British snobbery', *Times Educational Supplement*, 30 March 2001, pp. 22–3.

UCAS (2001) 'Annual statistical tables 2000', site accessed 9 July 2001.

Westaway, J. and Rawling, E. (2001) 'The rises and falls of Geography', *Teaching Geography* 26(3): 108–11.

Further resources

The awarding bodies

Assessment and Qualifications Alliance (AQA)
Stag Hill House, Guildford, Surrey GU2 5XJ, Telephone 01483 506506
E-mail postmaster@aqa.org.uk   Website www.aqa.org.uk

Edexcel Foundation (Edxecel)
Stewart House, 32 Russell Square, London WC1B 5DN, Telephone 020 7393 4500
E-mail enquiries@edexcel.org.uk   Website www.edexcel.org.uk

Oxford, Cambridge and RSA Examinations (OCR)
1 Hills Road, Cambridge CB1 2EU, Telephone 01223 553998
E-mail helpdesk@ocr.org.uk   Website www.ocr.org.uk

Other useful contacts

Department for Education and Skills
PEU, PO Box 12, Runcorn, Cheshire WA7 2GJ, Telephone 08700 002288
E-mail info@dfee.gov.uk   Website www.dfee.gov.uk/qualifications

Learning and Skills Development Agency
3 Citadel Place, Tinworth Street, London SE11 5EF
E-mail enquiries@lsagency.org.uk   Website www.lsagency.org.uk

Qualifications and Curriculum Authority
29 Bolton Street, London W1Y 7PD, Telephone 020 7509 5555
E-mail info@qca.org.uk   Website www.qca.org.uk

The Geographical Association
160 Solly Street, Sheffield S1 4BF, Telephone 0114 296 0088
E-mail ga@geography.org.uk   Website www.geography.org.uk

Tourism Concern
Stapleton House, 277-281 Holloway Road, London N7 8HN, Telephone 020 7753 3330
E-mail info@tourismconcern.org.uk   Website www.tourismconcern.org.uk

The Tourism Society
1-2 Queen Victoria Terrace, Sovereign Court, London E1W 3HA, Telephone 020
    7488 2789
E-Mail tour.soc@btinternet.com   Website www.toursoc.org.uk

2 Geography in (and out of) the classroom

This section considers some responses that are available to teachers when faced with the demands of teaching Geography in (and out of) the classroom. It starts by discussing the processes involved in planning and then investigates issues such as assessment, resources and the use of ICT, and makes links to current initiatives such as inclusion and literacy, as well as looking at issues that are more subject-specific, such as mapwork and fieldwork. In some cases material was written specifically for this book – Gill Davidson's chapter on planning for enquiry, for instance, and David Job's discussion of new directions in fieldwork. Some chapters have stood the test of time – Margaret Roberts' classic account of reading, writing and talking in Geography is as relevant today in the pursuit of literacy across the curriculum as it was in 1986 when it was first published. In other chapters, there are collections of published articles linked to the main title. This in part reflects the wealth of material, in journals such as *Teaching Geography* for instance, that is available to support new (and more experienced) teachers of Geography by the sharing of good practice.

5 Continuity across the primary–secondary interface

| Continuity after the National Curriculum
Bill Marsden

Introduction

The transfer between the primary and secondary phases of schooling in England and Wales has long been one of the most problematic events in the educational experience of students. They continue to face potentially subversive separations in terms of both content and teaching style. In the case of Geography, little serious attention has been given to more than the rhetoric of continuity. Szpakowski, for example, found that secondary schools regarded it as of low priority in comparison with, say, Mathematics. The fact that work in Geography in feeder primary schools was perceived as being disparate in quantity and quality also discouraged secondary schools from taking much notice (Szpakowski 1985). Similarly, Williams more recently (1997) identified conflicts in curriculum culture between upper primary and lower secondary schools. It may, therefore, be useful to look at the key concepts which have been identified by Derricott (1985) as underpinning genuine curriculum continuity. These are: transition, liaison, continuity of planning, consistency, and structure.

- Transition was defined as the process of moving from stage to stage, the key feature being to make this a gradual adjustment rather than a dramatic break, as at 11+.
- Liaison meant establishing sets of procedures between schools, which might include exchange of documentation about students; the mutual organisation of activities for students and teachers; and cross-phase academic and pastoral staff consultation.
- Continuity referred to the acceptance of an overall curriculum plan on the basis of agreed aims and objectives, content, skills, methods of assessment, and so on.
- Consistency was a linked concept, demanding that students had equal opportunity in their entitlement to contact with established ways of knowing, such as geography.
- Structure was defined in different ways, including the nature of the organisation of the environment of learning, the sequencing of material,

and the psychological structuring (eg. in moving during the 8–13 age range from the more concrete to the more abstract; in recognising the need for differentiation.

(Derricott 1985: 12–19)

The impact of the National Curriculum

Bennetts (1995) contends that the inclusion of Geography in the National Curriculum was an important step forward in continuity, ensuring that students would have a 'sustained encounter' with the subject at least from the ages of 5–14. 'It is no longer acceptable for geography teachers to ignore what students have learnt in primary schools, nor for secondary schools to devise humanities courses in which geography is only a weak component' (Bennetts 1995: 75). But the pre-Dearing experience of the National Curriculum did not provide much evidence that the desired intentions were implemented in practice. Fry and Schofield's valuable survey of Year 7 Geography (in 1993) found that some of the basic principles of continuity were not applied. It showed, for example, that detailed liaison between departments was not generally given priority by secondary schools who were preoccupied with the amount of work needed to get the new Key Stage 3 courses off the ground. Some primary teachers felt that their best efforts were wasted, believing that secondary schools judged that they needed more or less to start up from scratch. The concept of levels associated with the Statements of Attainment (and later level descriptions) tended to hinder rather than help. Secondary teachers had to envisage children entering Year 7 at any level from 2 to 5. The fact that primary schools are no longer required to make a formal end-of-Key Stage 2 judgement in Geography may equally encourage secondary teachers not to take the primary Geography experience too seriously.

There are, of course, examples of successful cross-phase liaison being implemented. Smyth (1993) recounted the procedures of one local education authority for promoting continuity in geography as involving:

- regular combined inservice training meetings;
- the sharing of schemes of work;
- the formation of cluster groups; and
- the transferring of records.

The critical point was made that all aspects needed to be conducted in a spirit of partnership.

Secondary-phase teachers of Geography will, for the foreseeable future, find students entering Year 7 not only at different levels of achievement (in respect of innate ability and attitude), but also from differing situations (in respect of consistency of provision in Geography). Good practice in primary Geography is mostly found where there are capable co-ordinators who have received strong LEA sustenance (Morgan 1995). Some teachers have benefited from skilled local authority adviser support across the curriculum, including major in-service training (including GEST) provision. At the other extreme, some in other LEAs are almost wholly denied these advantages, particularly in non-core subjects.

At the same time, secondary geography teachers should not negatively stereotype what students can bring to their Year 7 work from primary school. They might take account of the Ofsted report findings for 1994–5, which indicate that 80 per cent of geography lessons at Key Stage 2 were found to be satisfactory or better, and nearly 25 per cent good or very good (Ofsted 1996). A comparison with HMI Findings in the 1980s shows that geographical work in primary schools has generally improved considerably.

Transition and structure

The remainder of this chapter is concerned with transition and structure, two of the most important key concepts associated with curriculum continuity. Before the National Curriculum, students found themselves on the edge of a kind of tectonic plate at the primary–secondary transfer, unless they attended middle schools. Thus, in some primary schools children aged 10 or 11 were taught according to an ideology devised essentially for 5- to 7-year-olds. At the same time, in some secondary schools, students of 11 or 12 were offered a geography course based on the future requirements of the more academic 15–16-year-olds. Earthquakes and Richter scales are perhaps not bad metaphors for the impact of this educational discontinuity.

While the National Curriculum's stress on the interdependence of geographical skills, places and themes offers a potentially helpful framework across Key Stages, it would appear that a trend has evolved in which places (particularly at the local scale) are emphasized in the primary phase, and themes, often issues-based, in the secondary phase. This reflects the competing ideologies identified above. Away from the transition years, such differences, if present, may not be too problematical. But what happens at the plate margin between Key Stages 2 and 3, in terms of the concepts of transition and structure, clearly is. For evidence to support or refute the above observation, two sources of evidence will be considered: first, *Teaching Geography* and *Primary Geographer* and second, textbook series.

'Teaching Geography' and 'Primary Geographer'

Relevant detail can be garnered from *Teaching Geography* and *Primary Geographer*, two of the Geographical Association's most successful ventures of the last two decades. The former was started in the late 1970s and the latter a decade later. Both publications provide a fascinating insight into the interpretation of teachers, advisers and lecturers as to what should be emphasized in National Curriculum Geography in the two phases. Taking the issues of each journal from 1989 (the year in which *Primary Geographer* was initiated) to 1996, the emerging emphases were analysed on the basis of a rough page count (of over 1,000 pages in the case of *Teaching Geography* and over 500 in *Primary Geographer*). The approximate proportions of coverage found under the chosen headings is revealing (see Table 5.1). There are interesting comparisons and contrasts. The contention of this article, that there is an emphasis on places at Key Stages 1 and 2 and themes at Key Stages 3 and 4, can be sustained on the basis of this evidence. Places emerged more strongly in *Primary Geographer*, with a wide range of articles on locality studies at home and abroad. Places were not neglected in *Teaching Geography*, but themes were more

Table 5.1 Percentage coverage of selected topics in two GA journals, 1989–96

Topic	'Teaching Geography'	'Primary Geographer'
Skills[a]	18.5	22.0
Places	14.0	32.0
Themes[b]	25.5	16.5
National Curriculum[c]	24.0	14.0
Cross-curricular	6.0	2.5
Resources	6.5	13.0
Other[d]	5.5	negligible

Notes
a   Includes enquiry, fieldwork, and IT, as well as maps and photographs
b   Includes issues, development education, values and attitudes
c   Includes associated curriculum planning and assessment
d   Includes history of geographical education, methodology not associated with the National
    Curriculum, geographical education abroad, etc.

dominant and the preoccupation with issues was particularly apparent. Interestingly, development education made up 17.5 per cent of the 25.5 per cent of thematic material found.

There has been an understandable preoccupation in both journals with National Curriculum matters. Special issues were published on, for example, the Dearing proposals. However, aspects of assessment have been given greater attention in *Teaching Geography.* This characteristic may well become even more evident as an end-of-Key Stage assessment no longer applies at Key Stage 2. What is perhaps more surprising is that more space is devoted to cross-curricular matters in *Teaching Geography,* though it has to be said that much cross-curricular activity is masked in local locality study work in the primary phase. What is less surprising is the greater stress laid on advice on resources for the non-specialist teachers of Key Stages 1 and 2, though here it must be pointed out that the formal reviews section of *Teaching Geography* was not included in the calculations, while the less formal advisory one of *Primary Geographer* was.

One very encouraging feature of both journals is the excellent range of colour maps and photographs, including full-page spreads. However, there is a relative scarcity of larger-scale maps in *Teaching Geography.* Also of concern is the tendency in *Teaching Geography* to emphasize work at the 14–19 age-range. Although many articles overlap the Key Stages, and some are useful for Key Stage 3 even if they are not highlighted as such, the fact remains that less than 10 per cent of contributions to the journal were dedicated to Key Stage 3. This includes one recent edition almost entirely devoted to that phase. Is there not here a suspicion that Key Stage 3 may be regarded as lacking intrinsic worth, being seen, rather, as merely a preparation for the external examination years?

Textbook series

The problems discussed above emerge more starkly when the nature of Key Stage 3 textbooks and the ideology they appear to reflect are considered. Lambert and Butt (1996) have rightly criticized the undifferentiated comment on secondary textbook series. As they point out, these texts are dissimilar in critical ways. Some are intellectually more imaginative, professionally more flexible, and geographically more distinctive than others. But it can be argued that many, if not most, appear to follow a particular approved secondary comprehensive school, late-1970s/early-1980s 'wisdom', in both educational and social contexts. This approach has a different set of origins from the approaches more characteristic of the primary texts.

In the best current primary geography practice, many students have been introduced to a more distinctive geographical culture. This is one that reflects good educational and social principles in dealing not only with the real world in general, but also with real people interacting in real places: a humanizing process. The most successful schools have become accustomed to working with a range of maps, from picture maps and plans to large-scale Ordnance Survey maps (including historical), then moving on to smaller scales. A similar progression is planned in the use of photographs.

On their transition to Key Stage 3, however, there is the suggestion not only of under-expectation about what primary students may have achieved, but also over-expectation about what they are ready for. On the evidence of many of the textbook series, students will enter abruptly a more formal and less vivid world characterized by maps of countries and continents and few at the local or larger scale. They face too a dominance of issues-based work on double-page spreads, typically presented in the form of sound-bites from 'talking heads', and cartoon strips. These, at best, decontextualize and oversimplify issues and, at worst, dehumanize them (see Marsden 1992).

This is in no way to decry the importance of issues-orientated work, but rather to suggest that in Years 7 and 8 at least it should be encountered in real-place and in-depth case studies. Such activity should evolve from an extension of the locality-study principle of Key Stage 2, with which students will be familiar, into widening regional studies. A characteristically geographical 'real-life interacting with real-place approach' is, of course, in line with the statutory preamble in the Key Stage 3 Programme of Study: 'thematic studies should be set within the context of actual places … the studies should involve work at local, regional, national, international and global scales, and provide coverage of different parts of the world' (DFE 1995).

Similarly the 'place' requirements include the chosen country's 'distinctive characteristics and regional variety'. Therefore, many issues could well be built into this part of the Programme of Study for Years 7 and 8.

The influence of Geography in higher education

Another serious problem is that for the last two decades incoming teachers have been ingrained with particular, and often fragmented, approaches to Geography in their graduate studies. The modularization of higher education has led to increasingly specialized and bounded academic experiences. What graduates bring to their PGCE courses is therefore disparate. While Walford hopes the 'placeists' among them will grow in number, only 6 per cent were in this category in his recent survey (Walford 1996). Similarly, Barratt Hacking found the influence of systematic environmental/ humanistic/welfare geography, and physical geography, more dominant than anything to do with place study (Barratt Hacking 1996). So the newly trained environmental enthusiasts (rather than distinctive geographers?) could well find themselves very comfortable with more general globalized approaches at Key Stage 3.

Conclusion

It may well be that issues-based (or issues-dominated) work will remain prevalent in the later secondary years. However, what is sorely needed for Key Stage 3 is a recognition of where children are at the beginning of Year 7, as well as where they will be going at the end of Year 9. This should be based on the principles of transition, liaison, continuity, consistency, and pedagogical structure. In sum, there should be a bottom-up rather than a top-down approach to continuity between the primary and secondary phases of schooling.

References

Barratt Hacking, E. (1996) 'Novice teachers and their geographical persuasions', *International Research in Geographical and Environmental Education* 5(1): 77–86.

Bennetts, T. (1995) 'Continuity and progression', *Teaching Geography* 20(2): 75–9.

Department for Education (DfE) (1995) *Geography in the National Curriculum: England*, London: HMSO.

Derricott, R. (ed.) (1985) *Curriculum Continuity: Primary to Secondary*, Windsor: NFER/Nelson.

Fry, P. and Schofield, A. (eds) (1993) *Geography at Key Stage 3: Teachers' Experience of National Curriculum Geography in Year 7*, Sheffield: Geographical Association.

Lambert, D. and Butt, G. (1996) 'The role of textbooks: an assessment issue?', *Teaching Geography* 21(4): 202–3.

Marsden, W.E. (1992) 'Cartoon geography: the new stereotyping?', *Teaching Geography* 17(3): 128–31.

Morgan, W. (1995) 'Four years of Key Stage 2 geography', *Teaching Geography* 20(3): 108–11.

Ofsted (1996) *Subjects and Standards: Issues for school development arising out of the Ofsted inspections for 1994–95 – Key Stages 1 and 2*, London: HMSO.

Smyth, T. (1993) 'Linking across the primary–secondary interface', *Teaching Geography* 18(4): 175–6.

Szpakowski, B. (1985) 'Continuity in geography between primary and secondary schools', in R. Derricott (ed.) *Curriculum Continuity: Primary to Secondary*.

Walford, R. (1996) '"What is geography?": an analysis of definitions provided by prospective teachers of the subject', *International Research in Geographical and Environmental Education* 5(1): 69–76.

Williams, M. (1997) 'Progression and transition in a coherent geography curriculum', in D. Tilbury and M. Williams (eds) *Teaching and Learning Geography*, London: Routledge.

11 Some curriculum initiatives in Hampshire
Barbara Jones

[…] The experiences of the Hampshire Geography Team, working (in both an advisory and inspection capacity) in the county's primary and secondary schools, found that the statutory requirements are being met in the vast majority of secondary schools. However, there are occasions when secondary schools are less successful in building on what students have learnt in primary schools and plan a term of teaching geographical skills, out of context, in the first term of Year 7.

It is recognized and acknowledged that secondary schools draw from a large number of partner primary schools (often termed a pyramid structure) and have to contend with the problem of a lack of consistency of curriculum coverage at Key Stage 2. Nevertheless the issue of delays in some students' progress must be addressed. Year 6 teachers occasionally talk of their despair when students, on visiting their former primary school, tell the teachers that they are yet to cover new work in Geography after their first term at secondary school. Members of the Hampshire Geography Team have had conversations with Year 7 students which confirm this view.

The Geography Team considered this issue and decided, towards the end of the 1997 summer term, to undertake some research into links between secondary and primary schools for curriculum liaison in Geography. A questionnaire was sent to all primary and secondary schools in Hampshire local education authority. There were three main findings:

1   Of the potential 58 pyramids only 18 (31 per cent) had regular curriculum links with regard to Geography.
2   The main focus of pyramid meetings was discussion of the curriculum and assessment, and Ofsted inspections, visits and reports.
3   All the schools involved recognized the value of links – however, a number of frustrations/weaknesses were listed. These included:
    • the time involved in travelling to the meeting and that of the meeting itself;
    • timing of meetings – they were usually held at the end of a (usually) busy day;
    • poor attendance at meetings;
    • meetings were often considered a low priority;
    • there was often no secondary school representative;
    • a number of confidence issues;

1 When was the Pyramid Group first established?
2 Who was involved in setting up the group/meetings? (e.g. Were any headteachers/deputies for both phases involved or was this a personal initiative?)
3 Who now convenes the meetings? Is this a shared or revolving responsibility?
4 Who decides/determines the agenda?
5 Where is the meeting held?
6 How frequent are meetings? What time do they start and how long do they last?
7 To what do you attribute continued existence/success?
8 What has been your most successful venture? (Please provide as much detail as possible, and separately if you prefer.)
9 What is your biggest problem/threat?
10 Would you be prepared to write up a 'Case study' for inclusion in the report?

Figure 5.1 The modified questionnaire sent to secondary schools

- meetings often degenerated into 'moan and groan' sessions;
- other curricular demands – especially in small primary schools; and
- there was often a lack of focus for meetings.

The main issues identified were as follows:

- the most successful groups involve all phases;
- 'strong' leadership from either the primary or secondary phase is crucial to a group's continued existence;
- the support of headteachers from both phases is helpful in sustaining a group's continued existence;
- the lack of involvement of a secondary school representative in some groups is regretted (these were primary phase-initiated curriculum groups);
- attendance is usually better at meetings where some school time is involved;
- tiredness at the end of a busy day in school partly explains waning interest and attendance.

Some pyramid groups were successful, with groups in existence for a number of years. After some discussion the Geography Team agreed that it needed to confirm which secondary schools were involved in successful links. To this end a modified questionnaire (Figure 5.1) was sent to the 18 secondary schools which were involved in these links to establish more clearly why some pyramid groups were more successful than others. All 18 schools were also invited to submit a brief report (Figure 5.2 shows the reports of two schools).

Case Study 1: Richard Aldworth Pyramid

This pyramid has operated for eight years. In that time we have addressed many important issues.

In the past we have co-ordinated the content across our schools as this was a problem when I was first appointed to Richard Aldworth School, e.g. making sure that map skills were not taught twice; making sure that if the same countries were studied that content was deeper when they were repeated.

In recent months we have created a glossary of geography terms to be used across the pyramid (made with non-specialist teachers in mind). This has proved very popular.

We have also worked on information technology and assessment. On the latter we are working on making common level mark schemes across the Key Stages. This will allow standardization across schools and across Key Stages within the National Curriculum.

The attendance and interest in the geography pyramid has declined since the core subjects received greater emphasis. It is feared in the group that this interest will decline further in future with the focus on Literacy and Numeracy. Surely Geography will provide a useful context for these!

Andy Housden

Case Study 2: The Cowplain–Horndean Pyramid Group

The Cowplain–Horndean group has operated with varying degrees of success. The most successful ventures to date have been based around large-scale projects, sometimes requiring a day's in-service training and always requiring input from all the schools involved. The strength of the group lies in producing an activity or project that meets the following criteria:

- the activity/project suits as many group members as possible
- the activity/project has adequate time planned and given over to it
- the focus is pre-agreed and understood by everybody
- each member has an input resulting in the sharing of good practice.

Within the last three years the group has had a fair amount of success meeting these criteria. Outlined below are two of the tasks undertaken, their objectives, time taken, content and benefits. These are available from the author for viewing.

1 Using Your Locality – 1995/96

Time   One meeting and one in-service training day

Objective   To construct a pack that resources the study of localities at Key Stages 1, 2 and 3. The resources focused on the school site or local area.

Content   The pack includes guidelines on the National Curriculum, infor-
            mation on where to obtain aerial photographs, maps, digital
            map data and fieldwork guidelines. Specific resources include…
            information on how to use the school site, use of photographs
            trails, examples of activities, a summary of available resources
            from the Ordnance Survey, Hantsnet, Met Office, etc., general
            base maps.

            Each geography co-ordinator was supplied with a pack.

Benefits   The project has supplied an excellent resource base from which
            a variety of locality-based tasks can be planned. Reports to date
            have been favourable.

2   KS1, 2 and 3 Moderation Bank – 1996/97

Time   1.5 meetings

Objective   In the light of the need to report on a student's level at the end
            of Key Stage 3, we decided that a cross-moderated bank of
            work, representative of each Key Stage, would be useful. It
            would also illustrate progression through each Key Stage.

Content   Each member was invited to bring along a sample of work.
            Using blank assessment forms, the group assessed and
            discussed each student's work. Copies were made of these and
            some accompanying notes which outlined the elements that
            informed the reader of its appropriate level. The task was
            deemed difficult, especially as many of the pieces were taken
            out of their lesson contexts.

Benefits   A portfolio of work is now available to each member school. It is
            currently held by the group chair.

Finally, the group's work has been complemented with curriculum
mapping and the sharing of guidelines and good practice.

Chris Pooley, Horndean Community School

Figure 5.2 Two Hampshire LEA pyramid case studies

Responses

Of the 18 Hampshire LEA secondary schools contacted nine responses were
received. (The numbered points below relate directly to the numbered questions in
Figure 5.1.)

1   Of these nine groups five have existed since 1991 (the introduction of the
    original National Curriculum); two others were started in 1994 and the
    remaining two in 1996.

2   Five groups owe their foundation to joint initiatives of primary/secondary headteachers; three to the personal initiative of the secondary head of department and one to a history focus developed jointly by the county history inspector and a humanities head of department – this group now has a humanities focus. In one pyramid group there was agreement between all headteachers of the pyramid schools to fund liaison meetings on a rotating basis.

3   Once initiated by headteachers, subsequent development has been left to the head of department in two-thirds of the groups. In the remaining one-third the primary headteacher, the group chair and a group consensus now convene meetings.

4   In most groups the agenda is jointly agreed. In one group it is left to the secondary head of department. Two groups have their meeting agenda determined by the local headteachers and in the remaining group it is a joint group affair with headteacher input, and is usually in accordance with particular development needs.

5   Meetings in six cases are held at the secondary school. In some instances this is because of its central location, while in others it is for the convenience of using the resources of the secondary school. In three groups the meetings rotate from one school to another.

6   Currently only three groups meet once a term. In the remaining groups it varies between once or twice a year. Most meetings are held after school, though two groups have had the opportunity to meet in school time – one group was funded for their initial meeting and another was planned into the in-service training timetable. Most meetings last for between one and one and a half hours.

7   There is reasonable consensus that the pyramid groups have been successful. However, two schools feel that the meetings have limited value for them and benefit primary schools more. The apparent lack of confidence felt by some primary teachers in one group has made them reluctant to share materials. Two responses stress the importance of good relationships, mutual interest and trust, and relevance:

>   Regular attendance – definite pre-agreed tasks and agenda with concrete aims and outcomes … Dynamic chair helps!

>   Having a sense of purpose in producing a work pack on the local river for use in the primary sector.

8   Not all groups could boast of a successful venture! Five groups were involved in work linked to standardizing children's work to National Curriculum levels. Other activities have included the sharing of planning documents, creating a localities pack and agreeing definitions of the local area. One response states:

>   We used to meet once a term and I felt that we achieved little [so] I started an initiative about map skills. All feeder schools get Year 6 to do a map skills test for us. The last initiative came about last year. A teacher

from one primary school asked my advice on producing a pack on the local river. We have now finished this. A focus has made meetings much more meaningful.

Conclusion

This research confirms that relatively few schools in Hampshire are involved in active curriculum links for Geography across the primary/secondary phase. Where links do exist the involvement and continued support of headteachers in both primary and secondary schools are significant features. In those cases where support from the headteacher is absent, the commitment of the secondary school head of department is crucial to the link. Also important for the continued existence of a group are meaningful agendas and well-organized meetings with a practical focus (see Figure 5.2). The attitude of the secondary head of department in appreciating and handling the potential lack of confidence of some non-specialist teachers in primary schools is imperative. Such an attitude helps establish trust and a climate for productive interchange of information between the phases. Furthermore, students in secondary schools (especially those in Year 7) would benefit from a reconsideration of the continuity issue. This would help to facilitate a smoother transfer from Year 6 to Year 7.

Postscript

This article was drafted and written in autumn 1997, before the announcement of proposed changes to the primary curriculum, issued on 13 January 1998 (DfEE News 006/98). Therefore, this update has been added in response to the changes announced by the Secretary of State for Education. In his announcement Mr Blunkett made it clear that whilst focusing on Literacy and Numeracy, primary schools must still fulfil the statutory requirements of a broad and balanced curriculum (Education Act 1996). This clearly means continuing to offer the foundation subjects including Geography.

Any modification to Geography in the primary curriculum should, therefore, continue to contain those aspects of the subject which provide the basis for cross-phase continuity and which run through from Reception and Key Stage 1 to Year 9 in Key Stage 3. Whilst there is currently no legal requirement for schools to assess children's attainment by levels at the end of Key Stage 2, teachers are expected to comment and report to parents annually about progress in the subject. Reference to the booklet *Expectations in Geography at Key Stages 1 and 2* (SCAA 1997) should provide primary teachers with a helpful benchmark of progress by the end of the Key Stage. According to the *Expectations*, at the end of Key Stage 2, children will be able to:

- explain the character of places and their similarities and differences, by referring to physical and human features;
- know the location of key places in the UK, Europe and the world;
- explain patterns of physical and human features;
- recognize how selected physical and human processes cause changes in the character of places and environments;

- describe how people can affect the environment and explain the different views held by people about an environmental change; and
- undertake geographical investigations by asking questions and using a range of skills (including use of maps), resources and their own observations.

The recommendations below combine the findings and conclusions for this report with those from *Maintaining Breadth and Balance at Key Stages 1 and 2* (QCA 1998). There is considerable overlap between those elements of continuity already identified and the QCA end-of-Key Stage 2 expectations. The Hampshire Geography Team consider that, in order for children to continue to make progress in Geography, it is essential for both primary and secondary teachers to be familiar with those elements of the subject that recur at all Key Stages and to ensure that these should be built upon from one Key Stage to another. If there is no common understanding and little or no cross-phase consultation we anticipate children's experiences of Geography could either become fragmented or suffer increased and unnecessary overlap. The findings from our research suggest (we fear) that, in Year 7, Key Stage 3 teachers may attempt to over-compensate for what they perceive is a reduced preparation for the secondary phase. Consequently, members of the Hampshire Geography Team feel that Key Stage 2 to 3 liaison is now even more important. Therefore, we offer the following six recommendations, founded on the good practice evident in Hampshire school pyramids:

1   the involvement and continued support of headteachers at both phases is crucial;
2   heads of department in secondary schools must be proactive in generating and maintaining subject liaison with as many feeder primary schools as is practicable;
3   that each liaison meeting has a meaningful agenda and is well organized with an agreed cross-phase, practical focus (for instance, a shared activity with a practical outcome);
4   that there is a common understanding of the aspects of continuity described in this article and the QCA end-of-Key Stage expectations. Furthermore, that Key Stage 3 teachers know what they ought to be able to build upon from Key Stage 2 to further the development of pyramid links;
5   the establishment of trust and a climate for the productive exchange of information are essential; therefore, secondary teachers need to offer sensitive support to their primary colleagues in the delivery of geography; and
6   secondary school teachers of Geography must not expect to direct the teaching and learning of the subject in primary schools and should be prepared to recognize the quality of work achieved by many primary school pupils.

Acknowledgements

The author wishes to thank HIAS colleagues and the schools in Hampshire which responded to the questionnaires.

References

Department for Education and Employment (DfEE) (1998) *DfEE News 006/98*, London: DfEE.

Qualifications and Curriculum Authority (QCA) (1998) *Maintaining Breadth and Balance at Key Stages 1 and 2*, London: QCA.

School Curriculum and Assessment Authority (SCAA) (1997) *Expectations in Geography at Key Stages 1 and 2*, London: SCAA.

6 Planning for enquiry
Gill Davidson

Introduction

There is common agreement amongst educators that effective planning is vital to success in the classroom. Lambert and Balderstone (2000) claim plenty of evidence of a very close relationship between the quality of the classroom experience and thoroughness in planning. There is much less agreement upon how to approach planning. Certainly it is true that planning can be personal and idiosyncratic and that, as Roberts (1997: 46) states, 'the way in which teachers plan is a matter of professional judgement'. In a review of findings from Ofsted inspections of Geography, Smith (1997) pointed out that good planning was a feature of the best teaching and that the best lessons were those that offered an opportunity for investigative work. QCA (1998) commissioned two focused studies to investigate how teachers in a range of schools were seeking to integrate enquiry into their geographical work. The studies revealed a wide range of interpretations of enquiry activities and different ways of planning these activities, once again highlighting that planning is a matter of professional judgement. However, it is useful for beginning teachers to start by using a model for planning and, once they are competent, to adapt it to their own needs. It is equally important to understand the principles underlying different approaches. This chapter outlines a particular approach to planning that promotes enquiry as the basis for learning and teaching Geography.

Geographical enquiry

Recent changes in the National Curriculum, GCSE and A/AS level criteria have reinforced the importance of geographical enquiry. National Curriculum 2000, to a large extent, offered a new start for geography teachers. Many writers agree that the form and structure of 1991 National Curriculum Orders had a negative impact on school-based curriculum development and planning in Geography (Rawling 1992, 1996; Naish 1997). The emphasis on facts, place knowledge and traditional skills presented an outmoded view of Geography which stifled innovation. Little attention was given to the process of learning, so it encouraged traditional approaches to both pedagogy and assessment, which were outcome-orientated. As a result the quality of teaching, learning and progression in geographical work in relation to other subjects were often criticized by Ofsted (1999). According to Rawling (2000) the Geography National Curriculum now offers teachers greater freedom to draw on new ideas and approaches towards a more dynamic geography curriculum. In addition to becoming

Route to enquiry (adapted from Naish et al. 1987)	Key questions (adapted from the National Curriculum 1995)	Stage in the learning process
Awareness/ perception	What do I think about it?	Reception/ stimulus
Definition	What is it?	
Description	Where is it?	
	What is it like?	
Analysis/explanation	How and why is it changing?	Processing information
	What are the implications?	
	What do different people think about it?	
Prediction/ evaluation	What is likely to happen?	
	With what consequences?	
Decision-making	What do I think should happen?	Storage
	What have I learned?	
	What will I do?	

Figure 6.1 Route to enquiry, key questions and stages in learning

more flexible, the National Curriculum promotes enquiry as process for learning and teaching Geography:

> Geographical enquiry is clearly outlined as an active, questioning approach to teaching and learning which includes values enquiry and is integrated with the development of geographical skills. It is also explained that geographical enquiry and skills are developed and used when studying the required content and not separately. All work in geography should include some element of geographical enquiry.
>
> (Rawling 2000: 121)

The above quotation echoes Roberts (1996) that enquiry is not an 'event'; it is the whole process of constructing geographical knowledge. The 'route to geographical enquiry' devised by Naish et al. (1987) to guide the School's Council 16–19 Geography Project is now widely accepted as providing the theoretical framework for this meaning of geographical enquiry. The 'route to enquiry' guides pupils through a series of stages in decision-making, using a framework of key questions. The 'route to enquiry' involves factual and values enquiry and is the framework in which pupils are encouraged to develop and justify their own values and responses. The questions have been largely adopted within the National Curriculum (see Figure 6.1).

Planning for enquiry is, therefore, planning to facilitate geographical learning that encourages pupils to ask questions, to search for answers using a wide range of skills and information, to construct knowledge for themselves and to recognize that knowledge is contingent and contentious. 'Enquiry promotes a view that knowledge should always be examined, questioned, re-examined and never taken as absolute and it encourages children to develop their own ideas and to articulate them' (Davidson and Catling 2000).

Clearly, there are many different ways of developing enquiry-based work in Geography (QCA 1998). Enquiry promotes active involvement of the students in learning, but it is helpful to recognize that there are variations in the degree of control the teacher may exercise in planning and structuring enquiry work. Naish *et al.* (1987) suggested that enquiry work might be located at a point along a continuum of teacher control and pupil freedom. The majority of geographical work in schools is guided by National Curriculum and examination requirements, which necessitate some element of control over curriculum content. However, there is a great deal of scope within these curriculum boundaries to develop an enquiry approach to learning Geography, and there are also opportunities through projects and individual studies to facilitate open-ended enquiry with greater pupil freedom. What is presented here is an approach to planning for enquiry, which is to a large extent teacher directed, to enable external curriculum requirements to be met, but it provides scope for pupil involvement in formulating questions, developing enquiry skills and suggesting approaches to investigation. The first example will illustrate how an enquiry approach can be reflected in planning for a single lesson and the second example will show how the route to enquiry can guide planning for a topic.

Curriculum planning

Planning the geography curriculum in a school takes place at different levels. Bennetts (1996) outlines a hierarchy of planning decisions from school level to individual teachers. Teachers are all guided by educational objectives; these are the goals for education and in their broadest sense are described as aims. For instance, the aims of the school curriculum as specified in the 1988 Education Reform Act are to:

- promote the spiritual, moral, cultural, mental, and physical development of pupils at the school and of society; and
- prepare such pupils for the opportunities, responsibilities and experiences of adult life.

Aims are general statements which give an overall sense of direction to a programme of teaching and learning. At school level, general policy statements provide guidance for the whole curriculum. These in turn influence policies for geography departments, which are then used to structure courses and schemes of work for the subject and are usually agreed by the course team. Individual departments usually have statements of aims for the subject, which reflect the educational values of the department by indicating the nature of geographical learning considered to be most worthwhile. These aims are translated into more specific objectives for individual courses and units of study. The specific objectives for Geography are informed largely by National Curriculum documents and GCSE and post-16 syllabuses and specifications.

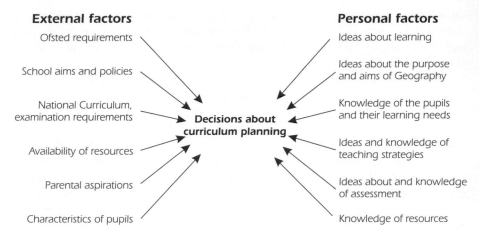

Figure 6.2 Key factors influencing planning decisions

Plans for individual lessons are generally left to individual teachers and it is at this level that most beginning teachers are introduced to planning. At whatever level, the process of planning involves making decisions, guided by aims and objectives, about how best to construct the curriculum to enable pupils to make progress in learning. It is a dynamic process and should be responsive to the pupils' needs as well as new ideas and practices.

There are many factors which influence planning decisions – some are external but many are dependent on the personal knowledge and understanding, values and perceptions of individual teachers. Figure 6.2 summarizes the key factors that are likely to influence planning decisions.

Thinking about learning

Research has demonstrated that the essence of being an effective teacher lies in knowing what to do to foster pupils' learning and being able to do it (Kyriacou 1991). Through careful planning many of the decisions about what to do can be made in advance and therefore provide the best opportunities for progression in learning. Notwithstanding that, it is important to remain flexible during the teaching stage.

Being able to plan for learning in Geography is predicated by an understanding of the learning process. It is important to be reminded briefly of some key ideas about learning which influence the approach to planning adopted here. Although there are many theories about learning, Claxton (1990) claims that there is common agreement that constructivist theories of learning now predominate. In summary:

> A constructivist view of learning perceives children as intellectually active learners already holding ideas or schema, which they use to make sense of their everyday experiences. Learning in classrooms involves the extension, elaboration or modification of their schemata. This process is one by which learners actively make sense of their world by constructing meanings.
>
> (Bennett and Dunne 1994: 53)

Pupils need to understand what it is you want them to learn and how it relates to previous learning in order to know where it fits into their current thinking.

Pupils need to understand why you want them to learn it so they are able to relate to the topic. They need to see the relevance of the topic.

Pupils need opportunities to make sense of and construct new knowledge for themselves by linking it to prior knowledge.

Pupils need opportunities to talk through their ideas in a supportive environment.

Pupils need appropriate learning challenges and activities presented in a structured and accessible form.

Figure 6.3 Conditions for learning

It is easy to detect a close link between constructivist theory and the enquiry approach in Geography. Barnes (1976) describes the process of learning as one where 'school' knowledge becomes 'action' knowledge. School knowledge is described as the curriculum knowledge we want the pupils to learn. Action knowledge is that which the learner makes their own and that which influences what they think and do. The job of the teacher is to facilitate the transfer of 'school' knowledge into 'action' knowledge by focusing on the process of learning. In order for this transfer to take place there are important conditions to be met as listed above (Figure 6.3). These are based on a constructivist view of learning (Vygotsky 1962, 1978; Driver 1983; Bruner 1986).

These conditions largely describe the characteristics that learners have in common and should be borne in mind when constructing plans for lessons. In addition, account needs to be taken of differences between learners and how their individual needs can be met. Gardner (1983) has defined seven distinct intelligences: logical–mathematical, linguistic, spatial, bodily–kinaesthetic, musical, interpersonal and intrapersonal. He suggests that as a result learners can respond in different ways to different learning challenges. There is also a good deal of research which shows that children use a variety of styles and strategies to help them to learn. Children's learning styles and strategies have a direct effect on the use they make of a particular learning experience. It is important in planning to give consideration to how teaching methods might take account of differences in pupils' styles and strategies (Adey *et al.* 1997). In a general sense this means offering opportunities for learners to learn in different ways by providing a wide variety of resources and activities. More specifically attention should be given to differentiation strategies that meet the needs of individual learners (Battersby 2000).

In order to aid planning for learning it is useful to think about learning in three phases (Figure 6.4). Figure 6.1 shows how these phases of learning can be linked to different stages in the enquiry process and the relationship to key questions outlined in the National Curriculum. This model can be used to aid planning for both lessons and schemes of work.

Phase one	Reception/stimulus	Engaging interest in the topic
Phase two	Processing information	Exploring issues and ideas, searching for answers, using various data sources and information
Phase three	Storage	Ensuring that new knowledge has been accommodated into pupils' thinking and they have made a personal response to it

Figure 6.4 Three phases in learning

Planning lessons

Lesson planning is usually the first level of planning that beginning teachers engage in, and lessons are usually derived from existing schemes of work. When presented with a topic to teach, a common approach for inexperienced teachers is to write a 'script', which is in the form of a list of 'content' interspersed with questions and activities. Emphasis is usually placed upon 'getting across information' rather than facilitating learning. This approach is understandable with beginning teachers who are often afraid to release control over the subject content. However, such habits can be avoided by approaching planning using a series of steps guided by questions as illustrated below. Figure 6.5 shows a plan for a single 45-minute lesson, which a trainee teacher was required to teach to a mixed-attainment, Year 8 class. The information given to the trainee was that the aim of the lesson was to provide an introduction to the value of the tropical rainforests. This plan will be used as an illustration of how these steps and questions can influence a particular lesson. The lesson is used merely for illustration of the planning approach and but the steps and questions can be used to guide the planning for any geography lesson that fosters enquiry.

Lesson plan: summary

Class: 8NH   Duration: 45 mins   Period: 2   Date:

Key questions

What is happening to the rainforests?
Where are the rainforests and how extensive are they?
How quickly are they being destroyed?
What is the value of the rainforests?
Should we do anything to protect the rainforests?

Resources

Video: Amazonia
OHT map of the rainforests
True or false information sheet on aspects of rainforest destruction

---

Computer link: Worldometers
Cards showing value of rainforest and scoring system

Learning outcomes

Knowledge and understanding

1   To know what tropical rainforest is like
2   To know that the tropical rainforests are being destroyed
3   To know the location of the tropical rainforests
4   To know and understand the size and extent of destruction of the rainforests
5   To know and understand the value of rainforest at local to global scale
6   To understand why people have different viewpoints about the value of the forests

Skills

7   To observe and extract information from a video
8   To work co-operatively in pairs and groups
9   To evaluate information

Attitudes and values

10 To understand that people have different viewpoints and opinions about the value of the rainforests
11 To recognize the interconnections between people's actions and the environment

Assessment evidence, opportunities

Ideas from pupils on video commentary (1, 2, 7)
Responses to true or false exercise (2, 3, 4)
Scoring for rainforest value (5, 6, 8, 9, 10)
Homework exercise (6, 9, 10, 11)

Lesson plan: structure

Time	Teacher activity	Pupil activity
10 mins	**Key question (KQ): What is happening to the rainforests?**	
	Play 3-min. introduction to Amazonia video without sound. Instruct pupils to observe the video and decide what they think the commentary shows.	Watch video. Take notes. Discuss commentary in pairs.
	Discuss commentary ideas in pairs.	
	Take feedback from some groups; discuss ideas; raise issues.	Give responses and ideas for video commentary; discuss issues.

Summary ideas

- The rainforest is vast and contains wide variety of flora and fauna
- The rainforest is being destroyed.

25 mins	**KQs: Where are the rainforests? How extensive are they? How quickly are they being destroyed?**

Give out sheets with 10 statements about the location, size and rates of rainforest destruction. Instruct pupils to work in pairs, using atlases, internet and fact sheets to discover which statements are true. (Select five pairs to use the computers.)	Work in pairs. Locate information in atlases, fact sheets and internet. Decide true or false statements.

Summary ideas

- Location of the forests
- Size of the forests
- Extent of destruction and areas most threatened.

40 mins	**KQ: What is the value of the rainforests?**

Ask for initial responses to destruction of rainforest.	Respond to questions; share ideas.
Ask for ideas about the value of the forests. Give out cards showing rainforest value. Ask pupils to individually give a score to the card (out of five according to value).	Evaluate information and allocate scores.
Pupils in groups of five. Work out total scores and discuss variations of opinion. Take total score from groups and record on the board. Discuss value placed on the rainforests and any variations of opinion. Discuss views about whether the forests should be protected.	Discuss ideas in groups. Work out total scores. Identify differences of opinion. Answer questions; share ideas.

Summary ideas

- Different reasons why rainforest is valued – global to local scale
- Variations of opinion about value and the need for protection

45 mins	**KQ: Should we do anything to protect the rainforest?**

Introduce homework activity – to investigate ways in which our behaviour may impact on the rainforests. Identify ways we might act differently to help protect the rainforests. Give out internet sites. Give personal opinion. Pack away and dismiss.	Listen, and record homework.

Figure 6.5 Rainforest lesson plan

Source: Adapted from a lesson devised by Nathan Monk, Prospect College, Reading.

Step one: What are the key questions that will structure the lesson?

> The principles of procedure implicit in the enquiry approach would first emphasise the importance of both teachers and pupils asking questions.
>
> (Roberts 1997: 44)

Once the topic to teach has been identified the next step is to think about the questions to ask about it. The questions provide a rationale for the information that will be presented in the lesson. Without the questions, pupils have no purpose for the activities. Slater (1993) places a great deal of emphasis on the importance of questions, and the dangers of presenting information without first asking questions:

> No real understanding takes place unless the answers to questions can be directly correlated to the questions. The argument for the maintenance of a close link between questions and answers suggests that knowledge and understanding are incomplete when the generalized answers alone and in bulk are presented to learners.
>
> (Slater 1993: 2)

By thinking about questions in this way the teacher will be more likely to pose questions to the pupils in the lesson, thereby stimulating enquiry. Questions are important to provide 'hooks' for learners to hang their knowledge on. The first stage therefore is to brainstorm questions and then to consider how many could realistically be addressed in the lesson. The second stage is to place them into a logical sequence, usually in a hierarchy of difficulty, so that there is progression evident within the plan. The route to enquiry illustrated in Figure 6.1 shows a general hierarchy for questions. In this lesson there are five questions, which guide the structure of the lesson.

What is happening in the rainforests?	Define
Where are the rainforests and how extensive are they?	Describe
How quickly are they being destroyed?	Describe
What is the value of the rainforests?	Analyse/evaluate
Should we do anything to protect the rainforests?	Decide

It is not always possible to include the hierarchy of questions in one lesson but it is important to be aware of the logic and sequence of the questions posed and also the progression in learning within the lesson.

Step two: What resources are available to help answer the questions?

No matter how innovative teachers are, they are always constrained by the availability of resources. A key aspect of enquiry is to help pupils become familiar with a

wide range of resources so that they know where to find information for themselves and can learn to analyse and evaluate information presented in different
forms. As Smith points out: 'Poor teaching may result from inadequate resources'
(1997: 126). A variety of resources used in a lesson will also appeal to different types
of learners and maintain interest, pace and motivation in the lesson. In this lesson
(Figure 6.5) a wide range of resources is used. Many teachers find it useful to
construct their own resources so that they can be tailored to meet the needs of the
lesson; for instance, this teacher, making use of information from other sources,
devised the card exercise used to evaluate the value of the forest. It is also important
at this stage to consider whether any resources will need adjustment to make them
more accessible to different learners. Differentiation by resource is a common
approach used in Geography.

Step three: What teaching and learning activities will best answer the questions? How should these be sequenced?

The key questions provide the structure for the lesson and are best written into a
sequence as seen in Figure 6.5. A sequence of questions helps to break up the lesson
into digestible chunks, making it more accessible for learners, and can also help the
teacher to plan for progression in the learning tasks. The questions also help the
teacher identify the transitions in the lesson. The type and nature of learning activities are guided by the nature of the questions, but in preparing activities the teacher
should be aware of the conditions for effective learning listed in Figure 6.3 and the
three phases in the learning process shown in Figure 6.4. It is helpful, as illustrated,
to use a divided page to show pupil and teacher activity so that the teacher can
monitor the variety of activities and the amount of time the pupils are passive and
active during the lesson. It can also help the teacher monitor his or her own behaviour during the lesson. Timings allocated to each section of the lesson help the
teacher to maintain pace.

An important feature in this lesson is the use of a stimulus at the beginning. The
teacher will play a short video clip from the BBC *Amazonia* series. The video will be
played without sound and show the extent of the rainforests, the vegetation and
wildlife and trees being chopped down. This is important in helping the pupils to
conceptualize rainforest and understand what it is they are learning about, before
beginning to investigate it. Pupils will be required to watch the sequence and then
decide what they think the commentary might be saying. This is a way of engaging
them in the topic and helping them to define the issue of rainforest destruction. It
also forms a good basis for an initial discussion of the issue and to raise the next questions in the sequence.

It is useful to consider different ways of stimulating pupils' interest in topics. This
can be achieved through music, cartoons, drama, artefacts and many others (see
Davidson and Catling 2000). The importance of stimulus is to engage interest and
for pupils to recognize that there are questions to be asked about the topic. This helps
them to see that it is relevant. Where possible, pupils should be encouraged to
generate questions themselves and for the teacher to use the pupils' questions to
structure the learning. If pupils are involved in generating the questions they are
more likely to see the relevance of the information and tasks.

Important features of geographical enquiry and learning are to involve pupils actively, in constructing new knowledge and in identifying the information needed. This approach is evident in the lesson plan in Figure 6.5. At the beginning, pupils will be describing the video images and so making sense of what they have observed. They will also be identifying an issue that is worth investigating. This is phase one of the learning process and involves stimulus and defining the issue.

They then move into the second phase of learning, which is processing information. They are required to find out the answers to a series of true or false questions by using an atlas, the internet and a fact sheet as sources of information. (This teacher was fortunate enough to have five computers in the teaching room.) They would then move on to the next question, which is to consider the value of the rainforests. The teacher will first ask the pupils for their own ideas before presenting them with some cards that describe the value of the rainforests from different perspectives. Pupils will then be asked to give their own opinions about how important each of the aspects is by giving them a score out of five. Pupils will be involved in evaluating the information and giving a personal response to it; there are no right or wrong answers. Their viewpoints and ideas are valued which will help to motivate and interest them in the topic. It will also help them to consider their own values and attitudes towards the rainforests. The teacher will then collate the scores and they can then discuss the value placed on the rainforest by the class and why they might have different viewpoints and ideas.

The third phase of learning, storage, is then accommodated in the homework exercise by asking the pupils to consider whether anything should be done to protect the rainforest and whether their own behaviour might be affected by what they have found out. This is important to give them an opportunity to respond to and accommodate the learning that has taken place in the lesson. This homework activity is also stimulating further enquiry by using the internet and giving a personal response to the content of the lesson.

A key principle for developing learning activities is that they should engage the pupils in thinking. Leat (1997, 1998) and Nicols (2001) describe a variety of valuable activities and principles that focus on developing classroom strategies to motivate pupils by encouraging them to ask questions and become independent learners who are excited by learning.

When devising learning activities it is important to consider whether any differentiation is needed to support different learners. This is known as differentiation by task.

Step four: What are the expected learning outcomes for the lesson?

Obviously it is important to establish a clear link between the key questions, the learning activities and the learning outcomes. Once the learning activities have been decided it is then possible to review them to ensure that the learning outcomes are appropriate, and meet the educational objectives of the subject. Learning outcomes describe what it is hoped the pupils will know, understand and be able to do as a result of engaging in the activities in the lesson. These are described in terms of knowledge, understanding, skills, attitudes and values.

Once each key question has been answered by undertaking the learning activities, it should be possible to anticipate the learning outcomes. For instance, in the lesson described the first question is: what is happening in the rainforests? By watching the video and discussing the images pupils will know what rainforest is like, and that the rainforests are being destroyed. They will also be engaged in skills linked to observation and extracting information from the video. The transition then occurs when the question has been answered. Planning in this way reinforces good classroom habits. By providing pupils with a key question the teacher is giving them the objective and purpose for the task. Once the task has been completed, the teacher should check understanding of the key points before summarizing ideas and moving on to the next question. Pupils will then be made aware of the learning outcomes at each transition phase.

Step five: What assessment evidence will be available to judge the success of the lesson?

An integral part of planning a lesson is thinking about the opportunities that will arise to monitor progress in learning and the nature of the evidence that will be available to make the judgements. It is important to ensure a clear relationship between the key questions, the learning activities, the learning outcomes and the assessment evidence as indicated in the plan.

When pupils are engaged in writing tasks, what they produce provides tangible evidence of their learning, but a good deal of evidence for assessment is informal. This is particularly the case when pupils are actively engaged in learning and the process is as important as the product. In the lesson shown in Figure 6.5, for instance, there would be very little recorded evidence of the pupils' learning. However, the teacher has noted the assessment opportunities that would arise in the lesson. He or she will need to be constantly evaluating pupils' responses to the tasks to judge whether learning has taken place and when to move on. On the plan the teacher has numbered the learning outcomes and linked these to the assessment evidence and opportunities.

By carefully monitoring pupils' progress in learning during the lesson the teacher is best placed to get to know pupils' individual strengths and weaknesses and to decide how to plan for the next stage in learning. Ofsted have recorded significant weaknesses in the use of assessment evidence by geography teachers, which this approach may help to overcome: 'The day to day assessment and its use to improve future lesson plans is unsatisfactory in one third of schools and needs to be strengthened' (Ofsted 1998).

Thinking about classroom management

It is not within the scope of this chapter to discuss issues relating to classroom management in any detail. However, it is worth remembering that when pupils are actively engaged in enquiry learning, using a range of resources, there are many more organizational issues to consider than in traditional lessons. During the planning stage it is important to think about the issues involved in managing and organizing the activities such that pupils' learning is maximized.

Successful, experienced teachers can make classroom management look easy as the lessons flow smoothly and without disruption. When watching such teachers at work, the complexities of the teacher's decisions and actions are not always obvious to beginning teachers. Successful, experienced teachers are able to draw upon a wide repertoire of established strategies and routines when deciding which actions to take at any given time. These routines are learned over a period of time and become internalized and implicit. Beginning teachers are unlikely to have such repertoires and must therefore give explicit consideration to such issues in planning.

Once a lesson has been planned using the steps above, it should then be reviewed with attention given to two aspects of management: firstly the organization of materials and resources, and secondly what the pupils will be doing. In the lesson example in Figure 6.5 for instance, there are many materials and resources to organize, such as the video player, the worksheets, the computers, the cards and so forth. At each transition there are materials to be given out and collected in, which need to be managed well in order to maximize the use of time in the lesson. It is important to establish routines for how this can be organized.

The second aspect of management involves what the pupils will be doing. Brown and McIntyre (1993), in their analysis of effective teaching, found that good teachers judge the success of their lessons in relation to two criteria: pupil progress in learning, and whether the pupils act in ways that were seen by the teacher as routinely desirable, referred to as a 'Normal Desirable State' (NDS). They found conceptions of NDS vary from teacher to teacher and at different stages of lessons. The concept of NDS can be very helpful for beginning teachers to consider when planning lessons. The lesson plan should be reviewed carefully, with consideration given to the desired pupil activities and behaviour at each stage and the actions the teacher might take to achieve these. For instance, at the beginning of the lesson (Figure 6.5) pupils will be watching the video. The likely activities required are quietly watching the TV while making some notes. The pupils will need to be in the best position to view the video. At various stages in the lesson the NDS will change, as pupils will be working in pairs, groups, individually and as a class, using different resources. The teacher needs to consider what actions will bring about the desired activities at each stage of the lesson. This process of thinking through pupil activity and teachers' actions is helpful for beginning teachers to consider at the planning stage because they do not have an implicit repertoire of routines to draw upon. However, during a lesson a teacher will need to evaluate constantly whether the actions taken are achieving the NDS required and to remain flexible in responding to the prevailing conditions in the classroom.

Planning schemes of work

The geography curriculum in most schools is divided into 'units of study' and described in schemes of work. Schemes of work are long- or medium-term plans and these are designed to ensure progression and continuity in learning over a period of time. They are usually devised by department teams and should be: 'a working document which summarises teachers' thinking about a course, providing a structure and offering guidelines for more detailed lesson planning' (Lambert and Balderstone 2000: 69). QCA (2000) have published exemplar schemes of work in

Geography for Key Stages 1, 2 and 3. Schools are encouraged to use as little or as much from the published schemes as they find helpful and to adapt ideas from them to meet their pupils' needs. These schemes are useful to show how the requirements of a Key Stage Programme of Study can be met. They also provide information on how wider curriculum issues such as Literacy, Numeracy, ICT and other cross-curricular elements might be incorporated into the geography curriculum.

Schemes of work are organized in different ways but should generally contain similar features to a lesson plan; key questions, teaching and learning activities, learning outcomes, resources and assessment activities. The process of thought involved in devising a lesson plan described on pp. 82–4 is similar for a scheme of work, but it involves less specific detail and a greater focus on progression and continuity in learning. Although most beginning teachers will work from existing schemes of work devised by their department teams, it is valuable to gain some experience of planning 'units of work' in order to develop understanding of planning for progression, within at least a topic. The content for a scheme of work will usually be based around places, themes, topics or issues that have been selected for study by the geography department.

The National Curriculum theme of 'tectonic processes' will be used as illustration here. There are many different ways of approaching this topic and it is often studied within the context of a place, for example Italy or Japan, or as a theme; for instance QCA (2000) have produced a unit called 'The Restless Earth – Earthquakes and Volcanoes'. Whatever context is chosen it can be approached within an enquiry framework and guided by a series of key questions. Once the topic for study has been decided, it is important to think about how it might be presented to pupils: 'the starting point for a study is necessarily a question, problem or issue' (Naish *et al.* 1987: 36).

Remembering the first stage in the learning process, reception (Figure 6.4), teachers need to motivate pupils to be receptive to new learning. Ideally, the pupils should be involved in the process of raising issues and developing the enquiry question so that they are more likely to see the relevance of the topic. For example, the theme of tectonic processes can be investigated within the context of a study of Italy. Italy is a familiar place; many pupils will have visited Italy on holiday, and Mt Etna is often in the news, so they will already be able to relate to the topic in some ways. In order to stimulate their interest in the tectonic processes affecting southern Italy pupils could, for instance, be shown photographs of Pompeii and raise questions about what might have happened there. An examination of recent video footage of Mt Etna, together with some maps to show the location of settlements in relation to previous lava flows, would begin to raise questions about the safety of living close to a volcano. These stimuli would generate questions, which could structure an enquiry around the question: 'Should people live close to the slopes of a Mt Etna?' Although Mt Etna is used as the main example, there are opportunities to draw comparisons to other volcanoes. In order to answer the enquiry question an investigation has to be formulated which involves both a factual and a values enquiry. The enquiry will be guided by questions, which can be formulated by the teacher and/or the pupils. Figure 6.6 shows examples of the type of questions that might guide the enquiry; the pupils may identify others. These initial questions should then be structured into a hierarchical sequence following the 'route to enquiry' identified by Naish *et al.* (1987) to ensure progression within the topic and the three stages in the learning process.

Theme	Tectonic processes
Stimulus	Photographs of Pompeii Video clips of news Maps of Mt Etna lava flows
Enquiry question	Should people live close to the slopes of Mt Etna?
Definition and description	What is a volcano? What is a volcano like? Where are there volcanoes? Where is Mt Etna? Where do people live around the volcano? Do people live close to other volcanoes?
Analysis and exploration	Why does the volcano erupt? How frequent are the eruptions? What damage is caused by volcanic eruptions? Why do people live near the volcano? What are the dangers? What has happened in other parts of the world? Can the dangers be minimized? What are the options available? What do people think about different options?
Evaluation and decision-making	What is the best option? Do I think people should live near a volcano?

Figure 6.6 A framework of questions for an enquiry

Once the enquiry question and a sequence of questions, as illustrated above, have been selected, a scheme of work can be devised using the questions as the framework. As with lesson planning it is useful to have a proforma to work with. Figure 6.7 is an example of how a scheme of work might be laid out and shows how the first few lessons of this enquiry might develop. Once the scheme of work has been completed in this way it allows the teacher to review the unit of work and make adjustments where necessary. A scheme of work should:

- provide opportunities to build on prior learning;
- show how pupils can make progress in their geographical understanding of key ideas and concepts related to the topic;
- be guided by a sequence of questions which are logical and sequential and aid decision-making;
- guide pupils through the three stages of learning and the route to enquiry;
- contain a wide variety of learning activities that meet the needs of different learners and are appropriate for the topic;

Enquiry question: Should people live close to the slopes of Mt Etna?

Key questions	Learning activities	Key ideas	Skills/attitudes	Resources	Assessment evidence
What is the issue?	Show photos of Pompeii Discuss possible explanations Video Mt Etna/maps Raise questions about living close to volcanoes Discuss structure of enquiry	Despite obvious dangers people live on the slopes of volcanoes	Extract information from photos, video, maps Raise questions Structure an enquiry	Photos of Pompeii Video of Mt Etna eruption Maps of lava flows	Questions raised
What is a volcano?	Share ideas Examine video of different volcanoes	Volcanoes are landforms There are different types of volcanoes	Identify key vocabulary Make observations Interpret diagrams	Video footage of volcanoes Diagrams of volcano types	Written descriptions Use of key vocabulary
What is a volcano like?	Info on different types of volcanoes Use video and info to write descriptions of volcanoes				
Where are there volcanoes?	Use the Internet to discover where volcanic eruptions have taken place Plot the locations on to a map Describe the pattern of volcanic eruptions	Volcanoes occur in particular locations along the lines of plate boundaries	Use the internet to locate information Plot info on to a map Describe a pattern	Internet sites/computers World maps Atlases	Maps

Figure 6.7 Planning for enquiry: exemplar proforma

- encourage pupils to be active learners, seeking answers to questions and developing a wide range enquiry skills;
- provide opportunities to make use of a wide range of resources;
- identify a variety of assessment evidence and methods that provide adequate opportunities for pupils to demonstrate their learning.

Conclusion

There is no doubt that planning for enquiry in Geography is a demanding and complex activity as there are so many considerations to be taken into account. However, it is clear that careful planning pays dividends in the classroom and pupils are motivated by classroom approaches which stimulate their interest and harness their natural curiosity. Ofsted have recognized that with such an approach 'geography appeals to learners' (Ofsted 1998). Planning is a dynamic activity and good teachers are constantly modifying their plans. It is important to remain flexible in the classroom, as Brown and McIntyre (1993) found in their discussions with good teachers:

> the teachers regarded their plans as almost infinitely flexible and implementation was crucially influenced by the conditions, which impinged on their teaching. Classroom events, behaviour, performance, availability of resources could all lead to the teacher readily changing his or her planned actions or goals in response to the circumstances of the moment.
>
> (Brown and McIntyre 1993: 47)

References

Adey, P., Fairbrother, R., Johnson, B. and Jones, C. (1997) *A Review of Research Related to Learning Styles and Strategies*, London: The School of Education, King's College.

Barnes, D. (1976) *From Communication to Curriculum*, Harmondsworth: Penguin Education.

Battersby, J. (2000) 'Does differentiation provide access to an entitlement curriculum for all pupils?', in C. Fisher and T. Binns (eds) *Issues in Geography Teaching*, London: RoutledgeFalmer.

Bennett, N. and Dunne, E. (1994) 'How children learn – implications for practice', in B. Moon and S. Mayes (eds) *Teaching and Learning in the Secondary School*, London: Routledge.

Bennetts, T. (1996) 'Planning your courses', in P. Bailey and P. Fox (eds) *Geography Teachers' Handbook*, Sheffield: Geographical Association.

Brown, S. and McIntyre, D. (1993) *Making Sense of Teaching*, Buckingham: Open University Press.

Bruner, J.S. (1986) *Actual Minds, Possible Worlds*, Cambridge MA: Harvard University Press.

Claxton, G. (1990) *Teaching to Learn*, London: Cassell.

Davidson, G. and Catling, S. (2000) 'Towards the question-led curriculum', in C. Fisher and T. Binns (eds) *Issues in Geography Teaching*, London: RoutledgeFalmer.

Department for Education (DfE) (1995) *Geography in the National Curriculum*, London: HMSO.

Driver, D. (1983) *The Pupil As Scientist?*, Milton Keynes: Open University Press.

Gardner, H. (1983) *Frames of Mind*, New York: Basic Books.

Kyriacou, C. (1991) *Effective Teaching Skills*, Oxford: Blackwell.

Lambert, D. and Balderstone, D. (2000) *Learning to Teach Geography in the Secondary School*, London: RoutledgeFalmer.

Leat, D. (1997) 'Cognitive acceleration in geographical education', in D. Tilbury and M. Williams (eds) *Teaching and Learning Geography*, London: Routledge.

—— (1998) *Thinking Through Geography*, Cambridge: Chris Kington.

Naish, M. (1997) 'Geography and education – knowledge and control', in H. Convey and H. Nolzen (eds) *Geography and Education*, Munich: University of Munich.

Naish, M., Rawling, E. and Hart, C. (1987) *Geography 16–19: The Contribution of a Curriculum Project to 16–19 Education*, London: Longman.

Nicols, A. (ed.) (2001) *More Thinking Through Geography*, Cambridge: Chris Kington.

Ofsted (1998) *Standards in the Secondary Curriculum 1997/98*, London: HMSO.

—— (1999) *The Annual Report of Her Majesty's Chief Inspector of Schools*, London: HMSO.

Qualifications and Curriculum Authority (QCA) (1998) *Geographical Enquiry at Key Stages 1–3*, London: QCA.

—— (2000) *Geography: A Scheme of Work for Key Stage 3*, London: QCA.

Rawling, E. (1992) 'The making of the National Geography Curriculum', *Geography*, 77(4): 292–309.

—— (1996) 'Impact of the National Curriculum on school-based curriculum development', in A. Kent, D. Lambert, M. Naish and F. Slater (eds) *Geography in Education: Viewpoints and Perspectives*, London: Cambridge University Press.

—— (2000) 'The Geography National Curriculum: what's new?' *Teaching Geography* 25(3).

Roberts, M. (1996) 'An exploration of the role of the teacher within enquiry based classroom activities', in J. van der Schee, G. Schoenmkeer, H. Trimp and H. Westbhenen (eds) *Innovation in Geographical Education*, Amsterdam: University of Amsterdam.

—— (1997) 'Curriculum planning and course development: a matter of professional judgement', in D. Tilbury and M. Williams (eds) *Teaching and Learning Geography*, London: Routledge.

Slater, F. (1993) *Learning Through Geography*, Pennsylvannia: NCGE.

Smith, P. (1997) 'Standards achieved: a review of Geography in secondary schools in England 1995–1996', *Teaching Geography* 22(3): 125–6.

Vygotsky, L.S. (1962) *Thought and Language*, Cambridge MA: MIT Press.

—— (1978) *Mind And Society: The Development of Higher Psychological Processes*, Cambridge MA: Harvard University Press.

7 Talking, reading and writing
Language and literacy in Geography
Margaret Roberts

Introduction

Language plays a vital role in every geography classroom. Pupils fill pages of exercise books and files with written work. They read textbooks, resource sheets, library books and worksheets. Teachers describe, explain, instruct, ask questions, encourage, reprimand and listen. Pupils listen, answer questions, discuss and sometimes ask questions.

Since the publication of the Bullock Report, *A Language for Life* (DES 1975), teachers and researchers have given increasing attention to all this writing, reading and talking which is taking place in our classrooms. The work which has been done so far is valuable to geography teachers for three reasons. Firstly, it provides examples of ways in which teachers can begin to investigate what is going on in their own classrooms. Secondly, the work suggests strategies for developing pupils' language skills. Thirdly, the research gives us insights into the way language enables us to learn. All pupils learning Geography already have some sort of world picture, however inaccurate or incomplete. They make sense of new experience and new knowledge in terms that they already know. They have to reconstruct new information in their minds to give it meaning. Most research suggests that the role of language is very important in the learning process. Geography teachers can help this process of reconstruction by careful planning of teaching and learning or they can prevent or hinder it by excluding some uses of language from their lessons.

This section draws upon the work which has been done on talking, reading and writing in the classroom to suggest investigations which teachers might carry out, strategies to use to develop pupils' language abilities, and types of activities which will help pupils to make sense of Geography for themselves.

Talking

Geography teachers who want to be more aware of the spoken language of their lessons could start by making some tape recordings. These will show that a lot more is going on than the teaching and learning of Geography. Teachers decide the kinds of talk which are permissible by pupils, who can talk, when and for how long. They are establishing the social context within which learning takes place. Underlying the surface meaning of classroom talk are messages conveying to pupils what teachers think is important about Geography and what pupils' part in the learning process should be. Often the meaning of a tape can be understood only with knowledge of previous pupil–teacher interactions. Also some messages are conveyed in gestures, others are conveyed more by intonation and pause. So listening to recordings needs to be done with caution.

A first step in analysing the tape could be to measure the amount of pupil and teacher talk. Is the balance consistent with our aims? Most teachers talk too much. Listening to teachers is a relatively passive activity.

> The thing I hated was listening to you talking … just standing in front of us all and going on. That's why people get bored.
>
> Comment by 14-year-old boy, on student teacher's lesson

Yet some teacher talk is highly desirable. It is a means of conveying excitement in the subject, of motivating pupils and of introducing pupils to the specialist language of Geography which is best done in talk where meanings can be fully explored. Research has shown that teachers are more conscious of their use of specialist vocabulary than of the general level of vocabulary and sentence structure.

> The teacher explained using all long words and none of us understood. When a boy said he didn't understand the teacher said the work was easy and he ought to understand it.
>
> Comment by 13-year-old girl on student teacher's lesson

Often the work is easy but teachers can make understanding difficult by using unfamiliar phrases such as 'limited by', 'the distribution of', 'in excess of', 'giving rise to', assuming that pupils understand. Listening to tapes of themselves can make teachers aware of the language they use and how much they make its meaning clear.

Most teachers break up their talk with question and answer sessions. There are many analytical frameworks to describe teachers' questions. They need to be used carefully. Often the meaning of a particular question can be understood only in the context of several exchanges or in the context of particular teacher–pupil relationships. Some sort of analysis, however, can indicate what we are up to when we ask questions.

It is worthwhile to consider two dimensions of questioning. Firstly, what type of *thinking* does a question encourage? Secondly, is the question *open* or *closed*? These two dimensions are shown in Figure 7.1 with some examples.

The first dimension (shown on the vertical axis) ranges from factual recall to hypothetical thinking. Research indicates that the majority of questions asked require factual recall or limited comprehension. Modern syllabus objectives emphasize comprehension, analysis and developing hypotheses rather than memory. Yet the message that we convey in our questioning is that memorizing knowledge is still of overriding importance.

The second dimension of questioning (shown on the horizontal axis) gives an indication of how much scope we are giving pupils to develop their own meanings. A closed question is one which has only one acceptable answer. An open question is one in which a range of answers is possible.

Most questions asked in geography lessons are closed. They are asking pupils to tell teachers what teachers already know. The teacher's purpose is to take pupils through a particular line of reasoning, in this way keeping control of the way geographical knowledge is structured. As pupils get older they become reluctant to

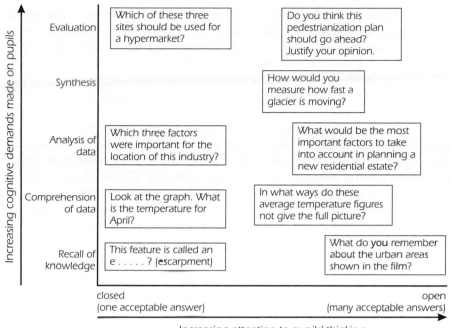

Figure 7.1 Two dimensions of questioning

take part in this curious procedure of telling the teacher what is already known. Teachers complain that they cannot get pupils to talk in class:

> It is infuriating. I ask questions and I know they know the answers but they sit there silently.
>
> Comment by student teacher

Open questions allow pupils to put into words what is in their own minds rather than guess what is in their teacher's mind. They enable pupils to make their own sense of new knowledge and to interpret it in the light of what they already know. Open questioning assumes that what pupils have to say, what they understand or misunderstand is important even if it does not fit the teacher's line of thinking. It leads to exploratory talk, to much better class discussion and to greater willingness on the part of pupils to participate. The difference between an open and closed question is often not evident in the words. For example, a teacher might ask, 'What do you remember about the shanty towns you saw on the film?' This could mean, 'I want you to tell me the things *I* think are important which I remember' (closed question). Or it could mean, 'I'm interested to know what kinds of things *you* remembered'. This is open because all recollections are valid. The essential difference is the intention of the teacher. Is it to understand the pupils' thinking or is it to limit the pupils to the teacher's thinking?

Similarly, 'Why do you think people moved to the shanty towns?' might invite the reproduction of information given in the film or it might invite the pupils' opinions, speculations, hypotheses. The differences are subtle, but if teachers listen to the way they question pupils, they can consider how much opportunity pupils have to express their own thinking and communicate their own ideas. Consideration of these two dimensions of questioning is also valid for teachers talking to individuals and small groups.

Class teaching, however well organized, gives limited opportunities for each individual to talk. Small group discussion is an alternative which has a lot to offer. Each pupil in a group of four or five has a chance to participate and to control the discussion and this can be motivating and stimulating. The pace of the talk can be related to individual needs. Transcripts of small group talk might appear initially very disappointing because the talk is hesitant, disjointed and tentative. Analysis by Barnes and others has shown that, in spite of this, pupils talking in small groups demonstrate high levels of thinking, of generalization and of speculation which are rare in class talk. Children are more likely to ask questions of themselves and each other. Group work also encourages social skills.

The following transcript is of four first-form [Year 7] (11–12-year-old) girls discussing their next move in the computer program *Treasure Island*.

Pupil A   If the wind doesn't change and we go along to 100, no to 270, and then if it takes us to 15, um, 9 – then if it takes us to 14.9, no – 15.9, sorry, then we go down here in this direction and that wind – and that will take us into port cos then we'd be blowing against that, wouldn't we? We'd be blowing against that. Get what I mean?

Pupil B   No Karen – it's north east now, not north west.

Pupil A   I know, I told you.

Pupil C   If we go down here.

Pupil B   Excuse me.

Pupil A   Then we're going to be shipwrecked cos it's blowing…

Pupil B   I don't …

Pupil C   Can I speak?

Pupil A   Wait a second. I'm just trying to tell her something. She can't seem to pick it up. We're here – right – 17.9. We go across … 270 degrees which should take us over to here somewhere for one hour. I don't know if it will take here, here or here, but it's worth a try to get there.

(Cummings 1984)

This brief extract from a lengthy discussion illustrates the ability of young pupils to make deductions from information given, to consider hypothetical situations (*if* the wind doesn't change), to correct themselves, to ensure that everyone understands and to correct each other. There are characteristics of this situation which encourage purposeful activity and which can be applied to any group activity. Firstly, there is a specific task, in this case to collect treasure. Secondly, the task is relatively open-ended, i.e. has many possible outcomes. Thirdly, there are materials and data to support the talk. The following tasks all have these features and involve group work.

Selecting or ranking exercises

Several possibilities are presented to the group. The task is either to select one or to place them in rank order.

- Allocating scarce resources; for example financing one of several schemes or allocating a council house to one of several applicants.
- Choosing a representative sample; for example slides or photographs can be chosen to illustrate particular aspects of an area.

Making a planning decision

- Choosing a route for a new routeway.
- Planning part of an urban area, for example an area of land for redevelopment, using cardboard cut-outs or wooden models which can be moved about on a base map. Manipulation of materials reveals more possibilities than drawing plans on paper and encourages a tentative approach where each individual can explore implications of decisions. Attention becomes focused on the resource materials which provide an alternative means of communication to support talk.

Devising a questionnaire

This can be a preparation for fieldwork. It is useful for groups to exchange draft questionnaires for criticism and revision.

Devising a method

Pupils are asked to devise a method for measuring, for example the flow of a stream or the movement of a glacier. This task prompts questions, arouses curiosity and may produce some ingenious methods.

Guesswork based on existing knowledge

Pupils can categorize a list of countries, for example according to specific criteria such as density of population, or proportion of people living in towns. Eavesdropping on these discussions gives insights into pupils' existing world picture and reasoning. It also makes the actual figures far more interesting.

Designing something

Pupils are asked to draw a sequence of plans, for example for draining an area of sea for reclamation. The role of the teacher is to assess the plans, feed in information when necessary and offer advice. This discussion precedes work on Dutch reclamation.

Preparing for a role-play exercise

Pupils are given roles to play and are provided with background information for each role.

Devising a marking scheme

This helps pupils clarify what is important and why. It is useful preparation for external examinations.

Teachers who have not used group work worry about the upheaval, the noise and the time it takes. If it is used frequently classes will organize themselves quickly and make it possible to have flexible group sessions lasting from as little as five minutes to a whole afternoon. Teachers who use group work value the greater pupil participation, the enthusiasm it generates and often comment that the discussion continues after the lesson, an indication of involvement.

Reading

The ability to read well has become increasingly important with the development of an enquiry approach to learning Geography. Pupils need to follow written instructions, to find out information, to skim through reference books, to read intensively and to evaluate what they read. What actually happens in most classrooms does not encourage the development of these skills.

The Schools Council Project on the Effective Use of Reading found that the time spent reading in social studies lessons, which included Geography, was only 15 per cent of each lesson. Most of this time was spent reading textbooks, worksheets and the pupils' own writing. The most significant finding was that over 80 per cent of the reading was in short bursts of less than 30 seconds. The authors of the report wrote, 'It is unlikely that "short-burst" reading provides pupils with an adequate means for developing a critical or evaluative approach' (Lunzer and Gardner 1979). Continuous reading was, however, frequently required for homework when pupils might not be able to get the help they need.

Geography teachers can help the development of reading skills firstly by being aware of the difficulties pupils have, secondly by providing a variety of reading materials, and thirdly by devising activities which enable pupils to read intensively and grapple with the meaning of what they read.

The difficulties of reading

Reading a text is more difficult than listening to spoken language because there are no additional clues to its meaning in intonation and gesture. Teachers can help by reading extracts out loud and by recording extracts on tape for poor readers in mixed-ability classes.

The actual process of decoding words and sentences is difficult for many. Geographical texts and worksheets contain many new words, both technical and general. For example, all the words in italics in this extract from a geography textbook might need to be explained: '*Irrigation* can *render* deserts green and *fertile*, as in the Nile Valley, and it can be used to *supplement* rainfall in the dry seasons in India.' Most geography teachers would ensure that children understood 'irrigation' and 'fertile', but what about 'render' and 'supplement'?

The length of some sentences and their unfamiliar structures make them difficult to read, as in this extract from another geography textbook:

Finally, in stage five, production is at such a high level and goods are produced so fast that, instead of concentrating on increasing production, industry concentrates on encouraging customers or consumers to buy more and more goods to use them up.

I am not arguing against the use of texts containing new vocabulary and long sentences, but I would suggest that teachers study texts to find out how difficult they are. One way of doing this is to apply a readability formula such as the Flesch Formula which is based on the number of syllables in words and the length of sentences. This gives a rough guide to the *minimum* reading age necessary to read the text. The use of readability formulae is explained in *Readability in the Classroom* (Harrison 1980).

Some children can understand the words and sentences, yet still make no sense of the overall meaning. The structure of non-fiction depends on linking words such as 'likewise', 'moreover', 'consequently', 'nevertheless', 'conversely and so on. If the significance of these words is not recognized, then comprehension is difficult. Comprehension questions tend to focus on the meaning of particular words or sentences. They rarely expect pupils to get to grips with the meaning of the text as a whole. The reading activities suggested on p. 102 involve the pupils in a close study of the structure and are therefore preferable to the random, piecemeal sampling of texts characteristic of comprehension questions.

Variety of reading materials

The use of reading materials other than textbooks can bring pupils closer to first-hand sources. Newspaper reports and letters, planning enquiry reports, travel brochures, foreign embassy and commercial handouts, autobiographical travel, writing and fiction can all contain information relevant to geographical enquiry. Some would appear initially to be more attractive than textbooks for pupils to use. They do, however, present two problems. Firstly, most have been written for adults and demand high reading ages, so can be used only with considerable support. Secondly, many are written from a particular viewpoint, which is evident in the selection of information and the underlying values. Teachers need to help pupils detect bias and to evaluate the text in the light of this. These particular skills should also be encouraged when pupils use textbooks which inevitably present a particular perspective on geographical information.

The use of fiction in Geography is particularly helpful in deepening children's grasp of remote experiences and difficult concepts. For example, Anita Desai's *Village by the Sea* conveys powerfully the experience of rural poverty in India and the search by a teenager for work in Bombay. Extracts could be read to illustrate aspects of the experience (e.g. the arrival of a newcomer to a large city) or of the Indian environment (e.g. the start of the Monsoon). The intention, however, is to explore the total experience so that pupils are encouraged to read the whole book.

The abilities to use the contents page and index of a book, and to skim through reference books for information, do not come naturally. They are best taught in context. If a geography teacher sets up an investigation or a project which demands these skills, then that is a good opportunity to teach and practise them.

Reading activities

The Schools Council Reading for Learning Project devised a series of activities which enabled pupils to study a text closely and to make sense of it as a whole. The activities were called DARTS: Directed Activities Related to Texts.

The texts used by the project were chosen by subject teachers to suit their own subject aims and objectives, while at the same time developing reading skills. The activities are done by pupils working in pairs so that they can reach agreement about the meaning of a text through discussion.

DARTS have two stages.

1   The pupils analyse the information given in the text according to categories chosen by the teacher. The pupils underline categories and in this way discover what information is in the text and how it is put together. Some texts are better analysed by dividing into segments.
2   When the analysis is complete the pupils reorganize the information into another form such as a diagram or a table. The reconstructed information should be in a simpler, more memorable form than the original text.

Several types of geographical texts are suitable for DARTS.

- Description of a mechanism or structure: e.g. a volcano; a power station; an HEP scheme; a fishing trawler.

    1   Pupils start by underlining the parts of the structure. A different type of underlining can be used to label the characteristics of the parts, e.g. the function.
    2   The information is reassembled on a diagram, either drawn and labelled by the pupil or given to the pupil with incomplete labelling. The task of labelling entails close reading of the text.

- Information about a classification: e.g. rock types; types of agriculture; uses of coal.

    1   Pupils underline different categories of information. Sub-categories can be distinguished separately with different types of underlining.
    2   If the text is mainly a classification, a hierarchical tree diagram can be made. If there is additional information about each category, a table is more suitable. If pupils are likely to need help, parts of the tree diagram or table can be completed for them.

- Texts describing a process or a sequence: e.g. making steel; a farmer's year; an ecological cycle.

    1   The stages in the process are analysed by underlining or segmenting, putting marks in the text dividing the stages.
    2   The information is reorganized into a flow-line diagram – drawn by pupils or a given diagram is labelled from the text.

The water cycle

Read the passage below carefully.

Underline in pencil *all the times that water is mentioned in any form (include rain, snow, hail and water vapour).*

Underline in biro *each time something happens to the water.*

*Work in **pairs**.*

Water falls from clouds in the sky as rain, snow or hail. Which you get depends on how cold it is. Some of this water soaks into the ground and some of it stays on the surface – like puddles in the playground. Puddles like these usually evaporate into the air in a few hours.

Some of the water that soaks into the ground is sucked up by the roots of plants and trees. This water evaporates through the leaves. When plants do this it is called 'transpiration'. Water also evaporates into the air from the sea, from lakes and rivers and from the ground itself. Water evaporates more quickly when it is warm. Have you noticed things drying more quickly on a warm day?

Most of the water that falls on the ground flows across the surface to make streams and rivers. Some water seeps through the ground into the rivers, too. Rivers flow down into the sea.

The water that evaporates into the air becomes invisible. It is called water vapour. If the air cools the water vapour might condense into water drop-lets which you can see as clouds.

Make a list of all the things that happen to the water (underlined in biro). Try to draw a picture showing these things happening. Put on your picture as many of the things that you underlined as you can.

Figure 7.2 Example of DART for 12–13-year-old pupils

- Texts developing an argument: e.g. advantages/disadvantages; problems/solutions.

    1   Different types of underlining are used to pick out the categories given.
    2   The information is reorganized into tables or lists.

Geography teachers can invent their own DARTS, consisting of analysis of text followed by reorganization of information, for any text.

An example of a DART is shown in Figure 7.2. It was used with mixed-ability second-form [Year 8] (12–13-year-old) pupils. All were able to do the first stage – analyse the text. The second stage was very demanding – far more stretching than copying a blackboard- or textbook-diagram of the water-cycle. The task required careful re-reading and linking of parts of the text. Weaker pupils needed help starting their diagrams.

The whole class   Extracts from written work can be made into a booklet so that the whole class can read them. Or extracts can be combined with maps, graphs and pictures to form a display. Flexibility in using different lengths of extract, i.e. words, phrases, sentences and paragraphs, makes it possible for everyone to contribute. Written work can provide the starting point for the next lesson. Extracts can be copied out and duplicated for group or class discussion.

Imaginary readers   Pupils can write letters, newspaper reports, etc. Or they can be asked to write for a younger child who knows nothing about a topic.

For a public audience   The following piece was written by a fourth-year [Year 10] girl as a speech to be made at a simulated public meeting. The imagined audience helped the girl sort out her arguments and suggested how they should be written.

> Against the construction of Killingholme Refinery.
> 1   The refinery will be built in an area which is popular with tourists. It's very unpleasant when you go to the coast and find out there is an oil refinery next to you, blowing pollution towards you. Most families go to the coast to get away from the city and the noise. They don't want to sit staring at a refinery all day.
> 2   People think that it will be much cheaper to build a refinery because it will put more men in jobs. But this is wrong. Money will have to be paid to buy and build the refinery and to buy the land to build it on. This money would be better spent on education and activities.
> 3   Oil slicks often occur and they cause many deaths of sea creatures. Just think back to 1982 – all the dead birds, fish and a few mammals on the beach.
> 4   The land is beautiful and if men build a refinery they will ruin the landscape.
> Conclusion
> The Humber Estuary and areas around should be thought of more than the oil industry.
>
> From a fourth-year [Year 10] girl's report

Encouraging first-draft writing

Children can be helped with the mechanics of writing if they start by making a rough draft. Words and phrases can then be changed, and meanings can be made clearer. The revision can be done in pairs or groups with teacher guidance.

Marking

Teachers' marking falls into three categories:

Evaluation   Work is judged as 'superb', 'excellent', 'disappointing', 'messy', 'careless' or 'untidy'. This type of marking emphasizes the teacher as examiner, especially if it is accompanied by a mark or grade. Pupils try to produce what the teacher values rather than explore what is in their own minds. They conceal lack of knowledge and misunderstanding.

Correction Errors of grammar, spelling and geography are corrected. This is helpful but if there are many corrections it can be discouraging. It is preferable to correct a few errors and to monitor improvement. Use of first drafts and preparation of work for a wider audience provides motivation for improving accuracy.

Comment Comments can focus on geographical thinking, on use of data, on reasoning, on value judgements and on misunderstandings. Teachers can question pupils on their writing and invite replies so that marking becomes a dialogue aimed at increasing understanding. Comments emphasize the importance of writing as a means of learning.

Should writing be seen as an end-product which takes place after learning, something to be assessed and corrected? Or should it be part of the learning process? How we mark children's written work indicates why we think writing is important.

Conclusion

Many geography teachers want to help their pupils' language development yet are uncertain how to do it. This brief resumé suggests three approaches which are common to talking, writing and reading.

- Investigate what is going on at present: what talk is taking place, what questions are asked, what written work is done, what reading ages the texts require.
- Encourage uses of language which enable pupils to make sense of Geography for themselves.
- Use the talking, writing and reading activities suggested to develop language skills at the same time as geographical skills.

References

Barnes, D. (1976) *From Communication to Curriculum*, Harmondsworth: Penguin.

Barnes, D. and Todd, F. (1977) *Communication and Learning in Small Groups*, London: Routledge and Kegan Paul.

Barnes, D., Britton, J. and Rosen, H. (1970) *Language, the Learner and the School*, Harmondsworth: Penguin.

Britton, J., Burgess, A., Martin, N., McLeod, A. and Rosen, H. (1975) *The Development of Writing Abilities 11–18*, Macmillan Research Series.

Casholan, A. (1979) *Language, Reading and Learning*, Oxford: Blackwell.

Cummings, R. (1984) 'Pupil talk in groups during a CAL simulation game', unpublished MA dissertation, University of London,.

D'Arcy, P. (1978) *The Examination Years. Writing in History, Geography and Social Studies*, East Grinstead: Ward Lock Educational.

Department of Education and Science (DES) (1975) *A Language for Life* (The Bullock Report), HMSO.

Harrison, C. (1980) *Readability in the Classroom*, Cambridge: Cambridge University Press.

Lunzer, E. and Gardner, K. (1979) *The Effective Use of Reading*, London: Heinemann.

Lunzer, E., Gardner, K., Davies, F. and Greene, T. (1983) *Learning from the Written Word*, Oliver and Boyd.

Marland, M. (1977) *Language Across the Curriculum*, London: Heinemann.

Martin, N., D'Arcy, P., Newton, B. and Parker, R. (1976) *Writing and Learning Across the Curriculum 11–16*, East Grinstead: Ward Lock Educational.

Mercer, N. (ed.) (1981) *Language in School and Community*, London: Arnold.

Richmond, J. (1982) *The Resources of Classroom Language*, London: Arnold.

Spencer, E. (1979) *Writing Matters: Across the Curriculum*, London: Hodder and Stoughton.

8 Thinking through Geography
David Leat

Introduction

In the schools of England and Wales there are many really hard-working and exciting secondary school geography teachers, producing high-quality teaching materials and stimulating their pupils. They use innovative teaching methods, going well beyond normal expectations. Nevertheless, I would argue that there is a particularly serious problem in some geography teaching. Essentially, there is too much concern with teaching and not enough with learning, too much emphasis on substantive aspects of Geography and not enough on the intellectual development of pupils.

On the surface, the continuing improvement in General Certificate of Secondary Education (GCSE) results would tend to indicate that my argument is wrong. If there is a problem, what are the symptoms? First, although I may harbour some doubts about the Ofsted (Office for Standards in Education) school inspection process, a report from the Chief Inspector of Schools on the teaching of Geography (Ofsted 1995), based on a large sample of English schools, paints a worrying picture. It is reported that the quality of teaching was good or better in only 42 per cent of lessons. Video evidence of geography teaching that inspectors judge as satisfactory leads one to question the figure of 17 per cent that inspectors regarded as less than satisfactory. Nearly all lessons ought to be good with only an occasional lapse into the satisfactory. Some of the weaknesses detected are fundamental: challenge, pace and motivation in lessons were often unsatisfactory; weak subject knowledge, over-reliance on textbooks, undemanding activities and insufficient attention to real places and particular circumstances were common.

Second, one can raise doubts about the quality of textbooks that are currently popular. The uncertainty surrounding the introduction of the National Curriculum and its associated assessment procedures had a natural consequence in a desire among teachers to find a safety net: a series of textbooks that would support them through a period of substantial change. Geography is often taught in secondary schools by non-specialists, frequently overburdened senior managers, especially in Key Stage 3 (KS3), and they often want a book that can be picked off the shelf. Books written to be virtually 'teacher-proof', requiring minimal skilled intervention by the teacher, do not increase teacher professionalism and actually serve to encourage the creation of an unspoken pact in which teachers demand little, for which, in return, the pupils do not misbehave.

Finally, many pupils get low grades at GCSE and some who are entered for the examination fail to get any grade at all. While it is unfair to blame the individual teacher, or indeed the community of teachers, it does represent a collective failure by the prevailing educational system: eleven years of compulsory education should not leave pupils with GCSE grades D, E, F and G unless they have serious learning difficulties. An analysis by the Avery Hill Project team of pupils' examination papers in the Avery Hill GCSE (Midland Examinations Group/Welsh Joint Education Committee) showed that approximately 40 per cent of candidates gained no marks on the case-study element of questions in the 1990 structured questions paper (Battersby *et al.* 1995). While lamenting this evidence, one must applaud the boards for undertaking the analysis.

Another approach

To generalize, perhaps grossly, curriculum planning and development have tended to proceed on the assumption that differences in ability are irremediable and that therefore a specific curriculum for the less able has to be devised. Thus, we have setting and streaming, selective schools, tensions between academic and vocational education and a concern for summative assessment that concentrates on sorting the sheep from the goats. This is a conservative (small 'c') approach that assumes that intelligence, whatever that may be, is fixed. In my twelve years as a school teacher I worked largely on that assumption! One adapted the curriculum to fit the pupils so that they could cope easily with it.

However, there is another perspective that can make pupils, teaching and schools look very different indeed. This view is underpinned by substantially different assumptions – that intelligence is not fixed and can be developed, and that the curriculum for lower-achieving pupils should be aimed at changing the characteristics of the learners, so that they can enter into the mainstream curriculum experienced by the rest of the school population. This is a very value-laden view, but there is a growing body of evidence that provides some substantiation for it. It is also clear, though, that there are substantial barriers at teacher, school and government policy levels to implementing this alternative view.

By way of a brief summary, the strongest evidence for the success of the 'changing the pupil' approach comes from the Cognitive Acceleration in Science Education project (CASE). There is evidence that CASE materials, when used appropriately in Years 7 and 8, or 8 and 9, improve GCSE results in Science, Mathematics and English two or three years later. The other thinking skills programmes that are used in British schools are Somerset Thinking Skills, Instrumental Enrichment, Philosophy for Children, and CoRT (Cognitive Research Trust) Thinking Skills. For both Instrumental Enrichment and Philosophy for Children there is good evidence to demonstrate gains in achievement and motivation where the programmes are implemented well. A useful summary of the programmes, their theoretical underpinnings and the research evidence is provided by Adey and Shayer (1994).

Cognitive acceleration in school Geography

Since 1992 I have been working with the assistance of some outstanding former University of Newcastle PGCE students and local geography teachers to develop a geography curriculum that teaches thinking. This work and the group involved in it have come to be called Thinking Through Geography (TTG). We have drawn heavily on the CASE model, but have made some adaptations. Using various definitions of thinking (Nickerson *et al.* 1985), TTG has set three broad aims:

- to devise adaptable strategies and curriculum materials that make geography lessons more stimulating and challenging;
- to help pupils understand some fundamental concepts in Geography in an explicit way so that these can be transferred to new contexts; and
- to aid the intellectual development of pupils so that they can handle more complex information and achieve greater academic success.

We have developed more than twenty strategies and six units for KS3 and, in the process, identified and clarified a number of principles for curriculum design and teaching. These principles are briefly described below and further elaborated in the teaching example.

Constructivism

Constructivists argue that we all learn largely through the framework of what we already know (Driver 1983). New information will be understood only if it can be interpreted through existing knowledge structures. An important principle, therefore, is getting pupils to access their existing knowledge or to provide concrete experiences that will serve as the framework for their understanding of a topic or issue. It is well understood that pupils are assisted in their understanding of, for example, condensation by reference to breathing on cold windowpanes, but it is less well appreciated that their understanding of conflict in National Parks can be assisted by reference to conflict and its resolution within families.

Challenge

The failure of most geography textbooks and much geography teaching is that they fail to challenge pupils. The pupils are given work that they can easily do (busywork); there is an unwritten contract between some classes and teachers: easy work in return for no trouble. Challenge, or work that makes you really think, is essential to intellectual development. The challenge may sometimes take the form of cognitive conflict, whereby pupils' existing understanding is established and then challenged by new experience or evidence. In many instances the challenge is provided by one of the strategies invented, gathered, developed and widely tested by the TTG. Examples include concept mapping, who/what/where/why/when, classifying, speaking graphs, relational diagrams, and reading photographs. Many of the activities deliberately include some ambiguity and an important part of many tasks is the process through which pupils clarify the task.

Talk between pupils and between teachers and pupils

Talk is a prerequisite of much learning and many of the activities are designed to be undertaken by groups. This emphasis on language and group work provides one of the pillars of differentiation in the materials. This will be familiar ground to teachers who have used materials from Development Education Centres and Action Aid. Attention has to be given by teachers to creating an environment in which pupils are encouraged to give their views and ideas and to be taken seriously as conversational partners. (For a fuller discussion, see Wells 1987.)

Concept elaboration

School Geography revolves around a relatively small number of key concepts. The materials and teaching style make these concepts very visible and potentially transferable, facilitating their elaboration over time. Examples include planning, systems and causation.

Debriefing

The materials provide learning experiences. Within this context the role of the teacher changes. Teachers encourage pupils to explain their work, help them to understand the significance of what they have done, and put names to the reasoning patterns that they develop. This can be likened to providing pupils with a filing system to help them to retrieve knowledge, concepts and ideas.

Metacognition

This is becoming an overused term that can be taken simply to mean an awareness of one's own thinking. The aim, through teachers' debriefing, is for pupils to be able to recognize types of problems or situations and select and apply appropriate strategies or reasoning patterns. More broadly, however, it may be conceptualized as making thinking, or 'how you tackled a problem', a legitimate and valued focus for discussion within the class. In this way pupils move towards being autonomous learners (Brown 1987).

Transfer

Once a strategy, concept or reasoning pattern has been established it is necessary to compare it against other contexts in Geography, other subjects or everyday life so as to encourage transfer. To give a very simple example, after an activity in which pupils have been making decisions, there is an opportunity for the teacher to introduce the word 'factor' as something that influences decisions, as part of the debriefing process, and they can use the example of the factors that influence where people go for holidays as a context from everyday life. (For a fuller discussion see Perkins and Salomon 1988.)

Appealing to all the senses

We are becoming increasingly aware of the need to develop pictorial, symbolic, photographic, concrete and even aural resources to appeal to those for whom text is a barrier. At present, olfactory resources have defeated us, but they remain a challenge.

A worked example

Flooding is a familiar topic in KS3. The Programmes of Study (Department for Education 1995) specify that pupils should be taught 'the causes and effects of river floods and how people respond to and seek to control the flood hazard'.

Phase 1

Imagine that your home gets flooded to a depth of two feet or 60 cm.

1   Make a list of all the damage that might be done by the water, both inside and outside the house.
2   If the flooding lasts on and off for a week, what further problems might be created for you and the rest of your family, especially if your neighbour-hood is flooded?
3   If you have an hour's warning, what could your family do to reduce the damage and problems caused by the flood? Who might you need to contact for help?
4   What would you expect the emergency services, council, government and public utilities to be doing to help?

Commentary

This homework is employing a constructivist approach because it is drawing upon pupils' knowledge of their own homes as a starting point. They would be encouraged to crawl around on their hands and knees to see what is below the 60 cm mark. They could be encouraged to talk to their parent(s)/guardian(s) about the difficulties that might ensue and what help could be expected. Disbelief has to be suspended by those who live in blocks of flats or on hills!

Phase 2

At the start of the next lesson the pupils would be asked to form groups of between two and four members to pool their data. A time-limit of five to ten minutes needs to be set. Pupils are then asked to generate some categories of action for 'How people respond to and seek to control the flood hazard'. This could be framed as 'Look at all the information that you have got. Try to put it into groups of things that people do to reduce, escape from, repair and prevent damage from floods'. Depending on the pupil group, the teacher may have to do some preparatory work on the notion of categorizing, but most KS3 groups will find this accessible.

Commentary

The talk between pupils is crucial at this stage as pupils, sometimes clumsily, extend their understanding of the possible effects of floods and the human response. Pupils are talking themselves into meaning. Furthermore, the classifying activity is challenging, there is no obvious answer and it is not something that they are routinely asked to do. Importantly, however, they are still working from their own knowledge base; no new content has been introduced by the teacher yet.

Phase 3

The teacher now asks one group, perhaps not the most able, to outline their categories. He or she then calls on another group who may have a somewhat different grouping and gradually encourages the class to consider whether any improvements can be made, but without giving what they consider to be the best or right answer. The types of category generated are diverse, but one can expect some of the following: moving goods and people, emergency rescue, repair services, community (friends, family and neighbours) action, financial assistance, local council services, and flood prevention. Following this, the pupils are then presented with an extended piece of text on the floods which affected the village of Singleton in southern England in January 1994. The piece focuses on the experiences over one week of a couple whose home was flooded. The pupils are asked whether their categories fit the evidence of the human response in this case.

Commentary

Here is a further opportunity for challenge. Do the categories fit or do they need amending? It is important that the teacher creates an atmosphere in which it is acceptable and even desirable to change one's ideas by positively reinforcing those who make some amendment. Debriefing is another principle that surfaces here as the teacher tries to draw out extended answers without trying to impose a teacher version.

Phase 4

The scale and context are now shifted radically to Bangladesh, a developing economy sorely troubled by floods. A traditional view might suggest that several weeks need to be spent giving a background geography to Bangladesh. In this case, it is considered more appropriate to be concise. Atlases can be used to locate Bangladesh and identify the main rivers and their source in the Himalayas, whose snowmelt and rainfall play such a large part in the regime of the rivers. It may be sufficient to tell pupils that Bangladesh is a very poor country, where the majority of the people live at very high density in rural areas, in a largely subsistence economy. Whatever decision is reached, the next task for the pupils is: 'For a flood of a similar size to the Singleton flood, will Bangladesh or Britain be worse affected?' Pupils are encouraged to use their categories as a basis for this difficult comparison.

Commentary

Here is a further opportunity for challenge as the pupils measure the rigour of their categories in the new context and struggle with the evaluation of the differential impact of flooding on different societies. There is a strong values dimension present as assumptions about Britain and Bangladesh are exposed. The stark difficulty facing them is that there is no clear answer. The Bangladeshis perhaps have less to lose in physical terms, but does their smaller capital base make them more vulnerable and is the relative value greater? Are they used to such disasters and take them as a matter of course? Are the British more vulnerable because our technological society is thrown out of synchrony by the loss of power supplies and piped water? Which society recovers more easily? Furthermore, pupils are asked to consider whether they wish to adapt or change their categories. It is very encouraging when pupils do change their categories as it is a positive marker that cognitive conflict has taken place as a result of some serious thinking. Obviously, talk between pupils has been important again.

Phase 5

Finally, the teacher has the task of encouraging the pupils to see that their categories have a wider relevance. Do the categories fit the human response to other natural hazards such as earthquakes, tropical storms, droughts and fires? Do they need any further amendment? Do they perhaps fit domestic disasters such as car crashes and burglaries?

Commentary

The teacher is bridging the outcomes of this activity to other contexts in debriefing the pupils at the end of the activity, drawing from their categories a framework that helps them understand planning in the context of hazards, i.e. that planning can be under-taken by individuals, organizations and governments and that some of this planning relates to prevention and some to dealing with the aftermath (pupils' versions may vary from this). They may also start to address prediction. They are beginning to put flesh on some of the characteristics of planning and therefore to understand the concept better. If the shape of their thinking seems valuable in other circumstances, then, in the view of the pupils themselves, thinking about thinking may begin to look like a rewarding activity. When one begins to think consciously about thinking then one is entering the state of metacognitive awareness. In this state, transfer of learning from one context to another without external assistance becomes more probable, especially as the teacher has introduced other contexts – earthquakes, droughts and even car crashes – to which the new learning can be applied.

It is important to realize that these materials and tasks ask for substantial changes in thinking and classroom behaviour from teachers. We, TTG members, do not find this change easy and, for example, we are at an early stage in developing our debriefing skills. The kernel of the change is in the pattern of interaction (discourse) in the classroom as open questions become more common, pupils are allowed to take the initiative, and the teacher is no longer the sole arbiter of correctness. Moreover, subject matter shifts in importance; it is still crucial but it becomes more the means to the end rather than the end itself. Pupils' intellectual and social development has become the prime focus.

Intellectual development and performance in Geography

Some pupils are better at Geography than others. Some of this variation is accounted for by interest, motivation and quality of teaching, but much of it must be attributed to intellectual development. Piaget's description of stages of development (Piaget and Inhelder 1969) identified concrete operations and formal operations. Formal operational thinkers have substantial and important advantages in dealing with schoolwork: they can deal with (operate on) the relationships between more than two variables, they can formulate hypotheses, and they can synthesize apparently unconnected information. One needs to think about the implications of this for GCSE geography teaching. Some tasks that pupils are set are impossible for them because of their level of intellectual development.

It is helpful to be more specific about performance in Geography. To clarify this, I have analysed the difference in quality in the work of pupils, across the ability-range from a number of schools, in a common task. This task involved giving pupils 30 pieces of information on separate cards about the Kobe earthquake that occurred in Japan in 1994, which not only provide a background to the causes of the disaster but also give a strong narrative thread concerning the members of a particular family, the Endos. The pupils were asked why one of them dies and the other survives. It is a very open task, initially tackled as a group activity and later as an individual written task.

Three clear levels emerged with some exceptional performance beyond the range at both ends.

Level A

The written response consists largely of statements from the cards, with little apparent sequencing. There may be some rudimentary linkage and some inference – going beyond the given data – especially in the case of the named characters. The meaning or implication of many data items is not clear from their use for they are frequently just copies. There may be some misinterpretation of the data items.

Level B

The significant difference at this level is that the linkage between the information is generally good; there is some sequencing and direction to the narrative. Words and phrases, such as 'because', 'so', 'then', 'which meant', and 'this caused', become more frequent, indicating that one piece of data is linked to another and relationships are being understood. Quantification and qualification begin to appear, making the explanation more specific and detailed. However, the narrative is largely at the level of the trigger or more superficial causes of the death and destruction: the earthquake struck; the construction of the house was inadequate; the emergency services had problems; and there were many fires. Some misinterpretation of the data is to be expected.

Level C

At this level pupils' answers are more specific, more detail drawn from their pupils' geographical knowledge is given, and misinterpretations are less common. Second, there are more frequent generalizations as pupils begin to go beyond sequencing of information to group data together to isolate contributory background factors such as the lack of preparation induced by a perception of low risk, rather than giving a narrative. There is more inference, going beyond the given data, and speculation, indicating that they are making more connections with their existing knowledge. They thus demonstrate understanding.

These differences not only provide a framework of assessment, they also signal the need for a certain approach to curriculum development. The level C pupils are those likely to get grades A and B at GCSE, so more pupils ought to be operating at this level. It is fairly certain that there would be a strong correlation between the levels obtained in this task and the Piagetian levels and between both of these and eventual GCSE results. (For more on intellectual levels and levels of outcome in pupils' work, see Biggs and Collis 1982.)

Conclusion

The argument in this chapter is that a geography curriculum developed on the principles outlined above and using procedures like those in the worked example has a far greater chance of bringing pupils to perform at level C than the sterility that characterizes many textbook series and classrooms observed in Ofsted inspections. The alternative model presented here is more likely to equip pupils to handle complex information and relationships, tackle challenging tasks and transfer learning to new contexts. It is also more likely to keep them interested. Some things are excusable in education, but boring pupils is not one of them.

References

Adey, R. and Shayer, M. (1994) *Really Raising Standards*, London: Routledge.

Battersby, J., Webster, A. and Younger, M. (1995) *The Case Study in GCSE Geography: Experiences from the Avery Hill Project*, Cardiff: Welsh Joint Education Committee.

Biggs, J. and Collis, K. (1982) *Evaluating the Quality of Learning: The SOLO Taxonomy*, New York: Academic Press.

Brown, A.L. (1987) 'Metacognition, executive control, self regulation and other more mysterious mechanisms', in Weinhart, Franz, Kluwe, and Rainer (eds) *Metacognition, Motivation and Understanding*, London: Lawrence Erlbaum Associates.

Department for Education (DfE) (1995) *Geography in the National Curriculum*, London: HMSO.

Driver, R. (1983) *The Pupil as Scientist?*, Milton Keynes: Open University Press.

Nickerson, R.S., Perkins, D.N. and Smith, E.E. (1985) *The Teaching of Thinking*, Hillsdale NJ: Lawrence Erlbaum Associates.

Office for Standards in Education (Ofsted) (1995) *Geography: a Review of Inspection Findings 1993/94*, London: HMSO.

Perkins, D.N. and Salomon, G. (1988) 'Teaching for transfer', *Educational Leadership*, 46: 22–32.

Piaget, J. and Inhelder, B. (1969) *The Psychology of the Child*, London: Routledge and Kegan Paul.

Wells, G. (1987) *The Meaning Makers: Children Learning Language and Using Language to Learn*, Cambridge: Cambridge University Press.

9 Teaching about the language of maps

Paul Weeden

> Maps and plans are extremely useful ways of storing and communicating information about places and the people who live and work in them. There is a 'language' of maps, and pupils can be helped to understand and use it just as they can be helped with any other language development.
>
> (Beddis 1983: 5)

Maps are an important form of communication, and for some authors graphicacy has been placed alongside numeracy, literacy and oracy as the fourth 'ace in the pack' (Balchin and Coleman 1965). This chapter looks at the centrality of maps to geography teaching and how maps are used as a communication system. An outline of the properties, elements and purposes of maps is illustrated by three examples of strategies children use to 'read' maps. The final section considers how theories of cognitive development inform progression in learning through maps.

The centrality of maps

Geography studies the relationship between people and the earth and in particular considers place, space and environment. In investigating places and geographical themes, geographers describe and explain the patterns and processes they observe in the world around them. Thus investigation of spatial patterns and the development of locational knowledge form distinctive and central parts of the discipline, with the map in all its forms being a vital tool in this process. What must be remembered, however, is that maps are merely one form of communication or evidence used by geographers and 'in the investigation of a place, all kinds of evidence, literary, statistical, cultural are examined' (Daugherty 1989: 30).

The map as a communication system

Most geographical literature includes a variety of maps which need to be 'read'. The clarity of the message depends on the skill of the map-maker in presenting the information and the user's ability to read and interpret the signals. The model of the map as a communication system (Figure 9.1) demonstrates the need for a common understanding of map language, otherwise there will be confusion and misunderstanding. As with any language the common conventions and the structure have to

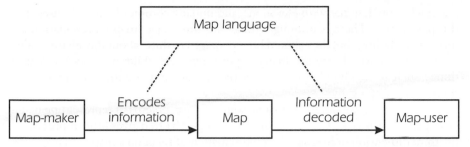

Figure 9.1 A simplified map communication system

Source: Gerber and Wilson 1989: 198.

be learnt if the message is to make any sense. There is considerable evidence that children do this best through a structured programme involving practice both in the individual elements and in synthesizing them.

Decoding maps involves learning how to 'read' a map. Unlike reading a book there is no conventional method for reading a map (e.g. from left to right across the page), so skilled map-readers may use strategies such as initial random scanning to identify features or familiar names and then focus on their area of interest or they may look for larger recognizable patterns. Beginner map-users need clear guidance on where and how to start reading the map.

The Geography National Curriculum (DFE 1995) lists the making, using and interpreting of maps as the map skills that children should learn. The author suggests that these terms are loosely defined and proposes four strands of learning through maps – using, making, reading, and interpreting – defining these command words more precisely as:

- using maps – relating features on a map directly to features in the landscape;
- making maps – encoding information in map form;
- reading maps – decoding successfully the elements of map language; and
- interpreting maps – being able to relate prior geographical knowledge to the features and patterns observed on the map.

The properties of maps

If systematic learning through maps is to occur, both teacher and pupil should be aware of the essential basic properties of maps that determine most map skills development programmes. Gerber and Wilson (1989: 202), in describing a sequential mapping programme for secondary-age children, propose four essential properties of maps that need to be understood – *plan view*, *arrangement*, *proportion* and *map language*. These properties should form the basis of mapwork skills development for any age-group and can be introduced individually and then integrated.

Plan view (perspective and relief)

Maps are drawn looking vertically down on an area, which enables the user to see features which may be hidden from them on the ground. The concept needs to be introduced and practised because the plan view is an unfamiliar viewpoint. Children are much more familiar with elevations, and initially commonly draw houses from this perspective. There is nothing wrong with this 'naive' map representation as a form of symbolism, but they should be encouraged to think about the 'picture' of the house from above. There are many opportunities for children to look down on things, such as high buildings, planes, aerial photographs and images on television, films or computer games.

Vertical aerial photographs illustrate some of the problems in representing height or slope on a map as the two-dimensional photograph often gives little impression of the third dimension of height. The representation of relief on a map is an important but difficult idea for children to deal with. Contours, the commonest form of relief representation, are also the commonest cause of confusion for most map-readers as they form complex patterns and are often obscured by other features or create 'noise' that is distracting.

Arrangement (location, direction and orientation)

Places or features on maps have a location that can be both absolutely defined (by a system such as grid references) and described in relation to other places (left of, north of, etc.). This enables map-users to locate specific places more easily and quickly on complex maps. Direction can be absolute (using a constant reference system – N, E, S, W) or relative to the user's position. The concept of absolute space means that objects or places stay in the same relationship to each other and are not affected by the position of the map-user (an important map-using skill is orienting the map to match the arrangement of observed objects).

Proportion (scale, distance and selection)

Maps reduce the size of objects on the ground so that the object can be represented on a small piece of paper. It is usually important that relative size is maintained, but in some cases important features are drawn larger than their true scale (e.g. roads on Ordnance Survey maps). Distance can be measured using a scale, but involves numerical manipulation and often requires a series of complex procedures. Scale is therefore another area of difficulty for many map-readers. The reduction in size means that some detail will be lost, involving the map-maker in selection of items to be included. Thus, while aerial photographs record everything seen at a particular time, maps are generalizations which, in improving clarity, can result in bias and omission.

Map language (signs, symbols, words and numbers)

Maps show information by the use of signs and symbols, and extra information is available through the use of words, letters and numbers which help decoding and interpretation. Skilled map-users learn not just to read the symbols but also to interpret the spatial patterns by drawing on their geographical knowledge.

When learning map language it is helpful to recognize that map symbols and information can be classified into three types – points, lines or areas. The symbols used can be classified on a continuum from pictorial to abstract with the more abstract symbols generally being more liable to misinterpretation. Figure 9.2 shows a

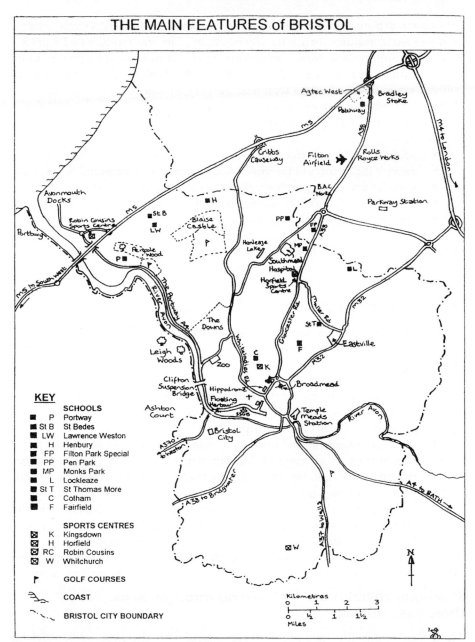

Figure 9.2 A map showing a range of symbols and information

Source: A. Wright, Cotham Grammar School, Bristol.

map that employs a range of point, line and area symbols. The key helps in the interpretation of the symbols but in this case some symbols have been omitted because the features are named. The point symbols range from pictorial symbols such as the aeroplane representing an airfield to an abstract symbol for a sports centre. The line symbols range from representing features seen on the ground such as roads or rivers to more abstract features such as the city boundary. The area symbols on Figure 9.2 are pictorial and concrete (wood, golf course) but other maps might represent more abstract features such as areas with high pollution levels in a city. Written information can range from letters (to represent schools), to words (names of important places), to numbers which can relate to features such as grid lines or spot heights.

To summarize, children should learn that maps usually:

- adopt a plan view perspective;
- arrange the features in the same relationship as they are found in real life;
- keep features in accurate proportion to their real size;
- involve the selection of information; and
- employ a recognizable map language.

Conventionally, maps also have a title, a key to define the symbols, an indication of orientation (direction indicator) and a scale line.

The purposes of maps

The ability to encode and decode information on maps is useful not just in Geography but also in everyday life. Maps are used in a wide variety of contexts which can be classified into four main functions:

- location, enabling the user to find a place (e.g. in an atlas, on a street map);
- route-displaying, allowing the user to get from A to B (e.g. a road atlas, underground map or street map);
- storing and displaying information, allowing the user to isolate and sort information from a wide range of different items (e.g. OS maps), or to consider patterns and relationships of selected information (e.g. distribution maps); and
- problem-solving, helping the user to solve problems by interpreting or inferring from the information provided (e.g. why a road does not take the most direct route or where to locate a factory). Skilled map-users have learnt to 'see' the landscape from the information on the map.

(adapted from Catling 1988: 168 and Wiegand 1993: 19)

Strategies children use for learning through maps: three case studies

These case studies illustrate the thinking strategies children use while working with maps. Each case study is accompanied by a short commentary that both considers the thinking strategies used and indicates some problematic areas in working with maps.

Locational knowledge

Jane (Year 4, age 8) is locating places and features she has been studying on a map of the British Isles. She remembers that England, Wales and Scotland are the names of the countries of Great Britain and that Scotland is above England, and Wales is a bump to one side. She knows that London is a city and that a city is smaller than a country. She uses the key to find out the symbol for a city. She remembers the approximate location of London, having looked at a road atlas when she went there with her family. She knows a river is a wiggly line on a map and that London is on the River Thames. She unsuccessfully guesses where to locate Birmingham, her home town, as she only knows it is north of London.

Jane's thinking involved recalling from her memory the names of several places and features. To locate the places successfully, she had to classify the different features and have some understanding of the terms 'country', 'city', 'river'. Her recognition of the shapes and arrangement of features in the British Isles enabled her to synthesize this knowledge, while the words in the key gave her extra clues in decoding the map. She had difficulty with locating her home town, Birmingham, partly because there are no recognizable features nearby, and because her awareness of distance is poor.

The route from home to school

Thomas (Year 6, age 11), when asked to draw a map of his journey to school as part of a topic on his locality, says, 'That's easy'. He starts by trying to visualize the journey, and seeing whether he can fit it on the paper. Home is marked first in one corner of the map and the roads on the route drawn sequentially and topologically until he reaches school, which is squeezed into the far corner of the sheet. Considerable thought is required to clarify relationships and there are some mistakes, rubbings out and redrawings before the route is complete. When asked to add on further detail, he includes nearby roads, their names, pictorial symbols, a key and a direction arrow. He works out the direction of south, from his knowledge of the position of the sun at midday at his home, and is then able to work out the rest of the compass points.

Thomas, in his thinking, used daily experiences stored in his memory to problem-solve. This ability to recall his mental picture of the area combined with a clear understanding of map properties enabled him to work out logically the arrangement of familiar roads and to create a recognizable map. He had difficulties with distance, so the map was not drawn to scale (roads nearer home were over-emphasized), and he ran out of space on the paper as he approached the school. He demonstrated the difficulties most people have in drawing mental maps, because of the need to recall and synthesize complex patterns and arrangements. However, he also showed how useful mental maps are for teachers in giving information about pupils' knowledge and understanding of map skills and places.

Interpreting patterns

David (Year 11, age 16), when asked to describe and explain the patterns on a map as part of a GCSE examination question, starts by analysing the question. He decides the key words are 'redevelopment area', finds the symbol for this in the key, and locates the areas correctly on the map. He describes their arrangement (in a tight ring around the city centre) and draws on his knowledge of urban 'models' to recall the main features of this area. He also applies this knowledge by picturing a redevelopment area in his home town and remembers that the older buildings have been knocked down and rebuilt. He does not immediately use the scale to help him work out how far from the city centre the areas are; rather, he senses their proximity and only later confirms it. He recognizes the line around the city as a boundary of some sort and uses the key to identify it as the city boundary.

David's thinking involved a complex interaction of knowledge recall and synthesizing information from the map. His familiarity with maps enabled him to recognize the pattern of the redevelopment areas and to put them into a meaningful context. He moved quickly from description into the processing of his stored geographical knowledge and was able to read and interpret the information on the map in a sophisticated manner.

These case studies illustrate how map language is used in the making, reading and interpretation of maps. Jane and Thomas show how they can draw on their own memories and perceptions of places, arrange their thoughts and synthesize information to complete the task. They are both familiar with the main properties of maps but demonstrate some of the difficulties of encoding information on to a map. In decoding the information on the map David illustrates clearly the difference between map-reading and map-interpreting. The symbols on the map can be read like the words in a book, but they have little meaning unless they can be combined to make 'sentences'. If the map-users have other geographical knowledge they can draw inferences and make interpretations – more akin to 'reading between the lines' in a written passage.

The case studies demonstrate how learning through maps involves developing map skills in a range of contexts. They illustrate how pupils when using maps have to combine thinking about the maps themselves with their knowledge of Geography, and that the best map-based activities will encourage work that is purposeful and appropriate to their age.

How theories of cognitive development inform progression in learning through maps

Geographical education has always been concerned with the systematic teaching and learning of map skills. There are many detailed accounts of appropriate teaching and learning programmes, such as Boardman (1986), Catling (1988), Gerber and Wilson (1989), Foley and Janikoun (1992), Wiegand (1993) and Catling (1995). This section will not outline a Programme of Work but looks instead at some of the theories of cognitive development that inform our understanding of progression in map skills, and indicates how these theories can be related to learning.

Theories of cognitive development

Meadows (1993: 197–251) suggests there are three major current models of cognitive development: Piaget's model of stages, information processing models and Neo-Vygotskian models. The most influential of these for learning through maps has been Piaget, although there has been criticism of the way that Piaget's work has been misused by some educationalists who, by slavishly adhering to fixed stages, have under-estimated children's abilities in using maps.

Piaget's model

Piaget's work is based on a biological model of adaptation. The child, or indeed the adult, is all its life actively trying to make sense of the world, just as any organism must try to adapt to its environment (Meadows 1993: 198). Piaget's model has been characterized by educationalists as suggesting that thinking develops in a series of stages: the sensori-motor, pre-operational, concrete operational and formal operational stages. These stages of development follow an invariant order and each stage can be associated with a certain mental age, so that a mental age of 8 typically goes with the concrete operational stage, while a mental age of 4 is associated with the pre-operational stage. This relatively simple model has been discussed and elaborated by authors such as Boardman (1983) and has led to a sequential programme for the development of map skills which has been adopted in many schools. It is clear from this experience that most children benefit from starting to learn about maps in a concrete manner in an environment they are familiar with (classroom, school, locality), and only at a later stage moving on to more abstract maps. However, it must be remembered that Piaget did not see his model of stages as a teaching model and it is now recognized as merely one way of thinking about cognitive development.

Information processing

Information processing models use the metaphor of the brain as a computer and there has been some work done simulating children's spatial abilities with computers (Spencer *et al.* 1989: 19). The case studies in this chapter illustrate how skilled map-users operate like computers and are able to make connections between observed patterns and stored knowledge. The speed of the information processing will depend upon experience, practice and ability. The links between this model and a teaching and learning programme for schools have not been explored in the literature.

Neo-Vygotskian models

Meadows (1993: 236) suggests that both Piagetian and information processing models emphasize the psychological structures inside people's minds while Neo-Vygotskian ideas have the premise that social interaction is paramount. If, as Vygotsky suggests, language has the power to shape mental development and social interaction is a prime way in which people learn – 'what the child can do co-operatively today she will be able to do individually tomorrow' (Knight 1993: 26) – then this has implications for learning.

In contrast to Piaget the Neo-Vygotskian model has an underlying belief that education can accelerate development, which leads to the concept of 'scaffolding' learning. For instance, the concept of plan view can be introduced by looking down on objects arranged on a desk and discussing this view. Rhodes (1994: 111) has shown how, in making choices about best routes for different transport networks, relief models and maps can be used by Year 6 children, working in groups, to interpret relief and slope patterns.

In most cases these children are thinking at, or just beyond, their most advanced, current understanding (Vygotsky's 'zone of proximal development' (ZPD)) and engaging in learning through social interaction.

An important idea that emerges from these three theories, an idea of increasing importance in understanding how we think, is the concept of metacognition.

Metacognition

While some pupils may develop map skills by a process of osmosis through exposure to maps, learning for most is aided by clear and focused guidance, particularly if they are helped to 'think about their thinking' (metacognition). Knight (1993: 35) describes metacognition 'as helping children to be conscious of what they know and can do and then teaching them how to draw purposefully on that knowledge and to deploy it when working on problems'. Teachers can encourage pupils to think about their learning by asking, 'How did you reach that answer?', or challenging them to justify an answer. Orienteers do this when they discuss and analyse their route-finding after an event. Often there is a choice between a shorter, direct route, that may be slower because it goes through dense woodland, and a longer, faster route along paths. By analysing the advantages and disadvantages of each route the orienteers are increasing their familiarity with the range of information on the map and their ability to make successful interpretations. Discussion and disagreement can lead to metacognitive conflict and hence metacognitive advance (Meadows 1993: 81).

Conclusions

Geographers regard maps as tools that enable them to communicate knowledge and understanding of place, space and environment. In particular, maps enable a consideration of the spatial patterns that are central to Geography. To develop their familiarity with maps fully, children should have the opportunity to use, make, read and interpret maps in a variety of contexts. Any programme of teaching and learning developed should introduce the four basic properties of maps (plan view, arrangement, proportion and map language) separately, but find ways of relating them to each other. Children can be helped with their understanding of map language if they recognize that map symbols can be points, lines or areas and are on a continuum of complexity from pictorial to abstract.

Children learn more effectively from maps if they have a clear idea of the purpose of the task being undertaken. These tasks can be linked to the four main purposes of maps (location, route-displaying, storing and displaying information, and problem-solving). In addition, successful interpretation of maps requires not just recognition of symbols and patterns but the synthesis of information from the map with other geographical knowledge.

Finally, our understanding of cognitive development suggests that children should work initially from direct experience (particularly with younger children or when introducing new or difficult concepts such as scale or relief), only later moving on to more abstract maps, and that they should be encouraged to think actively about their thinking (metacognition) since this aids the process of synthesizing and developing interpretation skills.

References

Balchin, W.G.V. and Coleman, A.M. (1965) 'Graphicacy should be the fourth ace in the pack', *Times Educational Supplement*, 5 November 1965.

Beddis, R. (1983) 'Introduction', in T. Johnson (ed.) *Maps and Mapwork – A Practical Guide to Maps and Mapwork in the Primary School*, Bristol: RLDU.

Blades, M. and Spencer, C. (1986) 'Map use by young children', *Geography* 71: 47–52.

Boardman, D. (1983) *Graphicacy and Geography Teaching*, London: Croom Helm.

—— (1986) 'Map reading skills', in D. Boardman (ed.) *Handbook for Geography Teachers*, Sheffield: Geographical Association.

—— (1989) 'The development of graphicacy: children's understanding of maps', *Geography* 74: 321–31.

—— (1991) 'Developing map skills in the National Curriculum', *Teaching Geography* 16: 155–8.

Catling, S.J. (1979) 'Maps and cognitive maps: the young child's perception', *Geography* 64: 288–96.

—— (1988) 'Using maps and aerial photographs', in D. Mills (ed.) *Geographical Work in Primary and Middle Schools*, Sheffield: Geographical Association.

—— (1995) 'Mapping the environment with children', in M. de Villiers (ed.) *Developments in Primary Geography*, Sheffield: Geographical Association.

Daugherty, R. (ed.) (1989) *Geography in the National Curriculum*, Sheffield: Geographical Association.

Department for Eduction (DFE) (1995) *Geography in the National Curriculum*, London: HMSO.

Foley, M. and Janikoun, J. (1992) *The Really Practical Guide to Primary Geography*, Cheltenham: Stanley Thornes.

Gerber, R. and Wilson, P. (1989) 'Using maps well in the geography classroom', in J. Fien, R. Gerber and P. Wilson (eds) *The Geography Teacher's Guide to the Classroom*, Melbourne: Macmillan.

Knight, P. (1993) *Primary Geography, Primary History*, London: David Fulton.

Matthews, M.H. (1984) 'Cognitive mapping abilities of young boys and girls', *Geography* 69: 327–36.

Meadows, S. (1993) *The Child as Thinker*, London: Routledge.

Rhodes, B. (1994) 'Learning curves ... and map contours', *Teaching Geography* 19: 111–15.

Spencer, C., Blades, M. and Morsley, K. (1989) *The Child in the Physical Environment*, Chichester: John Wiley.

Wiegand, P. (1993) *Children and Primary Geography*, London: Cassell.

10 Towards deeper fieldwork
David Job

Purposes of fieldwork

Like any other aspect of teaching Geography, the way we organize fieldwork is strongly informed by our values, preferences of learning styles and priorities as well as the needs of our students and curriculum requirements. Figure 10.1 lists a selected range of fieldwork purposes, partly sifted and paraphrased from the geography and environmental education literature but added to by groups of practising teachers during a number of workshop sessions. It is not intended to be comprehensive and includes some repetition, but a quick glance soon reveals the wide range of intentions we collectively have in mind when venturing into the field with students. These include aspects of personal development, emotional and aesthetic experience and more transformative intentions, some of which lie beyond the scope of the formal curriculum.

Scanning the list and simply adding ticks or crosses can be helpful in clarifying one's own priorities, as well as adding further purposes from a personal perspective. A more discriminating and flexible approach is to copy and cut out the list, discard any purposes that are deemed inappropriate, add further purposes from one's own priorities, then arrange in a diamond ranking pattern to distinguish those purposes to which we attach a greater or lesser importance. (This activity can be usefully undertaken by groups of teachers prior to the planning of fieldwork programmes, in order to recognize differing personal viewpoints before moving towards a consensus.)

The order in which the statements are listed in Figure 10.1 is intended to show some degree of groupings. One workshop came up with the following general classification:

- Statements 1–5: Curriculum-focused purposes with an emphasis on knowledge and understanding.
- Statements 6–10: Deeper ecological perspectives.
- Statements 11–15: Purposes pertaining to personal and social development.
- Statements 16–20: Purposes to stimulate action for change.
- Statements 21–26: Purposes relating to sensory and aesthetic sensibilities.
- Statements 27–32: Skills-related or vocational purposes.

A modification of this classification is presented in Figure 10.2, which also refines broad purposes into more specific aims and objectives.

1 Understanding geographical processes through scientific investigation.
2 Increasing conceptual understanding in Geography through personal experience.
3 Becoming familiar with hypothesis-testing and data-collection through direct experience.
4 Developing an understanding of the interactions between physical and human systems.
5 Enabling pupils to apply knowledge gained from fieldwork and first-hand case studies to examination answers.
6 Establishing a relationship with places based on emotional responses.
7 Developing deeper insights into the natural world.
8 Enhancing a respect for the natural world.
9 Appreciating the complex interconnections that make up the web of life.
10 Valuing nature and landscapes for themselves rather than for their usefulness to humans.
11 Offering physical challenges in order to build confidence and resilience.
12 Developing co-operative and communication skills through participating in group work.
13 Increasing motivation and commitment to Geography.
14 Promoting camaraderie and social fusion among a student group.
15 Developing a sense of adventure and an interest in outdoor pursuits.
16 Empowering pupils to become autonomous citizens by knowing how to discover, learn and evaluate.
17 Encouraging students to develop more caring social attitudes through developing empathy with disadvantaged people.
18 Developing a radical critique of society through investigating inequalities and environmental abuses.
19 Encouraging students to become active citizens involved in creating a better world.
20 Encouraging more liberal attitudes and empathy through exposure to different cultures and social groups.
21 Cultivating sensory and emotional response to environments leading to greater aesthetic sensitivity and appreciation.
22 Acquiring the ability to 'read' a landscape.
23 Promoting the sensitivities required to appreciate a sense of place.
24 Appreciating the diversity of landscape.
25 Offering opportunities for students to express their personal responses to environments.
26 Immersing the learner in the landscape.
27 Providing opportunity for experiencing enquiry learning at first hand.
28 Gaining experience in a range of field techniques which can be transferred to personal investigative work.
29 Collecting data which can then be used in practising statistical and IT skills.
30 Developing map interpretation and navigational skills.
31 Acquiring and practising skills relevant to the world of work.
32 Experience in using new technology to investigate the environment.

Figure 10.1 A selection of fieldwork purposes

Broad educational purpose	Related fieldwork aim	Examples of specific fieldwork objectives
Conceptual (knowledge and understanding)	Supporting the geography curriculum through promoting geographical knowledge and understanding	Reinforcing geographical terminology through tangible examples
		Identifying and defining geographical questions, issues and problems
		Understanding relationships between sets of geographical factors
		Understanding the processes underlying geographical patterns in space and time
Skills related	Developing organizational and technical aptitudes relevant to both Geography and the world of work	Planning a geographical investigation or enquiry
		Developing geographical skills which can be transferred to individual enquiries, coursework and employment
		Practising and applying technical skills (including IT) in a real-world context
		Developing skills in locating, retrieving and processing information
Aesthetic	Developing sensitivity to and appreciation of landscape and nature	Developing a sense of place
		Developing an ability to 'read' a landscape
		Encouraging emotional responses to environments
Values related	Developing awareness of a range of viewpoints in relation to social, political and ecological concerns	Recognizing and respecting the values of others
		Clarifying and justifying personal values
		Seeing the wider social and ecological effects of changes in the environment
Social and personal development	Promoting self-confidence and an ability to work co-operatively	Developing co-operative and communication skills through participating in group work
		Encouraging a sense of adventure
		Building confidence and resilience through offering challenges
		Promoting camaraderie and social fusion through participation in a common endeavour

Figure 10.2 A summary of fieldwork purposes

Source: Job 1999b.

Clearly different fieldwork purposes require the application of different strategies. The approaches adopted by geographers have evolved in interesting ways over recent decades since the descriptive 'field excursion' of the early days of fieldwork in the post-war years. A dramatic shift towards hypothesis-testing and quantification consequent upon the quantitative revolution in Geography characterized much fieldwork development during the 1970s. Subsequent reactions to what was seen as an over-enthusiasm for measurement, often resulting in somewhat reductionist studies, included the enquiry approach adopted by the Geography 16–19 project in the 1980s with its emphasis on environmental and social concerns (Naish *et al.* 1987). Elsewhere reaction shifted to a deliberate focus on sensory experience as a pathway to environmental understanding and commitment (van Matre 1979). In the UK a comparable approach to urban fieldwork was developed in numerous issues of the *Bulletin for Environmental Education* (BEE), copies of which are now much sought after and hard to find. In some quarters a general shift towards more pupil-centred field experience has characterized the last two decades of the twentieth century, with a concern to ensure that fieldwork activity begins with pupils' personal experience of environments (Hawkins 1987) rather than the prescribed, teacher-led fieldwork exercise.

Fuller reviews of the evolving approaches to fieldwork are available elsewhere. Kent and Foskett (2002) provide a review based on experience in higher education. More anecdotal descriptions of the various genres of fieldwork which have evolved over recent decades have been compiled (Job 1999a).

There is some evidence to suggest that the more pluralist approaches of recent years, with the inclusion of both quantitative and qualitative experience, may be narrowing somewhat, perhaps returning to the more prescriptive quantitative field exercises of a previous era. This may be in part attributable to the growing emphasis on the assessment of fieldwork through the presentation of coursework at GCSE, AS and in some cases A2. The assessment criteria, which inevitably influence the fieldwork process and outcomes, tend to require:

- focus on a clear hypothesis or fairly narrowly framed research question
- the application of quantitative techniques
- the presentation of findings in tabulated and graphical displays
- the use of statistical analysis in interpreting findings.

With a few notable exceptions, there is little encouragement to work with qualitative data, demonstrate a sense of place or focus on issues of social or environmental concern.

While these closely structured frameworks of assessment with definable criteria to distinguish levels of achievement enable reasonably objective assessment to be undertaken and moderated, they inevitably influence the strategies that teachers adopt in organizing fieldwork and, thereby, pupils' experience of fieldwork, possibly in constraining ways.

It is interesting to review the wide-ranging purposes identified in Figure 10.1 in relation to the coursework assessment criteria of the different examination specifications. Equally, it may be pertinent to review the summary of fieldwork strategies in Figure 10.3 and consider which would be appropriate and which would be less appropriate in meeting the criteria for assessed coursework.

Strategy	Aims	Characteristic activities
The tradi- tional field excursion	• Developing skills in geographical observation, recording and interpretation • Showing relationships between physical and human landscape features • Developing the concept of landscapes evolving over time • Developing an appreciation of landscape and nurturing a sense of place	Pupils guided through a landscape by a teacher with local knowledge, often following a route on a large-scale map. Sites grid-referenced and described with the aid of landscape sketches and sketch maps to explore the underlying geology, topographical features, the mantle of spoil and vegetation and the landscape history in terms of human activity. Pupils listen, record and answer questions concerning possible interpretations of the landscape.
Field research based on hypothesis- testing	• Applying geographical theory or generalized models to real-world situations • Generating and applying hypotheses based on theory to be tested through collection of appropriate field data • Developing skills in analysing data using statistical methods in order to test field situations against geographical theory	The conventional deductive approach involves initial consideration of geographical theory, leading to the formulation of hypotheses which are then tested against field situations through the collection of quantitative data and testing against expected patterns and relationships. More flexible variants of this approach encourage students to develop their own hypotheses based on initial field observations, thereby incorporating some elements of enquiry.
Geographical enquiry	• Encouraging pupils to identify, construct and ask geographical questions • Enabling pupils to identify and gather relevant information to answer geographical questions and offer explanations and interpretations of their findings • Enabling pupils to apply their findings to the wider world and personal decisions	A geographical question, issue or problem is identified, ideally from students' own experiences in the field. Pupils are then supported in the gathering of appropriate data (quantitative or qualitative) to answer their key question. Findings are evaluated and the implications applied to the wider world and personal decisions where appropriate.

(continued on next page)

Strategy	Aims	Characteristic activities
Discovery fieldwork	▪ Allowing pupils to discover their interests in a landscape by themselves (rather than through a teacher) ▪ Allowing pupils to develop their own focus of study and methods of investigation ▪ Encouraging self-confidence and self-motivation by putting pupils in control of their learning	Teacher assumes the role of animateur, allowing the group to follow its own route through the landscape. When pupils ask questions these are countered with further questions to encourage deeper thinking. A brainstorm then identifies themes for further investigation in small groups. This further work has arisen from pupils' perceptions and preferences rather than those of teachers.
Sensory fieldwork	▪ Encouraging new sensitivities to environments through using all the senses ▪ Nurturing caring attitudes to nature and other people through emotional engagement ▪ Acknowledging that sensory experience is as valid as intellectual activity in understanding our surroundings	Structured activities designed to stimulate the senses in order to promote awareness of environments. Sensory walks, use of blindfolds, sound maps, poetry and artwork are characteristic activities. Can be used as an introductory activity prior to more conventional investigative work or to develop sense of place, aesthetic appreciation or critical appraisal of environmental change.

Figure 10.3 A review of fieldwork strategies

Two issues in particular seem to emerge from such considerations:

- the future role of sensory experience and qualitative data collection in fieldwork; and
- the role of fieldwork in citizenship, the development of social and ecological critique and participation in change, particularly in relation to the emerging agenda of education for sustainability.

The remainder of this chapter is concerned with ways of attempting to meet specified curriculum requirements through fieldwork without losing sight of deeper, broader and to some extent more radical intentions.

Justifying qualitative fieldwork experience

The first of these issues concerns the relative importance of experiences which engage the 'head' and those which touch the 'heart' in pupils' experience of fieldwork – or, in the language of educational research, the relative significance of, and relationship between, the cognitive and the affective dimensions.

Kent and Foskett (2002) review research that highlights the important relationship between the two. The research of Harvey (1991) into the outcomes of A-level geography fieldwork provides further substantial evidence (summarized in Job 1996). The concepts and ideas learnt through geographical fieldwork are more memorable, it is suggested, where the senses, feelings and emotions have been engaged as well as the intellect. Yet a review of much fieldwork practice indicates a strong inclination towards the cerebral and conceptual and some neglect of the emotional, a constraint identified by a number of fieldwork practitioners reacting to an overdose of quantification:

> we feared entrapment by the idea that things are only real if they can be measured. Many of life's most rewarding, enriching and heartfelt experiences can barely be put into words, let alone placed on a scale. If we relied too much upon the usual processes of collecting and testing, what would happen to our goals of instilling a sense of wonder, a sense of place, and a reverence for life? If we failed to develop appreciations in our haste to convey understandings, if we overemphasized analytical skills at the expense of deep natural experiences, what would we gain – people who could take life apart, but cared nothing for keeping it together?
>
> (Van Matre 1979)

The rationale for engaging the 'heart' during field experiences rests in part on research which suggests that conceptual learning, perhaps using quantitative techniques, is all the stronger if arising from some kind of emotional engagement. Our natural initial response to places and landscapes is one involving the senses rather than analysis or explanation. Furthermore, as van Matre proposes, the experience that touches the heart is perhaps the key to the development of caring attitudes and actions – about the earth, its creatures and each other. The recent appearance of articles in *Teaching Geography* which take as their theme 'Awe and Wonder' in Geography (Ross 2001) or the use of drama, poetry and artwork in the field (Caton 2001) are a healthy sign of renewed interest in the more emotive and sensory experiences of fieldwork.

Fieldwork and the sustainability agenda

A second but not unrelated issue concerns the potential of Geography, particularly through fieldwork, to contribute in very significant ways towards the emerging and, as seen in some quarters, increasingly urgent sustainability agenda. Geographical fieldwork as environmental education has long been promoted but has often been short on significant or tangible outcomes. The dominance of somewhat tired urban models and rather predictable downstream river studies in a recent sample of AS coursework suggests that students may be engaging even less in topics which address environmental and social concerns than was the case a few years ago. Stephen Sterling, in a recent critique of education in relation to the sustainability agenda (Sterling 2001), proposes that education is largely behind other fields in developing new thinking and practice in response to the challenge of sustainability. Sterling views education, globally and nationally, as having been hijacked by the

New Right and the forces of neo-liberalism. Stated bluntly, the consequence, intentionally or otherwise, has been to create a population with restricted skills oriented largely to the new technologies that serve the global economy, the consumerist values which sustain corporate wealth, together with a lack of critical judgement, thus limiting the emergence of dissenting voices.

If there is any validity in this viewpoint then the implications for any of us involved in fieldwork (or indeed education as a whole!) are substantial. As soon as we venture outside the classroom and experience the real world we hopefully encounter beauty and harmony, but invariably we also find evidence of ecosystems which are falling apart, landscapes degraded by the junk of consumerism, and social structures in town and countryside which are losing cohesion. Having exposed the ecological and social wounds, do we have also responsibilities to guide our students into the healing process?

The two themes of this reappraisal of fieldwork – restoring the emotional dimension and developing a deeper critique of the world – are strongly interwoven. The ability to care and heal draws to some degree on understanding the workings and wholeness of the earth. The motivation to care and heal may spring rather more from experience, which touches the soul and the heart.

Qualitative starting points for fieldwork

In reporting research into the relationship between enhanced geographical understanding (cognitive gain) and experiences pertaining to the senses (affective gain), there is an emphasis on the significant contribution of the latter to the former (Kent and Foskett 2002). Yet while there are ample sources to draw upon for fieldwork techniques to promote geographical understanding, there are few guidelines which focus on the affective dimension. In the context of Simon Ross's experience with students amid the grandeur of the Icelandic landscape, the sheer drama of the physical setting cannot fail to move us spiritually. In more subtle or more familiar settings, however, it may be helpful to undertake structured but open-ended activities to raise awareness, stimulate perceptions or, where appropriate, encourage critical thinking about an environment.

Steering cards – an introductory activity to a fieldwork area

Examples of stimulus cards for a rural environment are presented in Figure 10.4. These might be used in an introductory session to generate questions and deeper thinking about an unfamiliar landscape. They lend themselves to small group explorations, possibly following a prescribed route with the instruction to turn up at timed intervals or specified locations along the route. The emphasis here is to promote observation, deeper perceptions, sense of place, awareness of temporal change and critique of human impacts as well as encouraging students to express opinions and feelings about their individual experience of place. More geographical questions are not intended to elicit 'right' or 'wrong' answers, but rather to stimulate thinking and subsequent discussion.

How does this landscape make you feel?

Face north, then east, then south, then west. In which direction would you take a photograph if you wanted to show someone who had not been here what this place is like?

How might the view in front of you have looked:

10,000 years ago?

100 years ago?

10 years ago?

What clues can you see in the landscape that might tell you what rock type you are on?

Imagine you have been kidnapped, transported blindfold and dumped at this spot. On removing your blindfold, what clues in the landscape would tell you:

a) which country you were in?

b) which county/region you were in?

Suggest two ways in which people have enhanced this landscape and two ways in which they have degraded the landscape.

What three features of this landscape would you most like to see conserved and why?

What three features of this landscape would you most like to remove or change and why?

In what ways is this landscape used by people?

Which uses would you describe as mainly sustainable or unsustainable?

What natural hazards (if any) can you identify in this landscape?

What features in this landscape might be the result of past processes?

Find two processes in the landscape (physical, ecological or human) that might be contributing to global environmental change.

Observe the view around you over the next two minutes. What events take place? Which of these events are attributable to nature, which to human activity?

Close your eyes and listen carefully. What is the first sound you notice? What are the second and third sounds you notice? Which are a result of human activity and which arise from nature?

Choose three words that epitomize (sum up) this locality.

Figure 10.4 Discovery cards for a rural environment

Note
Further examples of sensory or qualitative fieldwork activities are described in the case study developed on pp. 142–4 ('Deeper into the woods'), while fuller rationale and exemplification are available elsewhere (van Matre 1979; Job 1999a).

Using literature in the field

Mountain pass

Over this small brave road, the wind blows. Tree and bush are left behind, only stone and moss grow here. Nobody has anything to look for here, nobody here owns anything, up here the farmer has neither hay nor wood. But the distance beckons, longing awakens, and through rocks, swamp and snow, they have provided this good little road, which leads to other valleys, other houses, to other languages and other men.

At the highest point in the pass, I stop. The road descends on both sides, down both sides the water flows, and everything that is side by side up here finds its way down into two different worlds. The small pool that touches my shoe runs down towards the north, its water comes at last into distant cold seas. But the small snowdrift close beside it trickles toward the south, its water falls toward the Adriatic coast down into the sea, whose limit is Africa. But all the waters of the world find one another again, and the Arctic seas and the Nile gather together in the moist flight of clouds. The old beautiful image makes my hour holy. Every road leads us wanderers too back home.

(from 'Wandering' by Hermann Hesse 1920)

Aside from the vivid exemplification of the concepts of watershed and water cycle, the strength of such writing lies in the connection made between the uniting character of the water cycle and the human experience of departing and returning, thereby bridging the assumed separation between the physical and the spiritual. The usual detachment between physical process and human experience is broken down. When read to a group (or better, by a member of the group to their companions) at an appropriate location in the field, such writing can function as a starting point for individual or group enquiries. Within this simple piece of prose we might find, through subsequent discussion, the seeds for catchment comparisons, downstream variations or political concerns in relation to the management of water resources.

Ted Hughes's 'River in March' encompasses ideas about hydrographs, soil erosion and concepts of water storage (even if the speculative attempt to quantify things may depart somewhat from real measurements). Yet the language enriches our experience of rivers and helps break down the usual detachment between ourselves and what we study in the field.

The River in March

Now the river is rich, but her voice is low.
It is her Mighty Majesty the sea
Travelling among the villages incognito.
Now the river is poor. No song, just a thin mad whisper.
The winter floods have ruined her.
She squats between draggled banks, fingering her rags and rubbish.
And now the river is rich. A deep choir.
It is the lofty clouds, that work in heaven,
Going on their holiday to the sea.
The river is poor again. All her bones are showing.
Through a dry wig of bleached flotsam she peers up ashamed
From her slum of sticks.
Now the river is rich, collecting shawls and minerals.
Rain brought fatness, but she takes ninety-nine percent
Leaving the fields just one percent to survive on.
And now she is poor. Now she is East wind sick.
She huddles in holes and corners. The brassy sun gives her a headache.
She has lost all her fish. And she shivers.
But now once more she is rich. She is viewing her lands.
A hoard of kingcups spills from her folds, it blazes, it cannot be hidden.
A salmon, a sow of solid silver,
Bulges to glimpse it.

Ted Hughes ('Season Songs')

We all have our favourite writers and it would be presumptuous to offer a prescribed list relevant to fieldwork.

Fuller accounts of qualitative techniques as starting points for fieldwork are offered in *New Directions in Geographical Fieldwork* (Job 1999a).

Sustainability – is fieldwork missing the point?

In a compelling critique of the prevailing educational paradigm from an ecological perspective, Stephen Sterling (2001) asserts that education is largely behind other fields in developing new thinking and practice in response to the challenge of sustainability. In North America, Orr (1993) perceives higher education as, overall, participating and acquiescing in planetary degradation and social disintegration rather than countering these trends. Geography is often regarded as the curriculum subject through which ecological and social concerns are best explored. However, a not uncommon experience when conducting issue-based fieldwork is that information is gathered which identifies evidence of negative environmental impact or social injustice, but the process of change is either not explored or is insufficiently explicit to enable pupils to consider how they might involve themselves in the process of change.

A model of outdoor experience originally put forward by Hawkins (1987) asserts a stage of personal involvement and action as the culmination of investigative work. The framework that he outlines (summarized in Figure 10.5) proposes an initial phase of acclimatization in which the learner identifies his or her own focus in the landscape for subsequent investigation, a second phase of more conventional investigative work, and the third stage in which the implications of findings are transformed into concern for the environment investigated and personal or collective action to ensure its well-being.

A similar phase of personal commitment was proposed as the culmination of the process of geographical enquiry in the development of the 16–19 Geography Project's 'route to enquiry' (Naish *et al.* 1987). The framework for enquiry put forward involved, in its latter stages, a personal justification for supporting one of a range of options or viewpoints in the investigation of issues, followed up by a deci-

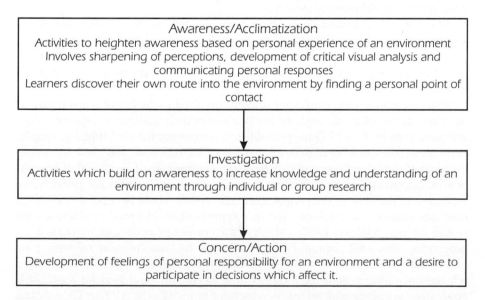

Figure 10.5 A teaching–learning model for outdoor experience

Source: Hawkins 1987.

sion to influence outcomes and decisions through some means of personal action. The implication was that geographical enquiry was not a detached academic endeavour but an evaluation of issues and viewpoints which subsequently entailed personal decisions, commitments and actions.

I recall some fieldwork that I was involved in developing recently on farming systems. A largely fun, 'foody' introductory experience (based on the blindfold-tasting of organically and conventionally raised produce) led to comparative investigations of a range of environmental variables on organically and conventionally farmed land. Convincing evidence was gathered of generally more sustainable systems on the organic farm over a wide range of variables which encompassed soil organic matter, earthworm counts, water quality, wildlife habitat, employment, energy use, system structure, distribution and packaging. Conversely, conventionally farmed land on otherwise physically similar sites showed evidence of depleted soil organic matter, instances of soil erosion, degraded hedgerows and stream-water nitrate concentrations in excess of EU limits. Yet the only significant concluding action point from the student group seemed to be that we should change our shopping habits and buy organic produce, a conclusion which appeared to miss most of the deeper issues as well as being socially divisive.

We had failed to critique the enormous environmental costs of air-freighting fresh organic produce halfway around the world; we had not considered the economic obstacles to organic conversion; we had not critiqued the distorted accounting of conventional economics which makes chemically grown produce artificially cheap; we had not considered the collective power and vested interests of agribusiness in maintaining chemical farming through influencing farm policy. In short, we could not adequately consider the possibilities of change without viewing the findings of our fieldwork as part of a broader and deeper picture involving underlying economic and political systems.

To reach more substantial conclusions we would not only need to have developed a wider critique of how things operate in a holistic sense, but we would also need some exposure to the alternative ways of organizing food production and distribution that have the potential to obviate problems resulting from conventional production and distribution systems.

What alternative ideas would our students involved in the farming investigations need in order to follow through the implications of their findings, to explore change and participate in change? Quite probably sources outside the established geography curriculum. We would need to develop our own awareness of, and make accessible, the ideas of the New Economics whereby the environmental and social disbenefits of activities are incorporated into the accounting system (Douthwaite 1999). Some awareness of the ideas of the permaculture movement would be helpful in showing how communities can establish their own systems of healthy food production even within the city (Molison 1988). (Much of the practice of permaculture reads like a geography textbook!) Simon Fairlie, following his involvement of setting up sustainably based communities in the countryside, shows us how to deal with a reluctant planning system for those wishing to reclaim rural land for sustainable productive purposes and set up new communities (Fairlie 1995). Though less familiar to mainstream Geography, works such as these are rich in geographical relevance. Their idealism excites young minds while countering the nihilistic responses which can arise from the repeated wringing of hands over the state of the planet.

The example of the organic farming fieldwork serves to illustrate that re-orienting fieldwork to address the deeper aspects of sustainability issues has a number of prerequisites which have ramifications throughout the curriculum. The implementation of the final 'action' stage in Hawkins' model of outdoor experience requires both a foundation in radical critique and the inspiration and ideas that come from an awareness of some aspects of our alternative culture, which is generally where small-scale sustainable solutions are already being worked out.

Towards deeper fieldwork

The term 'deeper' fieldwork is applied tentatively. The intention is not to imply that established fieldwork practice is superficial, but rather to indicate the possibility of experiences which:

- take us deeper into our inner world by engaging emotions as well as the intellect;
- seek the underlying causes of ecological or social dysfunction; and
- promote thinking about different ways of being and doing which offer a more sustainable future.

To a degree the term is lifted from deep ecology, a genre of ecological thinking which explores ecological ideas in the context of a social, spiritual and cultural framework.

The approaches developed here draw heavily on Hawkins's model of outdoor experience by offering initial activities that draw on individual experiences, then lead into more conventional investigative activity. The implications of findings are then followed through into a more transformative phase of both personal and societal change and commitment.

The examples offered are partly based on a nascent fieldwork venture taking shape on the upper sections of the Tarka Trail in North Devon. The purposes of this project are to develop innovative approaches to fieldwork while participating in the revitalization of a depressed rural locality.

The locational context is a remoter rural region of mainly small farms, with some traditional extractive industry in the form of clay working. The farming economy, currently reeling from the impacts of foot-and-mouth disease, was already in difficulties, in part through the breakdown of local systems of processing and distribution and increased transportation costs to far-flung dairies and abattoirs. Somewhat removed from the traditional tourist haunts of the North Devon coast, a number of agencies are promoting the development of 'green' tourism, partly through the development of a network of cycle and walking routes based along a former railway line. The National Cycling Network of which the Tarka Trail forms a part has yet to be evaluated and developed as a resource for fieldwork. The opportunities for allowing students to work more autonomously away from traffic hazards as well as the possibility of utilizing greener forms of transportation during fieldwork may be substantial.

Deeper into the woods

An initial engagement takes place through sensory experience in three woodland environments, all accessible either on foot or cycle along the Tarka Trail. We are encouraged first to inhale the humic aromas beneath a towering canopy of varied deciduous standards, ancient trees which have long witnessed the passage of rattling clay trucks descending to the Torridge estuary but now experience the changing seasons with little intrusion but the passing groups of cyclists and walkers. 'Magic spot' comes next, where we spread out and find a chosen place within the wood for informal meditation, the only requirement being to return with three words to describe our experience of the wood. The group comes together to construct a collective haiku using words contributed from the individual experiences. Two-metre lengths of string are then issued which are used to trace out a nature trail (microtrail) as it might be designed for an ant, with eight points of interest along the way. This initially seems a little like returning to primary school but as we begin to notice detail at the micro-level, the value in drawing attention to the intricate teemings and textures of the forest floor becomes apparent.

Close by, the trailside embankment bears a contrasting cover of sprouting ash and hazel coppice, in places a low canopy, open with wildflowers beneath; other areas are taller, dense, shaded and closed, obstructing the view south to the distant Dartmoor skyline. A short bike-ride away, adjoining a tumbling tributary of the River Torridge, is a mature stand of Douglas fir, equally majestic in their way to the ancient oaks, but offering a darker, more Nordic experience.

Subsequent creative work based on the woodland experiences suggests we all respond rather differently and have varying feelings and preferences concerning the three woodland environments. But how do these contrasting environments differ in other respects? Which offers greatest diversity of habitat? What is there here which we might eat? What useful medicines lie within the forest? Which system is most effective at renewing itself through nutrient cycling? Which has the greatest capacity to lock up atmospheric carbon and what useful timber resources does each offer? What sort of timber might be harvested, in what quantities and with what impact on the forest? Brainstorming generates a wealth of research questions, some of an academic nature but several relating the impact of different management policies or the effects of different woodland types to other environmental sub-systems, recreational value and resource potential for the local economy. Each of these research questions allows a small group to pursue a manageable and tangible investigation involving all three woodland types while contributing to the larger endeavour of considering the most sustainable way of managing woodlands. Answering this wider question inevitably involves debating the deeper sustainability issues – sustainable for what purpose? Sustainable for whom and over what time span?

The subsequent fieldwork activity entails the more familiar application of fieldwork techniques – canopy and soil invertebrates, forest productivity, soil horizons, groundflora, forest hydrology and the water quality of woodland springs are all investigated using largely quantitative methods while informal interviews are undertaken with a local woodsman and charcoal burner and a herbalist to discover the value of woodland species as a source of both useful timber and traditional remedies.

Group presentations, which incorporate both artwork and the results of investigative work, provide some answers to the individual research questions. The conifer plantation wins hands-down on productivity but leaves a few doubts concerning biodiversity and nutrient cycling and some evidence of acidification of soil and water resources. The towering oak standards seem to move us most and inspire the most lyrical poetry, and sustains the greatest diversity of invertebrates, while the large hardwood timbers, it seems, would make some glorious timber-frame buildings, but some questions emerge as to how the productivity might be sustained, or indeed how the timber might be harvested without harming the rest of the forest. Some ambiguity emerges over the trailside coppiced woodland – lots of diversity where recently managed, but the older stand seems too dense for the groundflora apart from blocking off the views from the trail (some cyclists we met complained that parts of the trail were a bit like cycling along a green tunnel). The smaller, more manageable timbers that could be harvested from the mature coppice had a wide range of potential uses, and the woodsman interviewed was beginning to make a living from a range of greenwood products harvested from the trailside, as well as a charcoal business supplying a local store.

Some consensus emerges that a renewed coppicing effort might not go amiss: opening up the views, boosting the biodiversity and creating a useful resource – small to medium greenwood timbers for fence posts, greenwood crafts, hazel stakes for straw-bale building. Fuel wood from a sustainable source was also much needed for the bio-fuel burner that provided heat for cooking and much of the hot water for showers in the bunkhouse where the group was staying.

Time for action! Armed with bow saws, billhooks, leather gauntlets and bike trailers we trundle to a nearby patch of thickly overgrown coppice under the guidance of the local woodsman. Training is given in the safe handling of tools and the method of cutting the ash boughs without killing the remaining coppiced 'stool'. As the trimmed poles of hazel and ash of varying diameters are lashed to the trailers, we leave behind neat, squat coppiced stools where, next spring, new shoots will sprout and wild flowers will flourish in the open spaces between. Beyond the plot where we've been working, the tor-studded whaleback summits of the Dartmoor skyline are visible through the gap we've created. A sense of new growth and creation from the harvesting of the old is strong. Within each harvested load are the resources for making useful and beautiful objects – and for warmth, if we don't mind returning some of the sequestered carbon back to the atmosphere!

Back at base is the chance to learn further skills during the evening while creating objects to take home, perhaps as gifts, but objects that offer a recollection of the woodland experience. Our woodsman demonstrates the pole lathe, powered only by a foot-operated treadle strung to the whippy top of a growing sapling, to power the spinning shaft of the lathe. With a little time and practice, candlesticks, objets d'art, stools and even rustic chairs can be crafted from pieces of freshly harvested coppice timber. Participating in these kinds of creative activities can boost self-confidence through successfully developing new skills and creating objects of beauty. Such experiences also recognize and create opportunities for those students whose aptitudes are more kinaesthetic rather than logical or linguistic.

Aside from the fun and skills element, the coppicing and subsequent woodcraft activities have meanings which encapsulate several core elements of what sustainable practice can mean. These include:

- Engaging in activity which has long-term benefits
- Enhancing biodiversity
- Working co-operatively
- Valuing physical work as well as intellectual activity
- Participating in regeneration
- Linking economic activity to the sustainable use of local resources
- Self-reliance – making things rather than being dependent on commercial providers
- Exemplifying a negative or zero-net carbon system (carbon fixation > release).

This woodland experience is still in its infancy and awaits further evaluation. Comparable programmes are being constructed in the areas of farming and food production, micro-climate investigations in the context of sustainable energy production, and settlement studies in the context of rural regeneration. The methodology is awaiting a wider application and development in an urban context.

The intention of the case study outlined here is to offer a framework which achieves conventional objectives closely related to the curriculum, while also presenting deeper and more transformative experiences that address some of the underpinnings of both citizenship and learning for a more sustainable future.

Conclusion

In some quarters there is currently an enthusiasm for 'virtual' fieldwork, that is to say vicarious experiences of environments, data collection and interpretation which take place in front of a VDU screen. Enthusiasts point to the savings in time and cost relative to real fieldwork, obviating the demanding processes of risk assessment and care of students in potentially hazardous settings and the possibility of 'experiencing' a wider range of field environments, including more distant places. Whilst some of the investigative phase of fieldwork may be accomplished through these 'virtual' strategies, the sensory and emotional experience of whole landscapes and real people is entirely beyond the scope of any electronic simulation or representation, however sophisticated.

A further constraint of virtual fieldwork is that it takes place in an environment entirely detached from the elements and the natural world, in a setting which is physically passive and often socially isolating. Engagement in real fieldwork, particularly of the deeper kind, addresses almost the full range of intelligences and learning styles. To promote and justify real fieldwork, it needs to be demonstrated that the experiences offered include not only the development of cognitive skills but also the nurturing of aesthetic sensibility, creativity, critique, co-operative endeavour, caring and healing. These attributes, rather than technical and rationalist aptitudes alone, form some of the foundations for the growth of ecologically and emotionally literate citizens.

References

Caton, D. (2001) 'An encounter with nature', *Teaching Geography* 26(3).

Douthwaite, R. (1999) *The Ecology of Money*, Schumacher Briefings 4, Dartington: Green Books.

Fairlie, S. (1996) *Low Impact Development: Planning and People in a Sustainable Countryside*, Charlbury: Jon Carpenter.

Harvey, P.K. (1991) 'The role and value of A-level geography fieldwork: a case study', unpublished PhD thesis, University of Durham.

Hawkins, G. (1987) 'From awareness to participation: new directions in the outdoor experience', *Geography* 72(3).

Hicks, D. and Holden, C. (1995) *Visions of the Future: Why We Need to Teach for Tomorrow*, Chester: Trentham Books.

Job, D. (1996) 'Geography and environmental education – an exploration of perspectives and strategies', in A. Kent, D. Lambert, M. Naish and F. Slater (eds) *Geography in Education: Viewpoints on Teaching and Learning*, Cambridge: Cambridge University Press.

—— (1999a) *New Directions in Geographical Fieldwork*, Cambridge: Cambridge University Press.

—— (1999b) *Beyond the Bikesheds: Fresh Approaches to Fieldwork in the School Locality*, Sheffield: Geographical Association.

—— (2001) 'Fieldwork for a change', *Teaching Geography* 26(2).

Kent, A. and Foskett, N. (2002) 'Fieldwork in the school geography curriculum: pedagogical issues and development', in M. Smith (ed.) *Teaching Geography in Secondary Schools: A Reader*, Milton Keynes: Open University.

van Matre, S. (1979) *Sunship Earth – An Acclimatization Program for Outdoor Learning*, Martinsville IN: American Camping Association.

Naish, M., Rawling, E. and Hart, C. (1987) *Geography 16–19. The Contribution of a Curriculum Project to 16–19 Education*, London: Longman.

Orr, D. (1993) *Earth in Mind – On Education, Environment and the Human Prospect*, Washington DC: Island Press.

Ross, S. (2001) 'The geography of awe and wonder', *Teaching Geography* 26(2).

Sterling, S. (2001) *Sustainable Education: Revisioning Learning and Change*, Schumacher Briefings 6, Dartington: Green Books.

11 Inclusive geographies

| Differentiation in practice
Adrian Norton

Differentiation is the art of making the curriculum accessible to all students. Although there are many texts on differentiation with respect to Geography, few provide practical examples. This article attempts to address that imbalance. While differentiation can be achieved in a number of ways, here the focus is on the modification of resources which allow students to reach a similar learning outcome.

Preparing differentiated resources

The time and energy required to prepare for differentiation in geography lessons is frequently cited as a reason for relying on differentiation by outcome. However, the modification of existing resources to allow for differentiation need not involve too much extra work. The use of a word-processing package can make the modification of texts quick and easy to accomplish, and a flatbed scanner will help in the rapid adaptation of maps and diagrams. Although the initial preparation of differentiated materials does take time, once the task is complete the materials are ready for the next occasion. Extension tasks for more able students can be based around utilizing existing resources in a wider variety of ways, while the provision of extra resources for less able students may be necessary. Teachers should also evaluate differentiated resources from time to time and modify those which have not been employed successfully by students. Frequently the resources require minor, rather than major, modification.

To make materials accessible for less able students, follow a simple principle: 'provide progressively simpler information or diagrammatic help'. The resources described here are classified as 'Extension Resources', 'Grade 1 Resources', 'Grade 2 Resources', and so on (the higher the grade number the greater the amount of help or the simpler the level of text provided for the student).

Text aimed at more able students is frequently complex in nature, so it must be shortened and simplified for the less able. Resources aimed at less able students should use language at an appropriate level: in other words, vocabulary should be relatively simple, and sentences should be short and preferably contain only one piece of information. They should be written using clear, plain, lower-case lettering in a reasonably large font (and not include italics or a mixture of typefaces). 'White space', free from text and pictures, can also make the information look less forbidding.

There are a number of ways to begin an activity. For the China mapping task outlined on pp. 148–51, our preferred method is to use a card-matching activity. Students work in mixed-ability pairs to match geographical words from the text with their explanations: the word appears on one card and its matching definition is on another (e.g. 'irrigation' and 'providing water for crops where there would not otherwise be enough' or 'subsistence farming' and 'farmers who grow food only or mainly to feed themselves and their families'). The definitions on the cards differ from those in the text, so students must reach an understanding of the term in order to match the word to its definition. This can be done in a number of ways:

- Students can clarify their thoughts about some of the words by discussing them in pairs. Discussion of the matching activity answers also helps students focus on the resources and on the mapping task.
- Students can be encouraged to use a geographical dictionary before they start the activity.
- A class discussion or teacher explanation of terms may be used.

However, the first approach gets students to engage with the materials in a focused manner and they are able to clarify their own ideas.

Who gets what?

There are several ways of approaching this question. The teacher can decide which materials are appropriate for certain individuals or groups of students and hand them out. An alternative strategy, and one which I prefer to use because I have found it to work well, is to explain the purpose of the task and describe what the outcome should be in terms of what the students will learn and produce. I then hand out copies of Grade 1 resources to all students with the option of choosing the grade of resources which they feel is appropriate to their ability. The resources are labelled clearly as 'Grade 1 Resources', 'Grade 2 Resources', and so on. The significance of this is explained to the students. Additional 'Extension tasks' should also be labelled. The resources are placed centrally so that they are accessible to all students. In my experience students tend to use the materials that enable them to achieve the task, but which also present them with a challenge. They tend to work at the highest grade appropriate for them; few students immediately reach for the easiest materials.

Activity 1   Mapping

This activity forms part of a Key Stage 3 (Years 8 and 9) unit of work on China. Students have examined climate and relief in China. This activity can be described as a 'Directed Activity Related to Text' (DART, see Roberts 1986).

Instructions

- Hand out atlases, a copy of the Grade 1 text 'Feeding People in China' (Figure 11.la) but provide the opportunity for students to use the simpler Grade 3 text (Figure 11.1b), and a map of China.
- Ask students to use these resources and what they have already learned to delineate the two main farming regions in China on their map.
- Ask students to label the areas they have identified on their map to show:
  — what is grown in the farming regions; and
  — what farming is done in the rest of China.
- Extend this activity for more able students by asking them to use an atlas to help them annotate the map in order to explain why farming is like this (Figure 11.2a).
- Provide less able students with a blank copy of Figure 11.2b (this shows the country divided into the farming regions). They can shade in the different areas and include a key. This enables the less able students to achieve the same outcome. They can then label the map (Figure 11.2b).
- Students who require more help can be provided with blank copies of Figure 11.2b and a set of six cards (Figure 11.3). Students can place the cards on the different regions and label each area by copying the text from the card.

(a)

Feeding people in China

The Chinese population is growing very rapidly. In fact, there are so many people living in China that, for every five people in the world today, one of them is Chinese. To feed all of these people is a problem the Chinese government has to face.

Most farm work in China is done by hand and many people work long hours on the land in order to grow as much as possible. They use all the land which is capable of supporting crops and increase its richness by adding every possible fertilizer, including human waste. Sometimes they use a system of multiple cropping so that more than one crop can be harvested each year. Where rainfall is low, irrigation helps to give plants enough water and where the land is steep, terraces are built to provide flat steps of land which are easier to farm. So much land is used for arable farming that there is very little left for animals. The only animals found are usually those needed for farm work, e.g. oxen, and those that live off waste, e.g. chickens and pigs.

Most people live as subsistence farmers on the lowland plains of eastern China. This area occupies the land below 400 metres above sea level. North of the line of latitude 35 degrees North, farmers grow only one crop per year. This is usually maize, wheat or potatoes which are similar crops to those grown in Europe. South of 35 degrees North two crops a year are usually grown. Rice is the standard summer crop with wheat in the winter. Here there are also plantations of tea and mulberry. The remainder of the country is either desert and rock surface or meadow and pasture, although people do try to grow crops by diverting water to irrigate them, as the passage below (from 'Danziger's Travels') shows.

In this passage Danziger describes travelling on the road north from Charhlik through deserts:

> The Lop Desert is the driest area on the Eurasian land mass. It is a wasteland of shifting sand, where temperatures can reach 50 degrees Celsius, while the relative humidity remains at zero. The desert is lashed by sandstorms up to 80 times a year, and winds attain hurricane-like speeds. Although we didn't encounter anything quite so ferocious, the first part of our route did lie across desert. It gave way to a desiccated forest, where the drivers collected dead wood, During the work we all became covered with dust and sand. Then on again, until finally we reached fertile land – land reclaimed from the desert through a network of canals and sluices which at the time I was there were dry, but which stood ready to channel the waters of the Tarim River, which was fed by snow from the Tian Shan mountain range. Around this fertile land were the great shoulders of the sand dunes, soaring to several hundred feet in height.

(b)

Feeding people in China

Most people live as subsistence farmers. They live on the lowland plains of eastern China. This is the land below 400 metres.

The lowland plains of eastern China can be divided in two according to what crops are grown. Find the line of latitude 35 degrees North.

- North of the line farmers grow only one crop a year. This is usually maize, wheat or potatoes. These are similar crops to those grown in Europe.
- South of the line two crops a year are usually grown. Rice is the usual summer crop with wheat in the winter. There are also plantations of tea and mulberry grown in this area.

The rest of the country is either desert and rock surface or meadow and pasture. In this area where it is very dry people try to grow crops by redirecting water to irrigate them.

Figure 11.1 Examples of differentiated resources for Year 8 and 9 students undertaking Activity 1: mapping: (a) Grade 1 and (b) Grade 3

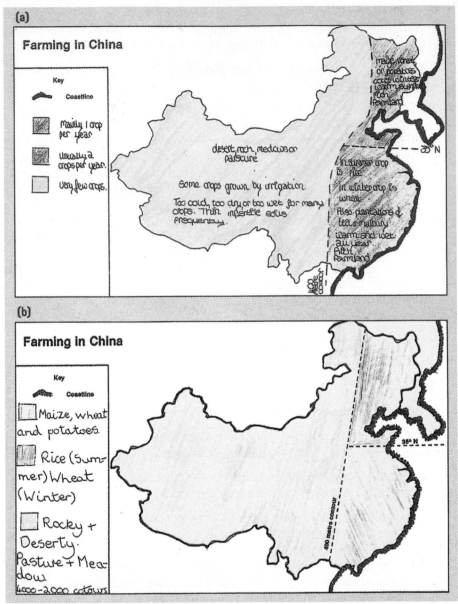

Figure 11.2 Example outcomes from Activity 1: mapping: (a) Grade 1 map annotated by a more able student as an extension task, and (b) Grade 2 completed map including annotations as a key (a base map is provided)

One crop per year Usually maize, wheat or potatoes	Lowland plains of Eastern China South of 35 degrees North
Lowland plains of Eastern China North of 35 degrees North	Remainder of country
Desert and rock surfaces or meadow and pasture Some crops grown by irrigating land	Two crops a year Rice in summer, wheat in winter Also plantations of tea and mulberry

Figure 11.3 Grade 3 resources for use in Activity 1: mapping

Table 11.1 summarizes the resources which are on offer to students of different abilities and the tasks they are asked to complete. All students thus complete a labelled map of China and have, ultimately, achieved the same outcome. However, the route to the learning outcome is different by virtue of the grade of resources used.

Table 11.1 Summary of differentiated resources used in the activities

	Extension	Grade 1	Grade 2	Grade 3
Resource				
Previous learning	yes	yes	yes	yes
Atlas	yes	yes	yes	yes
China map (unmarked)	yes	yes	no	no
China map with areas marked	no	no	yes	yes
Labels on cards	no	no	no	yes
Tasks to complete				
Annotated map	yes	no	no	no
Labelled map	yes	yes	yes	yes

Activity 2   Diagrams

This is another DART activity (Roberts 1986), devised for a unit of work about ecosystems at GCSE. In this activity students are asked to devise an annotated diagram of an ecosystem. As with Activity 1, the outcome is the same for all the Year 10/11 students; however, the resources they use are differentiated. The text (shown in Figure 11.4) is categorized as a Grade 1 resource. This resource alone should enable students to label their diagram.

Instructions

- Hand out copies of the sheet describing the ecosystem (see e.g. Figure 11.4) to all students.
- Ask students to produce an annotated diagram of the ecosystem described in this text.
- The task could be extended further by asking more able students to annotate the diagram to explain how the features illustrated are responses or adaptations to the environment.
- Less able students can use a diagram showing the basic features (Grade 2 resources) and be asked to label the features.
- Students who find the labelling activity challenging can be given Grade 3 resources (labels in the form of cards, see e.g. Figure 11.5). They place the cards on the appropriate parts of the diagram and copy the text from the cards on to the diagram.

Taiga

To the Equator-ward side of the tundra zone, summer temperatures begin to rise and trees begin to become important.

Evergreen conifers start to thrive, and they have certain adaptations suited for survival.

If water is available they can photosynthesize all year round.

The needles are a type of leaf that helps the trees to resist drought when water is locked up as ice or when strong winds increase transpiration rates.

The shape of the crown helps them to shed snow so the branches are not snapped off by the weight.

Large trees up to 40 metres high form a fairly continuous canopy that permits relatively little light to penetrate to the ground, so that a lower layer of trees is uncommon.

There is usually a fairly continuous ground cover of mosses and lichens.

Spruces are the dominant tree.

Because of the low temperatures, organic matter decays slowly, so litter tends to accumulate as a thick layer on the forest floor.

Figure 11.4 Grade 1 resource for Activity 2: diagrams

Source: Adapted from Goudie 1993.

Lots of evergreen conifers close together

Most of the trees are spruce trees

Lots of mosses and lichens grow beneath the trees

No trees grow beneath the big tree

Needles which have fallen to the ground to make a thick layer

Figure 11.5 Example of Grade 3 resources for Activity 2: diagrams

Activity 3   Written work

Key Stage 3 students at Howard of Effingham School study a unit on weather in Year 7, during which they are asked to write a weather forecast. The forecast is based on a copy of a relatively simple synoptic chart showing a depression crossing the British Isles. This is a challenging task. Once again the outcome is common to all students but the way in which they achieve it is differentiated. Some students will be able to complete the task using only the synoptic chart, so it is described as a Grade 1 resource. More able students are asked to forecast the weather using a synoptic chart from the day's newspaper or downloaded from the internet as an extension task. Where Grade 2 resources are provided, they indicate that students must write a sentence about each of the following aspects of weather:

- temperature;
- the nature and type of precipitation (is it rain, hail or snow?);
- cloud cover and type; and
- wind speed and direction.

The Grade 3 resources, provided for less able students, are issued in an envelope. These consist of a complete weather forecast cut into individual sentences. However, there are at least two copies of the information about each aspect of the weather: one correct and the other incorrect. This is designed to help less able students to write the forecast, while offering them the challenge of interpreting the data. This approach offers considerable flexibility: three, four or more incorrect statements can be included. Using the same approach, it is also possible to provide Grade 4 resources by including fewer sets of incorrect information in the envelope.

Conclusion

The provision of differentiated resources need not be a complicated and time-consuming task for teachers. The supply of a variety of graded resources and, where possible, allowing students to choose those they feel are most appropriate for their ability offer a positive learning experience for all. This approach enables all students to achieve a satisfactory outcome while experiencing appropriate yet similar learning experience in the geography classroom.

Note

The grading of resources discussed in this article has been devised by the geography department at Howard of Effingham School, Surrey – and is used widely in their geography teaching.

Acknowledgements

The author would like to thank Bob Digby (Lecturer in Education at Brunel University) for help in producing this article; Wendy Hendy at Howard of Effingham School for supplying Figure 11.4; students at Howard of Effingham school (in particular Jenny Briscoe) for use of their work; and Katy and James Norton for their help in producing and scanning figures.

References

Danziger, N. (1987) *Danziger's Travels Beyond Forbidden Frontiers*, London: Grafton.
Goudie, A. (1993) *The Nature of the Environment* (third edition), Oxford: Blackwell.
Roberts, M. (1986) 'Talking, reading and writing', in D. Boardman (ed.) *Handbook for Geography Teachers*, Sheffield: Geographical Association.

11 Disability and inclusive landscapes
Rob Kitchin

The ideas of social justice and citizenship have been key themes in many aspects of human geography since the early 1970s. Broadly, social justice studies have examined the distribution of material goods and power between people in a society, asking whether such distributions are fair and just, and how that society might be rearranged into a more just configuration. For example, David Harvey (1996) and David Smith (1994) explored inequalities between people in cities in relation to housing conditions, poverty, and access to employment and services, the reasons why such inequalities exist, and how this uneven development might be addressed. Citizenship builds upon notions of justice, and concerns the civil and welfare rights a State's subjects can expect – in other words what rights you can expect as a citizen of a country. Traditionally, questions relating to social justice and citizenship in western societies, whether something is good or bad, right or wrong, fair or unfair, have been avoided within the school curriculum. However, ideas of inclusion now form part of the secondary school curriculum, and the Programmes of Study in Citizenship at Key Stages 3 and 4 seek to encourage students to think about political, moral and social issues.

This chapter demonstrates how disabled people are often denied the same levels of citizenship, experiencing reduced levels of social justice in comparison to non-disabled people, specifically by focusing on access to the built environment. It can be argued that, in many western countries, disabled access to the built environment is only partially legislated for, therefore there is only partial obligation to provide access. Consequently disabled people only have partial citizenship, i.e. they only have partial rights to move about towns and cities. As well as detailing some of the problems, this chapter also considers ways in which students as geographers might intervene and try to make their environment more inclusive.

Disability, geography and exclusion

It is only since the mid 1990s that there has been a sustained attempt to start to map out the geographies of disability in relation to social justice, citizenship and exclusion (for an overview see Park *et al.* 1998 and Kitchin 2000). Despite this late start, a number of different issues have been investigated (Figure 11.6), although each of these topics is still highly under-researched.

What each of these investigations has revealed is that disabled people, by and large, experience different geographies from non-disabled people. In many cases, this

- Planning process and urban design issues, e.g. examining (1) the ways in which the physical environment excludes disabled people by denying access to certain locations; (2) how to design environments that are accessible to disabled people.
- Experiences of living within urban and rural environments, e.g. asking disabled people about what it is like to live in a location and some of the issues that concern them.
- Transport and mobility, e.g. (1) examining how accessible transport is for disabled people; (2) measuring the spatial behaviour patterns of disabled people (how far disabled people travel, how frequently, and by what means).
- Access to labour markets and schooling, e.g. examining how accessible, in terms of infrastructure and attitudes, labour markets and schooling are to disabled people.
- Siting of mental health facilities, residents' reactions and the socio-economic effects, e.g. examining the effects (social and economic) of siting mental health facilities in a particular location.
- Mapping and spatial ecology of disability, e.g. constructing maps of where people with different impairments are located, and then seeing if there is any relationship with variables such as social conditions, pollution or environment type.
- Learning and communicating geographic information, e.g. examining how people with visual impairments remember and learn spatial concepts such as street layout, and the routes between locations either through direct experience, or through secondary media such as tactile maps.
- Cross-cultural comparisons, e.g. examining the relationship between geography and disability in different places, in relation to both actual provision and legislation.

Figure 11.6 Some of the disability issues that geographers have examined

might be expected. For example, people with visual impairments perceive the geographic world differently from those with full sight, and wheelchair users cannot, for practical reasons, travel through many wilderness areas. Problems arise, however, when disabled people experience different geographies through no fault of his or her own. For example, it is now commonly argued that if a wheelchair user cannot enter a building it is because the building is inappropriately designed, not because of their impairment. In other words, it is the geography – the way the built environment is designed and built – that excludes many disabled people from full access to the towns and cities they live in.

What the studies in Figure 11.6 reveal is that there is a variety of ways in which disabled people are discriminated against in society, all of which lead to the *production* of very different geographies (Figure 11.7). The four points in Figure 11.7 indicate that there is an imbalance in how disabled people are perceived and treated. In other words, there is an imbalance in social justice and citizenship between disabled and non-disabled citizens.

1   Lack of access to power: Disabled people are generally under-represented in political positions at all levels (local, regional, national and international) and therefore lack a platform to give their views and change society.

2   Lack of access to social well-being: Disabled people are generally over-represented in poor housing, denied access to private and public transport, and find it difficult to take part in 'mainstream' social activities such as visiting the pub or cinema through poor provision and weak laws.

3   Lack of access to employment: Disabled people are often excluded from the labour market through discriminatory practices and poor levels of mobility. Where they do gain access it is usually in marginal positions undertaking low-paid, low-skilled work often on a part-time basis. This denies many disabled people prosperity and wealth, and their associated power.

4   Stigmatization through media images: Disabled people are often portrayed in the media as abnormal, 'freaks of nature' or 'charity cases'. This presents negative stereotypes that mean that many non-disabled people view and treat disabled people in unfair and discriminatory ways.

Figure 11.7 Four ways in which disabled people are discriminated against

Access to the built environment

There are many ways in which the urban environment disables people. For example, it is common for pavements to have kerbs at crossings rather than pavement-cuts and tactile markings, for cash machines to be placed too high for wheelchair users, and for places to be linked by inaccessible public transport. Even where there is provision for disabled people, it is often separate or different from non-disabled provision. For example, accessible public toilets are mostly separate from able-bodied toilets, and theatres and cinemas generally restrict wheelchair users to certain areas within the auditorium, usually towards the front or the sides. As a consequence, disabled people often encounter many more problems of mobility than non-disabled people.

All of the problems detailed above can be tackled with relative ease. For example, steps can be complemented with a ramp, cash machines can be placed lower, buildings can have lifts fitted, buses can be adapted, and so on. This reveals that the built environment is rarely 'natural' but is the product of people's values and actions. Indeed the built environment does not just occur – it is carefully planned. As such, if we wanted to make accessible environments, we could. The fact that environments are not accessible reveals important insights into how we, as a society, view and value disabled people. To geographers such as Rob Imrie (1996), inaccessible environments suggest that urban planning expresses a form of 'design apartheid' whereby planners, architects and building control officers are guilty of constructing environments which 'lock' disabled people out. This occurs, he suggests, because planners and architects are more interested in how a building looks or how it will be used by the majority of users, failing to consider the needs of disabled people. Here, environments and buildings are designed as if all people are the same (non-disabled). He argues that those that build and shape the environments we live in need to rethink the ways in which places are designed in order to make society more inclusive.

Investigating access

There are a number of ways in which the figures in this article can be used in the geography classroom, in the school buildings and grounds and for local fieldwork.

- Geography teachers can ask Key Stage 3/4 students to study photographs of inaccessible environments. Small groups of students produce brief descriptions of how ... the environment is inaccessible to wheelchair users. This could be followed by a whole-class discussion to clarify the issues. Students could then use this information and a simplified version of the access audit (Figure 11.8) to map accessible/inaccessible places for wheelchair users around the school buildings/grounds. They will need to decide on appropriate symbols and include a key on the map.
- Using the quotes in Figure 11.9 and a modified version of Figure 11.8, groups of Key Stage 3 or 4 students can make a second survey of the school grounds/buildings with the visually impaired person in mind.
- Students could then suggest ways in which the school environment could be made more accessible for: a) wheelchair users; and b) the visually impaired. The evidence could be presented either as a display, a presentation to the class or as a report to the headteacher.
- As a follow-up activity, groups of Key Stage 3 and 4 students can use these experiences as well as Figure 11.8 and large-scale maps, to gather evidence of accessibility and inaccessibility in an urban area (Figure 11.10). In the field, they should identify areas of good and bad practice, i.e. where kerbs are lowered, or where steps are painted in different colours. In this case the information gathered could be sent to the local planning office. The report could also take account of the views gathered from local people with disabilities, e.g. groups and/or individuals with specific needs. However, students should be instructed to respect people's privacy and/or anonymity at all times.

One way in which to find out how accessible an environment is, is to undertake an access audit. Take a walk around your local shopping centre and, using the checklist below, undertake an audit of:

- How many disabled people there are in relation to non-disabled people.
- How people with physical and sensory impairments would get to the shopping centre (e.g. is public transport accessible, are there disabled parking spaces?).

- How accessible the areas between the shops are for people with physical and sensory impairments (e.g. are there steps but no ramp, is there a lot of street furniture?).
- How accessible, both from the street and once inside, the shops are to people with physical and sensory impairments (e.g. are the aisles wide enough for a wheelchair, are there lifts between floors?).
- How the shops provide for people with learning and developmental disabilities (e.g. are the visual signs easy to understand, are items on sales colour-coded?).
- How many specialized services are provided in the immediate area (e.g. is there a shop mobility scheme, are there accessible toilets?).

The checklist below should help you focus on specific areas.

- Parking and approach
  — well-signposted and easy-to-find car park
  — designated car spaces for disabled people that are close to the building
  — trained staff available to help disabled people (with signs to indicate so)
  — accessible path from car park to buildings (e.g. dropped kerbs)
  — user-friendly path for people with sensory impairments (e.g. tactile paving)
  — obstacles (e.g. bollards/street furniture) highlighted by colour contrast and tactile surfaces

- Entrances to buildings
  — provision of both steps and ramp
  — handrails provided on both sides of steps/ramp
  — doorbell can be reached by all
  — audible/tactile/visible intercom
  — easy-opening door
  — level threshold across doorway
  — door-width sufficient to allow wheelchair access

- Reception and facilities
  — appropriate height of reception desk
  — adequate seating
  — publicly accessible toilets
  — map of site including levels of accessibility

- Circulation areas
  — adequate directional signage (tactile as well as visual)
  — corridors wide enough
  — level fire exits
  — suitable floor surface
  — tactile paths/guides

- Vertical circulation
  — lift large enough to accommodate wheelchair
  — doors open wide enough
  — appropriate height of control panel
  — appropriate alarm/phone height
  — audible and visible signage
  — suitable dimensions of treads/insets of stairs
  — handrails to both sides of stairs and in contrasting colours
  — stair nosing (edge of step) of a contrasting colour

If conducted as part of project work, photograph different environments and construct a poster documenting access in the shopping centre.

- What conclusions can you draw from your study?

Figure 11.8 Undertaking an access audit

Source: Ewart 1998.

Very simple practical ideas are needed, such as larger signs and painting the edges of all steps.

Larger signs are needed. Street signs in most towns are either too high or too low to read.

They should paint the kerbs; that would help. Sometimes I fall off even with the cane. I've been knocked down twice … Drivers don't realize even if you have a cane. They don't really care. It scared me a bit last time. I just lost the edge of the kerb.

Move lamp posts to one side of the pavement.

Painting a shop doorway would be good, like a yellow line by the door. I'm always walking into shop fronts looking for the door.

Tactile pavements need to be standardized and there need to be more of them.

We need consistency; they are not uniform. You can spot a white line on one set of steps and then take a tumble on the next. Positioning of signs needs to be better.

We need consistency in tactile markings at crossings and road junctions. They are good in some areas but they don't always end up at the pole with the button. Some go from the edge of the pavement to the inner shoreline, others just jut out into the path, so sometimes you can miss them.

Figure 11.9 Potential access solutions suggested by people with visual impairments

Source: Kitchin et al. 1998a: 43.

Making an accessibility map

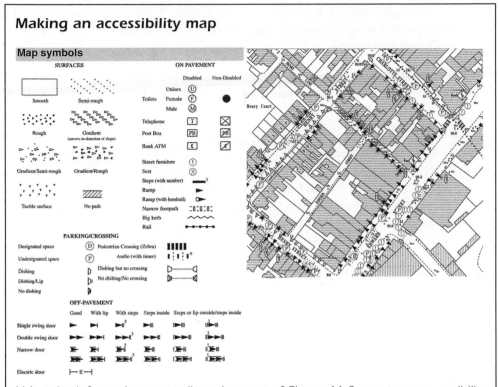

Using the information you collected as part of Figure 11.9, create an accessibility map of your local shopping centre. The map should try to be as inclusive as possible and will thus contain information suitable for people with different disabilities (e.g. wheelchair user, reduced mobility, visually-impaired). You could create maps dedicated to particular groups and then to merge them. Text should be in plain English and accompanied by visual logos (you may need to invent some) so that someone with a learning disability can understand the labelling.

Make sure you include details about the three parts of access: getting there, getting between the buildings, and moving about in the buildings.

The map should communicate issues of accessibility as clearly as possible, so take note of the following:

- provide a reference and a title (e.g. Accessibility Map of Metro Centre Shopping Centre)
- display at an appropriate size so that visual interpretation is easy and text readable
- make sure the map is uncluttered and contains the necessary information at an appropriate scale
- include a legend, scale and North arrow.

Figure 11.10 Instructions for constructing an accessibility map, with an example of a completed map

Other geographers, including myself (Kitchin 1998), have considered the messages that these inaccessible environments communicate to disabled people. As Napolitano writes:

> Good inclusive design will send positive messages to disabled people, messages which tell them: 'You are important'; 'we want you here'; and 'welcome' … if the way that disabled people are expected to get into a building is round the back, past the bins and through the kitchens, what does that message communicate? How will it make a disabled person feel?
>
> (1995: 33)

Here it is argued that the landscape is 'written' as a text, containing messages that we can read (see Cresswell 1996 for an introduction). We have all been taught how to create and read such messages, whether it is being apprehensive when we walk down a dark alley, or being quiet in libraries. In other words, when we look at an environment we recognize whether we 'belong' there and can decide what is appropriate behaviour in that context. In the case of disability, geographers are interested in how landscapes reflect the values of the people who designed them and who live there, and how such designs and values affect disabled people – how disabled people feel when they are trying to negotiate inaccessible environments, and how this affects their spatial behaviour (where they go). Such studies demonstrate that disabled people's spatial behaviour is not just affected by issues of accessibility but also by issues of acceptance, provision and attitudes. Understanding how geography disables people, then, is as much about understanding how the environment conveys messages of belonging and exclusion as it is about understanding the organization and structure of places. As Figure 11.11 demonstrates, teachers can use extracts from novels to introduce some of the issues that wheelchair users encounter. It details, in a humorous manner, the many different ways in which geography disables people and the messages of exclusion that the built environment can communicate to disabled people.

Towards a more inclusive environment

The argument being developed is clearly that there is a need to build a more inclusive society, that is, a society that has an enlarged concept of citizenship which respects and values all its members, including disabled people. As illustrated above, disabled people are often disabled by the fact that society in general, through its attitudes and actions, actively excludes them. Disabled people do not have the same access to what most people would consider basic rights such as education, housing, transport, employment, and the built environment.

If society is to become more inclusive then the built environment needs to be made more accessible. Making the environment more accessible and recognizing the need to cater for disabled people are now legal obligations in the UK for service providers and employers as part of the Disability Discrimination Act (1995). Because of their focus of study, and the skills they possess, geographers are in a key position to help the government and concerned citizens to identify particular problems and issues, determining what structural changes in the environment are needed and helping to enforce legislation. A number of inclusive projects can be initiated in rela-

Below is an extract from Ben Elton's novel 'Gridlock'. Read the extract and then answer the following questions:

1 How is Deborah portrayed in the passage?
2 What sorts of access problems does Deborah encounter?

Deborah [using a wheelchair because of a car accident] would come to realize that the only thing missing from doorways, steps, lifts, escalators, curbs, etc., in London, were neat signs saying Achtung! No Disabled People Allowed … For Deborah, once a warm and vibrant human being, exuding personality and soul, had become a fire hazard. Fire hazard, and specifically a fire hazard. Not obstruction, embarrassment or damn nuisance, but fire hazard.

The reason Deborah was so specifically a fire hazard was that in those two little words, the abled-bodied community let itself off the hook. It would of course be churlish to deny someone access to a theatre or pub because their chair would be difficult to get up a flight of steps, or because they might occupy more space than walking customers and hence are less profitable. On the other hand, to deny someone access because they are a fire hazard – well, there is a sensible and public spirited action. There is a fast route to the moral high ground if ever there was one …

Should Deborah, or anyone similarly afflicted, be so selfish as to complain about their effective ostracism from social and cultural life, what would she be doing but wishing pain or death upon the abled-bodied community? And let us face it, it is not their fault that she is in a wheelchair.

'It's the possibility of a panic that worries us,' people would patiently explain to Deborah. 'You have to ask yourself what your situation would be in the case of a rush or stampede.'

Very occasionally Deborah attempted to argue her corner, pointless though she knew it to be.

'Listen, bud,' she had said, as politely as she could manage, to the slightly punky young man who was refusing to sell her a ticket to a play to be performed in an upstairs room of a pub … 'It is Saturday afternoon OK? And I have just negotiated the entire length of Oxford Street. I dealt with it all; the tone deaf [idiot] playing two of the three chords of "Blowin' in the wind", who kindly had his guitar case full of five pence bits spread across half the pavement … I have got around ten broken paving stones that the council kindly put there to trip up blind people and snag wheelchairs. I have avoided the 1.5 million tourists standing in groups wondering how they just managed to pay £5.00 for a can of coke … I have circumnavigated the thousands of thugs from the city in pretend Armani suits who can't see you because they are so busy talking into their portable phones. So they bash you in the knees with their stupid briefcases, with reinforced steel corners, that are absolutely essential to protect the bag of crisps and a copy of Penthouse, which is all they have inside the case … I have detoured round the gangs of bored youths who hang around … outside each and every one of the identical fast food outlets offering identical [rubbish] in a bag and Tennessee Fried Dog; the crocodile of French schoolgirls with their beautiful Benetton jumpers tied round their

> waists, just at a nice level to get caught in the face; the endless men who stop dead directly in front of me to turn round and look at the French schoolgirls; … the road works; the bollards; the steaming piles of plastic bin liners; the taxis taking a little known short cut along the pavement; the bloke who stands around with a sandwich-board saying eat less meat and protein; and the strange bearded tramp waving his arms around and screaming [get lost] at everybody. All these things I have dealt with today, in a [blooming] wheel-chair, bud. I think I could just about handle 25 assorted teachers and social workers making for the door in an upstairs pub!'

Figure 11.11 An example of a representation of a disabled person and access issues

Note
Text in square brackets has been modified for language.

tion to focuses detailed in Figure 11.6. One such project, which builds on the activities outlined above, is to produce accessibility maps of the local area, as suggested in Figure 11.10. These highlight particular access issues that need to be addressed, and provide aids to local disabled people so they can plan more efficient spatial mobility. Such maps could also be used as evidence to lobby local councils, planning and design bodies for changes to the built environment.

Conclusion

The work of geographers around the world has shown that disabled people have more limited citizen rights than their non-disabled counterparts, particularly in relation to access to the built environment. As this article indicates, inaccessible environments are not 'natural'; they are made by people and can, with some forethought, be constructed in an accessible form. Although legislation has started to change the landscape, it is slow and partial. There are many opportunities for geographers to help speed up the process of developing inclusive landscapes in the form of more accessible environments by providing practical solutions that will help improve the quality of life of some disabled people. In doing so, geography students will be contributing to a more inclusive society as active citizens.

References

Cresswell, T. (1996) *In Place/Out of Place*, Minneapolis: Minnesota University Press.
Elton, B. (1992) *Gridlock*, London: MacDonald.
Ewart, K. (1998) personal communication. Centre for University Accessibility, University of Ulster.
Gleeson, B. (1999) *Geographies of Disability*, London: Routledge.
Harvey, D. (1996) *Justice, Nature and the Geography of Difference*, Oxford: Blackwell.
Imrie, R. (1996) *Disability, and the City: International Perspectives*, London: Paul Chapman Publishing.
Kitchin, R.M. (1998) '"Out of place", "knowing one's place": towards a spatialised theory of disability and social exclusion', *Disability and Society* 13: 343–56.

—— (2000) *Changing Geography: Disability, Space and Society*, Sheffield: Geographical Association.

Napolitano, S. (1995) 'Mobility impairment', in G. Hales (ed.) *Beyond Disability: Towards an Enabling Environment*, London: Sage.

Park, D., Radford, J. and Vickers, M.H. (1998) 'Disability studies in human geography', *Progress in Human Geography* 22(2): 208–33.

Smith, D. (1994) *Geography and Social Justice*, Oxford: Blackwell.

Websites

Centre for Accessible Environments: www.cae.org.uk
Disability Net: www.disabilitynet.co.uk
Disability Rights Commission: www.drc-gb.org
Newbridge Access Project: www.may.ie/staff/rkitchin/newbridge.htm
UK government disability website: www.disability.gov.uk

12 Assessment in practice

| Improving formative assessment
Nic Howes and John Hopkin

What is formative assessment?

Formative assessment is often referred to as the most important aspect of assessment, yet it is sometimes unclear what it is, and especially what it looks like in practice. Formative assessment of students' work informs future teaching and learning by giving feedback to students and teachers. The term embraces a broad range of day-to-day assessment strategies: for example, whole-class question and answer sessions or marking students' classwork. Formative assessment helps us to understand and make judgements about what students know, understand and can do, what their strengths, weaknesses and misconceptions are and what the next steps in their learning should be for them to make progress.

The counterpart of formative assessment is summative assessment, a term which refers to less frequent assessment which looks back on students' learning …: for example, at the end of a unit of work, when the assessments help establish students' learning over a period of weeks and set targets for future improvements, … [or] the end of significant stages in a student's education, such as end-of-Key Stage 3 teacher assessments, GCSE examinations and A-level examinations. The results of these summative assessments enter the public domain and are the focus of much comment outside the teaching and learning situation. The notional link between the two forms of assessment is that formative assessment helps teachers and students to follow a course of teaching and learning in the classroom, which leads each student to his or her best possible level of achievement in the next summative assessment.

Why consider formative assessment?

Formative assessment is an essential part of effective teaching and learning. All teachers regularly use some of its strategies, quite possibly without recognizing how they contribute to formative assessment. It would be a valuable exercise for teachers and departments to consider which formative assessment strategies they use now, and which others could be adopted. We would argue that using a broad range of formative assessment strategies is good practice. The essential value of recognizing formative assessment is that this will clarify the purpose of work on which students and their teachers spend much time and energy. This clarification will make it easier for teachers to help their students and parents to understand the purpose of tasks and how they are making progress. It will also make it easier for teachers to prepare documentation for inspections.

How does formative assessment work?

Teachers can use many strategies to ensure effective formative assessment. The strategies described here are developed in more detail, and with further exemplification, in *Assessment in Practice* (Hopkin *et al.* 2000). The strategies are complementary and may operate concurrently.

Questioning, intervening and reviewing

These are ongoing strategies which teachers use to monitor students' learning and inform further teaching.

For example, many lessons start with a quick review of work already covered. This might take the form of a short oral question and answer session which reassures the teacher that the planned lesson is taking place on a firm foundation of prior learning.

Observation of students' responses to work on a day-to-day basis

Example 1

A teacher noted that drawing a pie chart took a Year 8 class more time than the usefulness of the result warranted, because the students had difficulty converting percentages to degrees. The adaptation in the light of this observation was to use pie chart scales (transparent plastic circles marked in percentages) for this operation in future lessons.

Example 2

A teacher spent part of a Year 11 GCSE lesson explaining the difference between urbanization, counter-urbanization and re-urbanization. A subsequent homework based on a GCSE question asked students to explain what is meant by 'rural depopulation'; many students responded that rural depopulation equals urbanization. When the teacher returned the marked work to students an opportunity was taken to point out that rural depopulation is not necessarily due to urbanization. The example given was that it may be due to people leaving one rural area for another which offers better prospects (e.g. the Highland clearances).

Sharing learning intentions with students

Without understanding what teachers want them to learn and why, students do not have all the information they need to work effectively, or to evaluate their own progress. For teachers, clear learning intentions (or objectives) which are shared with students support their progress and are the cornerstone of good formative assessment. For example:

- Learning intention: to understand changes in urban land use.
- Words used: 'I want you to investigate how land is used in Birmingham city centre today, compared with in the 1970s. This will help you understand how some land uses in cities change, but other land uses stay the same.'

Sharing assessment objectives and criteria with students

This helps students to understand what they are aiming for in a piece of work and what their marks mean. One example is included here: Figure 12.1 shows one department's simplified marking criteria for Key Stage 3 investigations, which are displayed in teaching rooms.

Many teachers use GCSE and A-level criteria in a similar way, for example by holding a 'post-mortem' session when returning their students' marked scripts after 'mock' GCSE and/or A-level examinations. Handled carefully, such sessions can help students to write answers which fulfil the assessment criteria of the examination which they face.

Sharing examples of good student practice with other students

Figure 12.2 shows an example in which the teacher has printed a good response to a GCSE question from an unidentified student, together with the teacher's comments and marks. Copies of such marked responses may be occasionally distributed after a class has completed a GCSE question for homework. The strategy could also be applied after a 'mock' examination or rather more informally by discussing the strengths and ways of improving key pieces or work with students at any Key Stage.

Peer assessment and marking students' work with them

This strategy is widely used when marking tests which consist of short-answer questions; if students mark one another's work, under the teacher's direction, disputes which arise may serve to illustrate the assessment criteria and why some answers deserve more credit than others. If time allows, individual students will benefit from having their work marked by their teacher alongside them, explaining the assessment process in progress.

Written comments on each student's work

These are an essential part of formative assessment and should describe the strengths and weaknesses of the work and offer suggestions for future improvement (which could be in the form of target-setting). Examples from a Key Stage 3 investigation comment (level 5/6):

- you have made good use of wide-ranging specific examples of volcanoes;
- you should aim to make more use of informative labelled diagrams in future;
- you have described the features and causes of volcanoes but you needed to say more about the hazard which they present to people;
- you have made good use of ICT and your work shows promising written language skills.

	Foundation (levels 1–3)	Intermediate (levels 4–6)	Advanced (levels 7–EP)
		a range of places and themes at more than one scale	a wide range of places and themes at various scale
Places	describes features of one place compares features of different places	recognizes that features are produced by physical and human processes recognizes that people view places differently compares different places draws links between places	recognizes how change is produced recognizes how views influence decisions explains variation between places looks to future development of places demonstrates interdependence of places
Patterns and processes	describes patterns describes processes	describes and explains patterns describes and explains processes and their effects	shows how and why patterns change shows how change affects people and places
Environmental relationships and issues	gives own views about environment describes people/ environment interaction describes environmental management	finds others' views of environments recognizes that decisions cause change describes and explains environmental change/ management	shows understanding that people's values influence decisions and environmental policy engages with complex issues evaluates management strategies
Geographical enquiry and skills	uses teacher's questions uses resources from teacher follows teacher's instructions	uses own questions follows teacher's structure uses appropriate presentation techniques uses geographical skills uses geographical words	good independent questions asked well-planned enquiry good language, including terminology well argued confident use of skills and strategies

Figure 12.1 Mark sheet for student investigations

With reference to examples explain why many people live in areas of volcanic activity

Student's answer	Teacher's comment on answer
There are many benefits from living in locations of volcanic activity.	A quick general overview which addresses the question straight away: 'there are good things there as well as the volcanoes'.
Precious metals such as gold and silver came from mines developed in the volcanic rocks of the fold mountains that border the Pacific Ocean. In the past, many people made their fortune in that area. Today, minerals like gold, silver, copper, lead, zinc and sulphur are found here providing jobs and attracting tourists. In Chile there is a large copper mine and in Bolivia there is a silver mine and a tin mine. Sulphur is extracted from volcanoes in Bolivia too.	The minerals are the basic point but the answer is developed by naming some of the minerals and starting to explain why they attract people to live nearby. Exemplification provided by linking three specific countries with specific minerals – cases and places.
Rich fertile soils develop on volcanic ash and lava. This leads to high crop yields in the coffee areas of Costa Rica, Guatemala and Columbia. In these areas the population is very high because of the availability of work. However, when a volcano first erupts, the ash destroys all crops. After weathering it turns into rich soil full of elements like potassium.	The basic point is rich soils but this is developed by making clear the link between volcanoes and good soils, and why good soils attract people. The answer also exemplifies by referring to a specific crop and three specific countries – cases and places again.
Geothermal heat obtained from heated rocks can be used to generate electricity. Places where stations can be found are California, northern Chile, Nicaragua and El Salvador.	The basic point is about hot rocks and electricity. The correct technical term is used (geothermal) and four specific countries are named as examples.
Peru has a thriving fishing industry due to the Peru-Chile trench. The trench causes upwelling of cold water which encourages the growth of fish food and so attracts many fish.	The basic point is about good fishing grounds and a specific country is named. The link with volcanoes is not fully made – to do this there needs to be a comment about the fact that the trench is where the Nasca plate is sliding under the South American plate, producing volcanoes.

(continued on next page)

Yellowstone National Park preserves spectacular mountain scenery with volcanoes and geysers. This attracts tourists wanting to visit the views and people wanting to climb and walk.

Tourism is the basic point and the answer is developed by explaining why volcanic areas attract tourists. Ideally, there should have been further development to say that tourists (temporary) attract businesses with workers who live in the area permanently. Names a specific location.

An excellent answer – not perfect but contains enough points to meet the maximum mark of 8.

An omission is the basic comment that people will tell themselves that they will not be affected by an eruption.

Figure 12.2 An actual example of a good answer to a GCSE geography question

Students reflecting on their own progress

This formative assessment strategy provides students with a structured opportunity to reflect on their progress at intervals. Figure 12.3 shows a self-evaluation form that a geography department gives each student to fill in after the return of his or her marked Key Stage 3 investigation.

Student's name: Date:

Investigation title:

Did you understand what you had to do? YES/NO

What did you find difficult?

What did you enjoy?

Do you understand the teacher's comments and/or mark?

What do you have to do to progress in the future?

Figure 12.3 Student's self-evaluation sheet

Source: The John Kyrle High School Geography Department.

Monitoring the results of formative and summative assessments

Most teachers will be familiar with the 'raising achievement' agenda, and formative assessment strategies may have much to offer in this area. Analysis of GCSE examination results, 'mock' examination results, homework and classwork forms the basis of ongoing monitoring of students' progress. The monitoring of each individual student across all subjects allows tutors and subject teachers to identify potentially problematic patterns of achievement and work to help students overcome difficulties as necessary.

Planning for effective formative assessment

The strategies described above will work best when the teacher has clear objectives for learning and an understanding of progression in Geography; the teacher needs to know what the students are expected to learn and how this represents an advance in learning.

Although much formative assessment is informal and intuitive, it is important that it is part of a system and linked to other strategies, so that any teacher can immediately answer the question, 'How do your assessments of students' work help future teaching and learning?'

It would be better still to include specific reference to the geography department's use of formative assessment strategies in the department's assessment policy and other documentation such as lesson plans and schemes of work.

References

Assessment Reform Group (1999) *Assessment for Learning: Beyond the Black Box*, Cambridge: University of Cambridge School of Education.

Black, P. and Wiliam, D. (1988) *Inside the Black Box: Raising Standards through Classroom Assessment*, London: King's College London.

Hopkin, J. (2000) 'Assessment for learning in geography', *Teaching Geography* 25(1): 42–3.

Hopkin, J., Telfer, S. and Butt, G. (eds) (2000) *Assessment in Practice: Raising Standards in Secondary Geography*, Sheffield: Geographical Association.

James, M. (1998) *Using Assessment for School Improvement*, Oxford: Heinemann.

Leat, D. and McGrane, J. (2000) 'Diagnostic and formative assessment of students' thinking', *Teaching Geography* 25(1): 4–7.

11 Assessing students' thinking
David Leat and Julie McGrane

[…] In 1998, Paul Black and Dylan Wiliam published a major review of the research evidence linking assessment and learning gains, *Inside the Black Box*. The title refers to the fact that learning is the result of what teachers and students do in the classroom. Standards can only be raised if teachers tackle their role more effectively. Direct help in this endeavour appears to be missing from current policies at secondary level. What happens in the classroom is, in systems terms, inside the black box. First, let us give you the good news. Black and Wiliam (1998) argue that, if teachers were able to adopt assessment practices that have been shown to raise attainment, then GCSE results would rise by at least one or two grades. The bad news is that both in Britain and in the rest of the world, Black and Wiliam (1998) claim, we do not use effective practices. The most important failings are as follows:

- Current tests encourage rote learning, even where teachers say that they want to develop understanding.
- The tests are not discussed between teachers, particularly in relation to what they assess.
- There is a tendency to emphasize quantity and presentation of work to the neglect of quality in relation to learning.

The Thinking Through Geography Group has developed a variety of teaching strategies which are designed to challenge students and use their existing knowledge. We would call them 'elastic tasks' because they can stretch or contract to accommodate the knowledge base that students bring to the task alongside their quality of reasoning. Thus they are highly differentiated. Furthermore, because they encourage reasoning, they are extremely powerful diagnostic and formative assessment tools. They are diagnostic because you can gain insight into the type and level of reasoning that a student is using. They are also formative because, with skill, time and patience, you can begin to move students' thinking, writing and achievement forward.

This also has to be seen within the context of target-setting and -hitting, which are beginning to dominate school agendas. There is a real danger that target-setting is reduced to data generation and analysis which is badly disconnected from the process of teaching and learning. Schagen *et al.* point out that 'given that the quality of classroom teaching is crucial to improving students' performance, some schools are reviewing the effectiveness of teaching and learning styles' (Schagen *et al.* 1997). This article seeks to encourage more geography departments to engage in that process.

Making animals: a generic strategy

One particularly intriguing Thinking Through Geography strategy is called 'Making animals'. It got this name because in its first incarnation students were asked to design animals for particular ecosystems. The 'Making animals' strategy has three important characteristics:

Students are given

- a *context* to work within;
- features to *choose* to design something to fit/operate within that context; and
- some *constraints* on their choice, for example the number of features, the amount they can spend if each item is costed.

The particular example used here is entitled 'Backpacking in Italy' (versions for Japan and Brazil have also been produced). It was trialled with a number of Year 8 and Year 9 classes. Students were given some brief details (context) about various holiday destinations in Italy, such as Rimini, Cortina and Milan. They were also provided with a list of things which they could take in their bag (choice – Figure 12.4), each of which has been weighed, but they are also given a weight limit of 7.5kg (constraint). Such tasks benefit from a good introduction or 'framing', to establish the relevance and purpose. In this case the framing might be supported by exploring with students appropriate clothes for their everyday activities.

The activity can then be explained, emphasizing the need to think carefully about where they are going and what it is like.

Initially students worked co-operatively in pairs, before doing a written task in which they had to explain their choices of items for the backpack. We would recommend that you listen to what students say, not just for interest's sake, but also so that you can use the 'eavesdroppings' in any debriefing you conduct. One of the best of questions overheard was, 'What does 11°C *feel* like?'.

The diversity of response was extremely varied. The most able students recognized the interplay of physical and human factors whilst some students struggled to register much about the environments.

Developing levels

The next stage was to look at students' work from a range of classes and identify levels of performance using the following steps:

1 Select five pieces of work that reflect the range of performance from the class or year group.
2 Place the samples in rank order, avoiding quality of spelling/writing or the number of facts as criteria.
3 Make notes on what it is that characterizes the five examples. What is it that makes the best one outstanding? What are the characteristics of the weakest piece of work?
4 Take another five and compare them against the original characteristics, editing the emerging criteria – which may mean inserting new levels, extending the range of performance or qualifying existing descriptions.

At last! The holidays have arrived and you are off on a backpacking tour of Italy. You have been planning the trip for months and have eventually decided on the route.

It has been planned carefully so that you can fit in as many different experiences as possible. You have decided to begin your trip in Milan (leg 1), travel east to Cortina (leg 2), south to Rimini (leg 3) and then south-west to Rome (leg 4) where you will end your trip.

Your task

You have to pack for the trip. You have a backpack that can only weigh 7.5kg when full. You will be visiting friends at the start of each leg of your trip so you will be able to repack. Use the table to help you plan each leg of your trip. Remember to plan your packing carefully as I can guarantee your bag always feels heavier than it looks so you do not want to be carrying anything unnecessary.

Contents	Weight
Malaria tablets	10g
Water bottle	50g
Money belt	50g
Sunglasses	50g
Socks	50g
Camera and film	50g
Swiss army knife	50g
Swimsuit/trunks	100g
Pack of cards	150g
Deodorant	150g
Hair gel/spray	200g
Perfume/aftershave	200g
Underwear	200g
Umbrella	200g
Shirt/blouse	200g
Mountain kit	200g
Sarong	200g
Sandals	200g
Mosquito net	200g
Shorts	250g
T-shirt	250g
Thermals	250g
Make-up bag	250g
Book	300g
Raincoat	300g
Washing kit (soap, toothbrush/paste)	300g
Sheet and sleeping bag	350g
Long skirt	350g
Towel	400g
Jogging bottoms	400g
Suntan lotion	400g
Shampoo and conditioner	400g
Dress	450g
Smart trousers	450g
Hairdryer	500g
Roll mat	500g
Fleece	600g
Jeans	600g
Smart shoes	700g
Jumper	700g
Trainers	800g
Travel guide	1kg
Walking boots	1kg
Boogie board	Carry under arm

Milan is Italy's most important industrial and financial centre and it is home of one of the world's best football stadiums. The cathedral is impressive, it has 100 spires, 1000 statues and holds 40,000 people. There are, however, problems with congestion and pollution like other big cities.

The most famous, fashionable and expensive Italian ski resorts, Cortina, is also one of the most picturesque as it is surrounded by the stunning Dolomites.

Summer
Average temperature: 24°C
Average precipitation per month: 60mm

Summer
Average temperature: 11°C
Average precipitation per month: 130mm

Rimini lies on the flat coastal plain with its golden beaches and lively entertainment.

Summer
Average temperature: 24°C
Average precipitation per month: 50mm

Built among the famous Seven Hills, Rome is the capital of Italy and one of the most cultural. Famed for the Roman Forum and the Pantheon.

Summer
Average temperature: 23°C
Average precipitation per month: 37mm

Cortina (leg 2)
Milan (leg 1)
Rimini (leg 3)
Rome (leg 4)

N

0   100
km

Figure 12.4 Resources for the 'Backpacking in Italy' activity

This is an imprecise science and on different occasions with differing pieces of work it is useful to focus on differing qualities within the work. There may be occasions when spelling and punctuation are included. Ultimately our two sets of criteria were combined to produce Figure 12.5, which includes illustrative extracts of students' work. We have deliberately not indicated which National Curriculum level our 'levels' might relate to, in order to reinforce the point that this is not a summative assessment exercise, but designed to help students make progress.

If you are genuinely interested in improving reasoning, it is really important to examine students' work to derive levels. This is because these levels provide you with a map to guide your decisions about teaching the whole class and particular individuals in order to raise attainment. You might regard them as rungs of a ladder, but the rungs are not marks, rather they are levels of reasoning.

It is important to re-emphasize the message from *Inside the Black Box*. The role of effective assessment is to close the gap between current and desirable performance. This is what target-setting has to be about. However, it only works if you can begin to translate the desire for better grades into achievable steps for students. The teacher must be able to recognize what interventions will encourage improvements in students' performance, whilst creating an environment in which students value this process and understand its purpose. In an interview for another project one student signalled this readiness by saying, 'How will you improve if you are not told how to do it?' Figure 12.6 provides some initial guidance for the actions which you can take to help individuals to close the gap between each level and the next. Although these levels have been generated in relation to the backpacking exercise they do represent reasoning and therefore can be adapted for other 'Making animals' exercises.

When and how to take action

Figure 12.6 represents a working hypothesis that can inform your actions and be updated and improved with practice. Having generated the levels which can be used in diagnostic assessment, it is too late for this to inform your teaching of the activity. This gives the message that diagnostic and formative assessment is a long haul, which has to be punctuated with intelligent decisions. Below we give some suggestions as to when you could begin to take formative action.

1   The information in Figure 12.6 can be used the next year or with another set or class working a few weeks behind schedule.
2   The information can be used whilst the task is being done. You can intervene with a pair if your eavesdropping or conversation with them shows reasoning at a particular level that you believe can be improved.
3   Levels can be used to inform the written feedback for students.
4   The levels can be made explicit to the students before the task.
5   Students can be given each other's work to mark against the criteria in the levels.
6   'Making animals' is a generic activity. If you have a couple of other versions of it during the year you could revisit the levels with the intention of accelerating students' reasoning.

Level A

- Reasons are given for taking items, but they tend to be general and not directly related to context.
- There may be some misinterpretation of the need for some items.

Example: '… I would take clean underwear for each day … I would need to take walking boots so my feet would not hurt me. I would take a travel guide so I would not get lost.'

Level B

- Some reasons are given which relate directly to the place/context. However, some context factors are not made very explicit.
- The context factors are not clearly linked to suggest a coherent appraisal of the place.

Example: 'I would definitely take something to keep me warm (no explicit reason) … I would take walking boots because I am likely to be climbing up large mountains so therefore I need a good grip (explicit). I need a roll mat to lie on or I will probably get a sore back (not explicit).'

Level C

- Most items are justified by a context/place feature, which begins to show an overall appreciation of place.
- However, students generally fail to be specific or use evidence to reinforce their justification.

Example 1: 'I would take with me a jumper, a fleece, walking boots, etc. They are all important for climbing a mountain in the snow. The jumper and fleece would keep you warm … The walking boots would help you have plenty of grip on the mountain. The sunglasses would help block out the sun that reflects off the snow.'

Example 2: 'I would take a swimsuit because I would be on the beach, suntan lotion because it's hot and I might burn … I would try to take light things so I wouldn't be too hot.'

Level D

- Students use some evidence to justify choices.
- Students recognize that one resort presents a range of activities and contexts.
- Students recognize that the combination of items should be compatible.

Example 1: 'I may take a raincoat as Milan has quite a high rainfall. Milan is a fashionable city so I would take trousers, a shirt, and maybe some smart shoes for the night-time.'

(continued on next page)

Example 2: 'Smart clothes are probably wise as it's a big city for shopping as well as site (sic) seeing.'

Level E

- Generalizations begin to emerge about the choosing process. There is some evidence of prioritizing and choosing on the strength of need.
- Students recognize the significance of averages, i.e. that they represent a range.
- Students draw on their own knowledge.

Example 1: 'You have to take certain things depending on where you are going. Some things you will have to take regardless of where you go.'

Example 2: 'The first place I am visiting is Cortina. As it is a cool place and the average temperature is 11°C I would take a jumper and a fleece to keep me warm, a raincoat to keep me dry as the average precipitation is 130 mm… It is a very fashionable place so I would take jogging bottoms and a t-shirt to look casual.'

Example 3: 'You wouldn't need a book or pack of cards, as you wouldn't be bored because of the lively entertainment.'

Level F

- Students give an overall reasoning strategy with plenty of detail to back it up.
- Students show evidence of having reappraised choices.

(Only two students achieved this level).

Example: 'You have to take certain things depending on where you are going and what you will be doing … So in conclusion, you should think about what you are doing so as to know what to take'.

Figure 12.5 Inductive levels for the backpacking exercise

The argument that we have been stressing here has three elements. First, activities which promote thinking tend to make students' thinking more visible and explicit. Second, once you have drawn students' thinking out, you can assess its quality both in terms of levels and individual performance. Third, you can use this information to help close the gap between current performance and potential performance. This is an immensely powerful notion around which to build your assessment practice, arguably a good theory.

If you want to go further you can start exploring Vygotsky's notion of a Zone of Proximal Development. This can be taken to mean the difference between what the child can do alone and unaided and what the child can do when assisted by adults or more capable peers (see, for example, Hedegaard 1996, for more detail). Now wouldn't you enjoy explaining that to the Ofsted inspector?

Level A–B

Diagnosis: Student does not perceive the importance of the context.

Action:
- Provide stimulus material which brings context into sharper focus. This could be photographs or descriptions (from holiday brochures or travel guides).
- Question on the lines of 'Have you thought of/about?' and direct their thoughts to features of the physical environment.

Level B–C

Diagnosis: Student is beginning to appreciate context, but it is not being very specific or detailed.

Action:
- Provide stimulus material as above.
- Try a mind movie (Leat 1998) – describe a scene for the students while they have their eyes closed and then ask them to 'run the movie' in their minds for a minute: what do they see, hear, smell and feel? When they are finished ask them what they both saw and felt, but get them to think about what they will need for a holiday in this kind of place.
- Try asking, 'Well if you need X, what else will might you need to go with it?'

Level C–D

Diagnosis: Student is getting a good grasp of the place but is not fully appreciating the personal implications of being there, or using evidence to back up their reason.

Action:
- Really press them on why they are taking things, particularly in relation to what they know about the place.
- Raise the question of the variations within the locality/resort or variations between times of day.

Level D–E

Diagnosis: Students are thinking more flexibly and putting themselves in the environment, but they are not yet using their existing knowledge to great effect and going beyond the given to speculate and generalize. They show no sign of an overall reasoning strategy. Level E students are processing in a qualitatively different way.

Action:
- Ask what they know about the place and push them to speculate on what this might imply, i.e., 'If the place is like that, what else would you expect?'

(continued on next page)

- Ask individuals or groups to explain how they have come to their decision.

Level E–F

Diagnosis: Students are using high-order thinking, but they show no evidence of conscious control of their thinking, or thinking about thinking (metacognition).

Action: Debriefing should help in the long run. You can start to ask the class about how they made decisions, which makes thinking about thinking explicit and visible.

Figure 12.6 Scaffolding moves for improving reasoning in the backpacking exercise

References

Black, P. and Wiliam, D. (1998) *Inside the Black Box – Raising Standards Through Classroom Assessment*, London: King's College.

—— (1998) 'Assessment and classroom learning', *Assessment in Education* 5: 7–74.

Davies, P. (1995) 'An inductive approach to levels of attainment', *International Research in Geographical and Environmental Education* 4: 47–65.

Hedegaard, M. (1996) 'The ZPD as basis for instruction', in H. Daniels (ed.) *An Introduction to Vygotsky*, London: Routledge.

Leat, D. (ed) (1998) *Thinking Through Geography*, Cambridge: Chris Kington Publishing.

Schagen, L. and Weston, P., with Hewitt, D. and Sims, D. (1997) *Hitting the Targets, A Report for the National Advisory Council for Education and Training Targets*, Slough: NFER.

||| Marking and homework
Sunday evening at the kitchen table
David Balderstone and David Lambert

Discussion with PGCE students over the years has revealed that there is an enormous diversity of assessment practice between secondary schools. It also reveals just as wide a variation in what student teachers understand they should be doing in relation to this aspect of their professional lives. What *is* universally acknowledged is the expectation that marking has to be done because it is 'important'. The perception that marking usually takes up a large chunk of teachers' waking hours is also prevalent. What is not generally agreed is the reason why marking is important or how it is best undertaken.

Setting homework for students is similarly understood by most teachers to be 'important'. Students are expected to spend a great deal of their time on homework. However, we doubt there is general agreement amongst students, teachers and parents about the reasons why we value homework, or what constitutes good or effective homework tasks.

Putting homework and marking together

But why link marking and homework? There are two reasons – apart from the fact that human nature dictates that Sunday evenings tend to be 'blighted' by these activities in households containing teachers, or students, or both!

First, in many students' eyes, the two are organically linked: they get given homework, they do it and then it gets marked. This is fair enough, although not all homework is necessarily 'marked', and not all that is marked is homework. Moreover, we could argue that not all homework *should* be marked.

Second, both of these aspects of schooling are publicly very prominent, but sometimes strangely out of focus. Parents, heads, inspectors and even government ministers are keen to promote regular homework and assiduous marking. These are highly valued aspects of good schools and may even be considered indicators of the standards they set. Notwithstanding recent reports from academics (Cowan and Hallam 1999) and Ofsted that homework can, in some cases, be useless or even damaging to the students' development, most teachers and students have no difficulty accepting that homework and marking are 'important' activities, although they are, paradoxically, often undertaken reluctantly ... on Sunday evenings at the kitchen table.

Consequences

As with many other aspects of teaching and learning, an extremely helpful principle that clarifies the functions of both homework and marking is that of 'fitness for purpose':

- What is marking for?
- What is homework for?

Being clear about purpose helps teachers and students justify to themselves the enormous amount of time they spend undertaking marking and homework. It raises the level of the 'consequential validity' of spending time in these ways. If we and the students know and understand why work is being marked the activity stands a greater chance of affecting and contributing to the learning process. In today's busy and bureaucratized circumstances, to measure the validity of one's actions by their consequences seems to make a lot of sense: if spending Sunday evening at the kitchen table is of limited or no consequence, there seems little point in doing it!

It reminds us of the red-faced gentleman in *The Little Prince* who was always too busy to talk. Instead he sat in his office all day long, adding up columns of figures and turning people away because he was 'busy with matters of consequence' (Saint-Exupéry 1979: 41–5). Ironic really because, little did he realize, his wretched figures were of no consequence whatsoever! We believe that there is a risk that an over-zealous commitment to test scores and rows of marks, all neatly tabulated in mark books, may reveal attitudes which the red-faced gentleman would recognize. The acid test is how we respond to the following questions:

- Have I become so busy with my bureaucratic duties that I have lost sight of the purpose of setting homework and marking students' work?
- Why set homework?
- Why mark students' work?

Ultimately, the only reason to do either of the last two points is because we believe that they have consequences. We teach better and the children learn better as a result. Collecting marks for completed homework in itself achieves little – remember the old saying that 'weighing the baby does not make it grow'. However, setting work for students to tackle independently and then marking it so that we get to know them as individuals (as if each student and teacher were 'talking' directly to each other) surely lies at the heart of an effective teaching and learning relationship.

The remainder of this article attempts to spell out in a little more detail some principles that guide good practice in the setting and marking of homework in Geography.

Spotlight on homework

In 1987, an HMI report (based on a survey of 251 schools) asserted that: '[Homework can seem to be] little more than a reluctantly enforced time-filler imposed on unenthusiastic recipients: its importance as a means of control appears to override its educational objectives' (DES 1987).

Activities	Resources
creative writing and drawing	television and radio programmes
comprehension of text exercises	atlas
manipulation of data	encyclopaedias and reference books
word-play activities	newspapers and magazines
essays	computer software/internet
data and information research	telephone directories, Yellow Pages, etc.
note-taking (e.g. from the television)	travel brochures
wider reading	postcards and stamps
interviews	timetables
memorizing and learning (spellings)	local maps (estate agents)
keeping a scrap book	utility bills – gas, electric, etc.
writing letters, adverts (for an audience)	local council publications
	advertising

Figure 12.7 Suggested homework activities and resources

Source: Grimwade and Martin 1997.

Is this still the case?

The report stressed the value of teachers marking homework regularly – at least in the sense that it should be carefully monitored. It therefore supported homework, adding to the famous view of the Inner London Education Authority (ILEA) which stated that: 'Over five years of secondary education, appropriate homework can add the equivalent of at least one additional year of full-time education' (ILEA 1984). What HMI warned against, however, was being too rigid about either the length or type of work set.

Is this warning still valid?

We think so, but it is one thing issuing 'warnings' or criticisms, and quite another to offer advice. Setting 'appropriate' homeworks is easier said than done. The Geographical Association has come to the rescue to some extent; for example, Grimwade and Martin (1997) provide lists of prompts which go far beyond the 'finish copying the map' variety (see Figure 12.7). These lists help provide practical purchase to what HMI were saying ten years earlier:

> Where homework involves more than routine tasks, it has at least one of the following characteristics:
>
> - it is closely integrated with and reinforces classwork and has clear curricular objectives;
> - it exploits the materials and resources in the environment and the community outside the school;

- it encourages independence, research creativity and initiative;
- it promotes the co-operation and involvement of parents and other adults.

(DES 1987)

In other words homework is different from classwork and it is, therefore, helpful to specify its learning objectives. Homework should sometimes incorporate independent thinking and research, creativity, problem-solving and such like. When the objectives are clearly specified, it is possible to show students what they have to do and why they need to do it to improve their learning outcomes.

Focus on marking

There is little doubt in our minds that clear learning objectives, expressed as outcomes, underpin effective marking. Too often marking seems aimless, bland and mysterious, largely because it is entirely norm-referenced: work is judged merely on the superficial criteria such as presentation and quantity, against the norm of that class or year group. However, there are minefields in wait for those teachers who want to do better and change the focus of assessment. For example, 'effort grades' have been invented to balance 'achievement grades'. Good idea? Only if one knows what effort the student has put in. But how can you be sure? And what about the poor student who continually gets good effort marks combined with poor achievement scores? 'Well meaning, but a bit thick' would presumably be the appropriate epithet, and thoroughly demotivating it would be too.

So ipsative marking has been introduced, whereby a student's mark is referenced entirely against his or her previous performance. Here, high achievement grades can be given for modest work if it represents progress. Encouraging? Possibly, in the short term, but in the longer term we would argue that such an approach is deceitful and therefore unhelpful, appearing to promise students prizes that are beyond their reach at that time.

Some departments have invested time and effort developing 'intelligent' or 'smart' marking which claims to analyse students' work. Rather than blitzing the work with red ink and corrections, the marking 'targets' just a small number of common misconceptions or spelling mistakes. This approach has much to commend it. Students can be encouraged to handle it successfully, for example, by learning three spellings to be tested next lesson. However, it can also mislead in its mission not to upset or demoralize the student, and such an approach could be mistaken for not really caring about detail. In their research report Black and Wiliam (1998) made the point that too much unfocused praise in feedback to students can be unhelpful.

In his 1998 Annual Report, the Chief Inspector of Schools and Head of Ofsted remarked that many teachers were not using the information gleaned from marking to raise standards: 'commonly for example, marks and grades are given without comment or explanation' (Ofsted 1998). In the worst cases, there were inconsistencies in the way work was marked between classes and colleagues, leading to an opacity and a mystery in the eyes of students. One reason why Black and Wiliam's research is important is that, unlike the Chief Inspector's report, it painstakingly tries to identify what constitutes effective classroom practice. Their review makes it plain that providing 'feedback', perhaps the single most important thing a teacher can do in order to raise standards, is more challenging than simply writing a comment at the end of children's work (Black and Wiliam 1998). Figure 12.8 provides signposts for improving formative assessment according to Black and Wiliam's review (1998). We maintain that marking makes an essential contribution to this.

Feedback should be about the particular qualities of his or her work, with advice for improvement. Avoid comparisons with other students. It should encourage:

- a culture of success;
- students to take risks, make mistakes;
- a reconstruction of the teacher-student 'contract of content' (where neither is challenged).

Students should be trained in self-assessment so that they can understand learning goals. This may take some time to achieve; the aim is to:

- break the pattern of passive learning;
- make learning goals ('the overarching picture') explicit;
- establish the desired goal – present position – way to close the gap mentality in students.

Opportunities for students to express their understanding have to be built into the teaching – to initiate interaction and allow the teacher to build up knowledge of the learners:

- teaching and assessment are indivisible;
- choice of tasks (the chosen teaching strategy) has to be justified in terms of the learning aims they serve.

Dialogue between students and teachers should be thoughtful and reflective, designed to explore understanding. Teachers can critically examine their questioning techniques:

- Are questions framed as only 'closed' questions?
- Do you include questions which encourage only guessing the 'right' answer?
- Is silence tolerated after posing a question?
- Are questions answered only by the usual few students?
- Do questions tend to 'level down' to ensure a response?

Tests and homeworks need to be interesting and relevant to learning aims.

- Are the questions set good ones? (Collaborate with colleagues.)
- Frequent short tests and marking are better than infrequent long tests and long gaps between marking work.

Figure 12.8 Suggested signposts for learning

Source: Black and Wiliam 1998.

Conclusion

We appreciate that the implications of the statements in Figure 12.8 take us beyond traditional marking. We also appreciate that what the statements suggest – thorough, regular, analytical marking leading to precise, individually tailored feedback – may seem like the last straw, such is the current pressure on the profession. However, we are not suggesting instant or quick fixes. Instead we propose a longer-term development driven by a clear sense of direction. Basically what underpins the above is evidence that shows the value of criteria referencing marking – and making sure that students are fully aware of, and can operationalize, these criteria.

References

Black, P. and Wiliam, D. (1998) 'Assessment and classroom learning', *Assessment in Education: Principles, Policy and Practice* (special issue on assessment and classroom learning) 5(1): 7–74.

Cowan, R. and Hallam, S. (1999) *What Do We Do About Homework?*, Viewpoint No. 9., London: Institute of Education, University of London.

Department of Education and Science (DES) (1987) *Homework: A Report by Her Majesty's Inspectorate*, Education Observed No. 4, London: HMSO/DES.

Grimwade, K. and Martin, F. (1997) *Homework in Geography* (Geography Guidance Series), Sheffield: The Geographical Association.

Inner London Education Authority (ILEA) (1984) *Improving Secondary Schools*, London: ILEA.

Ofsted (1998) *Standards and Quality in Education: Annual Report of Her Majesty's Chief Inspector of Schools*, London: The Stationery Office.

Saint-Exupéry, A. de (1979) *The Little Prince*, London: Mammoth.

13 Evaluating and using resources
Fred Martin and Patrick Bailey

Introduction

Geography is a resource-rich subject. Few if any other subjects taught in schools command and demand the use of such a rich variety of resources, in terms of both type of resource and range of geographical content. Failing to make full use of this range is to fail to take advantage of one of the key attractions that the subject has to offer. The aim of this chapter is to outline the range and sources of geographical resources, but also to raise issues relating to how these resources can be evaluated and used. Examples of resources are provided as illustration; they are not intended to form a definitive list of what is available.

National Curriculum background

Ideas about resources must be set in the context of the current geography National Curriculum Order. Although this now relates only to Key Stages 1–3, Key Stage 4 and more advanced courses should be seen as a continuum in terms of ideas, content, skills and the deployment of resources being used.

The present Order has removed much of the element of compulsion in terms of factual content and minutiae of other detail that was characteristic of the earlier versions. There are broad guidelines as to what must be taught as a minimum, though, even within the Programmes of Study, there are options with regard to the choice of topics and places. The separation of Level Descriptions from Programmes of Study creates a situation in which any topic, skill and place can be taught in any order to any level. Syllabus decisions can now be made based on criteria devised by teachers. This is a responsibility and a freedom to be welcomed. Resources are a key to enabling these choices to be real.

Textbooks and their uses

[…] Textbooks are likely to remain a core resource in most schools, but each school must decide about the role a textbook is to play. […] When choosing books for a department, it is important to remember that not all teachers of Geography are specialists in the subject. Books which provide plenty of examples and exercises for pupils can help to maintain a high standard of geographical teaching in departments where there are several non-specialists.

The frequency of lessons might also affect the choice of textbook; if there is only one geography lesson a week, a text comprising self-contained blocks of work will be necessary. Student profile in a class might also affect the choice of textbooks; for example, if there is a high absentee rate, it can be useful to choose textbooks in which the content is divided into short sections which can be used in several different sequences (though beware that brevity does not equal superficiality).

Language, layout and illustration

It is obviously important to choose books which students will be able to read easily and which help to improve their use of clear, direct English. The use of simple words and basic phrasing to convey complex ideas need not disadvantage more able students. Teachers learn by experience what level of language suits their students, but sometimes it is difficult to assess the level of a new book. You could run a sample piece of text through the 'read-ability check' facility offered by many word-processing packages, or make a rough assessment by means of Gunning's FOG (1952) Test. There are also several useful books on the subject (e.g. *Readability in the Classroom*, by Colin Harrison 1980).

In this context, topicality and 'relevance' present problems for the geography textbook author. Extracts from newspapers or other secondary sources lend authenticity to a textbook and provide ready-made resources, but many are written for an audience with a higher reading age than the readers of the textbook in which they appear. Again, teachers need to be aware of this, and be prepared to produce simplified versions of such resources if necessary.

Accessibility of content is clearly related to the book's layout. Books which have an open layout, an attractive design, short line lengths and plenty of sub-sections are more accessible than those with dense, overcrowded pages and few sub-headings. Larger print can be an advantage to students with special reading problems, though there is a danger that this can appear patronizing. It must also be possible for the reader to follow the flow of content on a page – this can be difficult where a two-column layout is used, or where the text is broken up by numerous illustrations.

Books rich in photographs and other visual resources may *seem* more accessible than books which have more text than visuals, but this is not necessarily the case. Photographs and maps, for example, may contain far more information than is required or can be identified or absorbed and students need as much skill to obtain information from illustrations as from text. Few 12–15-year-olds can be expected to possess the sophistication to interpret a seven-colour flow diagram of dairy farm economics, or a whole-page perspective drawing which shows 20 ways in which the UK environment is being polluted – to name two examples from otherwise useful publications.

Accuracy and balance

Geography books often deal with topics that are ethically and politically sensitive, and in recent years publishers have paid much attention to what some call 'political correctness'. In selecting photographs, cartoons and text authors and editors are sensitive to issues such as gender and race stereotyping and other forms of bias. Questions of the suitability of a resource in this regard are now mainly a matter for teachers to decide and all will have their own ideas of the degree of balance which they find acceptable.

Resources produced by such 'hidden persuaders' as transnational corporations, national embassies and pressure groups are open to accusations of bias and are often supplied to textbook authors free of charge in generous quantities. It is therefore important to check all potential book purchases for bias of various kinds. Clearly, students need to be made aware of bias and to learn to defend themselves from prejudice and hidden persuasion, so 'biased' resources can be valuable when used carefully by a confident teacher. [...]

Dealing with differentiation

In their promotional material, educational publishers will often describe their publications as being suitable for all students in a particular year, or, even more implausibly, throughout a Key Stage. Such claims need to be treated with caution; a textbook suitable for students in a potentially high-achieving class can surely not be suitable for all students in the same year; the same must be true for lower-ability students. A textbook designed for use in a mixed-ability class presents an even greater challenge.

The amount of factual material in a textbook, and the way it is presented, ought ideally to be different for different audiences. The nature of student activities and the amount of structured guidance given ought also to vary. Differentiation by outcome is sometimes, but not always, the most appropriate technique. Apart from other considerations, a single textbook does not usually have the space to cater for the range of ability of its readers, though some authors and publishers have attempted to deal with this problem in a variety of ways. One way has been to produce sets of photocopiable worksheets or supplementary material pitched at different ability groups; another has been to provide core and supplementary texts.

As a consequence of some of these inevitable imperfections, teachers need to be prepared to write additional materials to make textbooks more usable in their own classes. The need to do this should be built in to any time and cost equation relating to choosing a textbook. Extra material means more flexibility, but it also means more work, so a balance has to be struck between the two.

Cost effectiveness

Books are bought to be used, not held in stock cupboards, so it is important before buying them to consider their likely frequency of use. How many students will use a book in a given year and for how many weeks in that year, for example? Cost, of course, is an important factor; a salutary exercise is to calculate the cost of each page that you expect to use (which may be less than half a complete textbook) before making a commitment to buy a particular quantity.

When ordering books it is vital to consider the needs of the whole department. A set of books that cover sixth-form topics in depth, for example, would clearly be a bad buy if it meant 28 14-year-olds going without a set of new books which would last them for two or three terms.

Finally, there is the question of durability. If books are likely to be used intensively, they must be printed on good-quality paper and strongly bound.

Choosing and generating resources for courses

One of the features of the revised National Curriculum is the wide range of options it offers. At Key Stage 3, for example, all students do not need to study the same country; … they can select one of many types of ecosystem and economic activity, etc. This has bonuses and disadvantages. When assessing students' work, for example, apart from data-response questions, tasks need to be virtually content-free, though students will still require factual content to illustrate their ideas. This should not be too problematic given that the essence of good Geography is that it should be more concerned with ideas than transitory examples. Some GCSE examining groups have been setting tasks of this nature for years.

It may not be feasible to provide resources which enable students to choose any topic or place for their scheme of work, but it should be possible to provide enough of a range for them to make at least some choices. Some choice was always possible using reference books in the school library and single copies of other resources, and these should still be available. Now, however, access to computer databases on a network or on stand-alone multi-media machines makes the concept of choice more of a practical reality.

Sources of information

Information sources for school geography courses are vast and varied. There are specialist geography textbooks, dictionaries, journals and software etc.; resources for a wider audience, such as maps, census returns, photographs, satellite images, newspapers and television programmes; and resources produced for specific audiences which may have relevance to geographers, such as company reports, aid agency and charity magazines and publicity material from industry. Most geography teachers will be familiar with much of what is available, but for those who are new to the subject or to teaching it, the brief summaries below, and the information given at the end of this chapter, may be helpful.

Aid and development organizations

Although not always produced to a high standard, and sometimes too full and detailed, such sources are a rich seam for geographers. Some of the most useful are detailed case studies of specific issues or localities, mostly set in developing world locations. The resources include posters, photo packs and CD-ROMs, and often involve students in a variety of active teaching and learning styles that are lacking in standard textbooks.

Original data

All major industries, organizations and public bodies produce public relations material, and some is packaged with educational use in mind; much of this includes raw data. Sources include electricity and water companies, tourist boards, National Park authorities and oil companies. Foreign embassies and local government departments involved in attracting industry are variable but often exceptional sources of information. Much of this is very well produced, much of it is in English and is generally contained in public relations material (see above regarding issues of bias, etc.).

Newspapers and other media

One of the delights of teaching Geography is that it is such a topical subject. Events that were covered in yesterday's newspapers, or last night's television or radio, can be discussed in the classroom the next day and incorporated into the curriculum, thus bringing immediacy and relevance to the subject. Indeed, the National Curriculum now encourages the use of secondary sources of this kind and states that the study of issues at Key Stage 3 should have 'topical significance'. Examination syllabuses, too, encourage students to investigate topical issues at a range of scales, from local to global.

This emphasis on topicality places a responsibility on the teacher not only to be aware of current events and to be prepared to discuss them, but also to ensure that up-to-date resource material is available, catalogued and stored in such a way that it is accessible to all members of the department. It also requires students to be aware of world events and to build up their own knowledge base.

Newspapers are excellent sources of topical, local and international material (see Figure 13.1). At the tabloid end of the spectrum, the text tends to be less dense and has a lower reading age than the quality broadsheets, though reliability is questionable and brevity may mean over-simplicity. Back issues of some national newspapers are available on CD-ROM and with a relatively basic network capability can be used by many students simultaneously.

Audio-visual resources

TV and radio programmes provide another useful resource, though there are copyright issues involved in recording non-educational broadcasts. Films, likewise, are a popular resource and can be exploited by a geography teacher. One example, though dated, is *Crocodile Dundee*, which includes scenes of the Australian landscape that are hard to match in the classroom. Similarly, *The Piano* vividly illustrates the problems of penetrating the New Zealand rainforest.

Teacher groups

The education departments of many local authorities often produce resources related to their own area. They are usually produced by teams of teachers and serve to encourage teachers to develop their own skills in writing and producing resources.

Computers

The volume of information available on some CD-ROMs far exceeds the capacity of any textbook. Maps and statistical data for any country can be researched using a CD-ROM atlas (Figure 13.2), including such detailed information as a street map of New York, and satellite images can now be studied on a computer screen. Encyclopaedias are also available on CD-ROM and include photographs as well as text.

The number of schools with access to the internet and e-mail is growing enormously, permitting contacts with schools in other countries as well as providing access to a world-wide information system of almost unlimited capacity. As the use of such systems increases, however, teachers will be faced with the problem of infor-

Freezer lightning strike stuns mum

TERRIFIED Wollaton mother-of-two Carole Sculthorpe was today recovering at home after being struck by lightning when she reached inside her freezer.

Her near-miss came as freak storms left a trail of mayhem throughout Notts, stretching police and fire services to the limit.

By ALEXANDER COHEN

Firemen battled through the night to contain a fire started by lightning at Clipstone Forest and another at Langwith, near Warsop.

Around 25 hectares of land was affected in the two incidents.

Traffic throughout much of the county was gridlocked.

Chaos on the roads was caused by a combination of heavy rain and the rush hour.

Mrs Sculthorpe, 41, of Calderdale, was hit by lightning after it ran through her house, into the electricity system.

Cousin Susan Lylak said: "She was shocked and terrified.

"Flames jumped out and spread up her arms."

Mrs Sculthorpe was treated at the Queen's Medical Centre in Nottingham.

Aerial

Lightning also struck a house in Aston Green, Toton.

It travelled down the TV aerial and blew out the house's electrics.

No one was hurt.

The rain caused major problems too.

The Royal Mail sorting office in Beeston was forced to shut for five hours when the roof started leaking.

Firemen from Ripley and Belper battled to keep flood water away from the electrics at Budget Fabrics, Eagle Street, Heage.

And Asda in Front Street, Arnold was closed for 90 minutes after flood water came up through manholes.

The freak weather was also blamed for the death of hundreds of fish.

National Rivers Authority staff are working flat out to rescue distressed fish and re-oxygenate the water.

Flushed

Affected stretches include the River Erewash between Sandiacre and its confluence with the River Trent, which is also hit.

The storms flushed oil and dirt off roads, into drains and into the rivers, causing contamination.

At the same time, the thundery, oppressive conditions drew the oxygen from the water.

Fish are being moved to emergency holding pools.

The spokesman said: "It is a natural phenomenon but it has happened on an enormous scale this time."

Figure 13.1 A newspaper resource

Source: Reproduced by permission of 'Nottingham Evening Post'.

Notes

This article appeared in a Nottinghamshire newspaper in 1995. It provided a one-off lesson on a topic of current interest. It is, however, an example of a resource that could be used in a variety of ways with students. For example:

- Construct a flow diagram to show the effects of the period of thunderstorms.
- Imagine that a similar thunderstorm affected the area around your home. Write a newspaper article with illustrations on computer to describe what its effects might have been.

mation overload and how to manage it effectively; students need to be encouraged to discriminate between relevant and irrelevant (though interesting) information.

Information on CD-ROM can be displayed on a large screen in the classroom by using an LCD panel on an overhead projector and operating the CD-ROM by a

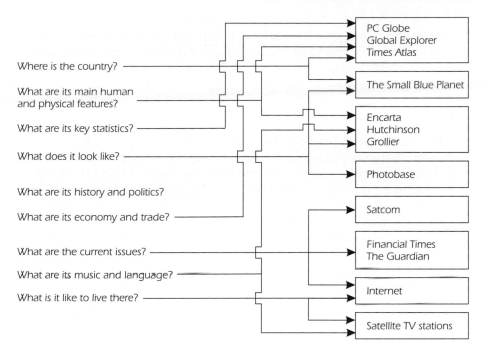

Figure 13.2 How to make a country study using CD-ROMs and other software

Note
Many items of information are on several CD-ROMs. Only some have been shown here for illustration.

hand-held remote control panel. Photos, text, animation and video clips can all be used either direct from disks, or put together as a preset trail. Unfortunately, this equipment is still very costly, so only very few schools can take advantage of it.

Some textbooks are already being translated into interactive format on CD-ROM and it can only be a matter of time before publishers sell their books in both printed and electronic versions, including a CD-ROM option with a range of interactive activities. This could be bought either as a disk, or downloaded via a modem immediately before the student needs to use it.

Resources produced in school

Opportunities to create high-quality resources in school are greater now than ever before. This applies to both teachers and students. Word processors with laser printers can be used to write, design and produce resources and worksheets; facilities such as 'cut and paste' make it possible to take text, photographs, and other extracts, then to incorporate them into new documents; video clips from a local field visit can be loaded into a multi-media computer to form part of a program; an ion camera that takes digitized images can be used to create photo banks that students can access on a network (Figure 13.3). The last has the advantage over slides that the students take control of both the selection of images and the time they want to study them. There is also the option for teachers and students to develop their own full multi-media resources.

Unique resources can be created in school using IT capability. The use of an ion camera and scanning are two techniques that can be used. Video and full multi-media productions are also possible using appropriate hardware and software.

Using an ion camera

An ion camera takes pictures in the same way as a camera. The difference is that the images are captured in a way that can be instantly loaded into a computer. Images can then be enhanced to obtain maximum clarity. Pictures of the local area or from field visits, for example, can be stored.

Images once installed can be changed by using a standard graphics package such as 'Paintspa' or 'Paintbrush'. This allows a pupil to add labels to an image, draw on additional lines and details or to remove parts of an image. A set of images, for example, can be produced to show different stages in the development of a sea stack. This technique can also be used to show what a landscape might look like if a proposed development took place.

A program can be created to store the images in a photo bank. These can then be accessed by a simple search facility. Text in the form of notes and pupil activities can be added to the program.

Scanning

Pictures and maps can be scanned into a computer. The quality of the images depends on the quality of the technology available. Line drawings are generally effective with this process.

Figure 13.3 Creating resources using an ion camera and scanning

Doing all this takes time, but the benefits in terms of student interest as well as educational attainment are potentially enormous. Perhaps the time could be found by reducing the hours spent on some of the other initiatives that have visited schools in recent years.

Existing resources

Over time, a department will build up a wealth of resources, and from time to time will face the question of what should be done with them. A good rule for resource management is not to throw anything away without first considering if it will be useful in five years' time. That way, when you decide to investigate a new topic or issue, many of the resources will already have been collected. The following is an example of how one geography department was able to take advantage of its existing resource bank:

A few years ago, the Aral Sea disaster began to make the news. At first it was only mentioned in journals such as the *Geographical Magazine* and *New Scientist,* then various quality newspapers ran articles on it. Television programmes such as *Horizon* came later, and then a schools programme followed even later in the year. Over a period of months we gradually filled a file on this issue without ever really setting out to build a resource bank on it. To cap it all, we found some old textbooks in the back of a cupboard, on the Soviet Union, which described the aspirations of the Virgin Lands schemes as they developed. Later, *Geofile* and *Geo-Active* distilled many of these resources into summary articles for students. However, an exercise we have carried out on other topics is to get students to write their own *Geofile* article by giving them selections of the original articles to research. We even produced a fictional letter from the publishers of *Geofile* commissioning an article from the head of department, who in turn enlisted student help on the project.

Enquiry skills and information exchange

Researching material requires enquiry skills; these must be developed before appropriate material can be selected and used to best effect. Research needs key ideas, structure, a knowledge of what resources are available and the ability to search and operate the relevant systems. Selection techniques are needed: more than ever now that students can print out reams of material from a computer simply by clicking a mouse.

Enquiry skills can be developed by asking students to write off to organizations for information and resources as part of their own learning experience through project work. As with textbook evaluation, teacher groups provide a good forum to exchange ideas, contacts, etc. Subject panel meetings could be held in different schools in rotation, with the first item on the agenda for each meeting being a briefing from the host departments on some of the resource material that the department has discovered. The local branch of the GA could provide such a forum if none exists in the local authority. Finally, there is the publishers' exhibition at the GA Annual Conference, where not only textbook publishers but numerous other organizations display their products and services.

Long-term planning

A long-term plan is needed to lead students towards the necessary enquiry skills. There are practical skills relating to the use of the department or school computer hardware and software, as well as using the library index system (that is probably also on a database). Students must be able to search for topics, then scan for relevant information. Coping with material at a wide range of reading levels is also likely to be involved. Research templates may initially need to be provided, so that students can be taught to think out how best to structure and present their work. Finding out just what new skills are needed and how they can be developed will involve a considerable amount of work.

Who is in control?

Most teachers are accustomed to being in control of what is taught. A framework of ideas will still be needed, but students now have access to a range of content in a way that is hard to control. Minimal control by the teacher could result in a high level of motivation and the discovery of new relationships between data. Subject boundaries could be seen as irrelevant by the students. An alternative scenario, however, is that the students become 'surfers' of disparate facts that serve no genuinely educative purpose.

Volcanoes can be studied using a range of different resources presented in a variety of different ways. This list is an example of how key questions can be answered by using this range.

Extract from the KS3 Programme of Study

Tectonic processes

- the global distribution of earthquakes and volcanoes
- the nature, causes and effects of volcanic eruptions

What is a volcano?
- Video for a basic introduction to volcanic activity

Where are volcanoes?
- Slides to show a world map of volcanoes and earthquakes
- Atlas

What are the different types of volcano?
- 'Encarta' CD-ROM encyclopaedia for categories of types

What do volcanoes look like?
- 'Small Blue Planet' CD-ROM for satellite images of volcanoes
- Textbook for photographs
- Photobase and 'Encarta' CD-ROMs for ground view photos
- Library books research

How big are volcanoes?
- GRASS database of volcanoes

Why do volcanoes erupt?
- Textbook information
- 'Encarta' and 'The Physical World' CD-ROMs for information

Why are volcanoes in some places?
- Atlas map of volcanoes and plate boundaries
- 'Small Blue Planet' CD-ROM for map of world plates
- 'Encarta' CD-ROM for cartoon animation

What happens when a volcano erupts?
- The Times and The Guardian CD-ROMs to research case studies

What comes out of a volcano?
- Textbook
- 'Picturebase' CD-ROM for information

What can be done to plan for an eruption?
- Decision-making simulation of Mount St Helens
- Tape and slide presentation of Mount St Helens

Figure 13.4 Resources for studying volcanoes at Key Stage 3

Note
A similar inquiry structure and set of resources can be written for earthquakes, and students offered the choice of either volcanoes or earthquakes to study. Considerable extra guidance, however, is likely to be required as to how information can be obtained from each type of source.

Many students are now more familiar than teachers with the skills needed to access computer data. They can create and print out complex graphs and manipulate data on spreadsheets, though they may lack judgement as to what is appropriate. New teachers should ensure that they are computer literate; more experienced and slow-learner teachers should make every effort to catch up. The department as a whole must exercise skill, imagination and ingenuity in its use of IT.

Conclusion

Teaching and learning Geography is in the process of change; the increasing range of resources is one of the forces that is enabling that change to take place.

The Geography National Curriculum offers opportunities to develop courses that are flexible in factual content and therefore flexible in the resources that can be used to support them. [...]

Different resources have been considered in this chapter in relative isolation from each other; they should, however, be considered as part of a total package. Textbooks, maps, slides, computer software and all the rest have a part to play in teaching and learning Geography (Figure 13.4) and will enhance its appeal and the effectiveness of teaching it. A balance between different types of resource and a choice of the most appropriate type for each activity needs to be achieved.

There are numerous references to IT throughout this book, and this should need no apology. ... Information technology ... is gathering momentum at such a rate that hardware is out of date as soon as it is purchased, as is much of the software. There is nothing futuristic about this chapter; much of what is described here is already happening in schools – indeed, there are probably even more creative uses for IT that have not been mentioned.

By the time the next edition is made available, probably on a world-wide superhighway, strategies will have been devised to cater for many of the questions that have been raised here. There is a lot to be done by the new entrants to the profession. By then, of course, there will be new issues to raise and new resource issues to explore.

Further resources

The following list is not intended to be either definitive or balanced, and provides examples only of information sources.

Journals

Geography and *Teaching Geography* The Geographical Association, 160 Solly St, Sheffield, S1 4BF. www.geography.org.uk

Geography Review Philip Allan Publishers, Market Place, Deddington, Oxford OX5 4SE.

GCSE Geography Review Philip Allan Publishers.

The Geographical Magazine (subscriptions) PO Box 425, Woking GU21 1GP.

General, topical and media resources

National Geographic National Geographic Society, 1145 17th Street NW, Washington DC 20036, USA.

The New Scientist Specialist Group, Kings Reach Tower, Stamford Street, London SE1 9LS.

The Times and the *Guardian* (on CD-ROM).

Aid and development organizations

OXFAM, 274 Banbury Road, Oxford OX2 7DZ.

ActionAid, Hamlyn House, Archway, London N19 5PG.

Christian Aid, Interchurch House, 35 Lower Marsh, London SE1 7RL.

Catholic Fund for Overseas Development (CAFOD), 2 Romero Close, Stockwell Road, London SW9 9TY.

Centre for World Development Agency, 128 Buckingham Palace Road, London SW1W 9SA.

Development Education Centre, Gillot Centre, Bristol Road, Selly Oak, Birmingham B29 6LQ.

The Commonwealth Institute, Kensington High Street, London W8 6NQ.

World Wide Fund for Nature (WWF UK), Panda House, Weyside Park, Cattershall Lane, Godalming, Surrey GU7 IXR.

Government and international organizations

United Nations Environment Programme (UNEP), POB 30552, Nairobi, Kenya (Europe: CP356, 15 chemin des Anemones, 1219 Chatelaine, Geneva, Switzerland).

World Health Organization (WHO), avenue Appia, 1211 Geneva 27, Switzerland.

Food and Agriculture Organization (FAO), Viale delle Terme di Caracalla, 00100, Rome, Italy.

United Nations High Commissioner for Refugees (UNHCR), CP 2500, 1211 Geneva 2 depot, Switzerland.

International Labour Organization (ILO), 4 route des Morillons, 1211 Geneva 22, Switzerland.

Note: Some UN agencies produce regular newsletters, for example *Refugees* from UNHCR. All produce reports on specific topics and places.

UK ministries and other national organizations

The Department of the Environment, Food & Rural Affairs, Nobel House, 17 Smith Square, London SW1P 3JR.

Overseas Development Administration, 94 Victoria Street, London SWIE 5IL.

The Countryside Commission, John Dower House, Crescent Place, Cheltenham, Gloucestershire GL50 3RA.

Office for National Statistics, Great George Street, London SW1P 3AQ.

The Forestry Commission, 231 Corstorphine Road, Edinburgh EH12 7AT.

Foreign embassies

These are listed in every library; several embassies also house organizations for tourism and economic affairs. Some produce regular newsletters, such as *Invest in France* from the Invest in France Bureau.

Sources of addresses

The *Europa Year Book is* an annual publication that contains names and addresses of embassies, government ministries and commercial organizations for every country in the world.

There are statistical handbooks and other sources of country data for many countries. As an example, the *Statistical Abstract of the United States* from the US Department of Commerce, Bureau of Census is an annual production.

Original sources

Electricity companies
Water companies
Meteorological Office, Bracknell, Berkshire RG12 2SZ.
The Institute of Hydrology, Maclean Building, Crowmarsh, Gifford, Wallingford, Oxon OX10 8BB.
British Tourist Authority, Thames Tower, Black's Road, Hammersmith, London W6 9EL.
County Planning Departments

Businesses and related organizations

Public relations material is available from almost every UK company and the trade organizations that represent them. A few examples are listed below.

BNFL (nuclear energy), Risley, Warrington WA3 6AS.
ICI (chemicals), Head Office, 9 Millbank, London SWIP 3JF.
Sand and Gravel Association (sand and gravel), 1 Bramber Court, 2 Bramber Road, London W14 9PB.
British Petroleum (oil and natural gas), 1 Finsbury Circus, London EC2M 7BA.
Rio Tinto Zinc (RTZ) (mining), 6 St James's Square, London SW1Y 4LD.

Sources of information about companies to be found in these and other directories:

Kompass, Company Information: CBI.
European Country Information: The London Business School.

14 Teaching Geography with televisual resources

Chris Durbin

Once there was chalk and talk; now there is a whole range of multi-media resources. Never has it been so important to ask what are the strengths and weaknesses of each medium for geography teaching and learning. [In this chapter], the focus is on the medium of televisual resources (that is television programmes, whether live broadcasts, recorded, or bought on video) – how to evaluate them, and how to use them in the classroom.

Research suggests that geography teachers like using television and video because they:

- bring distant places to the classroom;
- enable people's views to be heard, although they are often short sound bites;
- can explain a difficult concept or process using a combination of images, graphics and commentary;
- can relate the location of a place to a wider region or even the world, through a series of 'nested' maps; and
- can give a visual impression of change over time in relation to various geographical phenomena.

It is important to recognize that televisual resources have limitations and constraints, which is why support materials are also essential. It is difficult for televisual resources to:

- convey detail on maps and also specific locational knowledge;
- convey complex geographical data;
- give subtle and complex viewpoints about an issue; and
- allow enough time for the viewer to absorb complex information.

In short, television is not a medium which enables the user to dwell on things or to take in large quantities of information; a high-quality slide projected onto a screen, or multiple copies of photographs and maps, will often do the job much better. Tempting as it may be, we must not use television as a surrogate teacher; it is only one of several tools which teachers can use as aids to teaching and learning.

How should televisual resources be evaluated?

Every televisual resource is different and we must evaluate each in turn. Making time to do this is important, though more time-consuming than looking at textbooks, for

Evaluating televisual resources

Summary and timings of programme

Curriculum uses

Images	Clarity	very clear ☐ ☐ ☐ ☐ very unclear
	Appropriateness	very appropriate ☐ ☐ ☐ ☐ very inappropriate
Narration	Language level	very high ☐ ☐ ☐ ☐ very low
	Clarity of speech	very clear ☐ ☐ ☐ ☐ very unclear
	Clarity of explanation	very clear ☐ ☐ ☐ ☐ very unclear
Graphics	Explanation of	very clear ☐ ☐ ☐ ☐ not at all clear
Content	Geographical content	very accurate ☐ ☐ ☐ ☐ inaccurate
	Value position	biased ☐ ☐ ☐ ☐ unbiased
		represents one view ☐ ☐ ☐ ☐ represents many views

Other points of interest

Figure 14.1 An evaluation tick-list for televisual resources

example. A quick tick-list of criteria helps (see Figure 14.1) and this can be used by all members of the department. Sticking this tick-list to each video cassette box helps others to use it more easily and effectively.

How to make best use of televisual resources for teaching Geography

Given its popularity in schools, it is surprising how little research has been done on how children learn from the medium of television. The following experiment conducted by Margaret Roberts (1987) serves to illustrate one aspect of this.

A group of student teachers were shown a television programme and asked to take notes on what they learned from it. The programme was stopped after five minutes and the transcript of the commentary was read out. The students were asked to delete from their notes anything which they had written down during the programme that was in the transcript. Not a single student had anything left! They had made no record of what they had just seen.

This revealed that the students were not interpreting the pictures; they had behaved as if it was a simple dictation exercise. Visual information was not recorded.

The art of interpreting and describing pictures is intellectually demanding, but we as teachers must develop strategies to encourage it; it is important that children learn to develop their vocabulary from what they see on the screen as well as what they hear or read. Given the amount of time and money that television producers invest in selecting pictures for geography teachers, it seems an awful waste if they are not used to full advantage!

Think about the way you have used televisual resources in the past. Was the resource in the unit of work used:

- as a stimulus to a unit of work?
- to explain a process?
- to raise an issue?
- to illustrate an example or case study or a key idea?
- to compare another place with your local area (or another place you have been studying)?
- as a summary at the end of a unit of work?

It is suggested that you could use all these according to the fitness for purpose of each piece. Did you use:

- a whole programme uninterrupted?
- a clip in isolation?
- a series of clips with activities interspersed?

Whole programmes are good for providing a quick overview of a situation or place and are excellent for reinforcing learning. Clips are useful for very specific learning outcomes. Using more of the programme than the specific clip allows pupils a few moments to 'tune in'. A series of clips with activities interspersed enables an enquiry to take place. Often a geography programme follows a line of enquiry and is over before the pupils have assimilated the issue, let alone the case study and the relevant 'stakeholders' involved. It is important, therefore, to identify the breakpoints in a televisual resource which are often indicated by televisual chapter headings. Break-points are not always obvious; they may be rhetorical questions, musical 'stings', a switch of scene from ground to aerial shots (or vice versa), a screen of graphics or text. They are simply intended to break up the narrative of a programme. A teacher can use them to pause and allow pupils to 'do' an activity.

Here are some more questions you might ask.

- Did your pupils take notes?
- Did your pupils watch with no task?
- Did your pupils watch a section and then have a whole-class discussion?

- After watching a section did they move on to a related activity?
- Did you set a variety of tasks for different groups of pupils?

Taking notes on a programme can be a valid activity, but breaks in viewing are important to enable the learner to pause to recall. Allowing pupils to watch without a related written task is often appropriate, but always provide a thinking task and outline what task(s) will follow their viewing. Make time for discussion about particular issues raised by a programme, and intersperse discussion with viewing.

Often teachers attempt to do too many things after one viewing. They expect their pupils to get a visual impression of a country, to understand how it has changed in economic and social terms, to have empathy with the people featured and to understand key issues and processes. Some pupils may be able to achieve all this, but it is best to assume that most will not. Use the class as a team, with each pupil being responsible for a particular task designed to achieve a particular learning outcome.

In an article in *Teaching Geography*, Graham Butt (1991) called for teachers and pupils to be much more investigative in their approach to using televisual resources and listed a range of strategies for investigating the role of the film-maker. Media Studies is concerned with issues such as these, many of which are very relevant to the teacher of Geography.

In summary, there needs to be variety in the teaching strategies adopted when using televisual resources, and each strategy should be appropriate to the purpose. Below are some ideas for different approaches and specific activities for use in geographical enquiries relating to places and themes. While reading about these, it is worth thinking about active watching strategies that you might use to lift the medium from being one of passive entertainment to the powerful educational resource that we know it can be.

Exploring perceptions

Much of Geography is about facts, but much also is about perception. The way that we perceive distant places, for example, will depend to a very great extent on the visual images we are shown. Our pupils may have already encountered some of the places we teach them about, so we must take account of this, and of their perceptions of those places.

A brainstorming session, in which words that pupils associate with the place being studied are listed, is a useful exercise with which to begin. Television programmes about the place can be used as part of this process to make it more interesting, fun and informed. For example, you could begin by showing a clip from a programme about Japan with no commentary, just music. Pupils can then select adjectives that describe the images they see. These are written on the board or OHP, and then discussed. These words could also be written into a blank outline map (see Figure 14.2). The results will reveal the diversity of perceptions that pupils have – some will be 'negative' (dense, enclosed, depressing), some 'positive' (exiting, dynamic, rich).

Exercises like these help us to examine the things that influence our perceptions about places. They also help pupils to understand that the study of places is about attitudes and values as well as about facts (Durbin 1995), and that, when used on

THE SONG
THE BURNING SONG
THE DEMON VULTURES
THE HAZY TENTS   THE RAW
HORIZONS   THE DRUGGED SANDS   THE SCREAMING
THUNDER THE RATTLING BONES THE DUSTY MOUTHS
THE INFINITE EYES   THE DREAM POWER   THE CIRCLING
SKY THE TREACHEROUS BIRDS THE SHIFTING TOWNS   THE
SNARLING GUNS THE BURNING STORM THE VAST RIVER THE
CLAY DANCERS THE BLACK MASKS THE RICH SANDS   THE HAZY
DEMON THE SCREAMING SKIES THE VULTURES MOUTHS THE RAW
EYES THE THUNDEROUS SONG THE SHIFTING TRACKS THE VAST
CIRCLE THE RATTLING BIRDS THE DUSTY TENTS THE GUNS SNARL
THE STEAMING HORIZON THE BONE FOREST THE BURNING TOWNS THE
SAND FLOWERS THE TREACHEROUS INFINITE THE BLACK TRACKED THE
DANCERS SCREAM THE MASKED GUNS THE THUNDERS MOUTH THE FOREST
TOWN THE CLAY HUTS THE STORMS POWER THE DRUGGED RIVER THE
SHIFTING SONGS THE SKYS EYE THE RATTLING DREAM THE SNARLING DUST   THE
SANDS DEMONS THE BURNING BIRDS THE CIRCLING HAZE THE RAW BONES THE
RICH TENTS THE SCREAMING FLOWER THE STEAMING CLAY THE BLACK SAND
THE MASKED   DANCE THE TREACHEROUS HORIZON THE STORMS TRACK
THE RIVER THUNDER   THE SHIFTY VULTURES THE
FORESTS POWER   THE RAW SKY THE SCREAMING
EYES THE DREAM SONGS THE DRUGGED HUTS
THE HAZY TOWNS   THE BURNT CIRCLE   THE
GUNS MOUTH THE SNARLING BONES THE
INFINITE BIRDS   THE DUSTY FLOWERS
THE STORMS MASK THE THUNDERING
DEMONS   THE TENT DANCERS THE
RICH CLAY   THE SHIFTED POWER
THE SANDY RIVER   THE BURNING
TREACHERY   THE RATTLING TRACK
THE BLACK STEAM   THE POWERFUL
DREAM THE FLOWERING SONG THE
DRUGGED STREAM   THE DANCING EYE   THE
HORIZONTAL HUT   THE MOUTHLESS   SNARLS
THE TRACKLESS SKY   THE RAW   FOREST
THE TENT TOWN   THE HAZY   RIVER
THE INFINITE SHIFT   THE   BIRD
STORM   THE TREACHEROUS   DEMON
THE BURNING DRUG   THE   GUN
DANCE   THE SINGING
BONE   THE MASKED
RICH   THE BLACK
CIRCLING   THE
VAST DREAM
SINGING

Figure 14.2 A word shape (Africa) (compiled by Dave Calder)

their own, visual images (and music) have serious limitations, as well as being capable of manipulating our ideas.

Building descriptions

We all learn new vocabulary by picture and word association, and geography teachers share with their colleagues the duty to develop young people's vocabulary. In a study of contrasting regions in the USA the teacher and a class of 35 watched five minutes of a documentary programme about the Colorado river. She paused the programme on a vivid landscape and asked the class to annotate a pre-prepared outline sketch of the Arizona desert. On another occasion, the teacher used an envelope of adjectives and asked the class to select appropriate words to describe the landscape of the river Rhine. The pupils were then asked to create a 'wordscape' where the selected words are

Figure 14.3 A shape poem: me and Amanda (compiled by Colin West)

Source: Wes Magee 1989.

inserted, appropriately shaped, into an outline sketch (Durbin 1995). Many opportunities found in televisual resources can be used for developing geographical vocabulary in interesting ways, such as wordscapes and shape poems (see Figure 14.3).

Explaining geographical phenomena

Educational geography programmes usually include graphics designed to explain why things are like they are or why things are located in a particular place. Such programmes are also invaluable for illustrating change (Sharp 1995). Here are some ways of using television graphics:

Teacher A

Class of 11–12-year-old pupils

Task   To explain why there are different climates in different parts of the world.

Method   A television programme on the world's weather (designed for Key Stage 2 pupils), which included a graphic of a globe showing the sun's rays falling on the earth, was used. The class watched the whole programme once, were then given a list of 20 statements and were asked to decide which statements they thought were true; which not true; which they were unsure about. The class watched the programme again and were asked to write a commentary suitable for use by younger, primary school children.

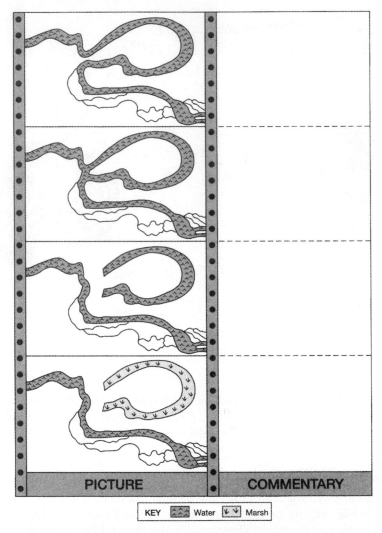

Figure 14.4 Storyboard: oxbow lake formation

Teacher B

Class of 11–12-year-old pupils

Task   To learn about the stages involved in the formation of an oxbow lake using differentiated activities.

Method   The class watched a clip from a BBC TV programme, *Le Rhône Sauvage*, showing the formation of an oxbow lake (see Figure 14.4). Immediately after the clip was shown, four different stages in the process were sequenced by the pupils. Pupils who completed this easily and quickly were given more complex explanations to add to the sequence. The final extension activity was to design a visual explanation for another river feature using a storyboard.

Figure 14.5 Two sound bites – one from a river engineer in the US Corps of Engineers and one from a representative of Friends of the Earth

Exploring issues

Geography teachers often use devices such as roleplay, debate, simulation and so on, to enable pupils to hear and evaluate a range of viewpoints about a particular issue. Pupils can then evaluate further the evidence (however partial/impartial), decide their own (or their character's) stance on the issue and qualify why they hold this viewpoint.

Televisual aids have particular value in this area of teaching. Unlike books they can be topical and show real people expressing personal opinions. They are also useful for providing thought-provoking and catchy sound bites (see Figure 14.5).

The sound bites shown in Figure 14.5 come from a *Horizon* programme called 'After the Flood' shown in 1994. The clip in which these people appeared was used in one class at the start of an enquiry into the impact of people on rivers. The pupils had to discuss the issue and to decide which viewpoint, if any, they agreed with. They then watched the programme in full, and were asked to note down any evidence which supported their view. The pupils went on to look at a range of other resources (books, etc.) to compare what they found with what they had learned from the programme.

Valuing people's views

Research (Sharp 1995) has shown that reactions to people from 'distant' places can be very confused and that pupils interpret what they see and hear from their own cultural perspective. Young people, therefore, need support from teachers when they are listening to people from distant places and must be alerted to listen carefully to the variety of viewpoints. They may need a transcript of what a person says. Profiles will also help pupils to get to know individuals better, and help them to understand and empathize with people in cultures different from their own. This is why it is important to provide some cultural background and to create a climate of empathy with people featured in the programme. Frequently, it is the priorities expressed by people directly involved in local issues which help pupils to understand why a place is changing in a particular way. These are much-valued aspects of all geography television programmes and significant efforts are made to set them up and get them right.

Active watching strategies

Television is mainly used passively in the home. Getting the most out of televisual resources in the classroom involves thinking and planning activities very carefully and imaginatively. Ask yourself: Am I trying to explore perceptions, set up a debate, show a sequence of events, give a case study? These are active watching strategies. As teachers we have a duty to make the most of television's learning opportunities and to develop it into an active learning experience. To enable us to do this we should ensure that we:

- try to appeal to a range of emotions in the pupil;
- give a clear briefing about what to watch for;
- set clear tasks before, during, and/or after clips; and
- allow enough time for thinking and responding in discussion, writing, drawing and so on.

Sources for geography teaching with televisual resources

Educational television

Both BBC Education (*The Geography Programme*) and Channel 4 Education (*Geographical Eye*) produce geography programmes for schools. These are targeted at the 11–18 curriculums for the constituent parts of the UK. Notable highlights from the BBC have been *Japan 2000*, *USA 2000*, *Brazil 2000* and *Investigating Britain*, and from Channel 4: *Geographical Eye Over Europe* and *Geographical Eye Over Africa*. Every year a wall chart is produced for heads of department showing repeats and new series. There are also broadcasts at night, usually a series *en bloc*. The BBC in Scotland, Wales (S4C) and Northern Ireland also produce programmes to reflect their own geography.

Support materials are available to accompany the series. Built around classroom geographical investigations, *Japan 2000* has an accompanying pack which comprises a set of photograph and map cards, a booklet of activity maps, data files and more in-depth information discovered in the research phase of these programmes. Channel 4 have produced sets of satellite images to accompany the *Geographical Eye* series. Some series are available for purchase on video. There are other commercial or charitable suppliers of educational material on video, but these are rare. This information is mailed directly to schools when it is published. The main sources of information are:

BBC Education Information Unit, BBC White City, 201 Wood Lane, London W12 7TS. E-mail bbc.education@bbc.co.uk

Channel 4 Schools Programme information is available from: Educational Television Company, PO Box 100, Warwick CV34 6TZ.

General television

There is a wide range of geography programmes on non-educational television. *Horizon* has provided a rich vein of physical and environmental geography over the years. … The Open University carries some excellent series for the study of Geography. These are not always appropriate to show in full to school pupils, but are useful in short clips or to update the teacher's own knowledge. Finally, do not forget the news and weather; topicality in Geography is very important. The Kobe earthquake in 1995 and the Scarborough cliffs landslip in 1993 are typical examples of topicality. The late-night weather reports are often longer and more detailed than others and also give information about the weather worldwide.

Copyright

Copyright status is complex; LEAs negotiate licences with, and pay fees to, the Educational Recording Agency on behalf of their maintained schools. For grant maintained and independent schools a separate fee must be negotiated. Details from:

Educational Recording Agency, 74 New Oxford Street, London WC1A 1EF.

A separate flat-rate licence for schools is also needed for Open University programmes. For further details contact:

Open University Enterprises Limited, 12 Cofferidge Close, Stoney Stratford, Milton Keynes MK11 IBY.

References

Butt, G. (1991) 'Have we got a video today?', *Teaching Geography* 16(2): 51–5.

Calder, D. (1981) *Continents*, leaflet published by the author.

Durbin, C. (1994) *Japan 2000*, BBC Education.

—— (1995) 'Using televisual resources in geography', *Teaching Geography* 20(3): 118–21.

Magee, W. (ed.) (1989) *Madtail Mini Whale – And Other Shape Poems*, London: Viking Kestrel.

Roberts, M. (1987) 'Using videocassettes', *Teaching Geography* 12(3): 114–17.

Sharp, C. (1995) *The Use and Impact of Schools Broadcasts*, NFER.

15 ICT in Geography

Introduction
Maggie Smith

It is clear that, as Hassell (2000) states, ICT provides 'a huge range of opportunities for enhancing the teaching and learning of geography'. Whether these opportunities are being fully exploited in schools is a matter of debate and concern – progress can, for a variety of reasons, best be described as 'patchy' (Fisher 2000: 52). However, Fisher argues that Geography is well placed amongst subjects in the curriculum to take the use of ICT forward in schools:

> Geography as an academic discipline has made use of computer-based data handling software, statistical processing packages and cartographic programs. Remote sensing data from satellites is organized and presented using computers. Simulations enable phenomena to be modelled and the interplay of variables to be examined, for instance the behaviour of water in a drainage basin. Beyond all these, geography has given its name to a powerful computer-based approach for the multivariate analysis and display of spatially referenced data: the geographic information systems (GIS), an application of great research and commercial significance.
>
> (Fisher 2000: 51)

With this background, Geography is able to provide a real context for the use of ICT in schools, enhancing learning for pupils by providing situations in which to explore, develop and present their understanding of geographical concepts, and providing support for teachers in their planning of effective geography lessons.

There are many guides to using ICT in geography classrooms – the references that accompany this chapter list a number of these. In this chapter the aim is to highlight three particular aspects of using ICT in Geography. First, in an article by Fred Martin, the issue of using ICT to raise achievement is explored. Martin gives an overview of the potential for ICT to promote learning in Geography and argues that raising the level of pupils' achievement can be done by increasing the quality of pupils' research skills and by providing pupils with an increased range of ways to process, analyse and present data.

Following on from points made in that article, there are case studies to demonstrate each of the two strands of ICT – the first of which, the use of information systems in the classroom, is outlined by Andrew Williams in his account of the value of geographical information systems (GIS) to the teaching and learning of Geography in schools. The second, the role of ICT in enhancing the presentation and understanding of work, is presented by Liz Taylor in a description of the ways in which she used a presentation package in the classroom.

References

Fisher, A. (2000) 'Developing the educational use of information and communications technology', in C. Fisher and T. Binns (eds) *Issues in Geography Teaching*, London: RoutledgeFalmer.

Hassell, D. (2000) 'Issues in ICT and Geography', in C. Fisher and T. Binns (eds) *Issues in Geography Teaching*, London: RoutledgeFalmer.

Using ICT to raise achievement
Fred Martin

The context

Raising achievement is at the top of the educational agenda. Using Information and Communications Technology (ICT) is one of the processes whereby raising achievement in Geography is possible. Since 1999, all trainee teachers have had to achieve a detailed set of standards in ICT. These standards relate to both technical competence to use hardware, software and peripherals, as well as the ability to use ICT for classroom work, administration and for their own professional development (DfEE 1998). The same standards form the basis of the New Opportunities Fund training that all teachers are currently undertaking (DfEE 1999a).

In case there is any room for doubt as to the importance of ICT, its use is now firmly and specifically embedded in the National Curriculum Subject Orders, including those for Geography (DfEE 1999b). The use of ICT has also become compulsory as part of the assessment criteria for GCSE Geography, though awarding bodies will need to work out just what this will involve. Exemplification documents for how the ICT standards can be applied to subjects have also been produced, though the examples provided in these do not have statutory status (TTA 1999). What they do provide is a wealth of ideas that aim to help teachers make appropriate use of ICT for subject work. Another useful source of ideas is the Contributory Database part of the Virtual Teacher's Centre (see 'References and website sources' on p. 220) where there are classroom resources available as files that can be downloaded.

The use of ICT can help raise achievement in a number of ways. This chapter demonstrates how it can be used as an aid to revision, a tool for fieldwork, a means for the teacher to create differentiated resources and for students to access differentiated resources and tasks, and a means of helping to motivate and to narrow the gender gap in performance.

Characteristics of ICT

The ideas in this article relate specifically to the use of computer hardware, peripherals and software, although ICT also includes other electronic forms. Four characteristics of ICT related to a computer's capacity are listed in DfEE documents (e.g. DfEE 1998: 4), as follows:

Geographical activities	ICT applications and key functions
Enquiry and research • statistical data • information • viewpoints	The internet, e-mail, CD-ROMS, fax: • geography websites • geography-related websites • links to experts and others Content-rich sites and disks: • geographical topics • atlases • encyclopaedias and newspapers
Map, graph and other graphic skills • drawing base maps • drawing quantitative maps • drawing graphs	Drawing programs: • basic and advanced drawing programs, e.g. maps, diagrams, sketches • geographical information systems Spreadsheets and databases: • statistical data in tables • developing graphicacy • mapping with data
Recording and processing data • field study data, e.g. qualitative, visual and quantitative data • data from research in secondary sources	Spreadsheet and database: • data in tables, e.g. use of palmtop computer on fieldwork • processing statistical data Data logging: • recording data (weather station, using sensors) • processing data Digital camera and scanner: • recording data (digital camera for fieldwork) • processing data
Analyse, interpret and communicate data and information (text) • writing essays and reports • 'word-play' activities • using writing frames • e-mail and fax messages	Word processing, desk-top publishing: • writing text • using drawing tools • sorting text and data Multimedia authoring: • writing text • using drawing tools • inserting images Presentation software, e.g. PowerPoint: • summarizing ideas and information • presentation templates and tools • inserting images
Hypothesis testing and simulation • asking geographical questions • modelling outcomes	Simulation and modelling software: • information research • data from a database • simulating complex systems Spreadsheets: • using statistical functions in models

Figure 15.1 The application of ICT in geographical activities

1   a computer's speed and automatic functions, i.e. to work quickly and carry out some functions automatically
2   capacity and range, i.e. to contain a large amount of material in a variety of media
3   provisional nature of stored data, i.e. to update data and information
4   interactivity, i.e. to involve the user by requiring decisions to be taken.

Each of these characteristics can help to raise achievement in the teaching and learning of Geography by raising the quality of students' use of research, recording, presenting and analysing the data. They can also contribute teaching methods and to how students learn.

Figure 15.1 provides a list of typical geographical activities together with the ICT applications that can be used for each one. It can be used as a basis for developing a geography department's portfolio of ICT equipment. Many of the ICT resources that form part of the whole-school's ICT resources that can be used in Geography are generic, including word-processing and drawing packages, image-processing packages, spreadsheets, databases or the world wide web. However, other resources are specific to Geography: for example, geographical information systems, weather data loggers and geography CD-ROMs. Effective use of ICT in Geography will involve students in multi-tasking between these different types of packages rather than regarding each as a separate entity.

Another key point is that raising achievement must mean more than simply improving the look of a piece of work, important though this is. The use of ICT must help raise the quality of the geography delivered and the students' performance. In many instances, students can do geographical activities more accurately and more efficiently using a greater variety of media. It might also he argued that ICT enables students to undertake a greater variety of geographical activities than using other teaching methods. What follows are examples of different approaches to raising achievement through the use of ICT in Geography.

Research and recording

Geography teachers use information to provide a rich context for delivering key ideas and for the development of geographical skills. Access to geographical information has traditionally been through textbooks and other library resources, supplemented by current newspaper articles and occasional video programmes on a topic. ICT does not need to replace these sources, however; it can help improve the quality and quantity of geographical information in a number of ways, for example:

- CD-ROMs and the internet can help increase the amount of information that is available, allowing a greater choice over what is relevant and what is appropriate for students of different abilities.
- Data and information that uses multimedia methods of display can be effective in helping to make resources accessible and more interesting, e.g. using animation to demonstrate complex processes.
- Search engines on the internet or an index in a CD-ROM can be used to search for information quickly and accurately.
- High-quality and current information is available from original sources, e.g. weather satellites.

- Some websites and CD-ROMs provide virtual field visits which allow students to 'move' through a distant landscape and collect information (e.g. the Nodak.edu website).
- Different types of geographical information are available more immediately, e.g. by the use of satellite imagery and processing software.
- Electronic mail can help students make new contacts for geographical information and ideas. This is especially useful when the views of people with different perspectives on an issue or topic are required.
- Research processes are made easier with the ability to 'copy and paste' relevant items from a variety of sources. This allows the student to analyse the information at a later date.
- Accurate data can be collected in the field by using data logging hardware and software, e.g. by using sensors linked to a data logger.
- Different data can be sampled over different periods of time, then presented as graphs and figures.

Access to information using ICT raises issues that need to be addressed. In order to deal with the increased amount of information available, students need to develop both their ability to undertake research and their skills in selecting information that is relevant to the topic or their project. They need also to be made aware of the issues of quality of the information, its reliability and the extent of bias in material. None of these is a new issue for geography teachers, however – what the use of ICT does raise is the importance of addressing them more immediately.

Where the teacher selects material for student use, it often limits access to the choice of information. ICT offers opportunities for students to make more of their own choices about the type and extent of the information they use. Their choice can be extended both to the details of content and to the methods to use it. For example, in order to develop their understanding of basic river processes, students could study any river from the information on different rivers that is available from websites and CD-ROMs. In addition, where students have a degree of choice on the selection of information, their ownership of the material is increased and they will be able to play a more active part in the enquiry process. Students can also be encouraged to select which type of software package they wish to use for analysing and presenting their work.

Processing and presenting data

Students can use ICT to process, analyse and present data in a variety of ways. This can range from the basics of making sure that the work is readable through to using the software packages to manipulate complex data, in tables and on maps.

Data handling

One simple way of handling or processing data is to put it in a table in a word-processing or spreadsheet package, then sort it using the 'Sort' tool. A more complex approach is to enter data in a spreadsheet or database and search for relationships or apply a variety of formulae to it. Both teachers and students will appreciate the speed at which this can be done on a computer, and the sheer tedium that can be avoided by

Figure 15.2 *An image taken using a digital camera during fieldwork. This has been annotated using a word-processing package*

doing so. Use of a computer removes the possibility of a mistake in the calculations, though there are several other possible sources of error that need to be avoided.

Presenting work

Students can use ICT to raise the standard of how they present their work by:

- editing text and images to improve their quality, e.g. by using a word processor to modify and rearrange text, or a photo-processing package to edit and label images (Figure 15.2)
- checking spelling and grammar
- using different types of packages to present their work: for example, by including different types of media in a multimedia authoring or presentation package.

Graphic skills

Basic generic drawing packages (e.g. Paint) can be used to produce attractive and accurate maps. Students who find cartography challenging or who lack basic drawing capabilities can achieve a high level of success using such packages. Colour shading can be changed until it is appropriate by clicking on an 'Infill' tool. Labels can be added to places where there is space. A map can be edited without the need to start from scratch, especially if the drawing package includes vector graphics, which are individually editable.

Geographic information systems (GIS) provide powerful mapping tools for drawing, processing and analysing the data (e.g. Mapmaker). Different layers of data can either be shown separately or combined to help identify relationships. Different styles of mapping

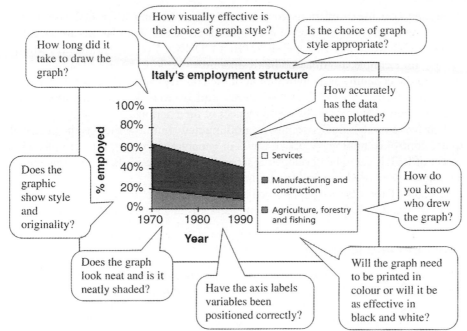

Figure 15.3 Assessment criteria for a graph drawn in a spreadsheet. Give this graph a mark

can be used to achieve the best visual effect. Unfortunately, few school geography departments have purchased GIS software; this is understandable on account of the cost involved, the complexity of use and the time it takes to teach students how to use it. Since this chapter is about raising standards, at this point it is worth asking if the use of GIS software would make for 'better' geography, if it might make it 'worse', or if it has no effect on the standard. Surely the first of the three options is the only answer.

Students can use 'Clip art' maps to produce base maps that are accurate and effective. Imported vertical air photographs or other scanned images can also be used.

Accurate and colourful graphs can be drawn using spreadsheet or database packages. The challenge is to teach students how to make appropriate choices between the different types of graphs they can use for particular sets of data (see Figure 15.3).

Special software packages have now been developed which allow students to record, process and present their fieldwork data: for example, work on rivers, sediments and slopes (e.g. Geopacks).

Modelling and simulation

ICT can help geographers ask 'What if …?' questions in order to apply geographical concepts to new situations, both efficiently and effectively. Students can model data using data-handling packages such as Microsoft Excel. By changing one or more variable in the data, changes to transport costs, for example, students can model the effects on industrial location. Any changes to raw data are automatically transferred to the graphs, thus combining modelling with the graphic presentation of the effects.

Students can use simulations to explore the effect of taking different decisions and improving their understanding of geographical processes. Simulations are available on both CD-ROMs and on websites. On a CD-ROM on Kenya (Matrix Multimedia), for example, a simulation helps students to explore the effects of their decisions on the economy and environment of the country. Similarly, a coffee-farming simulation from the Eduweb website allows students to make decisions about what to plant, then to appreciate the consequences of their actions.

Hardware models in Geography are nothing new, but now there is the potential to use control technology: to make waves or generate electricity, for example. This aspect of ICT is yet to be developed at secondary school level. Perhaps some enterprising software producer will rise to the challenge?

Using ICT for these geographical activities will help students to raise the standard in Geography and ICT. Other related teaching and learning issues are discussed below.

Teaching and learning

This section focuses on ways in which ICT can be used to help the teacher to present geography lessons and on how students can be helped to learn. The use of ICT may at least help to raise achievement in Geography by providing a greater variety of teaching and learning styles, because for some students the use of ICT offers better access to the work. For the teacher, ICT can:

- provide a means of creating attractive and effective printed resources such as worksheets and information sheets;
- allow him or her to adapt resources to achieve differentiation in the geography classroom;
- offer the opportunity to create on-screen activities – for example, to use 'drag and drop' techniques with words and images, to create writing frames and to make a wide range of resources instantly available; and
- present video, animations and photographs on a big screen by linking a computer to a projector (Treanor and Kilcoyne 2000).

For students, learning can be improved by:

- the use of software packages that contain interactive activities: for example, on how to use grid references or how to identify features of land use on a map or vertical air photograph (Geopacks 1999);
- allowing ownership of what is studied, provided students are given some choice in the subject content;
- providing the software tools to experiment and to edit work, and ensuring an improved end-product; and
- offering access to a variety of multimedia resources: for example, spoken and written text, sound and video extracts.

As with every other style of teaching and learning, the use of ICT needs to be done well for it to be effective. A combination of ICT training and experience is the only way to ensure that this is achieved.

Issues in raising achievement

Raising achievement by the use of ICT is not without its problems. Access to computer facilities and software is a major issue; however, the level of ICT skills of both teachers and students also needs to be addressed. To take advantage of the potential of ICT to raise achievement, what follows are ten practical ways forward:

1 Ensure that you receive training in the basic skills of ICT and make the most of NOF-funded training. You can then develop the ability to apply your skills to work in Geography.
2 Hardware, including peripherals, need to be accessible and available to staff and students both within and outside school hours.
3 Technician assistance is available in most schools – make sure that it is also accessible both during lessons and at other times.
4 Aim to build up a portfolio of software packages, which should include both generic ones such as mapping software and others on specific geographical topics.
5 Be creative in your use of generic packages, such as word processors and spreadsheets, to overcome problems of lack of subject-specific software.
6 Train students in the use of generic software so that you need to spend less time teaching its use in geography lessons and more time on the content of the lesson.
7 Ensure that the use of ICT is written into your development plan and schemes of work for Geography. Liaise with your ICT co-ordinator to make the most of skills learnt in other subject areas.
8 Create resources that make use of software packages; these can be a printed handout for students or for use on-screen. Staff can share this development work.
9 Ensure that students and colleagues have a clear understanding of the advantages of using ICT in Geography by including details in the departmental handbook and on the school intranet/website.
10 Share your vision of what makes 'good' Geography with colleagues and ensure that everyone is aware of their role in the whole-school ICT policy.

Achievement in Geography is usually measured by performance in examinations, which, of course, relates directly to the course content and especially to the assessment criteria. However, presently there are no specific requirements in the National Curriculum to, for example, use current data, understand how GIS work, model and run a computer simulation, or many of the other things that can only be done, or best be done, by the use of ICT. Without these requirements, work with ICT may not raise achievement in Geography to a measurable degree. The issue then is defining what makes 'better' Geography. In the search for this definition, some traditional skills or geographical content may need to be abandoned in order to make time for ICT work in Geography. While geographical resources may be infinite, time to teach Geography is not – this issue is yet to be debated.

Note

The websites and software mentioned in this article are intended only to be illustrative.

References and website sources

The Contributory Database is part of the Virtual Teacher's Centre: http://contribute.ngfl.gov.uk

Department for Education and Employment (DfEE) (1998) *Annex B to Circular 4/98*, London: DfEE (www.canteach.gov.uk).

—— (1999a) *The Use of ICT in Subject Teaching (NOF-funded training) Expected Outcomes for Teachers, Annex A1 (for England and Wales)*, London: DfEE.

—— (1999b) *National Curriculum Orders for Geography*, London: DfEE (also on website: www.nc.uk.net).

Eduweb, *Coffee Farming Simulation* (website: www.eduweb.com/agriculture/comag.html).

Geopacks *River Form and Channel Analysis* (software package), London: Geopacks.

—— (1999) *Mastering Mapwork*, London: Geopacks.

MapIT Ltd *MapMaker Student*, MapIT Ltd.

Matrix Multimedia *Kenya CD-ROM*, Leeds: Matrix MultiMedia.

NOF providers information on website: www.canteach.gov.uk

Treanor, C. and Kilcoyne, J. (2000) 'Fieldwork and geography on the big screen', *Teaching Geography* 25(2): 94–5.

TTA (1999) *Using ICT to Meet Teaching Objectives in Geography ITT – secondary*. (website: www.canteach.gov.uk)

Virtual Field Visits (website: www.volcanoworld.org/).

Weather Satellite Imagery (website: www.nottingham.ac.uk/meteosat/).

|| GIS in school Geography
Andrew Williams

Geographic information systems (GIS) provide us with a means of handling information about the world in an efficient and effective manner. GIS enable data on the physical and human environment to be brought together and analysed in an integrated way to help us make decisions about the organization of our world. As a result they are ideal for promoting an understanding of spatial relationships and patterns, for assisting in decision-making environmental management and for developing important information-handling ICT skills – all key objectives in contemporary geography teaching.

Geographical information and the world around us

Geographical information is of immense importance in every sphere of modern society and without it we would not be able to make sense of the world or address many fundamental questions, problems and issues that face humanity. Many of the major challenges that we face in the world have a critical geographical dimension: for example global climate change, increasing food production, vanishing natural resources, natural disasters or pollution. In addition, we are confronted by numerous geographical issues on a local scale, such as the siting of facilities (schools, hospitals and retail developments), the management of emergency services or the conservation of natural resources. In order to address these and many other complex issues, we need to collect, manipulate, analyse and communicate geographical information in ways that enable effective decision-making.

Geographical information is often presented as printed maps; these describe the location and qualities of virtually every facet of our planet. Historically maps have been used to solve geographical problems by illustrating relationships. For example, in the 1850s, Dr John Snow identified the source of a cholera outbreak in Soho, central London, by mapping the distribution of cholera deaths in relation to the sites of water pumps. Dr Snow found that a contaminated pump was at the centre of the cholera outbreak (Figure 15.4). However, maps are by no means the only visual medium; aerial photographs and satellite images are frequently used to convey geographical information. In addition, vast quantities of numerical and descriptive information, which have a geographical dimension, are now stored in databases around the world. Crime statistics, census data, voting patterns, consumer behaviour (generated by retail loyalty cards) and insurance premiums are all related to postcodes and thus can be located to specific places.

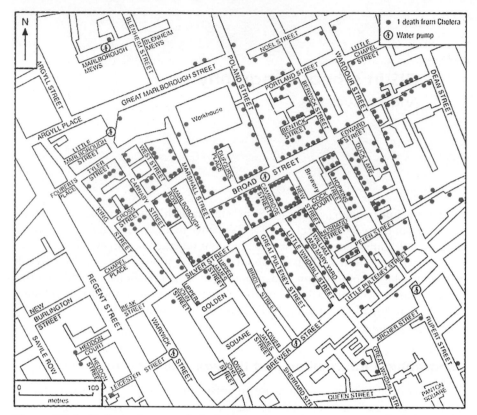

Figure 15.4 Dr Snow's map of cholera deaths and water pumps in Soho in the 1850s

The nature of many of the problems facing society and the overwhelming volume of information describing them present a serious challenge for decision-makers. GIS provide a means to handle this information in an effective way. GIS also enable different kinds of data describing our world to be brought together and analysed in an integrated way to assist in decision-making (Figure 15.5).

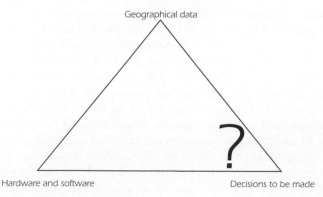

Figure 15.5 The components of GIS

GIS and society

A GIS package can be regarded as software that can capture, store, query, analyse and display geographical information. These systems range in scale from small in-car navigation systems to the massive computers used to provide weather forecasts. With the rise in computing power and the concomitant fall in cost, GIS software is more widely available on desktop personal computers. GIS are now big business; many government departments, local authorities, commercial organizations, and environmental groups now use GIS software for such tasks as land-use planning, market analysis, industrial development, the management of emergency services, transport planning, environmental impact assessment and wildlife conservation. These organizations use GIS to integrate information, solve problems, propose solutions and visualize scenarios, such as:

- the site of a new out-of-town shopping centre;
- the route of a controversial rail link;
- the social and economic characteristics of the population within an hour's drive of a new theme park; and
- clusters of disease incidents.

This provides career opportunities for students with knowledge of using GIS. A range of organizations, from charities, health authorities and police forces to transnational corporations, now employ people who have the ability to think geographically and who can apply their IT skills to problem-solving. In addition, new applications for GIS are emerging: for example, tourist information services, health monitoring and crime prevention. The technology pervades almost every workplace.

GIS as a tool for geography teachers

In schools and colleges GIS packages can enable students to explore and understand many issues in the geography curriculum. For example, students can examine patterns and features in physical and human environments, determine relationships between them, raise important issues and questions, and offer ways of addressing any problems.

The benefits of using Information and Communications Technology in geographical education has been summarized by the GA/NCET (now BECTa) as student entitlements (GA/NCET 1995). These entitlements can be applied more specifically to the role and potential of GIS in the geography classroom (Figure 15.6). In view of the key developments outlined below, the potential of GIS software as a tool to enhance teaching and learning in Geography should be considered.

- The forthcoming £230 million training programme for school teachers funded by the New Opportunities Fund (Hassell 1999) as part of the government's National Grid for Learning project will provide geography teachers with the opportunities to develop new skills and examine use of ICT afresh.
- The revised qualifications framework for 16–19-year-olds introduced in September 2000 (DfEE 1999) is likely to produce a more fragmented learning programme for many students. Several awarding bodies are examining the possibility of a free-standing introductory qualification in GIS which could be offered alongside AS level qualifications, GNVQ Part Awards and BTec modules.

Students of Geography are entitled to use IT ...	Students can use geographical information systems ...
... to enhance their skills of geographical enquiry	... to examine and analyse data collected through fieldwork
	... to develop important enquiry skills
... to provide access to a wide range of geographical knowledge and information sources	... to investigate vast quantities of information about the characteristics and location of specific places
... to deepen their understanding of environmental and spatial relationships	... to integrate geographical data from a variety of sources to look for patterns and relationships between different features in our environment
... to experience alternative images of people, place and environment	... to get a new perspective on the world by investigating digital maps and images for environmental variables such as relief, land use, transport networks and socio-economic characteristics
... to consider the wider impact of IT on people, place and environment.	... to investigate the most rapidly developing branches of the IT industry and illustrate the vital significance of Geography in understanding and managing the modern world.

Figure 15.6 Students' entitlements in relation to GIS

Source (column one): GA/NCET 1995.

- New specifications for Geography AS/A levels and (in due course) GCSE will include a more explicit reference to the role of ICT in promoting understanding in Geography. GIS software is an ideal tool for addressing IT competencies in the subject.
- All post-16 education will have to address opportunities for Key Skills to be developed. GIS provide a powerful vehicle to develop the IT Key Skill.

As Newcombe (1999) argues, GIS software is also an ideal resource for getting novice teachers started with using Information and Communications Technology in their geography teaching.

GIS in the classroom

Careful thought needs to be given to the most effective methods of introducing GIS into the geography classroom. One approach is to introduce GIS packages through a combination of teacher-demonstrations and small-group activities, with short follow-up revision exercises. Where resources and computer room access arrangements allow, these can be introduced over a period of two to four weeks.

Support for syllabus coverage

There are numerous topics in both GCSE and A-level Geography where GIS provide an appropriate resource to enhance understanding. These include:

- Hydrology – investigating the land-use zones that would be affected by a river flooding.
- Economic geography – identifying a suitable location for a new supermarket from demographic data.
- Biogeography – determining the rate and extent of vegetation destruction from multi-date satellite images.
- Urban geography – examining the spatial relationships between deprivation and crime in part of a city.
- Physical geography – using a digital elevation model to determine the relationship between rock type and relief in an area.
- Development geography – mapping patterns of development in more and less economically developed countries.
- Geomorphology – identifying areas with a high risk of slope erosion in a semi-arid region.

Analysis of fieldwork data

GIS packages are able to capture, manipulate, analyse and display data collected from a variety of sources including field measurement. For example, the location of visitors to a leisure facility in an urban environment can be mapped and compared with existing public transport, or data collected on the environmental quality in a region can be mapped and correlated to a quality of life index derived from census data.

Many GIS packages can import data from spreadsheets or databases, which allow students to utilize past records and examine changes over time.

Independent project work

Many project-work themes, relating to both the physical and human environments, lend themselves to the techniques of data manipulation, query, analysis and presentation available through GIS. Once students have been provided with some initial training in using the GIS software they may be able to use it for mapping and analysis purposes on their own data. Examination boards will always give credit for imaginative and intelligent use of new forms of technology if it genuinely supports geographical enquiry.

Figure 15.7 Contexts for GIS within the geography curriculum

Of course, the approach you use to introduce GIS into your geography teaching will depend on how they relate to the requirements of your school's or college's curriculum and your scheme of work. To get you started, Figure 15.7 outlines a number of contexts where GIS may be introduced within the geography curriculum.[1]

Conclusion

GIS are sets of software tools for capturing, manipulating analysing and presenting geographical data. The combination of a database element for storing information on attributes and a mapping function to display spatial data makes these powerful products especially valuable for examining the patterns that exist within and between geographical phenomena. The potential for using GIS to promote teaching and learning in Geography within schools and colleges is considerable. The changes to the curriculum and qualifications framework offer enhanced opportunities to utilize the GIS products developed specifically for the education market in an effective and meaningful way.

Note

1   The GIS for Teachers website (www.kingston.ac.uk/geog/gis_for_teachers) has been developed by the Kingston Centre for GIS to provide practical resources for schools and colleges. It includes introductory material outlining the principles and applications of GIS, information about curriculum developments relating to GIS, details of suppliers of GIS data and software, and information about forthcoming in-service courses in GIS.

References

DfEE (1999) *Learning to Succeed*, White Paper, London: DfEE.

GA/NCET (now BECTa) (1995) *Geography: A Pupils Entitlement for IT*, Sheffield/Coventry: GA/NCET.

Hassell, D. (1999) 'Will you get some training?', *Teaching Geography* 23(4): 198–9.

Heward, I., Cornelius, S. and Carver, S. (1998) *An Introduction to Geographical Information Systems*, London: Longman.

Newcombe, L. (1999) 'Developing novice teacher ICT competence', *Teaching Geography* 24(3): 128–32.

||| Using presentation packages for collaborative work

Liz Taylor

For some time I completely ignored the Microsoft PowerPoint presentation package[1] icon on my computer screen. However, after watching a television programme 'So what's ICT got to do with my subject?' (Channel 4 1999), I decided to investigate PowerPoint. The television programme included an excellent case study of a Year 7 English class preparing and giving a presentation on a set book. As the students had clearly benefited from the project, I decided to try it out in Geography.

Presentation packages help you plan and design a slideshow, which can then be delivered direct from a computer or printed on to overhead transparencies. (See Rogers 1998 for more detail about using PowerPoint and Hassell 1999 for information about projection hardware.)

The project

After spending a couple of hours familiarizing myself with the package (including experimenting with the range of wonderful backgrounds), I then devised a way of using it with my Year 10 middle- to upper-ability GCSE group. The students are required to undertake a research project on acid rain as part of their GCSE course, and this offered an ideal opportunity for experimenting with PowerPoint.

The project was structured over five one-hour lessons as follows:

- Lessons 1 and 2: setting up the project, research and production of storyboards.
- Lessons 3 and 4: producing and practising the presentations.
- Lesson 5: giving the presentations to the rest of the class.

Preparation

During the first lesson I used PowerPoint to brief the students on the aim of the project and the plan for the next five lessons. To set this up in a geography classroom I had to borrow the data projector[2] from the IT department and link it to my laptop. Using the presentation package in this way gave the students a clear idea of what they were working towards. They were keen to try out the technology.

The collaborative research was organized in a way that will be familiar to most teachers: groups of four students used text- and reference books in class and their own sources for homework to research the project (many students also found infor-

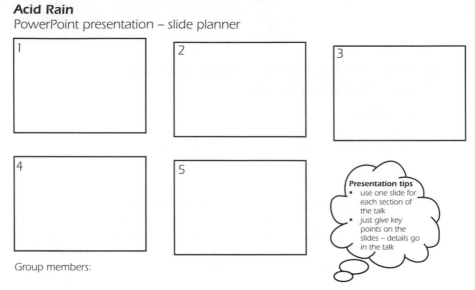

Figure 15.8 *Acid rain – PowerPoint presentation slide planner*

mation on CD-ROM encyclopaedias or the world wide web in their own time). The end-product was a five-minute group presentation on acid rain.

During the second lesson I helped the students plan their presentations and organize their ideas. We used the 'storyboarding' technique – students roughed out the sequence of slides in the same way that a film director may organize key shots for filming (Figure 15.8). Students were offered guidance on the skill of summarizing short points for the slides, so that each one provided a guide for the audience rather than a script for the speaker. To maintain the focus of their presentation, each group was permitted to use a maximum of five slides. We also discussed logical ways of dividing up the topic, e.g. introduction, causes, effects, solutions.

Production

The next two lessons were spent in the computer room using 20 networked computers. Initially, I described the process of making a slide using PowerPoint, then the groups worked at their own pace using the guide sheet (downloadable from the ICT Working Group page on the GA's website: www.geography.org.uk). I encouraged the students to enter the basic text first before experimenting with animation, backgrounds and sounds. Before long the computer screens were displaying psychedelic layouts. The students produced their presentation on PowerPoint, then practised integrating their slides with a verbal commentary. As this was the first time the students had used PowerPoint I encouraged them to experiment; however, I also provided guidance about effective colour schemes and simple layouts in order to focus on the message (Figure 15.9).

Many students incorporated graphics into their presentations by scanning in their own pictures and photographs found on the world wide web. Using the 'image'

1 Starting up
- Open Microsoft PowerPoint (double click on icon)
2 Set up your presentation
- Select 'blank presentation'
- Choose the layout most similar to your title slide (probably the top left one)
- Click OK
- Add your text in the appropriate places
3 Carry on with your slides
- Choose new slide, select the nearest layout, etc.
- Keep going until you have entered text into all 5 slides
- Choose View slide sorter to see all your slides in order
- Double click on any slide to alter it
4 Add a scanned picture from disk
- Insert Picture from file
- Change 'List files of types' to 'All files'
- Find the correct folder and click on your choice of picture insert
- Move the picture by dragging it and/or resize it by dragging a corner
5 Add a common design to your slides
- Format Apply design presentation designs [choose one] apply
6 Customize the background colour and pattern
- Format background click the down arrow choose the colour or fill effects you want apply to all or apply (just that slide)
7 View your show
- Slideshow View show
8 Change the way the slides move from one to another
- Slideshow slide transition choose from the list by clicking on the arrows apply (to that slide) or apply to all
9 Animate the way objects come on screen
- Slideshow preset animation or custom animation
- To see what it will look like, choose Slideshow animation preview
10 Save your presentation
- Put in your disk
- Click on the disk icon near the top of the screen
- Click on down arrow at top, choose 3½" Floppy A, type in file name and click on Save.

Figure 15.9 Handout: 'Using PowerPoint to make a presentation'

search in the search engine Altavista produced good results, but you must ensure that students are aware of copyright issues (Hassell 2000). There are also specially produced CD-ROMs that contain 'Clip art' and copiable images (e.g. the *National Geographic Photo Gallery*).

Each group's slides were saved on to individual floppy disks during the lessons. The finished work was copied on to the laptop's hard drive, so that the groups could access their material quickly during their presentations to the class.

Presentation

Back in the geography classroom for the fifth lesson, the groups were given ten minutes to practise using the laptop to control their presentations. Each group then delivered its presentation to the rest of the class. I assessed each one for presentation and content and gave brief written feedback to the groups. The students were encouraged to offer verbal feedback on the presentations and were impressed by the overall depth of content and professional design. At the end of the lesson we held a whole-class discussion on presentation skills.

Evaluation

What was gained in terms of the students' geographical learning?

At the end of the fifth lesson I was fairly confident that the students had a thorough understanding of acid rain. Sometimes this type of research project can result in students copying out a lot of information but not learning from it. However, in this case, as students were required to summarize key points for the slides and then provide a slightly expanded commentary for the audience, they should have acquired a deeper understanding of the topic. Most groups split their presentation so that each person focused on one aspect of acid rain; the danger here is that individuals learn about only one aspect of the topic. However, they were required to combine the information on to the computer as a group; this element of peer teaching helps to reinforce the learning process. To make sure that the students had all their group's information recorded in their books, they wrote up the case study in a later lesson. In retrospect, a more effective approach would have been to print out and photocopy one of the best sets of slides as handouts and ask the whole class to annotate them with the key information for homework.

Overall, the presentations were lively, varied and detailed, and the frequent use of images connected with key geographical phrases should have helped those who learn visually. However, next time I will devote some time to debriefing the students after each presentation, especially to pick up on some of the new information presented and go over any areas of confusion.

What was gained in terms of Key Skills?

The Key Skills of IT, Communication and Working with Others were vital to the success of this project. The students were accustomed to undertaking collaborative enquiry work and were keen to incorporate the IT element. They learned to use PowerPoint quickly, and the more confident users helped those who were less confident. This peer teaching was especially evident in some of the more sophisticated screen effects; for example, as soon as one student had learned how to produce 'flying bullet points' everyone else wanted them.

The professional appearance of the end-product really motivated the students to work together and keep to their deadlines. Having the slides as a visual aid helped those students who were more reticent to talk in front of the whole class as the display reduced the proportion of attention focused on themselves.

Conclusion

There are a number of advantages to using this approach in teaching and learning Geography. They include:

- deeper learning about the topic through researching, then actively selecting and refining information to enable peer teaching;
- the integration of visual (photographs, maps, graphs), oral and written information, catering for a range of learning styles;
- the development of Key Skills in IT, Communication and Working with Others; and
- the ownership of the learning process by the students and the production of a professional end-product resulting in higher levels of motivation and enjoyment.

Although the advantages listed above are true for any enquiry-based collaborative project, in my experience preparing a presentation has particular value. In particular it encourages students to select and summarize information – processes which require the higher-level skills of synthesis and evaluation. In addition, presentation packages offer an easy way of incorporating visual images, sound, animation and video, all of which are powerful tools in teaching and learning Geography.

Of course, it is not just secondary school students who can get a lot out of using presentation packages. Recently, I have been very impressed by the high standard of presentations produced by PGCE students for an assignment on 'selling' Geography to parents. Using a presentation package gives high-quality results for relatively little effort and, if used well, can benefit teaching and even public relations in Geography – so why not have a go?

Notes

1 Presentation packages: The Microsoft Office suite of software is installed on most school computers and most versions include PowerPoint. However, Lotus or Corel suites also include presentation packages with very similar facilities, and multimedia packages such as Hyperstudio or Illuminatus can be used in a similar way.

2 Data projection: Many schools now have data projectors and so many geography departments have access to them. If you have yet to decide which type to purchase, the BECTa website (www.becta.org.uk) includes a section with information on whole-class teaching with ICT. If you do not have access to a data projector, overhead projector transparencies, produced using a presentation package, look equally effective.

Acknowledgements

The author would like to thank the students of Netherhall School, Cambridge, for permission to reproduce their work in this article.

References

Channel 4 (1999) *ICT on Television*. The whole series is available on video. Visit: www.channel4.com/learning

Hassell, D. (1999) 'Whole-class computer activities', *Teaching Geography* 24(4): 198–9.

—— (2000) 'Developing your own web page', *Teaching Geography* 25(4): 200–1.

Rogers, S. (1998) 'Presentation software', *Teaching Geography* 23(3): 150–1.

Further resources

Altavista: www.altavista.com

National Geographic Photo Gallery CD-ROM. Available from Mindscape Tel: 01444 246333.

3 Geography for the twenty-first century

Some of the issues that are provoking current debate and discussion are the focus for this section. Citizenship, sustainable development and cultural considerations, for instance, are making demands on the geography curriculum and the first four chapters explore some of the ways geographers could or should respond.

Concerns for the future direction of geographical education are articulated in the last two chapters. Linda Thompson presents the 'customer' viewpoint as expressed in a survey conducted in Cheshire to determine young people's learning preferences in Geography. Ashley Kent discusses the 'outdated and inaccurate' images of Geography that still abound, and sets out a call to action from geographers in order to ensure the health of the subject beyond the next curriculum review.

16 Geography and 'race'[1]
John Morgan

Introduction

In recent years there has been a reappraisal of the role that geographical knowledge plays in the reproduction of the wider society. This reappraisal has been linked to an understanding that geographical knowledge is not produced in a vacuum, but reflects broader social and cultural patterns. For example, it is now widely accepted that, as an academic subject, geography played an important role in the projects of imperialism and empire. Peet (1985) suggests how geography lent scientific legitimacy to imperialist ideologies such as environmental determinism that explain why some 'racial' groups were more 'advanced' than others. Hudson (1977) argued that geography 'was vigorously promoted … largely if not mainly to serve the interests of imperialism in its various aspects, including territorial acquisition, economic exploitation, militarism, and the practice of class and race domination'. Many of these ideas found their way into school curriculums and textbooks and formed what might be called the 'Imperial Curriculum'. It is possible to argue that geography's rather unsavoury past was an aberration, and one that is well behind us now. After all, geography as a discipline has undergone a series of 'paradigm shifts', not least of which was the 'new' geography that established the discipline as a 'spatial science'. In addition, the incorporation of the children of immigrants from the New Commonwealth and Pakistan in the period following the Second World War has made teachers and textbook writers aware of the need for representations that are sensitive to different cultures. Generally, it might be argued, the gradual shift in consciousness, which has been brought about in large measure by the struggles of previously excluded groups to be recognized, has been reflected in the ways in which Geography is taught and learned in schools.

To an extent this is true. However, in this chapter I want to adopt a different stance and argue that school Geography still has the potential (if we are not careful) to promote 'racist' ideas (see Gill 1999 for further discussion). As I put it in earlier paper written with David Lambert:

> school geography tends to ignore questions of racialisation, emptying out the racialised meanings attached to processes of economic and social change in favour of a relatively abstract body of knowledge that counts as 'the geography curriculum'.
>
> (Morgan and Lambert 2001)

In order to illustrate this idea I want to discuss a number of themes or topics commonly taught in Geography at Key Stages 3 and 4. I provide short critiques of common ways of teaching about these topics, suggesting where they raise questions about 'racialized' knowledge. The aim is to highlight the subtle, often hidden, ways in which geographical knowledge tends to promote certain views of the world. It is hoped that these critiques can form the basis of 'reconstruction'. Indeed, although the following discussions make reference to examples of published textbooks and resources, these have been chosen because they reflect what I think are broad trends in school Geography rather than because I think they are examples of 'racism' in school Geography.

In selecting the examples to make my argument, I have chosen to focus on areas of the school geography curriculum that, at first glance, would appear to some to have little to do with questions of 'race'. By the end of this paper I hope to have persuaded you that, as geography teachers, we need to reflect upon the origin of ideas and concepts that, in school curriculums and textbooks, are often presented as 'common sense' or 'neutral'.

A theoretical note

It is worth noting the theoretical framework that informs this paper (see Morgan and Lambert 2001 for a fuller discussion). I adopt a 'social constructionist' approach that denies the idea that 'race' exists. Instead, 'race' as a social category exists only through language (this is not to deny the material force that racist ideas can have). From this perspective, geographical knowledge has, in the past and in the present, played its part in the construction of ideas about 'race'. Audrey Kobayashi (1999) provides a succinct statement of what constitutes anti-racism in geography teaching:

> Students need to be firmly theoretically grounded, to develop the concepts they need to analyse a complex social process such as racism. The more important theoretical challenge is to uncover deeply rooted essentialist notions of race, and to clarify the ways in which racialization occurs through social construction. In addition, students need facts, both as a basis for knowledge and to empower them in their anti-racist actions. They need to understand the history of racism in our society, and they need to be able to fix racism in terms of the concrete circumstances of life for racialized people.

Mapping urban spaces

My first examples are drawn from the study of urban structure that forms part of the study of 'settlement' in National Curriculum Geography. It is interesting to note that many textbooks use models and frameworks that have long since lost their currency in the study of urban geography in universities. Indeed, one of the most common ways in which school Geography represents urban geography is through the mapping of the disorder of real cities into imagined 'models' of the city. Thus: 'When we look inside cities our first impression is frequently one of disorder. The layout of buildings, the network of streets and types of land use often seem quite haphazard. However, on closer inspection order does appear' (Raw and Shaw 1996). In many textbooks, the division is typically between central business districts, manufacturing and residential districts: 'But do these areas have a spatial pattern? Geographers think that they have and they have developed a number of simple models to describe the spatial patterns of cities' (Raw and Shaw 1996).

The models most commonly used are based on those proposed by the Chicago School of Sociologists. Some textbooks (especially those written for GCSE courses) go as far as mentioning the names of those geographers (conveniently forgetting to mention that they were sociologists!). For instance, Waugh (1997) notes that the 'zonal' or 'concentric' model is associated with the work of Burgess, whilst the 'sector' model was associated with Hoyt. The distinctive 'zones' or 'sectors' are associated with particular activities and, by implication, particular groups of people. For instance, Taylor (1998) makes the link between the decline of manufacturing and poverty:

> This left inner city factories derelict, and the housing built for the workers was getting very run down. In Britain, many inner city areas were cleared in the 1950s and 1960s, and the people were re-housed in new flats or edge of town estates. Many inner city areas still suffer from lack of employment, poor road access and social problems.

Waugh provides a quite detailed mapping of the characteristics of land use in inner-city areas and on the 'edge of cities'. These land uses are associated with distinctive social and economic groupings:

> Burgess suggested, in his urban model, that the areas of lowest-cost housing were in the inner-city next to the CBD … The difference in the cost of housing has led to two distinctive groupings, both socially and economically, of people … those on low incomes tend to concentrate within the inner-city areas and those on higher incomes group together towards the edge of the city.

Waugh provides a table showing the socio-economic characteristics of people in different parts of the city.

Inner areas
- Elderly people living on low income, no longer with family, looking for cheaper housing.
- Young married couples with little capital and no family.
- Immigrants from overseas, especially those with limited money, education and skills.

Outer areas
- Those with high income now capable of buying their own home in suburbia.
- Those with higher skills and qualifications.
- Parents with a young family wishing for garden, open space and larger house.
- Immigrants who have established themselves over a period of time.

Though I suspect that textbook writers would argue that their accounts of the structure of cities has been necessarily simplified for a young readership, in reality these textbook writers provide a quite complex and detailed mapping of urban space. They are surprisingly exact and detailed in telling students who lives where, and underlying these descriptions are some powerful explanations. This results from a relatively uncritical reading and translation of these 'urban models'. I will consider these in turn.

First, within these textbook accounts there are underlying assumptions about human behaviour. It is assumed that competition for space is inevitable and universal, and that the residential decisions of human beings are based on rational economic knowledge. Thus, culturally specific ideas about competition, invasion and succession are elevated to the status of universal law. Second, the model is presented as a universal theory applicable to any city, when in fact it was actually time-space specific. There is an important issue here about the 'ethnocentricity' of much geographical discourse. Third, the models legitimate capitalist processes of economic competition. Finally, the models contain implicit moral judgements, which geography teachers would have to be very careful to guard against. For example, the whole thrust of the Burgess model as presented in these textbooks is to suggest that the sensible option is to seek to move away from crowded, dense, narrow and poor-quality inner-city environments towards the quiet, less dense, spacious and better-quality urban environments of the suburbs (or, as Burgess called them, the 'clean bright suburbs'). In this way the model contains an 'assimilationist' view of society in which, over time, immigrant groups establish themselves and come to 'fit in' with the norms of the majority population.

The discussion so far has focused on an aspect of school Geography where questions of 'race' are not explicitly raised. They form a 'hidden' aspect of the discourse. In fact, geography textbooks tend to avoid explicit discussions of 'race'. I will now turn to examples of geographical accounts that *do* deal with the issue. For example, *Geography in Place 1* (Raw and Shaw 1996) contains the following account:

> Many western cities have large ethnic minority groups. Leicester is a good example: nearly one in three of the city's population belong to an ethnic minority group. Most of these people are of Indian origin. They first settled in the 1960s and 70s to work in the hosiery and knitting industries. This Asian population is highly concentrated in the inner city. We call this *segregation* and it is typical of many ethnic minorities, in UK cities.
>
> We can explain ethnic segregation in a number of ways. First there are positive reasons: people want to live close to those who share their culture, customs and language, and use local services such as temples, mosques and ethnic food shops found in these areas. Second there are negative reasons, in particular the need to feel safe within a society which may often be hostile to minority groups. In Leicester and other cities with large Asian minorities, like Bradford and Wolverhampton, Asians are often attracted to the inner city because of its affordable terraced housing. As a rule they do not have a tradition of renting housing from the local authority.

David Waugh's account is as follows:

> Figure 9.18 [not included here] lists immigrants as one of the groups more likely to live in the lower-cost housing areas. Questions on the ethnic origins of people living in Britain were first asked in the 1991 Census.
>
> In this census people were asked if they considered themselves to be white, black Caribbean, Black African, Indian, Pakistani, Bangladeshi, Chinese or from another ethnic group. The census showed that 5.5 percent of the UK population was non-white: 2.7 percent southeast Asian, 1.6 percent black and 1.2 percent Chinese. It also revealed that nearly 50 percent of that non-white population had been born in the UK.
>
> With the exception of the Chinese, the 1991 Census confirmed that over two-thirds of each of the major ethnic groups were living in the major conurbations in England. Indeed, the proportion living in conurbations, especially that of Greater London, was continuing to rise.
>
> The census also confirmed that even within conurbations, most ethnic groups were concentrated in inner-city areas. However, different ethnic groups tended to concentrate in different parts of the inner city: e.g. in London, Sikhs concentrate in Southall, Jamaicans (black Caribbeans) in Brixton, Indians in Camden and Bengalis in East London. In other words, each ethnic group segregates itself from other ethnic groups.
>
> An ethnic group will concentrate in an area that it finds to be attractive; that is, where there is affordable housing available, and where there are jobs that suit their skills and culture. Later migrants are likely to join people of their own ethnic group because they share a similar background, e.g. language, colour, religion, customs, diet, education and dress.

Again, these representations of the 'black' community in Britain found in geography textbooks are problematic. True, they attempt to steer away from controversy by sticking to the 'facts' about the distribution of black people in Britain. However, it is their failure to offer plausible explanations that is most worrying, especially when the explanations they do offer are at odds with what many geographers studying this issue suggest. For instance, Susan Smith (1987) argues that patterns of segregation cannot be seen as arising from chance, or just as a result of income differences or low incomes. Instead, segregation has been sustained through the racist assumptions and practices of individuals and government bodies through 'institutional racism'. She shows how central government policies, including the sale of the housing stock, housing legislation, the policies and practices of local authorities, the role of financial institutions such as mortgage lenders and estate agents have all sustained the pattern of racial segregation by restricting black households to inner-city areas. Smith argues that in the 1980s the emergence of the 'New Right' brought with it 'new racism', in which social divisions were explained as a product of cultural difference and individual choice rather than white superiority. In the textbook extracts quoted above, the impression is given that 'segregation' is largely a product of the choices made by immigrant groups (*they* 'choose' to segregate *themselves*). As a result, pupils are denied the opportunity to learn about the structural context in which race thinking develops. It is difficult to avoid the conclusion that this is an example of how ideas expressed in geography textbooks reflect and contribute to broader discourses about race and racism that exist and flourish beyond the classroom (for recent accounts of the geography of racial segregation in Britain see Peach (1996) and Phillips (1998)).

My final example in this discussion of how the issue of 'race' is treated in 'urban' geography is of a coverage that seeks to pay more attention to the issue. It seeks to adopt a positive tone, whilst explicitly recognizing the continued existence of prejudice and racism. *Geography and Change 14–16* has a section entitled 'Changing communities'.

> The population of cities in Britain is made up of many local communities. These communities include people who have moved to the city from other parts of Britain or from other countries. People in all these communities have the same basic needs of shelter, food, clothing, warmth, employment and security.
>
> (Flint *et al.* 1996)

This is an interesting textual manoeuvre. The focus in this paragraph is on the basic 'sameness' of all people. Britain is made up of communities, and these communities are the same whether they are made up of people from Britain or elsewhere. The next section goes on to discuss Britain's black and Asian population. It provides some historical background and relates the immigration of people from the NCWP to the employment shortage in the economy. Their housing choices are explained through reference to the structural issues of housing shortages and racism:

> Housing in these cities was in short supply and no extra provision was made for the newcomers, so many of the immigrants and their families were forced to live in run-down, overcrowded conditions. They also faced prejudice both at work and in the community, partly because most British people knew little about the newcomers, their countries of origin and their culture.

The subsequent text does not gloss over continuing difficulties, but does offer a more positive picture of race relations: 'A number of suburbs in large cities have become multi-racial with generally better conditions and there have also been a few changes in the workplace to try and prevent discrimination'. Here we have an example that, within the confines of a textbook format, adopts a 'positive image' approach. Whilst the text does seek to provide a balanced and more historical account of 'race relations', pupils might be asked to consider in a more critical way the notion of 'community' as used in this account.

Migration

Any discussion of 'race' in relation to school Geography should consider the question of migration, not least because the issue of 'asylum seekers' has been elevated to a high status in contemporary political debates. Within school Geography, migration is studied is part of the triad of economy–settlement–population. In terms of the approach taken, study of migration in school Geography has traditionally been concerned with the identification of general 'laws' or generalizations about the

behaviour of groups of people. An important concept is that of 'push–pull' and identifying the factors that lead people to move from one place to another. There is much
potential for the study of data sets (aided by the availability and use of ICT). These
general statements about population movement tend to be framed in terms of individual choice. Thus, where theory is introduced, this is based on models that stress
rational choices and individual agency.

This is, of course, a simplification, since the 'softer edge' of human geography,
sometimes explicitly called 'humanistic' geography, seeks to recognize the movement of people as a lived experience, encompassing hard material imperatives and
contradictory cultural stories. The advantage of this approach is that it avoids the
temptation of understanding population movements as a problem to be contained.
In liberal versions of school Geography, the focus is on accommodation or the recognition that there needs to be a respect for all groups. The problem with such an
approach, however, is that it tends to rely on a language that is inherently problematic, with notions of 'hosts' and 'migrants', 'majorities and minorities', 'guests' and
'illegals'. In all cases, newcomers are seen as a problem demanding a solution. A
major problem with constructing our understanding of migration in this way is that
it tends to draw distinctions between 'us' (who are already here) and 'them' (who
want to come to 'our' country).

This tendency can be seen in the section 'People on the move' in *People, Cities and
the Countryside* (Burgess and Tapsfield 1990). The section 'Out and In' starts by
defining the terms 'emigrant' and 'immigrant', before informing the reader that the
section is concerned with the patterns of emigration from Jamaica and immigration
into Britain. There is a map that shows the main destinations of Jamaican emigrants
prior to and after the 1940s. The text explains that Jamaicans have been leaving their
island in large numbers since the 1860s. The photograph shows a steep-sided valley
that is inhospitable for farmers, and pupils are asked to look at the photo to find
reasons why the 'rapidly growing' Jamaican population found it difficult to make a
living from farming in this area. There is an account of one migrant's experience of
coming to Britain. The text then goes on to describe UK government policy towards
migrants ('To be an immigrant you must ask to be accepted in another country').

The following section ('Making a new life') considers the experience of Jewish
migrants in Britain, focusing on their choice of location upon arrival and subsequent
'dispersal'. In explaining the reasons for the existence of distinct 'Jewish areas', there is
a balance between positive reasons (e.g. traditions) and negative reasons (e.g. racism).

I think there is much to be recommended in this approach. The use of original
sources is useful. However, the questions provided are generally closed and lead
students to what the authors consider to be acceptable answers. The main problem,
as far as I can see, is the way in which the text addressed 'immigrants' as 'others' to be
measured and observed by the white reader:

> We have seen that Jews have lived in Britain for a long time, and also that many
> of them wish to retain their strict religious traditions and customs. Newspapers,
> TV, radio, our friends, MPs and lots of others often talk about such groups as
> 'ETHNIC GROUPS'.

A number of issues are raised here. First, there is the question of representation in such textbooks. As I have suggested, the tone of the textbook account is such that the textbook author and assumed reader are 'white'. In order to make this address problematic, we need only ask the question of how this text might be received by a child who identifies him or herself as Jamaican or Jewish? Second, the text makes it clear that people 'belong' to certain places – they have origins and 'homes'. In the case of the Jamaicans, the text suggests, there is always the possibility of return to the homeland. Third, and closely linked to this, is the idea that there are people who have distinct 'cultures' which they seek to preserve and maintain. Whilst this may be true of some people, it does not necessarily correspond with the experience of young people in multicultural societies such as Britain, where there are strong trends towards 'cultural mixing' and 'borrowing'. Indeed, a better place to start might be to ask the question of how migration has led to notions of 'hybridity', especially in relation to popular cultural forms such as music.

Whose country?

My final example is the way in which issues of 'race' are tied up with the representation of rural space. I want to argue that, although issues of 'race' seem far removed from the neutral topic of changing settlements, a more critical reading raises important questions about whose geography is being represented in school Geography. Consider the following example from a recent textbook, which has a section about the growth of Hilton village. The section starts by asking two questions:

1   Why are people protesting about building in the countryside?
2   Why can't people build houses just where they want to?

The context for the example is the UK government's estimate that an extra 4.4 million new homes will be needed in England by 2011. The textbook explains this need as the outcome of changes in the population structure: 'People are living longer, and more people are living alone … In addition, each year 90,000 people move away from towns and cities to live in the country'.

After a discussion of the concepts of 'greenfield' and 'brownfield' sites, the section discusses the tensions that development brings between the 'locals' and the 'newcomers'. Alongside colour photographs of the 'older' and 'newer' housing in the village, sociological pen-portraits of the long-standing residents of Hilton and the newcomers who 'have a rather different lifestyle' are provided. The focus is on the changes that have taken place in the village, linked to transport, and services such as the post office and school. Having considered the changes that are taking place in the village of Hilton, the section provides some cartoon-characters that represent the views of some of the villagers. The final activity is an enquiry that asks pupils for their ideas on how they would like to see the community develop: 'To create a settlement that does not split the community into "locals" and "newcomers", but which tries to keep the existing community spirit'.

An important part of their brief is the preservation of the existing countryside. This example is typical of the way in which settlement in rural areas is treated in many school geography textbooks. In many accounts, there is an underlying theme of 'tradition' versus 'modernity', which is variously expressed in the binaries of old/new, nature/culture, and country/city. Though these textbooks resolve the tensions in different ways, it is important to note how these are tied to broader cultural ideas about the nature of rural areas. Lola Young notes that much of the concern about cities and the countryside is to do with the rate of rapid, visible change. She argues that much of the concern about new developments such as housing, telegraph poles, roads and so on is less to do with what these are and more to do with the meanings attached to them. These developments are not in themselves a problem but signify change, something that unsettles and disrupts, serving to remind people of 'the differences between an imaginary ideal past and a demonised present' (Young and Pollard 1995).

This 'imaginary ideal past' tends to feed into a 'national environmental ideology' which associates rural areas with the nation and ideas about national belonging. After all, the word 'country' has the double meaning of both the 'countryside' and the 'nation':

> the countryside, as it is represented by those who have a privileged place within it, is the essence of Englishness ... it is those parts of national territory that are pictured as stable, culturally homogenous, historically unchanging which are taken to represent the nation in nationalistic discourse.
>
> (Sibley 1995)

These words raise alarm bells when we begin to consider the narratives of change and decline which are found in geography textbooks about changing settlement, especially in the light of the argument, made by a number of geographers in recent years, that the countryside is popularly perceived as a 'white' landscape: 'Representations of the countryside are controlled by white (mainly male and middle-class) people. They construct images reflecting a concern with the reproduction of a mythical and nostalgic white heritage' (Aygeman and Spooner 1997). The role played by schooling in reproducing this rural heritage has been noted. The argument is that people of colour are effectively written out of rural history, and denied a similar sense of attachment to the countryside (and, by implication, to the nation).

Mapping moral geographies

In all the examples discussed in this paper, I have drawn attention to the ways in which school Geography performs a 'moral mapping'. What I mean by this is that school geographical knowledge has the potential to include and exclude perspectives, and contains subtle messages about who belongs where. An important part of my argument is that, if we as geography teachers fail to consider the ways in which geographical narratives found in school serve to locate pupils, then we risk closing down their range of meanings at the very moment when we are asked to prepare children for a changing world. There is little space to develop these ideas further here, but a preliminary conclusion would suggest that geography teachers at all levels need to think carefully about whose geography is taught in schools, who constructed that knowledge and why, and whether there are other constructions of geographical knowledge that might better serve the interests of the students we teach.

Note

1   This chapter could just as easily be written about geography and 'gender' or 'class'. The important point it tries to make is that what counts as 'geographical knowledge' is never 'innocent'. It has been produced by particular people under particular circumstances, and, as teachers, we need to be aware of this.

References

Agyeman, J. and Spooner, R. (1997) 'Ethnicity and the rural environment', in P. Cloke and J. Little (eds) *Contested Countryside Cultures: Otherness, Marginalisation and Rurality*, London: Routledge.

Burgess, D. and Tapsfield, A. (1990) *People, Cities and the Countryside*, London: Collins.

Flint, D., Punnett, N. and Flint, C. (1996) *Geography and Change 14–16*, London: Hodder and Stoughton.

Gill, D. (1999) 'Geography', in D. Hill and M. Cole (eds) *Promoting Equality in Secondary Schools*, London: Cassell.

Hudson, B. (1977) 'The new geography and the new imperialism', *Antipode* 9: 12–19.

Kobayashi, A. (1999) '"Race" and racism in the classroom: some thoughts on unexpected moments', *Journal of Geography* 98: 176–8.

Morgan, J. and Lambert, D. (2001) 'Geography, "race" and education', *Geography* 86(3): 235–46.

Peach, C. (1996) 'Does Britain have ghettoes', *Transactions of the Institute of British Geographers* 21(1): 216–35.

Peet, R. (1985) 'The origins of environmental determinism', *Annals of the Association of American Geographers* 75: 309–33.

Phillips, D. (1998) 'Black minority ethnic concentration, segregation and dispersal in Britain', *Urban Studies* 35: 1681–702.

Raw, M. and Shaw, S. (1996) *Geography in Place 1*, London: Collins.

Sibley, D. (1995) *Geographies of Exclusion*, London: Routledge.

Smith, S. (1987) 'Residential segregation: an example of English racism?', in P. Jackson (ed.) *Race and Racism: Essays in Social Geography*, London: Allen and Unwin.

Taylor, L. (1998) *Population and Settlement*, London: Hodder and Stoughton.

Waugh, D. (1997) *The UK and Europe*, Windsor: Nelson.

Young, L. and Pollard, I. (1995) 'Environmental images and imaginary landscapes', *Soundings* 1 (Autumn): 99–110.

17 Geography and Citizenship
Stephanie Turner

Introduction

Traditionally geography teachers have taught about planning, environmental issues and global citizenship. They have raised awareness, developed attitudes and encouraged responsible behaviour. With Curriculum 2000 the part played by geographers in citizenship education is acknowledged, and geographers are well placed to take on the whole of the citizenship curriculum. When geographers deliver Citizenship, it will need to be explicit in order to satisfy Ofsted.

Some examples of Geography that are also relevant to Citizenship include the study of the local area, local environment and local community. Geographers encourage responsible action, such as developing a school environmental policy or taking part in recycling schemes. The links between local and global are demonstrated and participation in Local Agenda 21 is encouraged. The role of voluntary bodies is explained; education officers and resources contribute to learning Geography and Citizenship. There is an appreciation of world problems such as population growth and the uneven distribution of food, water and other resources. Planning issues are a vehicle for much Geography at local and national levels. An appreciation of location, which can so often be a prerequisite to understanding, is firmly grounded in Geography. Geographical enquiry methods are eminently suitable to Citizenship, which often begins with research.

Professor Crick in his report (1998) defines citizenship education as social and moral responsibility, political literacy and community involvement. It is the way these three themes are inter-related that distinguishes and defines Citizenship. Aspects of Citizenship that may enhance Geography include discussions, debates and decision-making, all tools that will be useful in Geography. Decision-making and how the system works in the local council, in parliament and in world bodies are relevant for geographers. Human rights feature in both subjects, and understanding of rights and corresponding responsibilities are valuable for both. The allocation of resources and how the media present information again apply equally.

Citizenship at Key Stage 3 has three strands:

1 Knowledge and understanding about becoming informed citizens
2 Developing skills of enquiry and communication
3 Developing skills of participation and responsible action.

Geography contributes to all of these and enables Citizenship to be developed from existing teaching within schools.

The National Curriculum documents for Geography and Citizenship (DfEE/ QCA 1999a 1999b) both suggest how Citizenship may be integrated into geography teaching. Linda Thompson (2000) has provided background information on the introduction of Citizenship and its relationship to Geography, and help with curriculum planning. The initial guidance to schools (QCA 2000) advises that Citizenship will be delivered through discrete citizenship provision, through the whole-school ethos, and through other subjects including Geography.

> *Geography*: topical issues concerning environment, sustainable development, population, economic activity, development, resources – at scales from local to global; interdependence of places and the idea of global citizenship; skills of geographical enquiry, including communication and analysing and evaluating evidence.
>
> (QCA 2000)

Citizenship: A Scheme of Work for Key Stage 3 (QCA and DfES 2001) contains material of interest to geographers including:

- Unit 10: Citizenship and Geography: Debating a global issue. (Is the Amazon rainforest being developed or destroyed?)
- Unit 18: Developing your school grounds.
- Opportunites for developing Citizenship through Geography (subject leaflet).
- Getting involved: extending opportunities for pupil participation (booklet of ideas).

A recent publication, *Citizenship through Secondary Geography*, edited by David Lambert and Paul Machon (2001) provides explanations of key ideas in Citizenship, the pitfalls to avoid in teaching Citizenship through Geography and many practical teaching suggestions.

Citizenship being taught through Geography is here illustrated by the following case studies:

1 Valuing the school environment
2 Developing a school environmental policy
3 Planning in the local environment
4 Global citizenship.

Valuing the school environment

Introduction

An important aspect of Citizenship is playing a part in the local community and caring for the local environment. Students may begin by studying and caring for the environment of the school. Traditionally, geographers have made use of the school grounds as a site for weather-recording instruments and a resource for fieldwork. However, there are opportunities to do much more: to survey and map the school buildings and grounds, to consult pupils in other classes, to plan and implement changes and to develop and monitor a policy for the school environment. Even a concrete playground can be transformed by designing and painting an accurate sundial where a student's shadow can be

Figure 17.1 Children in a school nature garden putting the finishing touches to a statue they have made from recycled materials. (Copyright: Nelson Thornes/Chris Kelly)

used to tell the time throughout the year, as Tam Giles explains in *Playground Sundials* (n.d.). Figure 17.1 shows students putting the finishing touches to one of a number of life-sized statues they have made from recycled materials for their school grounds.

Consultation

Consultation is increasingly encouraged in our society where organizations consult their members, companies consult their customers and local authorities consult residents on their local plans. The best way to learn about consultation is to take part. Students may be encouraged to respond to any local consultations taking place. They can also conduct a consultation themselves.

In one school, students undertook a playground survey to coincide with planned maintenance work at the school. Groups of students drafted short questionnaires,

Figure 17.2 *Children in a school nature garden planting one of the many trees for which they have raised funds. A security fence encircles the school grounds to deter vandalism. (Copyright: Nelson Thornes/ Chris Kelly)*

evaluated them and voted on the best features for a consultation. To help ensure the success of the consultation a small pilot survey of one class was undertaken, as happens in official consultations.

Fellow students in other classes were asked:

- what they most valued about their surroundings
- what they would most like to change
- to rank a list of proposed changes.

As it was impractical to consult every student in the school, some sort of sample was needed, again as often happens in consultations. Students were asked to consider the following questions:

- How many students from each class?
- How to ensure they represent the views of the whole class?

- Can co-operation be guaranteed or is it always necessary to have a prize draw?
- Who else needs to be included: headteacher, caretaker, school council, school governors?

The results of the consultation were analysed and displayed graphically to inform the rest of the school. The school was able to make minor changes to the playground when resurfacing work took place. There was increased planting, including a willow tree structure incorporating some seating. In Figure 17.2 students are planting one of many trees for which they have raised the funds. A security fence encircles the school grounds to deter vandals, an aspect of Citizenship worthy of discussion.

Planning changes

Another school used London Wildlife Trust's *Create a School Wildlife Garden* (Turner 1996), a planning-for-real resource, to plan changes to the school grounds. Groups of students made the case for different designs, then voted for their preferred design and discussed amalgamating ideas from several groups. Discussion, reasoning and negotiating skills were developed. Pupils were encouraged to reflect on what they were learning in Citizenship, in Geography and the overlap between the two.

Funding the changes

While it might be possible to afford minor changes from planned maintenance and to undertake some of the work with the help of older students and supportive parents, it is likely that finance will be needed. Geographers are used to dealing with economically developed and developing areas, reflecting the uneven distribution of wealth and poverty. Citizenship requires that students become financially literate. One way to achieve this is to involve students in costing and in raising the funds for school grounds changes.

Establishing the costs should not be difficult and students can be encouraged to research catalogues and to seek quotations for works. Raising the funds is a more daunting task, but again a reflection of community projects. Possible sources of funds include:

- sponsored event – walk, silence, read
- school event – performance, demonstration, fête
- Parent/Teacher Association
- school governors or allocation from school funding or school council
- local companies
- voluntary bodies, especially environmental charities such as Learning through Landscapes, local Wildlife Trusts or Groundwork Trusts
- local charitable trusts.

If students are to raise the money themselves, then you may wish to encourage them to donate a proportion of the funds to a charity of their choice. This may encourage support for their fund-raising campaign and educate students in considering others less fortunate than themselves. Grant-giving bodies issue guidelines and are usually willing to assist applicants. Even if funding is not secured, students will learn from the experience not just financial realities, but also something of the voluntary sector in society.

The local paper may be willing to publicize your campaign to raise funds for developing the school grounds, and to publish progress reports. Again the part played by the media in society is an important aspect of Citizenship. Geographers have often used topical events, and the reporting of them, to enliven their teaching.

In the school discussed on p. 249, students were helped by London Wildlife Trust, a conservation charity, to secure £2,000 from a local charitable trust to develop a tiny wildlife garden, including a small pond, in a corner of the playground.

Recording the changes

It is recommended that students keep a record of changes, to reinforce the learning process. They should record the initial consultation, the decision-making process, the planning, costing, funding, implementation and the celebration of the result. 'Before and after' photographs and comments will help remind students of what they have achieved. It is important to celebrate the opening of the new garden, to thank those who have supported the class in their project and those who have helped fund it, and to congratulate the students themselves who have persevered with a long and demanding project. Students can send a press release to the local paper inviting a reporter to the opening event. Alternatively, a press release and photograph can be sent afterwards to publicize the good work. Literacy, Citizenship and Geography are combined in raising the self-esteem of students.

Caring for the school environment

Students who have been involved with the planning and implementation of the new garden will have ownership of the garden and should be encouraged to care for it. Students can draw up a policy for the care and use of the garden. Ideally, the care of the garden will be part of the planned maintenance of the school grounds. Failing that, the more green-fingered students may be encouraged to volunteer time to maintain the garden, which should be low-intervention maintenance to preserve the area for wildlife. All should be encouraged to observe the wildlife, the changes to the plants, the insects, butterflies and birds and the evidence of small mammals. Students are observing the wildlife of the pond in Figure 17.3. The area can soon become a resource for the whole curriculum. Sharing it with other students in other classes can encourage good Citizenship.

Avoiding litter in and around school is an ongoing and lowly task, but a first step in caring for the environment. Participating in the Eco-schools scheme is also strongly recommended. Eco-schools will send schools a free copy of their handbook which provides a structure for shcools to follow and resources to support teachers. Schools have developed other possibilities, ranging from a vegetable garden to a school allotment. Produce can be cooked and eaten, or sold. A herb garden or a sensory garden may be a smaller, more manageable project. The opportunities for Citizenship and Geography, as well as other subjects, are still there.

Figure 17.3 Children observing and studying wildlife in the school pond. (Copyright: Nelson Thornes/Chris Kelly)

Developing a school environmental policy

Introduction

Caring for the school environment described above is a good preparation for developing a school environmental policy. The aim of the policy is for the school to behave in an environmentally friendly way and for the behaviour of the school to reflect the curriculum being taught. As developing a policy involves learning by participating and persuading others to become involved, then it is highly relevant to the citizenship curriculum. One way to develop a policy is as a series of topics, such as energy, water, recycling and purchasing policies, which can then be amalgamated into a school environmental policy. It may be possible to gain inspiration from existing environmental policies, such as those of companies, local authorities or voluntary organizations.

Energy

This is a popular starting point, because saving energy will also save money and this can provide an incentive for action in addition to studying. In one school, students researched the school's energy consumption from copies of its electricity bills, and were surprised by the costs involved. They obtained information from the energy-supply company, the local authority energy-saving department and a local voluntary body encouraging energy conservation. They surveyed the school buildings to identify where saving could be made. They designed posters to remind fellow students to switch off lights and to close doors and windows.

It was necessary to monitor consumption throughout the year to establish what savings were being made. The school itself also sought advice on modifying its heating and lighting to save energy in its three-storey Victorian building.

This project on energy was linked to work in Geography on finite resources, and on forms of renewable energy: solar, wind, tide and geothermal energy. For Citizenship there was behaving responsibly to conserve resources and participating in improvements for the benefit of the whole school community. There was experience of persuading others to change their behaviour and to co-operate, and the encouragement that the money saved could be invested in further energy-saving measures.

Water

Geographers teach about the water cycle and about water supply. They contrast areas of the world that suffer from drought with those which suffer from flooding. There is now awareness of climate change, and the belief that global warming will bring rises in sea level and more flooding of low-lying areas. Large dams to store water in reservoirs change environments and lead to conflicts downstream, and cause controversy whenever they are proposed.

To bring things closer to home, students studied the school's water supply, establishing consumption from the school's water bills. Students researched how much water is used, how much it costs and where potential saving could be made. Seeking the whole school's support followed on from the work on energy. Though the monetary saving may not be so great, behaving as responsible and active citizens will enhance learning. Again there were opportunities to enlist the support of voluntary bodies and statutory ones such as the Environment Agency.

Recycling

Linking to work on finite resources, students can research their own and the school's use of resources that can be recycled, especially paper. Students could investigate local authority recycling schemes to see if the school can participate. Alternatively, the school could become the focus for community recycling schemes.

In some areas collection of high-grade white waste paper from schools and businesses results in a small profit for the schools, though not the businesses. The aim should be responsible behaviour and school and local community participation, rather than to make a profit. If funds are raised, then students should decide, in a democratic manner, how to spend them on improving the school environment.

Purchasing policy or consuming

Students can research environmentally friendly products, of which recycled paper is probably the most obvious. They can look at their own and the class's purchasing habits. Is it possible to purchase locally produced goods to save transport costs and support the local community? Is it desirable to buy nationally made goods to protect jobs and working conditions? What are the dangers of purchasing goods from abroad, from trainers produced in sweatshop conditions to exotic foods and flowers which export water that is badly needed in those countries? You may also be brave enough to tackle the ethical and environmental issues involved in school drinks machines in particular and fast food in general.

Responsible global citizenship is the aim, with the realization that decisions taken locally affect what happens globally. 'Act locally, think globally' is the slogan of Agenda 21, the programme for sustainable development agreed at the Earth Summit at Rio de Janeiro in 1992. In this country Agenda 21 is being implemented through local government. There is a Local Agenda 21 Co-ordinator in your authority whose remit is to advise citizens, including students, on how they may become involved. He or she may be willing to visit your school to work with students. Alternatively, your students may be able to join in a local youth environmental forum.

Conclusion

Studying the topics above has provided the building blocks for a school environmental policy. An outline policy used successfully by schools includes:

- To care for the school buildings and grounds
- To conduct a regular environmental audit of the school
- To conserve energy
- To conserve water
- To recycle paper, glass, cans, and food waste
- To purchase environmentally friendly products
- To help others to learn the importance of caring for the environment
- To take part in local community environmental initiatives.

The development of one school environmental policy is shown in Figure 17.4.

Students should consider the implementation and monitoring of the policy. All members of the school community need to be involved. Questions to consider include:

- How can the rest of school be informed and the policy be promoted to them?
- How will it be implemented?
- Who will monitor the implementation?
- How can the policy be updated in the light of changing circumstances?
- Is it necessary to set up a school environmental forum or environmental action group, or is this a matter for the school council or one of its sub-committees?

A school environmental policy can be the foundation of integrating Citizenship and sustainable development into the whole school through Geography. It will amply repay the investment of time and effort to get it established. There are several publications and voluntary bodies to help with the task (see list on p. 261–3).

Planning in the local environment

Geographers make use of local planning issues to enhance their teaching of Geography, and teachers of Citizenship are beginning to see their value for engaging students' interest in matters affecting their community. Land-use planning is highly developed in this country, a consequence of the relative shortage of land in these densely populated islands and the conflicting demands of different uses and users.

Figure 17.4 Developing a school environmental policy. A boy summarizes the policy developed by the class. (Copyright: Nelson Thornes/Chris Kelly)

For geographers the advantages of teaching about land-use planning include:

- Land-use planning is spatial: it relates what is happening to precise locations.
- It is local, relating to a particular local authority.
- It involves change and therefore opinions about the best way forward or even about whether to change at all.
- It should be topical and relevant to today's students.

For teaching Citizenship, land-use planning offers pupils opportunities to:

- consider events happening within the local community
- study changes which are subject to local democratic process
- study local plans, with the help of the planning officer

Figure 17.5 *Children visiting a council planning department. The Planning Officer explains the importance of drawing up plans. (Copyright: Nelson Thornes/Chris Kelly)*

- attend local council meetings where plans are being discussed
- discuss, debate and decide
- participate in local decision-making.

Local authorities prepare local plans, and county plans or district plans or both. These designate broad zones for different land uses such as residential, retail, commercial, industrial and, crucially, areas to be protected from development and preserved as open space. The Local Plan consists of a map and a document of policies, and is available in local libraries and in Planning Departments of local authorities. Members of the public can view their Local Plan, and it may be possible to take a whole class to the Planning Department by arrangement. In Figure 17.5, the Planning Officer is explaining the local plans to the students.

Householders and businesses wishing to make changes to their property apply to their local council for planning permission, which is decided on the basis of how the proposed development accords with the existing local plan. The Local Plan is subject to almost constant revision, a long-winded process, since there is much consultation of drafts and an Examination in Public. Local authorities usually welcome interest and participation in the planning process.

For the teaching of Geography and Citizenship, it is the proposals for change that provide opportunities for learning. Any change offers possibilities for gathering evidence, discussion, disagreement and weighing the balance of advantages and disadvantages. New development – a housing estate, an out-of-town supermarket, a bypass or other new road, even the erection of a mobile phone mast – will provide views for and against.

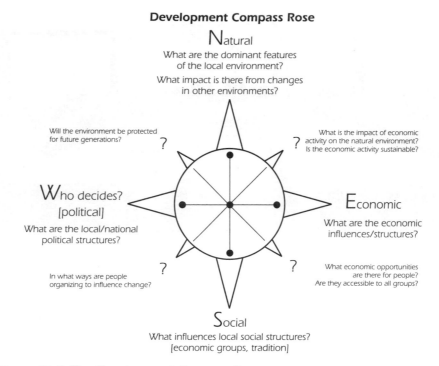

Figure 17.8 The Development Compass Rose

Source: Adapted from DEC Birmingham and DEC South Yorkshire 1992.

Global citizenship

Introduction

Geography students study a range of different places, at different scales and at varying stages of development. They are therefore well placed to study global citizenship. Becoming a responsible global citizen involves learning what it is like to live in other parts of the world, and developing an understanding of how decisions taken locally affect what happens globally. This study looks at what resources are available to help teachers with this work and how they can avail themselves of help provided by people and organizations working in this field.

Development education

There is a long tradition of development education, which precedes environmental education and the more recent education for sustainable development. Geographers have been at the forefront of development education, working for education to eliminate poverty and unfairness, and for an accurate understanding of life in developing countries, rather than the simplistic and stereotypical picture sometimes presented. Many counties and large cities have Development Education Centres (DECs), which provide resources and people to help teachers and students, and which involve teachers and students in education projects. The

Development Education Association in London co-ordinates the work of the development education centres and can provide information of your nearest centre (see Further resources p. 261–63).

Development Education Compass Rose

Figure 17.8 shows the Development Education Compass Rose first developed by the DECs in Birmingham and South Yorkshire in a project supported by UNICEF UK, and published in *It's Our World Too* (1992). The Compass Rose provides a framework of key questions about a place:

- **N**atural – What are the main features of the local environment?
- **E**conomic – What are the economic influences?
- **S**ocial – What influences local social structures?
- **W**ho decides? – What is the local and national political structure?

The relationship between the main points is shown by the questions on the diagonals. The Compass Rose works best if you apply it first to the familiar local environment, and may raise new questions and a different way of looking at things. It emphasizes the importance of the political decisions that are taken about places and integrates Citizenship and Geography. It can then be applied to any and every place being studied, perhaps using one of the many photo packs produced by DECs, international charities, the Geographical Association and education publishers. When the Compass Rose questions have been applied to a number of places in different parts of the world, then the similarities can be discerned. People in different countries, at different stages of development, face similar situations and problems, though the solutions may vary. Students can design their own framework of new questions, preferably with the directional titles, to further their understanding of global similarities, differences and inter-relatedness.

UN Convention on the Rights of the Child

The United Nations made a Convention on the Rights of the Child in 1989, which the UK ratified in 1991. All the countries of the world have signed up to the Convention except two: Somalia and the USA. It is a long document of 54 articles, many saying how adults will look after children. It can be summarized as:

- Provision – adults should provide for all children's needs
- Protection – adults should protect children from all harm and danger
- Participation – children are entitled to take part in decisions made about them, including being told about this Convention.

Though much of the Convention has been incorporated into our laws and it is an important aspect of Citizenship, it is not explicit in the National Curriculum. UNICEF has produced a short guide to the Convention in plain English and a number of other useful publications for teachers (see contact details in Further resources on p. 263).

Geography teachers using the Convention to teach Citizenship will want to link rights to responsibilities, and encourage students to understand that every right has a corresponding responsibility. UNICEF has also produced a musical on children's rights, *Thursday's Child*, which covers all the main articles of the Convention (UNICEF 1999). It includes a copy of the 'Wants and Needs Game', a set of cards with needs (from food, shelter, someone to take care of them, to education and freedom to practise one's own religion) and wants (including the latest consumer goods), and blank cards for the students to define themselves. Groups of students may rank the cards and justify their choices. The teacher then introduces levels of austerity, to force the less necessary choices to be discarded. This is then repeated until basic needs have been distinguished from mere wants. Jonathan Hart describes using this and other games at St Christopher School in Letchworth (Hart 2000). The UN Convention provided a framework for a whole term's work.

Organizations for global citizenship

In addition to DECs, the Development Education Association and UNICEF, there are other non-governmental organizations (NGOs) that provide an education service for teachers and students. OXFAM, Christian Aid, Save the Children, ActionAid, World Wide Fund for Nature (WWF) and others are active in promoting development in the less economically developed parts of the world. Their resources are based on work in the field, and are accurate, topical and relevant and a boon to busy teachers. All the organizations mentioned produce catalogues of resources for primary and secondary teachers. Other organizations with a campaigning focus, such as Friends of the Earth or Greenpeace, have information leaflets on a range of topics. It is helpful if only one letter from the class is sent to each organization, to minimize demands on the organizations. The NGOs also have websites, where students may search for information.

The NGOs also provide Education Officers to visit schools and work with students, often free of charge. Education is separate from fund-raising and is concerned with raising awareness rather than raising funds. It works best when teachers work with an Education Officer to plan a contribution to the geography and citizenship lessons. Education officers will tailor their work to your requirements and answer students' questions. For Geography, first-hand information about places being studied, their problems and the role of development agencies can make an invaluable contribution to students' understanding.

For Citizenship, students may appreciate the role of voluntary bodies in promoting development as well as providing aid when disaster strikes. They may contrast the work of the NGOs with that of governments and understand the independence of such bodies. Another important aspect is the work done by volunteers both overseas and in this country. Indeed the person working with your class may be giving their time to an organization they support. Students can explore the different ways it is possible to volunteer and support organizations other than by fund-raising.

Conclusion

As the case studies show, Geography in school, in the local community or when learning about distant places, has much to contribute to Citizenship. Studying the local community involves discussing, debating, deciding, participating and consulting. Comparisons can be made between the role of the school council and that of the local council and of parliament. Land-use planning offers the opportunity to consider local environmental issues, study local plans with the help of the planning officer and to take part in public consultation processes. Global citizenship links local and global, and provides opportunities to study fair trade and other aspects of globalization, including the responsibilities of citizens in the developed world. It also considers the role of international bodies such as the United Nations and voluntary organizations.

There are a number of voluntary bodies promoting and assisting with citizenship education, including the Institute for Citizenship, the Citizenship Foundation, Community Service Volunteers (CSV) and School Councils UK. The Institute for Citizenship is producing materials, with a range of partners, including books, CD-ROMs and online resources under the overall title *Activate!* (2001). One case study is 'Citizenship for Sustainability', which looks at consumption, food and sustainable communities. In June 2001 a new professional body, the Association for Citizenship Teaching (ACT), was inaugurated. ACT aims to promote citizenship teaching and learning by developing and implementing education programmes, organizing meetings and publishing a journal, *Teaching Citizenship*, three times a year. Contact details for these organizations are given at the end of the chapter.

This chapter has shown the importance of education in Citizenship for students in the twenty-first century and the valuable part that geographers play in integrating Citizenship into their geography teaching. There is a wealth of support for teachers from QCA and DfES; from professional organizations such as the Geographical Association and ACT; and from voluntary bodies working in the fields of citizenship and development.

Acknowledgements

The author thanks the Institute for Citizenship and Nelson Thornes for permission to include the photographs from *Citizenship for Primary Schools: Teacher's Resource Book and Photo Pack for Years 5–6*.

The photographs were taken by Chris Kelly at Columbia School, Tower Hamlets; by Radburn School, Letchworth Garden City; and of pupils from Stonehill School, Letchworth Garden City at North Hertfordshire District Council. Thank you to all involved.

Further resources

Association for Citizenship Teaching (ACT)
Ferroners House, Shatesbury Place, Aldersgate St, London EC2Y 8AA
www.teachingcitizenship.org.uk

ActionAid Education
Chataway House, Leach Road, Chard, Somerset TA29 IFA
01460 62972
www.actionaid.org.uk

Christian Aid
PO Box 100, London SE1 7RT
020 7620 4444
www.christian-aid.org.uk

Citizenship Foundation
Ferroners House, Shaftesbury Place, Aldersgate Street, London EC2Y 8AA
020 7367 0500
www.citfou.org.uk

Community Service Volunteers (CSV)
237 Pentonville Road, London N1 9NJ
020 7278 6601
www.csv.org.uk

Development Education Association
29–31 Cowper Street, London EC2A 4AT
020 7490 8108
www.dea.org.uk

Geographical Association
160 Solly Street, Sheffield S1 4BF
0114 296 0088
www.geography.org.uk

Institute for Citizenship
62 Marylebone High Street, London W1U 5HZ
020 7935 4777
www.citizen.org.uk

Learning through Landscapes
Third Floor, Southside Offices, The Law Courts, Winchester SO23 9DL
01962 846 258

Oxfam Development Education and Resources Centre
Ground Floor, 232–242 Vauxhall Bridge Rd, London SW1V 1AU
020 7931 7600
www.oxfam.org.uk/coolplanet

Save the Children Education
17 Grove Road, London SE5 8DR
020 7703 5400
www.savethechildren.org.uk

School Councils UK
Lawford House, 5 Albert Place, Finchley, London N3 1QB
020 8349 2459
www.schoolcouncils.org

UNICEF UK
55 Lincoln's Inn Fields, London WC2A 3NB
020 7405 5592
www.unicef.org.uk

The Wildlife Trusts
The Kiln, Waterside, Mather Road, Newark, Nottinghamshire NG24 1WT
0870 0361000
www.wildlifetrusts.org

World Wide Fund for Nature (WWF)
Panda House, Weyside Park, Godalming, Surrey GU7 1XR
01483 426 444
www.wwf.org.uk

References

Crick, B. (1998) *Final Report of the Advisory Group on Education for Citizenship and the Teaching of Democracy in Schools*, London: QCA.

DEC Birmingham and DEC South Yorkshire (1992) *'It's Our World Too' A Local-Global Approach To Environmental Education at Key Stages 2 and 3*, Birmingham and Sheffield: DEC Birmingham and DEC South Yorkshire.

DfEE/QCA (1999a) *Geography: The National Curriculum for England (KS 1–3)*, London: DfEE/QCA.

—— (1999b) *Citizenship: The National Curriculum for England (KS 3–4)*, London: DfEE/QCA.

DfES (2001) *Draft Scheme of Work for Citizenship*, London: DfES.

Giles, T., Hughes, A. and Minikin, G. (n.d.: 1995 or 1996) *Playground Sundials*, London: Remtel Design Service.

Hart, J. (2000) 'The rights of the child as a cross-curricular topic at Key Stage 2', *New Era in Education* 81(2): 53–6.

Hertfordshire County Structure Plan (1989) *Consultation Document*, Hertford: Hertfordshire County Council.

Institute for Citizenship (2001) *Activate!*, Cheltenham: Institute for Citizenship and Nelson Thornes.

Job, D.A. (2001) 'Citizenship and sustainable development: fieldwork for a change', *Teaching Geography* 26(2): 67–71.

Lambert, D. and Machon, P. (eds) (2001) *Citizenship through Secondary Geography*, London and New York: RoutledgeFalmer.

Thompson, L. (2000) 'Citizenship', in K. Grimwade (ed.) *Geography and the New Agenda*, Sheffield: The Geographical Association.

Turner, S. (1996) *Create a School Wildlife Garden: An Interactive Teaching Package for Developing School Grounds*, London: London Wildlife Trust.

—— (2001) *Citizenship for Primary Schools: Teacher's Resource Book and Photo Pack for Years 5–6*, Cheltenham: Institute for Citizenship and Nelson Thornes.

UNICEF (1999) *Thursday's Child: Teacher's Handbook*, including 'Wants and Needs Game', London: UNICEF.

18 Teaching and learning about development

Tony Binns

Introduction

'Development' is a key concept, which I would strongly argue is, or certainly should be, an integral element – indeed a 'student entitlement' – at *all* levels of the education system from primary through secondary to further and higher education, and well beyond in the context of 'continuing education' and 'lifelong' learning (Binns 1995).

In this chapter I will examine the meaning of development and development education, and will raise issues and questions relating to how these are often taught today, and the potential for enhancing their position and role within the education system of the future. It so happens that, either by design or default, teaching about development in primary and secondary schools has generally been the responsibility of Geography and geography teachers, but at tertiary level the field of 'development studies' widens to involve practitioners from many social science disciplines, such as anthropology, economics, international relations, politics and sociology. But as such subjects are rarely taught in schools below A level, it is Geography which has a key role to play in laying the groundwork for more advanced study at a later stage.

What is 'development'?

The concept of 'development' is both complex and constantly being contested. There is no single definition of development; as Sachs suggests, 'Throughout the century, the meanings associated with urban development and colonial development concurred with many others to transform the word "development", step by step, into one with contours that are about as precise as those of an amoeba' (Sachs 1992: 10).

We might usefully examine just a few of the countless definitions of development which have been put forward:

- *Chambers English Dictionary*
  > The act or process of developing: state of being developed: a gradual unfolding or growth: evolution … Advancing through successive stages to a higher, more complex, or more fully grown state.
  >
  > (*Chambers English Dictionary* 1988: 386)

- *Dictionary of Human Geography*
  > A process of becoming and a potential state of being. The achievement of a state of development would enable people in societies to make their

own histories and geographies under conditions of their own choosing. The process of development is the means by which such conditions of human existence might be achieved.

(Johnston, Gregory and Smith 1994: 128)

- *Collins Reference Dictionary of Environmental Science*
  The process by which some system, place, object or person is changed from one state into another; the term carries the connotation that the change is in the direction of growth or improvement.

(Jones *et al.* 1990: 123)

My own favoured definition of development comes from the well-respected economist Dudley Seers (Seers 1969, 1971, 1979), who suggested in his seminal 1969 paper that:

Development is inevitably a normative concept, almost a synonym for improvement. To pretend otherwise is just to hide one's value judgements ... The questions to ask about a country's development are therefore: What has been happening to poverty? What has been happening to unemployment? What has been happening to inequality? If all three of these have become less severe, then beyond doubt this has been a period of development for the country concerned.

(Seers 1969: 4)

Seers felt strongly that a definition of development should also involve the 'true fulfilment of human potential', and in a later paper, written after the oil crisis and price hike of the 1970s, he suggested that 'self-reliance' should be another important goal of development plans (Seers 1979). In considering the question of individuals and groups being able to fulfil their potential, this raises many issues relating to the nature and quality of governance, as reflected, for example, in aspects such as freedom of speech, democracy and transparency in the formulation and implementation of government policies. Furthermore, it could be argued that the fulfilment of human potential is also severely constrained in poor countries by high rates of infant and child mortality, lower levels of life expectancy, as well as such features as the frequently low level of female participation in education systems.

Most importantly, development is quite definitely a 'social' as well as an 'economic' process, and it is unfortunate that, even after much debate over four decades, economic growth is all too commonly still regarded as being synonymous with development. Rostow's well-known 'Stages of Economic Growth' model (Rostow 1960), for example, is often wrongly interpreted as a development model. Rostow was more concerned with economic progress and increasing industrial investment, rather than with human welfare and variables regarded by those such as Seers as important indicators of development – poverty, unemployment and inequality. Furthermore, Rostow's model was based on the historical experiences of economic growth in Europe and North America, and it is, therefore, quite inappropriate to attempt to apply such a model to countries which have been subjected to colonial rule and whose economies (and societies) have been manipulated to serve the demand for agricultural and mineral resources from the growing manufacturing sectors in the metropolitan countries. Above all, it should be remembered that development both concerns and involves *people* and that development processes vary considerably in their impacts both socially and spatially.

Moving to the school curriculum context, it should be noted that the definition and understanding of the concept and process of development were not at all helped by reference to 'economically developing countries' in the first Geography National Curriculum Order for English schools. For example, at Key Stage 2, levels 2 to 5, students were required to 'study a contrasting locality in the United Kingdom and a locality in an economically developing country' (DES 1991: 37). The term 'economically developing' is problematic, not least because there are many cases of countries with rapidly rising Gross National Products, but where true development, in terms of a reduction in poverty and inequality, has just not occurred (Binns 1993; Potter *et al*. 1999). Rather than trickling down to the poorest and remotest communities, it is well known that increased economic wealth in reality often moves towards already wealthy urban-based élites, thus increasing inequality in a range of key development indicators such as life expectancy and infant mortality. So the term 'economically developing' wrongly implied both that economic progress is the essence of development, and also that such countries are actually 'developing', which is questionable, certainly in the case of a number of sub-Saharan African countries, which in relative terms are now far worse off than they were over thirty years ago at independence. Interestingly, the term 'economically developing' was not used in the 1995 revised curriculum, but instead reference is made to countries and parts of the world 'in various/significantly different states of development' (DfE 1995).

Contexts and perceptions

If we regard development as fundamentally a process which should lead to an improvement in living standards, then it is important to recognize that development can happen in so-called 'developed' countries as well as in poor Third World countries. Varying levels of poverty, unemployment and inequality are found even in the world's wealthiest countries, but too often we seem to find it convenient to ignore their existence at home. In schools, teachers far too often portray the poor Third World countries as riddled with economic and social problems, whilst showing reluctance to deal with such problems in the home context, regarding them, I would suggest, as too complex, politically sensitive and controversial. Yet poverty and homelessness are all too evident, for example, in large European and US cities, and a report published in the mid-1990s indicated that income inequalities between 1977 and 1990 had increased in the UK further and faster than in almost any comparable country and were greater than at any time since the Second World War. In fact, only New Zealand registered a greater increase in inequality during this period (JRF 1995). It is essential that in teaching about development, at whatever level in the education system, students be introduced to a wide range of locational contexts and case studies, including the home environment and society.

Another significant consideration in teaching about development concerns the different perceptions which both students and teachers have, particularly about unfamiliar peoples and environments. Even within the UK, those living in southern England, for example, through images conveyed in the media, often have distorted perceptions of what life is like in northern England, Scotland, Wales and Ireland. In broader spatial and temporal contexts, a complex chronology of terms has evolved from the colonial period to the present day, and it is unfortunate that many outdated and stereotypical views still persist. Drummond, for example, writing in 1888, typified views held about Africa at that time when he commented,

> here in his virgin simplicity dwells primeval man, without clothes, without civilisation, without learning, without religion – the genuine child of nature, thoughtless, careless and contented … The African is often blamed for being lazy, but it is a misuse of words. He does not need to work; with so bountiful a nature round him it would be gratuitous to work
>
> (Drummond 1888: 55)

More recently, sub-Saharan Africa has become synonymous with famine, drought, poverty, civil war and many other seemingly insurmountable problems, a region characterized by little progress in economic, social or cultural development (Binns 1994).

There has been a considerable, and indeed ongoing, debate on what is the best term to describe the world's poorest countries. In fact, the different terminologies present a semantic minefield, with many descriptive terms at best inaccurate and at worst pejorative. A recent text rejected all but three terms: 'South', 'Developing World' and 'Third World' (Robinson and Serf 1997: 7). The idea of the North–South dichotomy was a creation of the Brandt Report in 1980, but it is inaccurate in the way that the all-important dividing line includes geographically southern countries such as Australia and New Zealand in the North (Brandt 1980). Though the term 'Developing World' is positive and implies progress, it does imply that the rest of the world is not developing, and as we have seen there are many so-called developing countries which are also not developing!

Terms such as 'Third World' continue to be widely used long after they were invented, and their meaning has often changed with time. The concept of Third World was first used to describe the growing number of states that were neither aligned with the 'First, Western-capitalist world' nor the 'Second, Eastern-socialist world'. The French demographer, Alfred Sauvy, is sometimes credited with first using the term in 1952, but the Bandung Conference in 1955 has come to be regarded as the event which gave birth to the Third World (Berger 1994). Since the term was first coined, the so-called Third World has become much more diverse, including some of the world's poorest countries, such as Ethiopia and Mozambique, as well as the oil-rich Middle Eastern states and the emerging 'Asian Tigers' (South Korea, Taiwan, Hong Kong and Singapore). Furthermore, the collapse of state socialism in Eastern Europe, which was Sauvy's 'Second World', makes the tripartite division of the world even more redundant. Although some writers have argued that the term 'Third World' is now obsolete (Harris 1986), it is still widely used by non-governmental organizations (NGOs), and most people have some idea of the broad characteristics of Third World countries (Robinson and Serf 1997). As John Toye comments,

> The Third World is not, despite all that the development counter-revolution says, yet able to be dismissed from our minds. It is not a figment of our

imagination ready to vanish when we blink. It is a result of our collective lack of imagination, our inability in our present difficult circumstances yet to see ourselves as belonging to one world, and not three

(Toye 1987: 10)

So, in the absence of a more satisfactory label (if indeed a label is actually needed?), I would agree with others that Third World is the best we can do. As an albeit imperfect teaching tool, use of the term Third World could provoke useful educational debate on important issues related to development, such as perception and interdependence.

Perceptions are also changing as the process of globalization becomes ever quicker and more encompassing. Overseas travel, the growth and 'incorporation' of sizeable ethnic minorities in many 'rich' countries and, not least, the phenomenal success and potential of the internet, are just three factors which have helped to gradually change perceptions of distant peoples and environments. Whereas just two decades ago, stories, films and television programmes provided the only images of distant places, the young people of today are much more travelled than previous generations. In most school classes there will be at least one child who has possibly been to Florida or has experienced a safari or beach holiday in Africa. The greater 'ethnic mix', which is now a feature of so many of our schools, also provides an invaluable resource for generating study units and discussions on other cultures and livelihoods in such diverse places as Bangladesh, Nigeria and the Caribbean. Even the youngest children are fascinated by distant places and have an entitlement to be able to discover more about them, not least through the diverse cultural heritages of their classmates. Older students might be able to gain first-hand experience through overseas field courses and 'gap years' before, during or after university. Lastly, the internet now provides an invaluable resource for everyone to use (selectively!), as the facility becomes available to more students both in their school or college, and increasingly at home.

Why should we teach about development?

A statement from the United Nations in 1975 in itself provides a strong justification for teaching about development:

> Development education is concerned with issues of human rights, dignity, self-reliance, and social justice in both developed and developing countries. It is concerned with the causes of underdevelopment and the promotion of an understanding of what is involved in development, of how different countries go about undertaking development, and of the reasons for and ways of achieving a new international economic and social order.
>
> (UN 1975, quoted in Hicks and Townley 1982: 9)

The Development Education Association (DEA) sees development education as:

> a process which explores the relationship between North and South and more generally the links between our lives and those of people throughout the world.

It is also about recognising our global interdependence and that, for any change to take place, a change of attitudes and values is required by the North.

(DEA 1993: 1)

Both statements suggest that there is in fact a very fine dividing line between development education and what is sometimes referred to as 'global citizenship', which is currently the subject of much curriculum debate in the UK.

There are a number of compelling reasons why development education should be regarded as a student entitlement in our education system. First, from a humanitarian viewpoint, global inequality has never been greater. Should it not concern us all that, whilst average life expectancy in the UK and USA in 1995 was over 76 years, in the world's poorest country, Sierra Leone, life expectancy was under 35 years? (UNDP 1998: 128–30). Is it just and fair that an individual in one country can enjoy a life which on average is 40 years longer than another individual elsewhere in the world, purely because of where he or she was born and lives? Considering levels of economic wealth in the same countries, whilst the USA had in 1995 a per capita Gross Domestic Product of US$26,977 and the UK had US$19,302, Sierra Leone's per capita GDP figure was a derisory US$625 (UNDP 1998: 128–30). Many of the world's poorest countries and people are heavily dependent on farming and live-stock-keeping to provide family subsistence requirements and sustain their livelihoods. In Western Europe, where relatively few people now work in the highly mechanized agricultural sector, we have a situation of over-production of food, such that policies have been introduced to 'set aside' land for non-agricultural use. Yet in other parts of the world, including Eastern Europe, food shortages are a regular, if not everyday, concern. Commenting on Africa, Timberlake argues:

Africa's plight is unique. The rest of the world is moving forward by most of the normally accepted indicators of progress. Africa is moving backwards … The continent's living standards have been declining steadily since the 1970s. Its ability to feed itself has been deteriorating since the late 1960s.

(Timberlake 1985: 7)

One might indeed pose the question, why is there such considerable social and spatial disparity in the availability and accessibility of basic foodstuffs in the world today?

In the area of basic education, as reflected in levels of adult literacy, the UK and USA both had adult literacy rates of 99 per cent in 1995, whereas the figure for Sierra Leone was only 31 per cent. However, a particular concern is the sometimes vast differential between levels of male and female adult literacy, which is the case in some of the world's poorest countries, as well as those which are predominantly Muslim. In Sierra Leone, for example, whereas the adult literacy rate for males is 45 per cent, it is only 18 per cent for females. Even some relatively better-off countries show marked gender-based inequalities in educational attainment and literacy levels, such as Saudi Arabia, which, with a per capita Gross Domestic Product of US$8,516, has a male adult literacy rate of 71 per cent, yet only 50 per cent for females (UNDP 1998: 131–3). We need to encourage students to engage with such issues and ask what the underlying causes of such inequalities are and what strategies might be implemented (at different scales) to reduce them. Through introducing development issues, young people should hopefully develop empathy and concern for those less fortunate than themselves, and this should encourage consideration of the nature and significance of different 'personal geographies' in a development context.

A second reason why development education should be regarded as a student entitlement concerns the historical justification. The United Kingdom is today one of the world's leading economic powers and the home-base of many of the world's most powerful multinational companies, whose origins can often be traced back to the period of colonialism. Whilst the UK (like other European powers such as France, The Netherlands, Spain and Portugal) derived much of its wealth from the production of raw materials associated with colonial expansion, British culture and values were simultaneously disseminated throughout the colonies in the shape of structures and systems for the management of economies, health, education, law and order, transport and trade. Such influence also extended into areas such as the arts and sport – cricket is surely a good example of this! It is probably fair to say that long after gaining independence, in some countries and among some people who experienced British colonialism, there remains an enthusiasm for maintaining strong links with the 'mother country' through, for example, organizations such as the Commonwealth.

Development education can play a key role in promoting an understanding of Britain's (or indeed other rich and powerful countries') role in the world today and the historical processes which underlie this. Furthermore, present-day economic, environmental and social conditions can be located in a global context with a strong historical dimension. It has been a long-standing concern of mine that school History and history teachers have really failed to 'get to grips' with the origins of present-day inequalities in the world and temporal changes in development processes. Topics such as the growth of world trade, slavery, colonialism and neo-colonialism receive remarkably little classroom time compared with aspects of British and European history, which in some cases are taught repeatedly as children progress through the four Key Stages and on to A level. The position in schools is in sharp contrast to that in higher education, where issues such as the nature and legacies of colonialism are well up the agenda in both teaching and research undertaken by historians.

Development education in the UK

Development education emerged in the UK during the 1960s with the establishment of a number of development agencies, and has become a remarkably strong field of interest and activity over the past three decades or so. The latest Oxfam education resources catalogue lists no fewer than 45 Development Education Centres (DECs) in the UK, together with a further 12 in Ireland, some of which, perhaps most notably the DEC in Birmingham, were established as long ago as the early 1970s and have an impressive list of resources to support teachers and youth workers (Oxfam 1999). In addition to such centres, which are frequently operated by volunteers, various development agencies (NGOs: non-governmental organizations) also have sections working on development education and producing a wide range of resources: for example, Action Aid, Catholic Fund for Overseas Development (CAFOD), Christian Aid, Intermediate Technology, Oxfam, Save the Children, Voluntary Service Overseas and Worldaware. The strength of the development education 'movement' in the UK was reflected in the establishment in October 1993 of the Development Education Association (DEA), with some 250 affiliated member organizations and its headquarters in London. The DEA's twice-yearly *Development Education Journal*, together with its *Monthly Bulletin*, provide up-to-date news on events and publications as well as some stimulating articles. The DEA's stated mission is to:

- promote development education within all sectors of education
- support the network of practitioners through a range of events, publications and information services
- lobby key decision-makers to recognise the value of development education and to give it full support

(DEA 1996: 7)

As far as government support for development education is concerned, in 1976 the Labour Government's Ministry of Overseas Development established a Development Education Fund to promote wider public knowledge of international interdependence and a better understanding of 'worldwide social, economic and political conditions, particularly those which relate to and are responsible for, underdevelopment' (MOD 1978). An Advisory Committee for Development Education was also established to advise the Minister on the expenditure of funds for development education. However, with the coming to power of Margaret Thatcher's Conservative Government in 1979, development education became an immediate casualty of financial retrenchment at the new Overseas Development Administration (ODA).

In its short lifespan, the DEA has worked hard to influence government policy, and before the General Election in May 1997 was particularly active in lobbying political parties for a greater commitment to development education both in a future International Development Department and also as an integral feature in the revised National Curriculum (DEA 1996). In 1996, the UK Government's Overseas Development Administration allocated just £700,000 to development education, representing only 0.01 thousand US$ per capita, which was one of the lowest expenditures among developed countries, and well below the figures of 1.22 and 0.99 US$ thousand per capita allocated respectively in Sweden and The Netherlands. Following the 1997 General Election, the publication by the new Labour Government's Department for International Development (DFID) of its White Paper on International Development in November 1997 represented a significant step forward in recognizing the importance of development education. Section 4 of the White Paper (*Eliminating World Poverty: A Challenge for the 21st Century*) is concerned with 'Building Support for Development' and stresses the importance of popular education on development issues:

The British people should have accurate, unbiased, accessible information about the causes of poverty and inequality in developing countries, and about what the international community can do ... The Government therefore attaches great importance to increasing development awareness in Britain. Every child should be educated about development issues, so that they can understand the key global considerations which will shape their lives. And every adult should have the chance to influence the Government's policies.

(DFID 1997: 77)

The White Paper also proposed that the government would establish:

> a working group of educationalists and others (including the business sector, trades unions, the churches, the voluntary organisations and the media) to consider and promote awareness and understanding. We will work to ensure that global issues are integrated into the National Curriculum and that relevant teaching materials are available. We will examine ways of improving progress in other aspects of formal and informal education and youth work.
>
> (DFID 1997: 78)

In addition, a Development Policy Forum would be established:

> to allow individuals and representatives from all parts of society – academics, research institutes, the voluntary sector, the private sector and others – to share thinking and ideas for development and to draw on their wealth of knowledge and experience.
>
> (DFID 1997: 78)

In the latest proposals for the revised National Curriculum for English schools, published for consultation in May 1999, and implemented in September 2000, much emphasis is placed on citizenship and sustainable development, which are arguably key elements of both development education and geographical study. In the introduction to the Qualifications and Curriculum Authority (QCA) consultation document, it is suggested that curriculum changes being made will focus on a number of issues, including 'helping young people understand the world in which they live, and ensuring that they have a stake in society and their community by providing citizenship education' (QCA 1999a: 4). The Secretary of State's proposals on the revised curriculum, which accompany the QCA consultation document, suggest that:

> Citizenship encourages pupils to become helpfully involved in the life of their schools, neighbourhoods, communities and the wider world. It promotes their political and economic literacy through learning about our economy and our democratic institutions, with respect for its varying national, religious and ethnic identities.
>
> (QCA 1999b: 28)

Such a statement is very much in line with the ethos of development education.

Similarly, in the new curriculum proposals for Geography, it is stated that references to sustainable development 'have been strengthened to reflect the work of the (government-appointed) Panel for Sustainable Development Education' (QCA 1999b: 8). Geography, the consultation document argues:

> provides a link between the sciences and the arts and humanities, and contributes to environmental education and education for sustainable development. Geography develops understanding of physical and human landscapes and introduces pupils to different societies and cultures, enhancing awareness of global interdependence. It also promotes exploration of issues about the environment, development and

society, and provides opportunities for pupils to reflect critically on their place in the world and their rights and responsibilities in relation to other people and the environment.

(QCA 1999a: 144)

Even as early as Key Stage 1, pupils will be required to be taught the skills, knowledge and understanding through Geography to appreciate 'environmental change and sustainable development' and develop 'a framework of locational knowledge, with an ability to recognise how a locality is linked with other places in the world' (QCA 1999a: 146). With such objectives for the youngest school children, Geography is making a valuable contribution to development education, which is further developed in subsequent Key Stages and beyond, through A level and into higher education.

Some practicalities of teaching about development

As we have already seen, Geography is the most important vehicle for teaching about development issues in schools. I have examined in detail elsewhere a number of strategies which might be used with different age-groups of children (Binns 1993, 1996), but it might be useful to mention some possibilities here:

Role plays and simulations

With primary-age children in particular, there is much to be gained from setting up a simulation in which they make a 'pretend visit' to a distant country. I was involved with one very successful initiative, where we took 90 6- and 7-year-old children from an infant school in Hove (East Sussex) to the West African state of The Gambia for a day! The event arose out of a visit by a Gambian teacher to the school some months earlier. For several weeks before their 'visit' the children had been learning about people, wildlife and environment in Africa and The Gambia, and were actively involved in reading, writing and artwork, as well as making passports and designing hats to keep off the tropical sun. With the essential support of a group of Secondary PGCE trainees from Sussex University, who assumed a variety of different roles during the day, the children were given medical and passport checks before boarding the plane, gained more knowledge about The Gambia during the flight, and then visited three Gambian villages where they could ask questions about life and work, before dancing to Gambian music and listening to an African story at the end of the day (Binns 1993). The event was followed up later when the children moved into the neighbouring junior school, through establishing a letter exchange link with a Gambian school and using a series of laminated photographs for a work unit on the village where the school is located.

With older students, it might be possible to set up a role play or debate on an issue such as Third World debt, which is particularly topical in the light of the Jubilee 2000 campaign and its lobbying of western governments to cancel this debt, which amounts to about US$209 billion, more than twice the figure for 1985 (*The Guardian* 1999). The key 'actors' should be identified, such as the 'Heavily Indebted Poor Countries' (HIPCs), governments and local producers, global lenders such as the

World Bank and the International Monetary Fund (IMF), developed country governments and multinationals, and national and international development agencies. Important and challenging questions to debate would include the history of world debt: How did such indebtedness arise? What are the causes of debt and who is to blame? Should the debt be cancelled? Can the debt be cancelled? How can the future growth of indebtedness be stemmed? What is the effect of debt, and its possible cancellation, on poor people in Third World countries? Is debt cancellation a necessary prerequisite for the alleviation and elimination of poverty?

Artefacts and food

Many museums, as well as organizations such as the Commonwealth Institute, have collections of ethnographic artefacts which in some cases may be loaned to schools. Artefacts may provide a stimulus for examining many aspects of livelihoods in Third World countries, such as farming, fishing, rituals, cultural heritage and gender relations. Work on farming and food production could be initiated by actually examining foodstuffs produced in tropical countries such as mango, yam or rice. A visit to the local supermarket should reveal just how many products are imported from Third World countries. An audit of such produce may be conducted and a debate developed around such questions as: Who benefits in Third World countries from producing food for export? Is it more appropriate for such countries and their farmers to grow foodstuffs for home consumption rather than produce for export? What is the most appropriate strategy for alleviating poverty? Again, it is important to identify the 'actors' involved in such production and trade.

Visual aids

There is no shortage of high-quality photo packs and videos produced by the development education centres, NGOs and television companies. Students may be divided into small groups to discuss a photograph and present their views to the whole class. A good video might be used to promote debate. For example, the International Broadcasting Trust (IBT) and Yorkshire Television produced for Channel 4 a five-programme series titled *Geographical Eye Over Africa,* the second programme of which, *Nigeria: Dammed Water*, also has a linked photo pack (IBT 1995). Both the film and the photo pack address the important question of who actually benefits from large dams and irrigation schemes in poor tropical countries. Is such a type of development appropriate? This is a topic of much current interest and concern, and for sixth-form and higher education students there is no shortage of additional material about such development schemes, which can be used to raise further questions and provide useful case study material (see, for example, Adams 1992; McCully 1996). The controversial Three Gorges dam project on the Yangtze River in central China has generated much interest (see, for example, *National Geographic* 1997), and was the subject of a programme in a Yorkshire Television/Channel 4 series for schools in 2000. The points in favour and against this massive construction project, which will displace over a million people, yet at the same time help reduce flooding downstream and generate electricity sufficient to supply ten large cities, might be examined through debate or role play.

Poetry, books and music

These are particularly important types of resources which can help truly to 'engage' young people in a wide range of development issues. There is no shortage of poetry and novels written in English by African, Caribbean and Indian writers, for example Chinua Achebe's *Things Fall Apart*, *No Longer at Ease* and *Anthills of the Savannah*, which can help to shed light on many aspects of the colonial and post-colonial transformation in African countries, in this case Nigeria. With the phenomenal growth in interest and availability of 'world music' in the 1990s there is plenty of scope for building a unit of work on development around a particular song. For example, international migration from poor to rich countries might be studied, as epitomized in the song 'America' from *West Side Story*. Meanwhile, the Senegalese artist, Youssou N'Dour, in his album *Hey You!* sings about aspects of everyday life such as polygamy and the emancipation of women, as well as the problem of multinational companies dumping toxic waste in poor countries.

School links

Establishing a link with a school or college in a poor country can do much to develop empathy and promote global citizenship. By exchanging letters, artwork and photographs, children can gain a rich and personal insight into local issues and family life. Exchange visits for teachers and pupils are also becoming increasingly popular. The Geographical Association's International Committee has done much to initiate such links and exchanges.

Field courses

There is absolutely no substitute for direct experience. Having led many groups of sixth-formers and university students to Africa (The Gambia, Kenya, Morocco, Tunisia), I have never failed to be impressed by the indelible impact that such a visit can make on an individual. In the light of gloomy media reports about Africa, it is a great step forward in the learning process for students to become personally aware of the fact that, though Africans may indeed live in extreme poverty, they are frequently positive and forward looking and invariably greet visitors with a warm smile and handshake. With cheaper packages and greater accessibility, many schools and colleges are now taking students to Third World countries on fieldwork. Whilst there is so much to be gained from such visits, it is vital that they are sensitively placed in a broader learning context and that teachers should guard against them becoming predominantly voyeuristic. There is much to be gained from closely examining with students the ethics of such fieldwork.

Conclusion

The concept and processes of development are fundamentally concerned with the quality of life at home and overseas. Geographical education, particularly in schools, has played an absolutely vital role in promoting interest, understanding and debate in this important area, whereas too often other disciplines have 'stood on the sideline', displaying much potential, yet considerable reluctance, about becoming more involved. Getting to grips with development issues can do much to engender a sense of global citizenship in young people, whilst also strengthening awareness and understanding of a wide range of issues and values. In the context of an even more crowded curriculum, with recent initiatives in Literacy and Numeracy creating increased pressures on schools and teachers, it is vital that sufficient attention and time be devoted to development issues. There is great potential for more cross-curricular work, but it is likely that geographers will have to take the lead and convince their colleagues of the value of such collaboration. Fortuitously, the current emphasis on Citizenship and sustainable development might be viewed as a highly appropriate vehicle for strengthening the position of development work within the curriculum.

Issues and questions for discussion

- Is there a Third World?
- What is the most appropriate definition of development?
- How can myths and stereotypes be most effectively challenged?
- How can we best develop empathy, concern and action in young people – a sense of global citizenship?
- Why is there such little interest from other school disciplines and practitioners in embracing development issues?
- How might the teaching about development issues be strengthened in Geography, but also perhaps by exploring opportunities for more cross-curricular work?

References

Adams, W.M. (1992) *Wasting the Rain: Rivers, People and Planning in Africa*, London: Earthscan.

Berger, M.T. (1994) 'The end of the "Third World"?', *Third World Quarterly* 15(2): 257–75.

Binns, T. (1993) 'The international dimension in the geography National Curriculum', in C. Speak and P. Wiegand (eds) *International Understanding Through Geography*, Sheffield: The Geographical Association.

—— (1994) *Tropical Africa*, London: Routledge.

—— (1995) 'Geography in development: development in geography', *Geography* 80(4): 303–22.

—— (1996) 'Teaching about distant places', in P. Bailey and P. Fox (eds) *Geography Teachers' Handbook*, Sheffield: The Geographical Association.

Brandt, W. (ed.) (1980) *North-South: A Programme for Survival*, Report of the Independent Commission on International Development Issues (Chairman: Willy Brandt), London: Pan Books.

Chambers English Dictionary (1988) Cambridge: Chambers.

Development Education Association (DEA) (1993) *Launch Broadsheet*, London: DEA.

—— (1996) *The Case for Development Education: Why it Should be Funded and Supported*, London: DEA.

Department of Education and Science (DES) (1991) *Geography in the National Curriculum (England)*, London: HMSO.

Department for Education (DfE) (1995) *Geography in the National Curriculum (England)*, London: HMSO.

Department for International Development (DFID) (1997) *Eliminating World Poverty: A Challenge for the 21st Century*, White Paper on International Development, London: The Stationery Office.

Drummond, H. (1888) *Tropical Africa*, London: Hodder and Stoughton.

The Guardian (1999) 'Deep in the red', *Guardian Education*, 25 May 1999, pp. 10–11.

Harris, N. (1986) *The End of the Third World*, Harmondsworth: Penguin.

Hicks, D. and Townley, C. (1982) *Teaching World Studies*, London: Longman.

International Broadcasting Trust (IBT) and Yorkshire TV (1995) *Geographical Eye Over Africa* (five 20-minute programmes), and *Dammed Water: Nigeria* (a photopack for secondary Geography), London: IBT.

Johnston, R., Gregory, D. and Smith, D.M. (eds) (1994) *The Dictionary of Human Geography*, Oxford: Blackwell.

Jones, G., Robertson, A., Forbes, J. and Hollier, G. (1990) *The Collins Reference Dictionary of Environmental Science*, London: Collins.

Joseph Rowntree Foundation (JRF) (1995) *Income and Wealth*, York: JRF.

McCully, P. (1996) *Silenced Rivers: The Ecology and Politics of Large Dams*, London: Zed Books.

Ministry of Overseas Development (MOD) (1978) *Report on the Future of Development Education*, London: MOD.

National Geographic (1997) 'China's Three Gorges', *National Geographic* 192(3) (September): 4–33.

Oxfam (1999) *Oxfam Education Resources for Schools*, London: Oxfam.

Potter, R.B., Binns, T., Elliott, J.A. and Smith, D. (1999) *Geographies of Development*, London: Longman.

Qualifications and Curriculum Authority (QCA) (1999a) *The Review of the National Curriculum in England: The Consultation Materials*, London: QCA.

—— (1999b) *The Review of the National Curriculum in England: The Secretary of State's Proposals*, London: QCA.

Robinson, R. and Serf, J. (eds) (1997) *Global Geography: Learning Through Development Education at Key Stage 3*, Sheffield: The Geographical Association/DEC (Birmingham).

Rostow, W.W. (1960) *The Stages of Economic Growth: A Non-Communist Manifesto*, Cambridge: Cambridge University Press.

Sachs, W. (ed) (1992) *The Development Dictionary*, London: Zed Books.

Seers, D. (1969) 'The meaning of development', *International Development Review* 11(4): 2–6.

—— (1971) 'What are we trying to measure?' *Journal of Development Studies* 8: 21–36.

—— (1979) 'The new meaning of development', in D. Lehmann (ed.) *Development Theory: Four Critical Studies*, London: Frank Cass.

Timberlake, L. (1985) *Africa in Crisis: The Causes, the Cures of Environmental Bankruptcy*, London: Earthscan.

Toye, J. (1987) *Dilemmas of Development*, Oxford: Blackwell.

United Nations (UN) (1975) *Statement on Development Education*, New York: UN.

United Nations Development Programme (UNDP) (1998) *Human Development Report 1998*, Oxford: Oxford University Press.

19 Envisioning a better world
Sustainable development in school Geography

David Hicks

> Geography teachers in Britain have, over the past 100 years, played a significant part in opening the eyes and widening the horizons of those who have sat in their classes. In the new century, the need to draw attention to those horizons is surely not diminished?
>
> (Walford 2000: 311)

The new agenda

On any journey, as all good travellers know, the horizon shifts and changes. What once seemed distant and unknown in turn becomes immediate and known. Geographers, in particular, should be adept at scanning the horizon for possible opportunities and difficulties that lie ahead. Approaching fast as we move ahead into the new century are two interrelated areas of concern – the so-called 'new agenda' of citizenship and sustainability (Grimwade *et al*. 2000). Both, I wish to argue, should be of central concern to secondary Geography.

I have also previously argued that Geography requires a futures perspective. This should enable students to ask questions about probable, and preferred, futures for different issues and localities at a variety of scales (Hicks 1998). Both citizenship education and education for sustainable development raise crucial questions about the sort of future society that we wish to create. Indeed they remind us that Geography has a key role to play in 'teaching for a better world'. The questions this chapter addresses are:

- How might Geography respond to citizenship education?
- How might Geography respond to issues of sustainability?
- What part can envisioning the future play in geography teaching?

Geography and citizenship education

At first sight Geography and Citizenship may appear to share little in common; but this depends on what one sees as the purpose of Geography. For myself David Smith's words are as true for the new century as they were for the old:

> The well-being of society as a spatially variable condition should be the focal point of geographical enquiry. This simply requires recognition of what is surely

the self-evident truth that if human beings are the object of our curiosity ... then the quality of their lives is of paramount importance.

(Smith 1977: 17)

In essence, effective citizenship requires that a person (a) has some knowledge and understanding of public affairs; (b) is concerned about the welfare of the wider community; and (c) has the skills needed to participate in the political arena. In other words Citizenship explores the social and political *context* within which the struggle to achieve 'quality of life' takes place.

This renewed interest in Citizenship is not just a UK concern, as various cross-cultural studies show. In a nine-nation survey (from Europe, North America and Asia) Cogan and Derricott (1998) report that the experts consulted in each country reached consensus on eight characteristics of effective citizens.

1 Looking at problems in a global context.
2 Working co-operatively and responsibly.
3 Accepting cultural differences.
4 Thinking in a critical and systemic way.
5 Solving conflicts non-violently.
6 Changing lifestyles to protect the environment.
7 Defending human rights.
8 Participating in politics.

I would suggest that most of these characteristics are ones that effective geography teaching should be promoting. The same is true if we look at the new requirements for Citizenship. In the area of becoming an *informed citizen* Geography has much to offer in relation to the following:

- Rights: human rights, responsibilities, issues of justice and fairness.
- Identity: national, regional, religious, ethnic, identity and place.
- Change: local, national, international groups working for change.
- Global: social, political, economic and environmental issues.

Similarly, geographers have a major contribution to make in relation to *enquiry and communication skills*:

- thinking about political, moral, social and cultural issues;
- justifying a personal opinion about such issues; and
- contributing to class discussion and debate.

And, in relation to the skills of participation and responsible action:

- considering other people's experiences and views; and
- taking part in school and community activities.

Geography, if its practitioners wish, could make a major contribution, if not *the* major contribution, to citizenship education (Carter 2000). In order to help you

Scenario 1   Not for us

We don't actually feel that we contribute much to Citizenship and neither do we really want to. Anyway, it is not something that we have been trained for and to force Geography into this mould is to contaminate the boundaries of a well-established curriculum subject.

Scenario 2   Making changes

We could contribute more to Citizenship than we do and this is an idea we are prepared to entertain. A minor/major shift in the emphasis of our teaching could make this possible. This could enhance both our geography teaching and make a useful contribution to Citizenship itself.

Scenario 3   Doing it now

We are very aware of how Geography contributes to Citizenship, and we already teach in a way that promotes knowledge and skills for both these subject areas. Indeed, we feel that Geography and Citizenship are closely inter-related and that they add to, and enhance, each other.

Scenario 4   Stealing the scene

In our geography teaching we already make a significant and conscious contribution to Citizenship, and we now wish to take this even further. This would mean that Geography becomes the prime deliverer of Citizenship in school, with added support from history and religious education colleagues.

Figure 19.1 Four scenarios for Geography and Citizenship

judge whether this feels right in your school, Figure 19.1 presents four different scenarios. Which do you relate to most?

Geography and education for sustainable development

The National Curriculum includes a definition of education for sustainable development:

> Education for sustainable development enables pupils to develop the knowledge, skills, understanding and values to participate in decisions about the way we do things individually and collectively, both locally and globally, that will improve the quality of life now without damaging the planet for the future.
>
> (DfEE/QCA 1999: 25)

The report from the government's Advisory Group on Citizenship led to statutory changes in the secondary curriculum; however, the report from the Sustainable Development Education Panel was reduced to a single paragraph. The Panel's longer definition is more explicit, and provides geography teachers with phrases that clearly demonstrate how sustainable development relates to the geography curriculum:

> Education for sustainable development is about the learning needed to maintain and improve our quality of life and the quality of life of generations to come. It is about equipping individuals, communities, groups, businesses and government to live and act sustainably; as well as giving them an understanding of the environmental, social and economic issues involved. It is about preparing for the world in which we will live in the next century, and making sure that we are not found wanting.
>
> (DETR 1999: 30)

At first sight sustainability might seem more appealing to geographers than Citizenship, in that it refers to 'quality of life' and 'environmental, social and economic issues'. With its reference to future generations it also clearly involves a futures perspective.

The meaning of the term 'sustainability' is, of course, contested. Fien and Trainer (1993), for example, highlight differences in meaning between 'sustainable growth' and 'sustainable development'. Sustainable growth is seen as reformist, in that it relies on the greening of existing production and consumption, and high-tech solutions to both environmental and human problems. It reflects the dominant industrial worldview. It comes from a 'light green' perspective. Sustainable development, on the other hand, is more radical in that it argues the equal importance of social, environmental and economic goals. It reflects an emerging post-industrial worldview, and comes more from what might be called a 'red/green' perspective.

My amplification of the concept of 'sustainability' would also highlight the fact that traditional models of development narrowly focus on economic growth (GNP) as a measure of progress and discount various other 'costs'. This is one of the causes of *unsustainability* because:

- some individuals and groups benefit at the expense of others;
- people often benefit at the expense of the environment; and
- people today benefit at the expense of future generations.

In contrast, the notion of *sustainability* emphasizes:

- Human well-being – increasing levels of social and economic well-being for all and especially the least advantaged.
- Environmental value – higher priority on the need to protect the biosphere on which all life depends.
- Future generations – should inherit at least as much wealth, natural and human, as we ourselves inherited.

Education for sustainable development is thus much more than traditional environmental education, because it highlights the close inter-relationship between both environmental and human welfare. It is not a term that the public immediately understand, although once it is explained people are able to relate it to their own immediate interests.

Scenario 1   Not for us

We don't actually feel that we contribute much to education for sustainable development and neither do we really want to. It is not something that we have been trained for, and to force Geography into this mould is to blur the boundaries of a well-established curriculum subject.

Scenario 2   Making changes

We could contribute more to education for sustainable development than we do and this is an idea we are thinking about. A minor/major shift in the emphasis of our teaching would make this possible. This could both enhance our geography teaching and make an important contribution to the under-standing of sustainability.

Scenario 3   Doing it now

We are very aware of how Geography can contribute to education for sustainable development and we already teach in a way that promotes these principles in the classroom. Indeed, we feel that issues of sustainability lie at the heart of good geography teaching and always will.

Scenario 4   Stealing the scene

In our geography teaching we already make a significant and conscious contribution to education for sustainable development and we now intend to give this an even higher profile. This involves the head and governors publicly recognizing Geography as the prime deliverer of education for sustainable development.

Figure 19.2 Four scenarios for Geography and education for sustainable development

Geography, if its practitioners wish, could make a major contribution, if not *the* major contribution, to education for sustainability. In order to help you judge whether this feels right in your school Figure 19.2 shows four different scenarios. Which do you relate to most?

Envisioning preferred futures

Unless it is in creative writing, or the creative arts, we tend to dismiss the imagination as a serious tool for learning. Yet the imagination plays a central role in geography, alongside photographic, video and digital images of other people and places. When these are not directly in use it is the imagination that holds images of geographical features, local and distant places, probable and preferable futures.

Envisioning is a process, based on use of the active imagination, used by futurists and others to clarify preferred visions of the future. A sustainable world, for example, cannot come into being unless we can envision it in some detail. However, vision

Futures 'fieldwork' 2021

This activity should only be used after the following steps have been taken within the study of a particular locality or geographical issue:

1 clarification of the current problems to be resolved;
2 identification, by individual students, of three differences they would most want to see in their preferred future for this situation;
3 a brief introduction to use of the creative imagination.

Note: When reading the text below allow sufficient pauses for students to focus on their own images.

Since the future hasn't happened yet, it exists only in your imagination, awaiting its invention. If we do not clarify our choice of preferred future then we are likely to get somebody else's. We are going to use the creative imagination now to 'visit' your preferred future (for …) in 2021. Remember this is not about trying to predict the future but about exploring your most optimistic vision. You will need to get comfortable, relax and close your eyes – as if you were going to daydream, for example – but in this case it is for a particular purpose. Just let images arise in the mind's eye, allowing your imagination to act as a source of inspiration to you.

Imagine yourself following me out of the building where, instead of the usual scene, you are confronted by a high hedge stretching as far as you can see in either direction. Look at it in detail. What sort of hedge is it? How does it look, feel and smell? Set in the hedge you see there is a closed door. What does it look like? Look at the detail. On the other side lies your preferred future of 2021.

Hold your previously identified hopes for the future in the mind's eye and see where you find yourself as you step through the door. Are you inside or outside, in a town or in the country? A variety of images may come to mind; don't start judging them, just note them. Remember this is not an exercise in forecasting. Maybe you are in a place you knew back in 2001. If so, how has it changed?

In what ways is life in 2021 different from today? What is it that indicates that your desired future has actually come about? Be as specific as you can. How have things changed? How is life different? What are people doing differently in this place? What are they saying that is different? What are the words, feelings, colours and sounds? What do people say to you? Which of the images or ideas that come to you feels the most interesting? Focus on it and make it as concrete as possible.

How is this society or place different? How do you know that your preferred future has come about? What is the specific evidence? Look for details – for central images or themes. Search for the compelling, that which you can't let go of, which feels like the future speaking to you. Look for the detail which makes you say, 'Yes, this is how it should be!'

Remembering these details, turn back to look at the hedge and follow me again, through the door returning to this room in the year 2001. Without speaking to anyone else describe in an annotated sketch the main features of your preferred future.

Figure 19.3 Envisioning futures 'fieldwork' activity

without action will not bring about change and similarly action without vision has no clear goal to aim for. We need, therefore, many different visions of more sustainable communities if this paradigm shift is ever to be achieved.

Visions of the future can only exist in the human imagination. While it is possible, of course, for students to write down individually what their preferred future might look like, or for a group to discuss and record possible answers to this question, deeper and richer images nearly always emerge if these are arrived at through the process of visualization. At its most basic this involves students making a simple 'journey' using the inner eye to 'visit' each one's preferred future, led by the teacher. Students then write down or draw the main features of their preferred future. They are often surprised by the images that arise, and the similarities that occur in the group. It is, if you like, a sort of futures fieldwork in the imagination. Clearly this activity requires some structure and guidance, which can be provided by using the framework shown in Figure 19.3.

Figure 19.4 lists some of the key images that have emerged when people have explored their preferred futures using the process of envisioning described in Figure 19.3. Elise Boulding (1998), one of the pioneers of what are sometimes called 'futures workshops', has worked with countless business, community and activist groups in North America and Europe. She reports, in Figure 19.4, the common features of many people's preferred futures. As a result of Boulding's work, I became interested in the process of envisioning, and wondered whether students in the UK would have similar preferred futures (Hicks 1996). The most common features (including descriptors used by participants) are presented in Figure 19.5. The overlap between the findings shown in Figures 19.4 and 19.5 is striking. While none of the groups had set out specifically to focus on sustainable futures or citizenship, both are apparent as central themes. I have no doubt, of course, that captains of industry or venture capitalists might have quite different preferred futures. The similarities in this sample may, of course, come from the fact that when people are given the opportunity to reflect on their ideal community, and they use the creative imagination to do this, it taps into deeply felt human needs for security, community and social harmony.

- Lack of divisions based on race, age or gender.

- A non-hierarchical world.

- A strong sense of place and community.

- Low profile and widely shared technology.

- Especially in relation to communications and transport.

- People acting out of a 'new' consciousness.

- Education generally occurring 'on the job'.

Figure 19.4 Characteristics of preferred futures (Boulding)

Source: Boulding 1998.

- Green: clean air and water; trees; wildlife; flowers.

- Convivial: co-operative; relaxed; happy; caring; laughter.

- Transport: no cars; no pollution; public transport; bikes.

- Peaceful: absence of violent conflict; security; global harmony.

- Equality: no poverty; fair shares for all; no hunger.

- Community: local; small; friendly; simpler; sense of community.

- Justice: equal rights of people and planet; no discrimination.

Figure 19.5 *Characteristics of preferred futures (Hicks)*

Source: Hicks 1996.

New horizons …

So what happens if we try to draw together these issues of Citizenship and sustainability? Surprisingly it is not until Key Stage 4 that sustainability actually gets a mention in Citizenship, whereas the principle of sustainability can actually be explored from the early years onwards. In the past environment and development were seen as separate concerns; they are now seen as inextricably intertwined, so in turn the view of Citizenship and sustainability as somehow separate must now be challenged. A curriculum opportunity has been lost to bring them together in fruitful juxtaposition – an opportunity that geographers could now choose to grasp.

One of the major contributions Geography could make to human and environmental well-being would be to develop numerous detailed scenarios of more sustainable futures (Dauncey 1999). So many geographical themes and issues invite a futures perspective. On one level this is no more than asking what the impact of particular changes might be on students' future lives. More specifically it is about asking: What is the probable future here? What is the preferable future here? Since probable futures are often unsustainable this opens up the need for scenarios of sustainable futures – for the school playground, my street, my suburb, for this national park, this environment, global warming (Hicks 2001). It could be considered an educational crime not to give young people the critical tools for asking, and beginning to answer, such questions. We surely would not want to teach Geography for a 'worse world', or the existing 'unjust and inequitable world'? If this is the case it leaves us no choice but to teach for a 'better world', debatable though the meaning of that may be. Similarly, we can teach Geography for 'participation and action' or for 'alienation and inaction'. I have to say that the former seems the more worthwhile educational goal, as we travel into a turbulent and challenging new century.

References

Boulding, E. (1998) 'Image and action in peace building', in D. Hicks (ed.) *Preparing for the Future: Notes and Queries for Concerned Educators*, London: Adamantine Press.

Carter, R. (2000) 'Aspects of global citizenship', in C. Fisher and T. Binns (eds) *Issues in Geography Teaching*, London: RoutledgeFalmer.

Cogan, J. and Derricott, R. (1998) *Citizenship for the 21st Century*, London: Kogan Page.

Dauncey, G. (1999) *Earth Future: Stories from a Sustainable World*, Canada: New Society Publishers.

DfEE/QCA (1999) *The National Curriculum: Handbook for Secondary Teachers in England (KS3&4)*, London: The Stationery Office.

Fien, J. and Trainer, T. (1993) 'A vision of sustainability', in J. Huckle (ed.) *Environmental Education: A Pathway to Sustainability*, Australia: Deakin University Press.

Grimwade, K., Reid, A. and Thompson, L. (2000) *Geography and the New Agenda: Citizenship PSHE and Sustainable Development in the Secondary Curriculum*, Sheffield: Geographical Association.

Hicks, D. (1996) 'Preferred futures 2020: are students interested in sustainable future?', *Australian Journal of Environmental Education* 12: 41–5.

—— (1998) 'A geography for the future', *Teaching Geography* 23(4): 168–73.

—— (2001) *Citizenship for the Future: A Practical Classroom Guide*, Godalming: World Wide Fund for Nature (UK).

Sustainable Development Educational Panel (SDEP) (1999) *First Annual Report 1998*, London: Department of the Environment, Transport and Regions.

Smith, D. (1977) *Human Geography: A Welfare Approach*, London: Arnold.

Walford, R. (2000) 'Wider issues for the future', in C. Fisher and T. Binns (eds) *Issues in Geography Teaching*, London: RoutledgeFalmer.

20 Young people's geovisions
Linda Thompson

Introduction

One of the primary aims of the Geo Visions project is to explore the role of school Geography in developing the capabilities of young people in the twenty-first century. The project aims to do this so that Geography can help young people to lead fulfilled lives and encourage them to create a better world. Geo Visions provides a forum for debate and discussion, unconstrained by short-term objectives and immediate political concerns. It helps geographers to stand back from the minutiae of everyday demands, and encourages consideration of the big picture.

Several areas for investigation were identified by those involved in the first phase of the Geo Visions project:

- knowledge and understanding as a body of content prescribed by the National Curriculum for Geography (DfEE/QCA 1999) and its relevance to the lives of young people;
- young people as learners and an emphasis on 'deep learning' rather than content coverage;
- the influence of society, the changes that are currently reshaping the world and how young people make sense of a world full of uncertainties and multiple truths;
- disseminating Geo Visions ideas and influencing decision-makers: for example, awarding bodies, the Qualifications and Curriculum Authority, teacher trainers.

Many of these aspects are now informing the second stage of the Geo Visions project. Since November 1999, the Geographical Association has supported a group of geography educators to take Geo Visions further. Contributions are being sought from the wider geographical community. The group would welcome your involvement by conducting some research in your own school. It simply involves questioning your students about their geographical learning (see 'Wider involvement in the research' on p. 294).

Young people as learners

One Geo Visions group became involved in considering 'young people as learners'. This article explores some of this work undertaken in Cheshire schools. The group started by identifying a number of issues relating to the teaching and learning of Geography in schools.

- Do young people gain a positive and stimulating learning experience that goes beyond the limited diet of textbook-based Geography?
- Do they experience a broad range of learning approaches?
- Are some young people underachieving as a result of low teacher expectations and a lack of challenge and variety in Geography schemes of work, learning resources and activities?
- Have developments such as the National Curriculum and other external measures of achievement reduced school Geography to the lowest common denominator – 'What do I need to do to pass this test?'
- Does school Geography help young people to make sense of a world full of uncertainties and multiple truths? Does it reflect the diversity of reality?
- School Geography is still relatively successful in terms of, for example, A-level and GCSE uptake. Is this due to its diversity of content and affinity for a variety of learning styles?

Geo Visions members are committed to improving young people's learning and enjoyment of Geography by emphasizing its relevance to their lives and futures. The Geo Visions group acknowledges that it needs to know more about how young people learn in Geography in order to improve planning for teaching and learning. The group wanted to explore preferred learning styles and how young people develop the skills of critical thinking, enquiry, graphicacy and an understanding of scale. This is being addressed by bringing together published and unpublished research. Several lines of enquiry have been followed.

- How do young people learn and how can planning for this be more explicit?
- What do young people enjoy learning about and what are their preferred learning styles?
- What do young people need to learn about and to be able to do in order to make sense of the world and their role in it?
- What are their perceptions and opinions about their own future needs and imperatives?
- What is the role of 'values and attitudes' education in developing young people who are willing and able to be active global citizens?
- How can appropriate professional development opportunities support teachers in exploring such issues? How can this enhance teacher professionalism?

These lines of enquiry were, initially, investigated using a student questionnaire (Figure 20.1). An existing questionnaire devised at Keele University for a 'Student survey of school life' (Barber 1996) was adapted to explore the perceptions of a sample of students studying Geography in Key Stages 2, 3 and 4.

Methodology

All 47 secondary school geography departments in Cheshire LEA were invited to participate in the research project. Thirteen schools agreed to be involved:

Questions about Geography

Circle your year group: Year 5 Year 6 Year 8 Year 9 Year 10 Year 11

Circle: male female

(Circle one letter for each question: a. strongly agree, b. agree, c. not sure, d. disagree, e. strongly disagree)

1	I enjoy geography lessons	a b c d e
2	Geography lessons are always interesting	a b c d e
3	Geography is easy for me	a b c d e
4	Girls are better at Geography than boys	a b c d e
5	Geography is more important for boys	a b c d e
6	The teacher who teaches you Geography makes a big difference to whether you like or dislike it	a b c d e
7	I understand Geography better when we have discussions about it	a b c d e
8	I understand Geography better when I have to write about it	a b c d e
9	I understand Geography better when I can use a computer	a b c d e
10	I understand Geography better when I draw maps or diagrams	a b c d e
11	I learn best in Geography when I am required to solve problems, make decisions and give opinions	a b c d e
12	I enjoy doing fieldwork and surveys in Geography	a b c d e
13	The hardest part is carrying out research or investigations	a b c d e
14	I enjoy learning about physical (natural) geography	a b c d e
15	I enjoy learning about human (people) geography	a b c d e
16	I enjoy learning about distant places	a b c d e
17	I enjoy learning about environmental issues	a b c d e
18	I think Geography will help me to get a job when I leave school	a b c d e
19	I think Geography will be useful to me in adult life	a b c d e
20	I do not see the value of the work we do in Geography to my future	a b c d e

The most important things we learn or do in Geography to prepare us for life in the twenty-first century are:

1

2

3

4

Figure 20.1 The student questionnaire

Source: Adapted from Barber 1996.

- ten mixed 11–18 comprehensive schools
- one boys' 11–18 comprehensive
- one mixed 11–16 Roman Catholic high school
- one primary school with a strong tradition of geographical education.

The schools were invited to submit as many responses as they wished from students from Years 5–11 (with the exception of Year 7[1]). In total 1,056 student responses were received. The research described here is opportunist and circumstantial in its approach. This is often likely to be the case with small-scale research projects, carried out by teachers and without the involvement of higher education institutions. However, the findings of this project strongly concur with research undertaken by Michael Barber in 1996.

The questionnaire sought students' reactions across a five-point scale, from 'strongly agree' to 'strongly disagree'. Questions of a similar type were grouped, e.g. those that focused on student enjoyment of various aspects of content. Some questions aimed to discover students' perceptions about how they learn best, whilst others investigated what elements of the National Curriculum they enjoyed learning about. The final part of the questionnaire invited a free response to the question, 'What are the most important things you learn or do in Geography to prepare you for life in the twenty-first century?' Four numbered spaces were provided.

The questionnaires were completed in geography lessons with classes selected by the geography teachers. Teachers were asked to ensure that the students understood all of the questions and to point out that some questions were about whether students enjoyed certain elements of Geography whilst others wanted them to consider which learning approaches helped them to understand best. They were asked to give guidance as necessary without unduly influencing the student responses and to assure students that their responses would be confidential.

Feedback to schools

The student information was entered into a spreadsheet, classified by school, Key Stage and gender. The data was then displayed using graphs according to Key Stage and gender for each individual school and then for the sample population as a whole. The results presented in this article are for the whole sample as it was agreed that no individual school's results would be published to anyone other than members of the geography department concerned.

When the information from each of the 13 schools had been processed, the results were sent to each of the departments. A representative from each school was invited to a feedback session to evaluate the information and its potential for informing future departmental planning. This meeting enabled the teachers to compare their students' perceptions with those from other schools, thus providing them with a broader picture and useful reference points.

Research results

Although each school generated its own distinctive set of results, a number of generalizations can be drawn from the data.

- Despite the fact that 58 per cent of the girls and 53 per cent of boys in the sample claim to enjoy geography lessons, only 30 per cent of girls and 39 per cent of boys always find them interesting. When analysed by Key Stage, 54 per cent of students enjoy Geography at Key Stage 3 compared to 66 per cent at Key Stage 4. Few students claim to find Geography difficult (15 per cent at Key Stage 3 and 20 per cent at Key Stage 4).

- About 73 per cent of the students believe that their teachers have a powerful influence upon whether they like or dislike the subject. Students' responses to this show almost no gender difference. Even more importantly, 67 per cent from Key Stage 3 and a massive 80 per cent from Key Stage 4 agree. This factor may significantly influence student motivation and learning and is likely to affect uptake at GCSE and AS/A level. This issue was held to be particularly significant by some of the participating schools.

- 22 per cent of girls and 40 per cent of boys claim that they understand Geography better when using ICT. Some individual department results show greater gender differences in this area. It is also interesting that 39 per cent of Key Stage 3 students compared to 25 per cent of Key Stage 4 students claim to understand Geography better when using ICT.

- Boys and girls across the whole age-spectrum sampled agree that they can understand better through the use of discussion (only 8 per cent disagree at Key Stage 3 and 5 per cent at Key Stage 4).

- Only 11 per cent of students at both Key Stages disagree with the statement, 'I understand better when I draw maps and diagrams'. Boys show a slightly greater preference for learning via this approach (61 per cent of girls and 69 per cent of boys agree).

- The gender difference is less marked than expected in preferences for learning through written work. In departments where there is a greater variation this perhaps suggests a greater or lesser use of 'writing interventions', for example the use of non-fiction writing frames or 'scaffolding'.

- Claims about better understanding through the use of problem-solving and decision-making are not particularly apparent in either the Key Stages or from either girls or boys. During the feedback session a number of teachers acknowledged that this was not an approach used frequently in their department's geography lessons, particularly at Key Stage 4 where it is not required as an examination technique.

- Both boys and girls across the Key Stages express a slightly greater enjoyment of studying physical than human geography – 66 per cent of girls and 69 per cent of boys state that they enjoy physical geography, whilst 56 per cent of girls and 51 per cent of boys say they enjoy human geography. Students appear to enjoy the study of physical geography most at Key Stage 4 (71 per cent).

- There is a slightly stronger preference for carrying out fieldwork amongst the boys (75 per cent of boys and 70 per cent of girls). There is also a slightly stronger preference for doing fieldwork at Key Stage 3.

- Girls appear to enjoy studying environmental issues more than boys (59 per cent compared to 42 per cent).

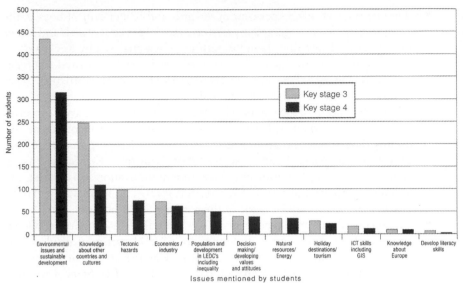

Figure 20.2 Graphed responses to 'How Geography prepares "us" for life in the twenty-first century'

- Students of all ages enjoy learning about distant places (59 per cent agree and 14 per cent disagree).
- While students of all ages and both boys and girls value Geography's role in contributing to their futures as adults they are less certain of its ability to support them in gaining employment. At Key Stage 3 boys have the stronger perception that studying Geography may lead to a future job. Sixty-two per cent of the students are able to see the value of the work they do in Geography to their future lives and 67 per cent believe that having studied Geography will be useful to them as adults.
- The final section of the questionnaire allowed students to respond freely about how they believe Geography is preparing them for life in the twenty-first century. In addition to those responses graphed in Figure 20.2, fewer than 50 responses were recorded for enquiry skills; fieldtrips and fieldwork; knowledge about other places in the UK; and developing oral and discussion skills.

In the analysis of the total responses many interesting patterns and anomalies peculiar to individual geography departments have been masked. In many instances it was these features that were most informative to the future planning of these departments.

Findings and further questions

It is likely that more questions have been raised than answered through the research carried out so far. The findings suggest that the following points may be important in curriculum planning.

- The key role played by individual teachers in determining young people's enjoyment of geography lessons and the implications this has for student motivation, behaviour, quality of learning ... and uptake of the subject at the subsequent Key Stage.
- The need to take account of young people's views about how they learn effectively when selecting learning activities and approaches.
- Young people value geographical education but do not always see its relevance to their current and future lives. They need to understand how they are a part of the phenomenon they are studying. Do teachers need to make their objectives more explicit to the learners?
- Young people are not always challenged enough by their geographical learning experiences.
- Decision-making and problem-solving activities occur infrequently in many schools (or students are not aware of them occurring). Nevertheless these are considered useful learning approaches by students who experience them.
- Teacher and student awareness of gender issues needs to be enhanced (an area relating to teaching and learning that requires further exploration).
- Young people generally enjoy learning about all aspects of the National Curriculum, but believe that education about environmental issues, management and sustainability are of paramount importance for their future lives as citizens of the twenty-first century. The revised Order for Geography (and the new Orders for Citizenship and Personal, Social and Health Education (DfEE/QCA 1999)) may provide a stimulus for curriculum development in this area.

Some of the issues raised by teachers in response to the research include:

- How valid is the research? A number of teachers were surprised by the lack of correlation between the students' views on 'what prepares them for life in the twenty-first century' and the curriculum/schemes of work that they had been taught. Several felt that the results for their departments reflected the more recently covered topics most and that students had 'forgotten' work covered earlier in the Key Stage. This in itself is an issue to be considered when constructing a Key Stage Programme of Study.
- Many teachers were surprised that knowledge and understanding of geographical content predominated in answers to the final question (see Figure 20.1) about the importance of Geography to life in the twenty-first century. Some were surprised that departmental initiatives focusing on the development of literacy skills, thinking skills and decision-making skills were not reflected in the student responses. One reason for this may be that teachers are less explicit about such objectives in their lessons than those relating to the development of geographical skills, knowledge and understanding.
- Was the research representative of a true cross-section of schools and students? How did teachers select classes? The involvement was voluntary and, although all schools in Cheshire were invited to participate, only thirteen chose to. The questionnaire required some time and effort to organize

on the part of the teacher. It also required the department to believe in the value of the project's outcomes. It is possible, therefore, that participating departments were those that tend to be more responsive to new ideas and teaching methods with more progressive approaches to teacher professional development. Thus the results may be biased.

Despite some reservations, all the teachers who participated felt there were aspects of the research outcomes that would inform their departmental development planning for 1999/2000. Several participants believed it would be necessary to discuss the findings with their senior managers with a view to extending the research within individual schools.

Note

1   Because the questionnaire was carried out early in the autumn term, Year 7 students were not asked to participate since they had only a limited experience of 'discrete' Geography.

Wider involvement in the research

We are seeking to involve a wide range of geographers in this debate and would welcome comments or responses to any of the issues presented in this article. The questionnaire (Figure 20.1) and graphs of results are available on the Staffordshire Learning Net (website: www.sln.org.uk/geography). Please send your responses to Diane Swift, Chair GeoVisions, c/o the Geographical Association, 160 Solly Street Sheffield S1 4BF.

References

Barber, M. (1996) 'Student survey of school life' (research report), Centre for Successful Schools, Keele University.

DfEE/QCA (1999) *The National Curriculum: Handbook for Secondary Teachers in England (Key Stages 3 and 4)*, London: DfEE/QCA.

Further resources

A leaflet explaining the work of the first phase of the Geo Visions project can be obtained by contacting Diane Swift, c/o Geographical Association headquarters (at the above address) or via e-mail: diane.swift@btinternet.com

21 Image and reality
How do others see us?
Ashley Kent

As we approach the end of the twentieth century, I wish to suggest that, across the world, Geography is often still perceived in an outdated and inaccurate fashion. We, as professional geographers, are convinced about and committed to its values, the ways in which it causes us to wonder at, analyse, understand and help propose alternative futures for our world. Our knowledge, understanding and perceptions of the discipline invariably contrast with those of fellow educators, parents, the public in general, employers, politicians and even our own students. This is a call to arms for geographers around the world and particularly those associated with the IGU Commission on Geography Education. It suggests that, at an international level, we geographers should research the perceptions held by non-geographers in our respective societies and, based on these, propose, share and carry out strategies for promoting up-to-date and accurate knowledge, understanding and thus perceptions of the study of Geography.

The comments which follow are based upon UK experience and writings but anecdotal evidence suggests that circumstances are not dissimilar elsewhere across the world. Concern about our image is not new. As early as 1976 Michael Naish reminded us that 'ignorance of the spirit and purpose of modern geography is commonplace: we need a public relations exercise'. Indeed, in 1971 Blachford forcefully declared that 'we must advertise the work of geography teachers. It needs to be advertised quite openly, blatantly, proudly and positively in order to dispel the many persistent misrepresentations and oversimplifications which are so frequently made with reference to geography and geography teachers'.

In a nutshell, Geography is frequently seen as being a burden on the memory rather than a challenge to the mind and is invariably associated with a catalogue of facts. A particularly typical and uninformed discussion was broadcast on BBC Radio 4 (22 January 1983) which described Geography as 'a species of dead end'. 'What other subject offers such a minimum of speculation, such limitless savannas of unleavened fact?' In that discussion Geography was held to be 'low in the hierarchy of acceptable subjects' and to be concerned with studying the 'eccentric, the odd and the absurd'. A survey by John Chiplen was reported in the *Times Educational Supplement* in 1984. He attempted a classification of some of the limited views of Geography that he discovered. He identified firstly 'Eiffel Tower knowledge', concerning the height and length of various features; 'Timbuktu knowledge' which concerns itself with gazetteer information about the location of places; and 'Colman's Mustard knowledge' which involves lists of the products grown or made in various towns, regions or countries. He concluded that 'geography appears to be particularly misunderstood and to be singularly unfortunate in not being able to shed the really obsolete, naive images of itself' (Chiplen 1984).

In Britain, from 1981 the joint Royal Geographical Society, Geographical Association and Institute of British Geographers Committee on Geography in Higher Education was 'increasingly concerned about the public's image of geography which it senses as often neutral, frequently obsolete and sometimes contemptible' (GA Council minutes, March 1983). The committee considered a number of needs and actions as a part of its deliberations. The identified needs were to:

1   bring the general public's, educators', employers' and decision-makers' attention to the nature and concerns of modern Geography and to the actual and potential roles of geographers;
2   present Geography as both exciting and relevant to issues which command widespread concern;
3   stress space, environment and their implications as the distinctive focuses of modern Geography;
4   present Geography as analytical as well as descriptive;
5   utilize the mass media in attempting to achieve points 1–4;
6   review at every level the geography curriculum and the methodologies of Geography both as preparations for Citizenship and in the light of the contemporary needs of society;
7   promote the adaptability of geography graduates as employees at a time when adaptability is increasingly seen to be a virtue;
8   promote in-service courses for those teaching Geography in schools in order to update the content and methodologies of Geography during a period when the entry of specialist geographers seems likely to be minimal; and
9   stimulate Geography within the continuing education sector.

The joint committee also suggested a number of actions designed to counter the situation as they perceived it. The actions they proposed at that time included:

1   preparing and maintaining a list of influential media contacts;
2   preparing and maintaining a list of geographers qualified, willing and able to speak or write effectively on specific topics, regions and places in such a way that they would satisfy the media requirements of brevity, clarity, relevance and immediacy;
3   encouraging existing groups of geographers to approach editors in television, radio and the press with specific suggestions for programmes and articles accompanied by the names of advisers and possible contributors/authors;
4   encouraging individuals to form links with the mass media on a personal basis with a view to offering information, opinion and comment on current issues of public concern;
5   adopting positive strategies equivalent to but different from 1–4, designed to revise the image and increase the perceived utility of Geography in

regional and national government and likewise in the world of commerce and industry; and

6 seeking the advice of public-relations specialists with a view to developing an integrated public-relations policy.

At least in Britain, it appears that only one piece of substantial research has been undertaken on images of Geography since that time, and that was by Bunce in 1984, while the issue has periodically resurfaced as indicated by the editorial in the *Journal of Geography in Higher Education* in 1989. Yet probably more regular and persistent than academic debate has been the negative stereotyping of Geography in the media. Two relatively recent examples occurred in January 1997 in the UK. First, in an article in the *Sunday Telegraph* newspaper (12 January 1997) entitled 'Marx seizes the rift valleys', Ross Clark argued that left-wing ideology had taken over the geography departments of UK universities. Basing his argument on papers produced at the Exeter conference of the Royal Geographical Society–Institute of British Geographers held a week earlier, he wrote: 'Geography has abandoned its original territory in favour of people and politics. In doing so, it is rapidly becoming not so much an academic subject as a general depository for Marxist academics who don't quite fit in any other university department'.

The focus of criticism shifted later in the month to school-level Geography when the following headlines made four national daily newspapers on 23 January 1997 to 3 January 1997:

- 'Geography goes west for schools' lost generation' (*Daily Mail*);
- 'Children cannot pinpoint London' (*The Times*);
- 'London moves to Aberdeen in schoolchildren's mixed up world' (The *Guardian*); and
- 'Half of Britain's children can't put London on the map' (The *Telegraph*).

This publicity was orchestrated by the press release from Microsoft Research the previous day entitled, 'British Children don't make the Geography Grade'. 892 children between the ages of eight and sixteen were interviewed about their 'geographical knowledge'. NOP Consumer Market Research carried out the research for Microsoft, publishers of the *Encarta 97 World Atlas*. Clearly, *Encarta* had a vested interest in such negative results being revealed! The research approach and instrument can be questioned but even so such results are profoundly depressing for geography educators especially when trumpeted so loudly in the national media.

That is not to say that Geography does not have its supporters, since, after all, our students both past and present represent our most effective advocates, and some influential members of the press such as Simon Jenkins stand up for the subject. Jenkins, in a number of editorials in *The Times* newspaper and articles, for example in the *Sunday Times* in 1988 and at the GA conference in 1992, has been an influential ally.

There has been a particular 'edge' to this issue in Britain since 1997 when a new government began reassessing the entire 14–19 school curriculum, and Geography had to demonstrate how it could contribute within both new and traditional curriculum structures. The latest approach asks geographers to specify the minimum entitlement of Geography for every 14–19-year-old.

Making the case for Geography (and enhancing its image) is not unique to Britain. In the United States of America, a social studies curriculum led to a demise of 'quality' geography education and necessitated an encouraging 'renaissance' of school Geography under the new Alliances subsidized by the National Geographic Society. More recently in South Africa, a new curriculum framework announced in February 1997 entitled 'Curriculum 2005' has removed traditional subject areas. The eight 'learning areas' include Human and Social Sciences, and Natural Sciences. Geography is having to make a strong case for its inclusion in at least those two 'learning areas'. Similarly in Australia, discussions at a national level led to the creation of 'key learning areas', one of which was entitled 'Studies of Society and Environment' and to which geographers were asked to pledge allegiance. Issues of state rights over education have resulted in almost continuous confusion over the status of Geography over the past decade which currently appears to have been resolved in favour of Geography in Victoria and New South Wales, the two most populous states, while the battle to prevent students being denied their 'geographical entitlement' still rages in Queensland. In all these examples, the case being made for Geography is one of image, relevance and status.

It appears that the concerns of the joint committee in Britain in the early 1980s are still with us at the international scale. In the late 1990s, I should like to propose a number of questions we as geographers should ask ourselves and actions we could take, based on Bunce's research.

Question	Possible action
1 In-school image: Do I as a geography teacher have sufficient dialogue with colleagues about recent subject developments, approaches and resources?	internal promotion of subject; keep headteachers briefed verbally and with documentation briefing colleagues
2 Parental image: Am I keeping parents informed about Geography's changing role?	handouts at parents' meetings; in-school displays of project work or fieldwork on open days
3 Public image: Is there anything I can do to make the general public more aware of the benefits of Geography?	displays of work in public areas, e.g. council offices, libraries, galleries; local press coverage of visits and departmental activities
4 Political image: Can I help to make politicians better informed about Geography's modern role and utility?	write to your local MP about the work you do; send him or her geographical articles of likely use and interest to him or her; brief him or her on departmental activities
5 Media image: How can I gain a higher media profile for Geography (in local press, radio and television)?	write letters and articles for newspapers and popular magazines; stimulate more local press coverage of your departmental trips and other activities

[...]

References

Blachford, K.R. (1971) 'Why is geography in the curriculum?' *Geographical Education* 1.

Bunce, V.J. (1984) 'An investigation into whether viewpoints and images of geography held by decision makers reflects its potential as a valuable medium for education', unpublished MA dissertation, University of London, Institute of Education.

Chiplen, J. (1984) 'Image, role and relevance', *Times Educational Supplement*, 13 April 1984.

Conolly, G. (1997) *Rediscover Geography*, Geography Teachers' Association of New South Wales Inc.

Jenkins, S. (1988) 'Geography puts on its glad rags at last', *Sunday Times*, 3 April 1988.

—— (1992) 'Four cheers for geography', *Geography* 72(3).

Kent, W.A. (ed.) (1990) *Selling Geography*, Geographical Association.

—— (1997) 'Challenging geography', *Geography* 82(4).

—— (ed.) (1999) *Promoting Geography in Schools*, Geographical Association.

Naish, M. (1976) 'Public relations', *Geographical Magazine* 48(4).

National Department of Education (1997) *Curriculum 2005*, National Department of Education, South Africa.

Walker, D. and Unwin, D. (1989) 'The image of geography' (editorial), *Journal of Geography in Higher Education* 13(2).

4 Research geography and professional development

The final section of the book goes beyond the classroom to take a brief glimpse at some of the current directions of research in geographical education. Michael Williams and Rod Gerber provide an overview of the range of research areas currently being undertaken, and this is followed by two specific examples of research studies – one into gender and one into children's perceptions. There is much here to stimulate thought about classroom practice and to encourage new (and more experienced) teachers to go beyond the constraints and pressures of the daily 'grind' and to help push the frontiers of geography teaching forward. In the final chapter, Ashley Kent provides encouragement for teachers themselves to take an active part in researching geography education by undertaking work towards a higher degree as part of their professional development – a move that is becoming increasingly important as part of a teacher's career progression.

22 An overview of research in geographical education

Rod Gerber and Michael Williams

Introduction

Across the globe, over the last three decades there has been a dramatic increase in the numbers of researchers in geographical education and their output is evidenced in bibliographies, books and theses, research conferences and symposiums, and articles in research journals. A brief glance at the British bibliography (Foskett and Marsden 1998) and the more recent internet bibliography produced by the National Council for Geographic Education (2000) in the United States indicates clearly the range of topics that have attracted the interest of researchers and demonstrates a variety of research methods. It is important that research reported in languages other than English should not be ignored and examples of such writing include the work of John Chi-Kin Lee (1998) in Chinese, Hannele Rikkinen (1997, 1998a and 1998b) in Finnish and Juan-Luis Klein and Suzanne Laurin (1999) in French. Many others could be quoted.

In this chapter we sketch out selected features of the context of research in geographical education with particular reference to their culture and community. We highlight the roles of both the Commission on Geographical Education of the International Geographical Union and national organizations. We then seek to identify broad trends in research in geographical education before outlining an agenda for future research studies.

Context

Elsewhere, we have listed a number of features of the research culture of geographical education (Williams 1998) and suggested three stages in its development: an incipient stage, an intermediate stage and a mature stage (see Table 22.1). Using this model it is possible for researchers to locate themselves in terms of the stages and indicate lines for progress in a cultural context. Published evidence suggests that most research in geographical education is being conducted at the incipient stage. Obviously, this is not a reflection on either the quality or quantity of the work being undertaken. Further, it does not indicate the influence that any researcher or group of researchers may have upon other researchers, curriculum policy-makers and classroom practitioners. What the model offers is a checklist against which individuals and groups can gauge their progress in establishing and strengthening the research culture of geographical education. 'The fundamental shift is from the

Table 22.1 Stages of growth in the culture of research in geographical education

Incipient stage	Intermediate stage	Mature stage
Individuals researching in isolation	Intra-institutional groups	International groups
Idiosyncratic and changing substantive focuses	Stable substantive focuses though subject to personnel changes	Enduring substantive focuses that are unaffected by personnel changes
Unfunded	Funded by local and national organizations	Funded by international organizations
Unsupported by a professional body	Supported on the margins of a national professional body	Central to the work of an international body
Dominated by immediate practical issues	Linking practical and theoretical issues	Dominated by universal theoretical issues
Focused largely on a single sector of a national education system	Focused on more than one sector of a national education system	Focused on lifelong learning in international context
Undeveloped specialist geographical education research language	Emergence of a specialist geographical education research language	Use of a sophisticated geographical education research language
Absence of textbooks on geographical education research	Introductory textbooks on geographical education research	An array of established textbooks on geographical education research
Lacking close ties with conventional educational disciplines	Developing ties with a number of educational research disciplines	Closely integrated into the educational research community
Lacking any sub-discipline strengths within geographical education	Emergent sub-discipline strengths within geographical education	Established sub-discipline communities within research in geographical education
No infrastructure of research-focused symposiums, conferences, web pages, journals and other publications	Developing nationally based infrastructure of research-focused symposiums, conferences, web pages, journals and other publications	Well-developed international infrastructure comprising symposiums, conferences, web pages, journals and other publications
Few opportunities for training in research in geographical education	Limited national opportunities for training in research in geographical education	Many international opportunities for training in research in geographical education

relatively isolated individual functioning in one institution to an international group of researchers collaborating on a single project' (Williams 1998: 2).

What the model also highlights is the need for a strong research infrastructure that includes frequent research-focused symposiums and conferences with publications appearing in referred specialist and general journals and on websites. Globally, there is a need for funding agencies, governmental and non-governmental, to include research in geographical education higher in their funding priorities. This is particularly important for those agencies that fund international research projects. Lacking this funding, it is not surprising to find that curriculum revision of geographical education is usually undertaken without recourse to prior research findings. Indeed, some commentators have pointed to the deliberate neglect of the geographical education community in the launching of major reforms, as in Australia (Lidstone 1998) and the Republic of South Africa (Smit 1998).

Without doubt, the organization that has been most influential in progressing research in geographical education beyond the incipient stage for many researchers is the Commission on Education of the International Geographical Union (ICU). In recent years the numbers participating in the symposiums on geographical education, held usually before the meeting of the World Congress every four years, has been increasing. More and more participants are attending from more and more countries. In addition, more continental and national symposiums are being arranged under the auspices of the Commission. Thus, in 1999, symposiums were held in Argentina, England and the United States. Details of the presentations can be read in the publications stemming from these meetings, e.g. *Teaching Geography in a World on Change* (Ostuni *et al.* 1999), the proceedings of the conference held in Mendoza, Argentina.

Every four years, the Commission prepares a list of projects proposed by participants, usually in international, collaborative groups. While the Commission lacks the funding to finance these projects, it lends its weight behind submissions for funding made to various bodies. Books, reports and journal articles are the products of these projects and a list of recent publications can be accessed on the Commission's website and listserve page. In 1991, the Commission launched the referred journal, *International Research in Geographical and Environmental Education,* edited by Rod Gerber and John Lidstone. The journal was initially published three times a year, but in 1999 a decision was made to extend the issues to four a year, reflecting the increasing number of quality papers being produced. The year 1999 also witnessed the establishment of a new American journal, *Research in Geographic Education,* edited by Richard Boehm and David Stea and sponsored by the Gilbert Grosvenor Center for Geographic Education at the South West Texas State University, San Marcos.

At the national level, in various parts of the world researchers in geographical education find organizations that enable them to communicate their interests with their peers and disseminate the findings from their studies. Such national groups include the UDE (University Departments of Education) Geography Tutors Group in England and Wales, the Geographie und Ihre Didaktik Group in Germany, the Australian Geography Teachers Association and the National Council for Geographic Education in the United States. In Europe many national organizations have been brought together under the former European Standing Conference of Geography Teachers' Associations, now referred to as Eurogeo. These organizations arrange national conferences and some publish journals and reports that include research in geographical education.

Table 22.2 Dichotomies in research in geographical education

Originating in practice	Originating in theory
Designed for a practitioner audience	Designed for a researcher audience
Intended to contribute to improved professional practice	Intended to contribute to improved research
Not linked to a social science discipline	Closely linked to a social science discipline
Single method	Eclectic
Atheoretical	Theoretical
Not rooted in a substantial scholarly literature	Rooted in a substantial scholarly literature

Current trends

In considering current trends in research in geographical education, the dichotomies listed in Table 22.2 are a useful starting point.

These dichotomies point to differences in motivation and purpose. In particular, they stimulate questions about who are and who should be the beneficiaries of research. Generally, there would appear to be little interest among geographical educators in undertaking research that is narrowly defined in terms of theory construction or the refinement of research methodologies. There appears to be a strong interest in practitioner-based research. Much research in geographical education originates in the contemporary school classroom, is not linked closely to a social science discipline and is intended to contribute to improved professional practice. A good example of this pattern can be found in the *Theory into Practice* series of booklets (Dove 1999; Leat and Nichols 1999; Walkington 1999), edited by Mary Biddulph and Graham Butt and published in 1999. As the blurb for the series states:

> The aim of *Theory into Practice* is to take aspects of current research into geographical education and deliver them directly to the classroom practitioner. Geography teachers from across the professional spectrum will be able to access research findings on particular issues which they can relate to their own particular context

There are perils for researchers who follow too closely a research agenda that is determined by policy-makers and practitioners. As stated elsewhere:

> Research in geographical education ought not, in my opinion, to become a political football used in a game where the goal posts are ever changing. Far better would it be if the research agenda was defined according to concerns for both improved research methodologies and substantive issues of an enduring and universal kind.
>
> (Williams 1998: 6)

The dissemination of research in geographical education has been diverse, but a survey of major databases and key journals reveals that major areas of interest over the past two decades have been as follows.

The development of policy in geographical education

What, how and why general education policies have been used to develop policies in different curricular areas in formal education have been of particular interest in countries around the world. Without wanting to single out any country in this regard, geographical educators have reported how their policy-makers have prescribed a diversity of policies on such issues as the principles of education for particular levels of education, e.g. for primary or elementary schooling, the implementation of fieldwork in school programmes or what should constitute a school curriculum. Detailed investigations are reported on the nature of these policies, their relationship to prevailing social priorities and the impact of different policies on the type of geographical education that is promoted in such policies. Sometimes, the studies report on the debate and challenges that have resulted from proposals for developing new policies, e.g. how the status of Geography is affected by particular policy pronouncements. Limited attempts have been made to produce comparative studies of the variations in these policies and cross-cultural impacts in different regions, e.g. South East Asian countries.

Learning and teaching in geographical education

Research on learning and teaching in geographical education has been quite comprehensive. It reflects a passion by researchers to focus on the learning and teaching of school children and, to a lesser extent, of students in higher education. It does not reflect a strong interest in learning and teaching in vocational/technical education or lifelong learning. The main sub-areas in learning and teaching that interest geographical educators include: different approaches to learning and teaching; teaching styles; children's development of geographical and pedagogical skills; the development by teachers and students of the basic forms of communication including literacy, numeracy, graphicacy and oracy; children's development of basic geographical concepts; and the development of values through geographical education, especially social and environmental values.

Many of these studies focus on either learning or teaching. Few of them attempt to relate learning to teaching. With the advent of the widespread use of new communications technologies in geography classrooms, the reconsideration of how teachers use these technologies to maximize learning in Geography, and of how students use these technologies to learn, has drawn the two sides of the teaching–learning experience together. A similar observation can be made about learning and teaching in cross-cultural contexts within countries or regions. Here, case studies of learning and/or teaching Geography were reported, but little attempt was made to reflect on any generalizations that may be evident across a range of similar studies in different cultural contexts.

The growing interest in learning and teaching Geography in higher education over the past decade is reflected in the increased popularity of the *Journal of Geography in Higher Education* and the number of studies that focus on learning and teaching in university or college geography classes. The increase in the number of interest groups in professional associations for learning and teaching Geography in higher education reflects the strong interest in improving learning and teaching across all areas of formal education. Maybe the next wave of interest will be to extend research in geographical education to learning and teaching in vocational education and lifelong learning?

Geography curriculum development

Changes in geography curriculums in different countries provoke researchers to study the variations of the changes to previous policies and practices, the implementation of these changes and the impacts of these changes on policy development and practice in learning and teaching in Geography. Since most of these changes to curriculums occur on a state or national basis it is usual to find many reports of individual curriculum developments. On a similar basis, these reports may be of special curriculum projects that have been developed as a government priority. Often investigations of these changes involve the collection of a considerable amount of empirical data from people who have experienced the change. This has involved the popularizing of a range of research methodologies, e.g. case-study methodology, naturalistic inquiry, action research, ethnography and phenomenology, to draw out the personal experiences of people implementing a different geography curriculum.

The impact of the diffusion of a curriculum innovation has been the focus of a string of studies in geographical education. This is often the closest that researchers come to thinking about geography curricular changes across different educational environments. An example is the impact of the High School Geography Project from the USA as it related to the investigation of the diffusion of inquiry methodology in the teaching of Geography in different parts of the western world in the 1970s and 1980s.

The implementation of an action research approach to studying curricular changes and developments in geographical education has been very productive. It enabled research studies to become research and development studies as educators conducted investigations into the implementation of a curricular change in Geography, reflected on their findings and then improved their curriculums on the basis of the results of their earlier study. This practice is in the mainstream of geographical education research in many countries.

Assessment and evaluation in Geography

Research into student assessment and wider aspects of evaluation in Geography is popular because of the influence of external examination systems in many countries. Studies of the variations in student success in examinations use differing methodologies depending on the goal of the particular study. For example, detailed investigations of student performance on different types of questions in an examination have been conducted using the most comprehensive experimental research designs to search for significant differences in student performance. However, in studies focused on the students' experience of, say, a field-based examination, a more qualitative methodology has been found to be more appropriate.

Investigations searching for the effectiveness and relevance of geography curriculums are reported regularly at geographical education conferences. They reflect the continuing thirst to determine the effectiveness of curricular innovations as expressed in different geography programmes. Using accepted techniques for programme evaluation, studies describe and interpret individual programmes based on surveys of participants or interviews with them. Sometimes these evaluations are conducted on a contract basis for an employing educational authority. At other times, professional associations undertake the evaluations on a voluntary basis. Strengths and weaknesses of the programmes are often included in the results of such evaluations. However, few of these evaluations are conducted on a scale broader than the single programme.

Teaching resources

The effectiveness of different types of teaching resources in geographical education has become a very popular research theme. In Geography, reported studies have focused on learning and teaching resources, including textbooks, video and audio-visual resources, maps and atlases, games and simulations, and computer software. They include the suitability of the resources for the learner, the clarity of the resources, how they structure the learning, aspects of attractiveness, relevance to the curriculum, and cost.

In studies in higher education, there has been strong interest over the past decade in how learning using remote sensing and Geographic Information Systems (GIS) has occurred and can be improved. At school levels, the emphasis has been more on how textbooks, atlases and individual maps are used and can be effective. In the 1980s, there was strong interest in using games and simulations to promote geographical education. More recently, this emphasis has changed to maximizing the effectiveness of computer software and multimedia programs in geographical education. New types of resources enter the educational market every day ensuring a continuing research focus on their educational qualities

Technology in geographical education

For some educational researchers consideration of technology in geographical education is a part of the section on teaching resources. Specifically this may be true, but it is also true that technology may be considered in the section on learning and teaching. Because of the dramatic growth in the use of advanced communication technologies in geographical education it is worthwhile to consider research into them as a discrete part of the research arena.

In the last decade, a number of geographical education research studies have focused on computers, specialized software for learning, remotely sensed spatial data obtained from earth satellites and the digitizing of spatial data through GIS software. However, there is currently a strong research interest in GIS software, together with geographical education through the World Wide Web and the internet, with a focus on multimedia learning.

These studies have placed a new emphasis on the teaching–learning process where teachers have become much more facilitative and learners much more active and independent. Not only have the styles of learning and teaching changed as the result of research into technology in geographical education, but the concept of literacy in geographical education has taken on a broader meaning to include information technology literacy, in conjunction with verbal, oral, graphic and numeric literacies.

Geographical education in differing social contexts

The study of Geography in different social contexts has attracted considerable research interest as the role and place of Geography in the formal education curriculum have been challenged over several decades. Several studies have been conducted into the role that Geography can play and has played in the areas of citizenship and political education, development education, intercultural understanding, peace education, industrial and/or business education and vocational education. Some of these studies have sought to demonstrate the differences between Geography and other subjects while others have set out to explain how geographical education can contribute to, say, citizenship education. The first set of studies has often taken a defensive stance, whereas the second has been more positive, searching for links between the two types of education that may strengthen them both.

Not totally forgotten, though fewer in number, are studies bridging different cultures on different scales and across regions and countries. These seek to demonstrate variations in geographical education as it has been implemented by different government policies at different administrative levels. When it comes to understanding the variations in the ways that geographical education is planned, implemented and recognized in different cultural settings, then the work of global organizations such as the International Geographical Union becomes very important as a facilitator of cross- and inter-cultural understanding through geographical education (see Naish 1990).

Geographical and environmental education

While geographical education is researched in differing social contexts, the largest set of comparisons is reserved for studies about geographical and environmental education. Most researchers agree that Geography is a discipline that integrates the physical and social sciences. However, many educators believe that the role of Geography in environmental education can be explained without having Geography operate as a separate subject or discipline. They argue that Geography can act as the link or integrator in a holistic approach to learning and teaching the social and physical sciences from a spatial perspective. Consequently, both camps of researchers and theorists have established separate journals to promote their viewpoints, e.g. *Geography* and the *Journal of Geography* promote a specific geographical approach, whereas the *Journal of Environmental Education* and *Environmental Education and Information* promote an integrative approach.

Research futures

There is little doubt that the study of people's interaction with their earth and with other planets will continue to be an important aspect of human endeavour. Also, there is little doubt that technologies will continue to improve and be applied to formal and everyday learning situations. Geographical education in some form will continue to be important for effective human existence. What then may be some pegs upon which to hang the organizers of future research in geographical education?

The seminal report, *Learning: The Treasure Within* (Delors 1998), by the International Commission on Education for the Twenty-first Century, offers one starting point. In this report, four pillars of education are identified:

1   Learning to know, e.g. acquiring the instruments of understanding, learning to learn and understanding the benefits of lifelong learning.
2   Learning to do, e.g. being able to act creatively in one's environment, having the competence to deal with many situations and working in teams.
3   Learning to live together, e.g. being able to participate and co-operate with other people in all human activities, managing conflicts and appreciating independence.
4   Learning to be, e.g. being better able to develop one's personality and act with greater autonomy, judgement and personal responsibility.

From these pillars, it may be deduced that international geographical education should seek to achieve the following things:

1   Improving teacher education through searching for new perspectives in geographical education by: developing new ways to bring the world into the classroom; developing new competencies in geographical education; learning what and how to teach; and promoting the professional development of geography teachers.
2   Using the resources of the information society to broaden geographical learning and teaching.
3   Emphasizing geographical education that is aimed at improving the art of people living together.
4   Refocusing curriculum development at all levels of formal geographical education to promote pedagogies to promote greater autonomy, judgement and personal responsibility. This would include developing learning strategies that are used in both post-industrial and developing countries such as guided participation.
5   'Rediscovering Geography' as a basis for effective lifelong learning in both formal and non-formal education.

These five clusters of emphasis offer researchers in geographical education a future agenda. Whichever themes they choose, researchers should take very seriously the view that we are groups of people who function within selected environments at differing scales. Therefore, while it is useful to know what one group of people comprehends in their geographical education, it is most important to develop an understanding of how regional groups and the whole world understand and practise geographical education. New communications technologies make international and global considerations much more realistic for researchers in geographical education, permitting cross-cultural studies to be achieved with greater ease. This will require much greater networking among geographical educators around the world, thus promoting a global geographical education community of scholars.

References

Delors, J. (ed.) (1998) *Learning: The Treasure Within*, report to UNESCO of the International Committee on Education for the Twenty-first Century, Canberra: UNESCO Publications/Australian National Committee for UNESCO.

Dove, J. (1999) *Immaculate Misconceptions*, Sheffield: Geographical Association.

Foskett, N. and Marsden, B. (eds) (1998) *A Bibliography of Geographical Education*, Sheffield: Geographical Association.

Klein, J.-L. and Laurin, S. (eds) (1999) *Education Géographique: Formation du Citoyen et Conscience Territoriale*, Sainte-Foy, Québec: Presses de l'Université du Québec.

Leat, D. and Nichols, A. (1999) *Mysteries Make You Think*, Sheffield: Geographical Association.

Lee, J. C.-K. (1998) *Theory and Practice in Environmental Education in Primary and Secondary School: Towards Sustainable Development*, published in Chinese, Beijing: Beijing Normal University Press.

Lidstone, J. (1998) 'Cultural studies and geographical education: are we losing the way?', in M. Ferreira, A. Neto and S. Conceição (eds) *Culture, Geography and Geographical Education: Proceedings of the Oporto Symposium of the Commission on Geographical Education of the International Geographical Union*, Lisbon: Universidade Aberta.

Naish, M. (ed.) (1990) *Experiences of Centralisation: An International Study of the Impacts of Centralised Education Systems upon Geography Curriculums*, British Sub-Committee of the Commission for Geographical Education, London: University of London Institute of Education.

National Council for Geographic Education (2000) *A Bibliography of Geographical Education*, Indiana: National Council for Geographic Education.

Ostuni, J., Lotfi, V., de Grosso, M. and de Becette, R. (1999) *Teaching Geography in a World on Change*, Proceedings of the International Geographic Union Commission on Geographical Education conference, Mendoza, Argentina 19–24 April.

Rikkinen, H. (1997) *Geography in the Primary School*, published in Finnish, Helsinki: Helsingin Yliopistin Opettajankoulutuslaitos (Department of Teacher Training, University of Helsinki).

—— (ed.) (1998a) *Geography in the Secondary School*, published in Finnish, Helsinki: Helsingin Yliopistin Opettajankoulutuslaitos (Department of Teacher Training, University of Helsinki).

—— (ed.) (1998b) *Geography in the Upper Secondary School*, published in Finnish, Helsinki: Helsingin Yliopistin Opettajankoulutuslaitos (Department of Teacher Training, University of Helsinki).

Smit, M. (1998) 'A paradigm shift in geography teaching in South Africa: the outcomes-based approach', in M. Ferreira, A. Neto and S. Conceição (eds) *Culture, Geography and Geographical Education: Proceedings of the Oporto Symposium of the Commission on Geographical Education of the International Geographical Union*. Lisbon: Universidade Aberta.

Walkington, H. (1999) *Global Citizenship Education*, Sheffield: Geographical Association.

Williams, M. (1998) 'A review of research in geographical education', in A. Kent (ed.) *Issues for Research in Geographical Education, Research Forum I*, London: University of London Institute of Education.

23 Corked hats and Coronation Street
Children's imaginative geographies

Sarah Holloway and Gill Valentine

This chapter contributes to the developing literature on childhood and national identity by considering the ways in which children imagine other nations. Focusing in particular on online interactions between children in twelve British and twelve New Zealand schools, the article explores their imaginative geographies of each other, and assesses the ways these visions are endorsed or contested by the children to whom they refer. The article not only illustrates the sources and importance of stereotypical understandings of landscape, people and patterns of daily life in other nations, but also the ways these may be contested through online contact.

Introduction

Debates about identity have been a key focus of interest in the social sciences for the past two decades (Rutherford 1990; Epstein 1998; Laurie *et al.* 1999). The key concern, in a variety of different disciplines, has been to dispute essentialist assumptions about identity, and argue that the differences between us are not the product of biological differences, but are made and remade through the processes of social construction. Within this overarching debate some differences, perhaps most notably gender and 'race', have received greater attention than others. Despite groundbreaking work by historians such as Ariès (1962), childhood has remained an essentialized concept in the eyes of many social scientists for longer than most other identities, not least because of the strength of socialization theory in sociology (James *et al.* 1998). Work within the new social studies of childhood has now recovered children from such biological discourses, and increasing attention is being paid by sociologists, social anthropologists and others to the question of children's agency in the constitution of different children's childhoods (James and Prout 1990; Mayall 1994; Qvortrup *et al.* 1994; Brannen and O'Brien 1996; James *et al.* 1998). This trend towards studying children as competent social actors is paralleled by work in children's and young people's geographies. Research in this field considers both the construction of childhood in and through different places, spaces, and spatial discourses, and the importance of these in children's everyday worlds (Holloway and Valentine 2000).

One set of issues which has attracted relatively little attention, either in children's and young people's geographies, or the new social studies of childhood more generally, concerns the relations between child, childhood, nation, national identity and nationalism. In a special issue of the journal *Childhood*, Stephens (1997a) suggested that this paucity of work is explicable given childhood's relatively recent recovery from biological essentialism, but argued that it was now time for a new area of study to be opened up. A two-fold agenda was proposed which would consider both the place of the child in national imagery, and the consequences of nationalist discourses for individual children. Though studies of childhood and nationalism are still limited in number, research which addresses both elements of this agenda is beginning to emerge both through articles in that special issue of *Childhood* itself (see Gullestad 1997; Hengst 1997; Koester 1997; Okely 1997; Povrzanovic 1997; Stephens 1997b) and elsewhere.

Mankekar (1997) and Conrad (1999), for example, both consider the place of childhood in national imaginations. Mankekar (1997) focuses on the ways in which ideas of childhood were classed, racialized and gendered in India through discussions about Ameena, a Muslim girl alleged to have been sold as a child bride. Conrad (1999), in her discussion of the JonBenet Ramsey murder, highlights the different ways the concept of child has been mobilized in nationalist discourse in post-war US political history. Similarly, a range of studies with both historical and contemporary focuses is beginning to emerge which considers the implications of nationalism for children's life-worlds. Gagen's (2000a, 2000b) analysis of nineteenth-century American playgrounds, for example, shows how assimilationist concerns about America's immigrant children led to the growth of supervised playgrounds whose activities were designed to produce appropriately gendered American citizens. Carrington and Short's (1998) ongoing research with children and young people in 1990s Britain highlights the fact that most British children define nationhood in concrete terms (for example being born, living or working within a country) rather than in terms of cultural homogeneity, with few children in their research expressing self-evidently racist, xenophobic or nationalist views.

Hengst's (1997) exploratory study of British, German and Turkish children's negotiations of 'us' and 'them' is a particularly interesting example of this second genre of work, which considers the implications of nationalism for children's life-worlds. Like Carrington and Short (1998), Hengst examines children's understandings of their own national identity. However, he also goes further and begins to tease out the ways in which children consider their nation to be thought of abroad, and how they value other people and places. His thesis is that children's sense of collective identity (being German, etc.) is constructed through their perceptions of their difference from others. The import of his argument – which owes much to post-structuralist and psychoanalytic debates about identity (Rose 1993; Sibley 1995) – is that we would do well to consider children's visions of 'others', as well as their understandings of 'self', when trying to elucidate the relations between 'children' and 'nation'. Interestingly, Hengst also goes on to suggest that the social collectives which children define for themselves may not solely be defined in terms of nation, but may recognize similarities across certain types of nations; for example, German children might consider other high-status, affluent European nations in terms of 'us' rather than 'them'.

In taking up Hengst's challenge to consider children's definitions of 'other' as well as 'self', we want to draw on Said's (1985) seminal work, *Orientalism*, which has had a considerable influence on the ways in which geographers have studied the form and implications of societies' knowledges about other people and places. Said's particular focus is on the ways in which western 'knowledge' of the Orient was central to the operation of imperial power and continues to be important in the post-colonial world. In other words, he considers the ways constructions of 'other' can shape and legitimate our unequal relations with different people and places. The specific aspect of his work that we want to draw upon here is the concept of 'imaginative geography'. Said argues that the construction of an imaginative geography, in which familiar space is mentally designated 'ours' and unfamiliar spaces as 'theirs', is a universal way in which groups define their own identity by reference to what they are not. In his words: 'there is no doubt that imaginative geography and history help the mind to intensify its own sense of itself by dramatizing the distance and the difference between what is close to it and what is far away' (Said 1985: 55). The boundaries established in this imagined geography, Said argues, need not be acknowledged by those defined as 'other', nor, as the following quotation illustrates, rest on any extensive or intensive knowledge of the 'other':

> The geographic boundaries [of imagined geography] accompany the social, ethnic and cultural ones in the expected ways. Yet often the sense in which someone feels himself [*sic*] to be not-foreign is based on a very unrigorous idea of what is 'out there', beyond one's own territory. All kinds of suppositions, associations, and fictions appear to crowd the unfamiliar space outside one's own.
>
> (Said 1985: 54)

The fact that these imaginative geographies may rest on fictions does not detract from their importance, as Said makes clear in the context of Orientalism, because they are part of a process through which dominant groups can define and exert power over those they define as 'other'.

Said's (1985) work, though open to refinement and critique, illustrates the power of our ideas about other people and places, and thus reinforces Stephens's (1997a) call for work on children and nationalism, and Hengst's (1997) more specific identification of a need for research which considers children's constructions of 'other' as well as 'self'. In this article we pursue this agenda through a focus on British and New Zealand children's imaginative geographies of each other.[1] Our aims are threefold. First, we want to map these children's imaginative geographies. In doing so, we take Said's term 'imaginative geography' in its broadest possible sense to include a consideration of how children imagine each other's nation in terms of place, people and patterns of daily life. Second, we want to consider whether the construction of imaginative geographies universally involves the 'othering' of distant people and places as Said suggests, or whether, as Hengst hypothesizes, children may imagine commonalities as well as differences in their constructions of other nations. Finally, bearing in mind Said's point that the imagined geographies may not be acknowledged or recognized by the imagined 'other', we want to examine whether children in the 'imagined' country endorse or contest other children's imaginative geographies of their nation.

Research context

This article draws on online interactions between British and New Zealand children which took place as part of 'The Link', a British Council-funded programme of cultural exchange between the two countries.[2] Britain and New Zealand provide a particularly interesting case study for the examination of children's imaginative geographies because of the historical and contemporary relations between the two countries. In historical terms, the relationship between the two countries is one of colonialism: British missionaries began to arrive in New Zealand in the early 1800s, and by 1840 the Maoris (who had first occupied New Zealand some time before the fourteenth century) were forced to accept British sovereignty. The colony achieved self-government in 1853, was made a dominion in 1907, but did not gain full independence until 1931. However, this history of colonization is now glossed over by the British, and 'The Link' is an example of an initiative designed to deepen and strengthen Britain's relations with New Zealand in the post-colonial world. In the words of Tony Blair, the British Prime Minister, in a publicity brochure for the scheme:

> Thanks to *The Link*, New Zealanders and Britons have been able to explore together shared values and interests, and to build partnerships for the future. We have updated our perceptions of each other as we face the challenges of the millennium.

> We think *The Link* has been a great success. It has created a fresh sense of one of the modern world's most mature relationships. It has been good to show old friends the new Britain.

> (Blair, cited in 'The Link' 1998: 2)

Projects for young people were of key importance to 'The Link', and in this article we draw on the experiences of children involved in just one of these, the 'Interlink' project. 'Interlink' was funded by the British Council but was developed and managed by Copeland Wilson and Associates Ltd (CWA), a specialist producer of educational learning materials in New Zealand. The aim of the project was to take advantage of new information and communications technologies (ICTs), mainly e-mail and the World Wide Web, but also video-conferencing, to bring children from Britain and New Zealand closer together. Twelve schools from each country (who covered the state and independent sector, as well as children with a range of educational abilities) were selected to take part in the project, and partnered with a school in the other country. In total, over 1,000 children aged 13 in these schools were then asked to undertake a range of educational activities – designed by CWA to complement the curriculums in each country – and share the results with the children in their partner school both by e-mailing individual children there and by creating web pages.

The activities designed by CWA were wide-ranging, but here we draw on the results of just three activities which enable us to address the aims of the article set out earlier. First, British and New Zealand children were asked to e-mail their counterparts descriptions of what they thought their country and people were like, and, second, what they thought a typical week and weekend day would be like for children in the other country. In both these activities children were asked to send their first impressions, rather than undertake prior research into the subject. In the third activity we draw upon in this article, children were asked to respond to their counterparts' impressions of their country and lifestyle, either by agreeing that it was an accurate reflection of their nation, or by pointing out misunderstandings or misinformed accounts of what their country was like.

The e-mail accounts this produced are not pure, unmediated insights into children's views (something we doubt could ever be achieved); some topics they might like to consider, such as the weather, landscape and what people look like, were suggested by the project co-ordinators,[3] and the amount of collaboration between pupils and the level of teacher involvement varied between the schools. Nevertheless, children's responses do give us an interesting insight into their imaginative geographies of people, place and daily life in another country which have, hitherto, been neglected within the new social studies of childhood. The broad contours of these imaginative geographies, and the ways in which they are contested by children in the nation to which they refer, are drawn out in the sections which follow and illustrated through the use of quotations from children's e-mails.

In the following section of the article we look first at British children's visions of New Zealand, and the way New Zealand children respond to these visions of people, place and daily life. In the subsequent section the roles are reversed, and we consider New Zealand children's visions of Britain, and the responses of their British counterparts. We draw the article to a close with a discussion of young people's often stereotypical understandings of other people and places, and examine the potential of online discussions for bringing children together in ways which can broaden their understandings of the world in which they live.

Children's imaginative geographies

Visions of New Zealand

Place

Most British children had a general idea where their counterparts' country was in the world. All placed it in the southern hemisphere, many locating it in relation to Australia, and some noting that it comprised two main islands:

> New Zealand is in the Southern hemisphere, on the other side of the world from us. We think you are near Australia.

> New Zealand is in the south of the Pacific Ocean, to the east of Australia.

> New Zealand is in the Southern part of the world, by Australia.

> New Zealand is an island and is surrounded by the Tasman Sea. The island is in the south east part of the world …

> New Zealand is in southern hemisphere, not too far from Australia. It is also not too far from Antarctica.

> New Zealand is two islands, a north and a south island, like Tasmania it is off the coast of Australia.

Taken at face value, these descriptions might seem to illustrate children's varying geographical competencies, their differing levels of knowledge about where New Zealand is to be found on the globe. However, in articulating where New Zealand is in a spatial sense, these excerpts from children also start to tell us something about how children envisage New Zealand's socio-cultural location. We discuss the cultural importance of Australia later, but first want to draw attention to the significance of being in 'the Southern part of the world'.

Clearly, the child that describes New Zealand as being in the 'south east part of the world' has been exposed to British maps, most of which project Britain at the centre of the world with the Americas to the west and Australasia to the east (see Wood and Fels 1993 on the power of maps). However, for many children the description of New Zealand as southern did not just reflect where they had seen New Zealand on a map; it also meant association with a range of stereotypical ideas about what it means to be from the South. Important for many British children is the idea that the South is hot, potentially beautiful, but also potentially dangerous as nature here is assumed to be untamed:

> New Zealand is South and close to the equator. Therefore it is hot. It is very near to the Australia.

> We presume that the climate is warmer and dryer than ours, because you are in the Southern Hemisphere.

> Very hot climate … palm trees and beaches, tropical rainforests.

> Your countryside is basically palm trees, mountains, beaches and deserts.

> Your country seems to be really dangerous, what with tornadoes, scorpions, poisonous animals, hurricanes and earthquakes.

Nevertheless, a minority of British children had more nuanced understandings of what it means to be southern. These children tended to appreciate that there was a diversity of climatic experience within the southern hemisphere, and one was able to pinpoint the climatic diversity which is experienced within New Zealand itself:

> The climate is the same as England because it is quite far south, It has more rain than us also.

> I also know that New Zealand is made up of two islands. The southern one is much the same as Britain climate wise, and the northern island is much warmer.

These more nuanced understandings were, unsurprisingly, more in tune with the descriptions of New Zealand children, who contested the conflation of South with hot through descriptions of New Zealand's varied climatic regime:

> Not all of New Zealand is hot, we have a temperate climate which is semi-tropical in the far north and quite cold in the south – Dunedin's climate is rather like Scotland. We often experience 'four seasons in one day', Or so the [Crowded House] song goes.

Alongside these ideas about the South, British children also envisaged the New Zealand countryside in terms of an agricultural landscape. Though there were differing ideas about the nature of New Zealand's physical landscape, there was universal agreement among British children that the land was populated by large numbers of sheep:

> The countryside is desert land and loads and loads of sheep, possibly more sheep than people … The climate is very hot and humid, with tropical storms etc.

> Not sure what the countryside looks like but the North Island is quite Hilly. I don't know about the South Island but it has lots of sheep.

> I know for a fact that New Zealand is hotter than England. I think one of your main industries would be farming e.g. sheep farming because when I buy lamb in the shop it normally says 'a New Zealand lamb'.

Their ideas in this regard resonate with those held by wider sectors of the population. As Johnston (1976) spelt out over two decades ago: 'The common but grossly over-simplified image of New Zealand is of a green and pleasant land with a population consisting largely of sheep, cattle and farmers.' These quotations from British children suggest that this impression is fuelled by large-scale export of lamb from New Zealand to the UK, a trade which British children come into contact with through trips to their local supermarket. This notion is an interesting one. Recent work in human geography has suggested that 'ethnic' commodities, including foodstuffs, are important in creating and reinforcing western ideas about 'exotic' others (Jackson 1999; May 1996). In this instance, the circulation of an agricultural commodity, lamb, which is a far from 'exotic' part of the British diet (being a staple of the home farming industry as well as a commodity bought on the global market), plays a crucial role in (re)creating children's images of New Zealand. Though New Zealand children were happy to admit that this image has some basis in fact, they were equally clear that the presence of large numbers of sheep in New Zealand does not mean that they are a nation of farmers:

> Even though New Zealand has lots of sheep, farmers most people aren't.

People

The notion that New Zealand is hotter than Britain also came through clearly in British children's descriptions of what New Zealanders look like. The vast majority of children imagined that New Zealanders look like British people, but with a better tan:

> We don't really know much about New Zealand, but we think it is hot and sunny all the time. The beaches are great and there are lots of cool things to do like surfing, and everybody has a tan.

> We reckon that you look like us but with a better tan!!!!

> New Zealanders look like us but have more of a tan and they speak Australian English.

> We think that you look like us but with a sun tan.

> People who live there are the same as us but maybe have a better tan. (What a stupid question to be asked 'What do the people look like?').

Their response is an intriguing one. The notion that New Zealand children 'look like us but with a better tan' depends on the construction of Britain and New

Zealand as white, racially homogeneous nations. This construction obscures the importance of racialized minorities in British society, and illustrates a lack of awareness among British children of New Zealand's diverse immigration history (Jackson 1998). This understanding of New Zealand as a white nation was disrupted by New Zealand children, some of whom responded to the idea that they 'have a better tan' by highlighting the 'racial' diversity of their own nation:

> You said New Zealanders would be very sun tanned and it is true that many of us are sun tanned as we like to be outdoors when it is sunny. But there are many races in New Zealand such as Europeans, Asians, Polynesians and Maori some of whom are naturally tanned, and some of whose skin is very sensitive to sun-burn.

Equally significant is the fact that whiteness – which is usually an unremarkable identity for many white people (Bonnett 1992; Frankenberg 1993; Jackson 1998) – is temporarily foregrounded in this discussion about what people from New Zealand look like. The discomfort at apparently being asked to remark upon whiteness, or perhaps the incongruity of seemingly being asked to describe what 'white' people look like, is evident in one child's aside: 'What a stupid question to be asked "What do the people look like?"' It is questionable whether this child would have made the same comment if she thought she were being asked to describe a racialized minority.[4]

In one sense, British children's lack of appreciation of the diversity of New Zealand's population is understandable given their more general ignorance of New Zealand's history and culture. This ignorance of New Zealand's history and culture is itself more difficult to explain, particularly given Britain's historic role as a colonial power, and the continuing importance of links between the two countries in the post-colonial era. Nevertheless, many British children were completely unaware of New Zealand's past, or Britain's part within it. Indeed, some were quite open about their lack of knowledge, and explained that to many British people New Zealand is simply conceived of as an off-shoot of Australia:

> We don't know anything about the history of New Zealand.

> Many people consider New Zealand as being an offspring of Australia and are not considered as being a country of its own.

Nevertheless, others did have a hazy idea about New Zealand's history, with developing understanding of the role and implications of colonialism.

> New Zealand is less than 200 years old being settled at about the time that Capt. Cook discovered the islands.

> The Maoris are the natives of the country and when the white people went over they nearly wiped them and their country out.

However, this did not lead most children to an appreciation of native culture (to use the terms employed in the 'Interlink' project) in New Zealand. Considerable numbers of British children thought the native population of New Zealand were Aborigines rather than Maoris, and the traditions of the two groups were also often conflated and confused with one another:

The native culture is Aborigine … They wear animal clothes and play the didgeridoo.

You obviously speak English and your native language. (Is it aboriginee?) We don't have a clue about your native culture.

You paint your faces, do dances and own sheep.

The native people are aborigines.

They do a war dance before every rugby game.

This labelling of Maoris as Aborigines, and confusion over and lack of respect for Maori culture, was something hotly contested by New Zealand children. The responses from New Zealand children which follow illustrate both some frustration with British children's attitudes, as well as pride in Maori identities and traditions:

Most of you are wrong about the culture, however. Aboriginals are Australia's indigenous people and have nothing to do with New Zealand really. Our indigenous people are the Maori, and I happen to be one. (And proud of it).

We wear clothing just like everyone else, normal western clothing. For actions songs and kapahaka groups we wear a Maori costume.

The 'cute little war dance' you mentioned is the Haka and it is performed at the beginning of rugby matches to challenge and scare the opposing team. The haka is an item of pride and mana (power), and it is complex to perform as it is made up of chanting and actions.

A similar conflation of Australian and New Zealand stereotypes also occurred where British children tried to describe the culture of the majority 'white' population. Corked hats in particular were a key symbol in children's imaginations:

Your national costume is that you either dress up as a kiwi or wear shorts and T-shirts, wear sandals on your feet and wear hats with corks hanging down.

The people who live there have a tan, are big and muscled with blond hair, wear hats with corks dangling from them, like surfing and sunbathing, are soccer and volley ball stars, drive around in open air cars and sporty land rovers, are farmers and love cricket.

We think you probably dress like Crocodile Dundee in Bermuda shorts and a hat with corks dangling.

In fact, this conflation of New Zealand with Australia was only avoided where New Zealand's rugby team was concerned, though their name – the All Blacks – which refers to the colour of their strip did cause other confusions:

We think that New Zealand are very good at rugby.

You won the rugby world cup in 1987.

We know you have a very good national rugby team, who are black, we think.

In total, this masking of New Zealand's location, and cultural traditions through British children's association of New Zealand with Australia and stereotypes which are primarily associated with Australia, was something fiercely contested by New Zealand children. They were insistent on asserting their own identities and tradition in the face of cultural assimilation by their more powerful neighbour, assimilation which was taking place in the imaginative geographies of children from a former colonial power:

> We are NOT part of Australia, in fact it takes three and a half hours by plane to get to Australia. So we don't have Kangaroos, koalas, poisonous snakes or hats with corks hanging down.

> We are not connected to Australia at all. We are our own independent country and Australia is one of our neighbours. Australians have a different accent to us. Kangaroos are native to Australia and the only ones found in New Zealand are in our zoos.

This contestation of Australian stereotypes was pursued with sufficient enthusiasm to produce apologies from the British children, who in the process have gained more nuanced understandings of antipodean life:

> Sorry for insulting you by calling you Australians.

> We are so sorry we even mentioned Australia and kangaroos.

A day in the life

What is significant about British children's notions about New Zealand children's daily life is that they consider it to be very similar to their own. Far from constructing a sense of themselves by dramatizing their difference from a far away 'other', as Said's (1985) thesis implies, these children construct a sense of sameness across distance in their imaginative geographies. For example, they think a typical school day will be regulated by time (James *et al.* 1998), and incorporate a range of lessons, with perhaps only the languages studied separating their experiences.

> I think on a Monday morning you would get up and get ready for school at about 8.00 am and go off to school at about 8.30 am. I think school starts at 9.00 am and at 9.10 am you go to class. Then I think you learn a lot of subjects, but I'm not quite sure what they are! I'm sure that you learn English, Maths, Geography and History; probably Science and P.E. I'm not too certain what languages you do, but you probably do Maori, maybe French or German, or Spanish too. Maybe you even do Japanese because of emigration. I would say school in New Zealand would be great because of the weather. The sun would be shining all year round; it would be great.

Similarly, they imagine New Zealand children's evenings to be taken up with homework, watching television and maybe seeing friends. Weekends are also assumed to be akin to those of British children, dominated by 'hanging out' with friends at home or in public spaces, shopping trips, homework, or visits to the cinema:

> Children from New Zealand would do the same things we do on a Saturday, like go to the nearest town or go for a day out at the park or cinema or something like that.

> What I think you do on Saturday is go to town and eat out with friends or family and go to the cinema sometimes. What I think you wear is short sleeve tee shirts, shorts and baseball caps because of the hot weather.

In terms of daily life then, Hengst's (1997) suggestion that children from high-status, affluent nations might define each other in terms of 'us' rather than 'them' does indeed appear to be the case. Rather than thinking of New Zealand children's lives as in some way 'other', British children imagine them to be very similar to their own. In fact, the only difference that British children seem to imagine between themselves and the New Zealand children is that New Zealand children will be able to do all this in better weather, leading to a slightly wider range of activities:

> On Saturday I think that the people from [partner school] go to the beach, go surfing, sunbathe and something like that.

Though some New Zealand children clearly do live within easy reach of a beach, and in areas with good weather during the summer, many do not. These children did not recognize this picture of themselves as sunbathing, surfing, barbecuing beings, which the British children painted:

> We don't leave school at 3 o'clock we leave school at 3.20 pm, and we DO NOT go to the beach and have a quick surf, in fact the only time we would go to the beach is at the weekend and most people in our class don't go to the beach regularly then either. We don't have many barbecues regularly either.

Visions of Britain

Place

Most New Zealand children, like British children, had a general idea where their counterparts' country was in the world. All could locate Britain in the northern hemisphere, and many positioned it relative to Europe as a whole:

> It is in North Western Europe.

> I know that England is an island like New Zealand, and I think that it is in the Atlantic Ocean.

> It belongs to Europe and it's on the other side of the world.

This positioning of Britain relative to Europe by New Zealand children lacked the symbolic meaning involved in British children's positioning of New Zealand relative to Australia. Though the New Zealand children's statements might be taken to mean that Britain is politically as well as geographically part of Europe, no overall understanding of 'Europe' seeps through their interpretations of the British landscape or culture. In short, the statement that Britain is close to, or part of, Europe is not meant to suggest that Britain is 'like' Europe in the same way as British children thought New Zealand was 'like' Australia.

Despite a general consensus that Britain is in the North, other aspects of Britain's physical geography were sometimes confused in the minds of New Zealand children. While some children were clear that Britain is made up of two principal islands, others were less sure and thought Britain was attached to a continental landmass:

> Britain is made up of two main islands that include Scotland, England, Ireland and Wales.

> We think England is about the size of New Zealand and that England is attached to a bigger country.

> Britain is not an island but it has neighbouring countries. Britain is in the Northern part of the world.

Indeed, one rather confused student thought Britain to be considerably bigger than it actually is:

> I think that Britain is about half the size of the world.

A similar picture of insight and confusion is evident when we consider New Zealand children's understandings of the British climate. On the one hand, the image of Britain as a very cold, wet, and rather dull place was strong in many children's imaginations:

> We think that your climate is cold, wet and misty with a little bit of sun.

> I think England is a pretty rainy place.

> The climate in England is much colder than ours.

> One thing I know is that it must be FREEZING!

> It's hot sometimes, but mostly cold, smoggy in the cities …

On the other hand, some children thought that cold and wet winter weather was accompanied by hot and sunny weather in the summer:

> We think that England has rolling hills and it's green and that they have blizzards and floods in the winter. In summer there is nice hot weather.

> We suspect that your weather conditions are very cold in the winter around 0 degrees, continual rain and knee deep snow. But in summer it's a different scene, blue sky and green grass, with temperatures around 25 degrees Celsius and up.

This rather pleasant picture of British summers was rejected by British children, who were happy to admit that Britain could be cold and rainy though not particularly snowy, but felt bound to explain that long hot summers are not a permanent feature of the British climate:

> In winter it is around 0°C, but the snow is not up to our knees. In winter it's not even up to our ankles, except on very rare occasions. In summer it is not 25 degrees and up. If we had 25°C, we would think that the weather was brilliant! As you can guess, this doesn't happen too often!

Some New Zealand children, like their British counterparts, imagined the others' countryside in terms of its agricultural landscapes. Some of the images they conjured resonate with romantic notions about the countryside which are part of British culture, and are arguably central to constructions of Englishness (Daniels 1993). However, given the confusion over the climate, some children also imagined rural areas where oranges grow and vineyards abound:

> We imagine that your country has lots of big green hills, lots of stone walls and castle-like buildings, and thatched crofts with whitewashed walls.

> We think your country has heaps of hills, lots of hedges, a few fruit trees – mainly apples and maybe oranges. There might be swamps and marshes and lots of ponds and lakes.

> We think the main economic activity in your country is mostly farming sheep and cattle. We also think that vineyards and wine making is a big industry in North Ireland.

What is particularly curious given the importance attached to the rural in studies of English landscape, and the fact that this aspect of the 'Interlink' project specifically asked children to comment on what the other nation's countryside might be like but did not (at that point) ask about the built environment, are the multiple ways in which New Zealand children imagine Britain as an urban society. Unlike their British counterparts, who largely kept to the countryside brief in discussing their images of New Zealand's agricultural landscape, New Zealand children also attach considerable importance to Britain's urban form. On the one hand, their images tended to stress the age of Britain, and the ways in which the long history of the country is evidenced in its built environment:

> The houses are old and of an older style than seen in New Zealand. They often have two storeys and no front or back gardens like *Coronation Street*.

> The towns are all made up of funny old buildings and cobblestone streets. People go around in dark clothes talking in funny accents about the soccer game yesterday or what happened on *Coronation Street* last night.

> I think the big cities would be a lot like L.A. (But not as big). The buildings would probably look more interesting with gargoyles and stuff like that.

On the other hand, British cities were also constructed as big, exciting and ultra-modern:

> I think most of England is big cities and that there is not a lot of countryside.

> I imagine Wigan to be a very big city full of skyscrapers and people. I guess you would have more TV channels than our 3 (as well as Sky). I bet you have world famous people that live close by.

These images stem, at least in part, from the ways children have read media images of Britain, thus confirming the suggestion in a range of educational and psychological studies (see Matthews (1992) for a review) that popular culture is an important source of environmental imagery for children. The keenness of British children living in cities to reinforce this image of 'cool' urban Britannia through reference to the cultural and sporting products of their own town further shows the importance of these media in children's imaginative geographies:

> Manchester is home to some of the world's greatest bands such as Simply Red, Take That, and Oasis.

> Manchester … has two football teams, Manchester United and Manchester City.

People

The ideas expressed by British children that New Zealand children are just like them 'but with a better tan' are paralleled in some of the ideas expressed by New Zealand children. Some New Zealand children, for example, describe English children as having rather pale skins:

> We think that people born in England speak natural English and have skin that is white as snow.

> They look like normal people with pale skin.

> Bit whiter than us, small (5ft 10)?

> We think that people in [Northern] Ireland are very pale with red or blonde hair.

> The people there are very fair and dress very tidy.

Nevertheless, other children do not conceive of Britain in such universally 'white' terms, and point to the 'multi-racial' nature of British society, as well as the variety of languages spoken:

> The people who live there are Caucasian, Negro, Pakistani: it's multi-racial and they speak English and Welsh.

> We think that some are fair skinned, some are dark skinned (from Africa), a lot of people are below the poverty line. We think most of them speak English but Great Britain consists of many languages, including Irish and Scottish.

The heterogeneity of Britain in New Zealand children's geographical imaginations comes through most clearly when they talk about British culture. The diversity they describe does not relate to the various racialized groups which some children described as making up the British populations, but rather the diversity of nations which make up Britain. Thus New Zealand children paired with a Scottish school had preconceptions of their culture based on their Scottishness, rather than their Britishness:

> We think your ancestors had long hair, wore kilts, did the highland fling, played the bagpipes and were sheep farmers (we learnt this from *Braveheart*).

> Our thoughts on your traditional dress is that you wear kilts and pompom hats.

Similarly, the New Zealand children paired with a school in Northern Ireland had specific ideas about what it means to be Irish:

> Most Irish go to either a Catholic, Protestant or Anglican church. For a night out on the town, you go to the pub or nightclubbing. From what we've seen in movies, you are very musical people. We think Irish people tell a lot of (Irish) jokes.

Children from these nations were happy with some, though clearly not all, aspects of this stereotyping:

Your impressions of Ireland and Irish people are mostly right. Most of the Irish people have red or blonde hair but there are a good lot of people with black hair as well. In Ireland people are very strict about religion. We are Catholics in [our school] and most of the people living in Derry are of the same religion (70%). Ireland has many churches and even though we might be thought of as church going, we aren't too religious.

In New Zealand children's quite sophisticated imaginative geographies of these nations within a state, the English, perhaps because of the history of colonialism, tend to be characterized by a class position, most notably through the idea that they are 'posh' or snobs:

We think that people look very posh and proper and that they act like that as well. We know that they speak English. They also sound very posh.

I think that you would be nice to talk to and very posh.

I think that you would do the same sports as us and you might play croquet too.

This definition of the English as posh was hotly contested by English students, whose strategy for denying this charge depended upon their location within England. Northern students tended to rely on regional stereotypes – most notably that southerners are posh – to reject the way they themselves were being stereotyped:

First of all up here in Manchester we are not snobby! We leave that to the southerners!

You may think we are posh but honestly we are not posh compared to people in the southern part of England.

Don't believe the stereotyping of English people, we don't talk posh. We talk in our gruff northern accent.

Southern students clearly could not use this strategy, and instead those ideas applied only to particular social groups, specifically the rich:

The rich people in England are well spoken and look posh. The clothes they wear may look old fashioned, but we are really up to date. Adidas jogging bottoms and tops are fashionable at the moment. In Harlow we are mostly smart but not posh.

A day in the life

In imagining British children's daily lives, most New Zealand children see British lifestyles as very similar to their own. The descriptions of daily life illustrated in the following quotes, therefore, have much in common with British children's descriptions of New Zealand life. The themes they stress are the regulated nature of school life (James *et al.* 1998) and 'hanging out' with family and friends at the weekend:

School lessons start at 8:50. They have subjects like Maths, English, History and Science. For lunch they have sandwiches but you can have dinners at school. School finishes at 3:30, they go home and then go out with their friends till about 7:30 and go home for dinner, after dinner they have homework and watch TV and finally go to bed.

> We think on an average Saturday that you would probably be listening to music, playing sport, going to the movies, shopping or meeting your friends, if you were at home you would most probably be watching television.

This attitude further reinforces Hengst's (1997) point that children from affluent, high-status nations may regard each other in terms of sameness rather than difference.

Unlike British children, however, New Zealand children imagine their counterparts undertaking these routine activities in contexts very different to their own. Most notably, New Zealand children imagine British children to have a different diet to themselves and to live in a different type of urban environment. The New Zealand children's association of a different nation with different dietary practices is hardly surprising in one sense, when we consider the long and complex histories which have produced a range of supposedly 'national' dishes in a range of countries (Bell and Valentine 1997). However, their vision of the British diet is striking because, while constructing the English in particular as posh or snobs, New Zealand children also assume that British children eat a range of foodstuffs, some of which might be associated with the upper classes, but many of which are more often associated with the working classes within Britain itself:

> We think that you eat mashed peas on top of pies, hot dogs, fish and chips and you like to have a cup of tea and a bikkie (like posh people) and also like to eat stuff like us like sweets and chocolate and you drink fizzy (fizzy is coca cola and lemonade).

> you eat fried potatoes, bacon and sausage for breakfast.

These notions about British food, and wider assumptions about British culture, are contested by British students:

> By the way, we don't watch *Coronation Street* all the time. We don't spend all our time in the pub (you have to be 18 to drink) and I don't eat fish and chips all the time.

This contrast in class position is also evident in the gap between how New Zealand children imagine English children to be in class terms, and where they assume British children live. While New Zealand children imagine the English to be posh, the houses they imagine them living in are those traditionally more associated with the working classes in Britain:

> We think you live in old brick houses or apartments, some may be joined together in rows.

> I assume your house is like the ones off *Coronation Street* as these are the only British houses I have seen.

> When I was ready I would hop on my bike and ride down [a] *Coronation Street*-like street and through downtown over cobblestone streets to my school.

This particular example again illustrates the importance of television and that the entertainment media more generally is shaping children's understandings of other places (see Matthews 1992). In this instance, *Coronation Street*, a British soap opera which many of the New Zealand children said their mothers watched, has had a defining influence on how children envisage the everyday environments of British children. These images are again rejected by the British children:

We all have back gardens except the people who live in the town centre. We also have very LARGE HOUSES.

Manchester is quite a big city, the third largest in England. It is not all like *Coronation Street* or *EastEnders*, anymore than New Zealand is like *Shortland Street*!

What New Zealand children do share with their British counterparts is the assumption, which is not usually correct, that all these daily activities will be undertaken in different climatic conditions, and, for Britain, that tends to mean in cold weather:

After school we would have a game of cricket and then watch TV at home. After dinner I would go to bed and wake up with snow on the doorstep.

I would have a shower (all ice cold) and stick on my uniform of trousers over shorts, double layer of woolly leggings, poloshirt, vest, sweatshirt, jersey, scarf, mufflers, woolly hat, shoes and mittens and go outside into the snow and walk the fifteen miles to school.

Conclusion: challenging visions

The picture of British and New Zealand children's imaginative geographies presented in this article builds upon the emerging interest in 'children and nation' within children's and young people's geographies, and the new social studies of childhood more generally (Stephens 1997a). To date, this literature has highlighted the need to examine the place of the child in discourses on the nation, as well as the consequences of nationalist discourses for individual children. This article draws on Said's (1985) conception of 'imaginative geography' to build up on this second strand of work, and in particular to take further Hengst's (1997) suggestion that we consider how children value other nations when researching children's own sense of national identity. Our route into this is broad and the empirical material reported in this article explores how children imagine other peoples and places, not only in terms of their national cultures and traditions, but also the physical geography of their country and the patterns of daily life.

Said's (1985) analysis makes clear that societies' images of other people and places are not simply of academic interest, but a powerful way in which groups define and relate to each other. The nations under consideration in this article are particularly interesting because of their long historical and changing contemporary relationship. New Zealand is a former British colony, but the two countries are now actively reworking their relationship in the post-colonial world. Indeed, the 'Interlink' project in which these children took part was part of a broader programme of events designed to update and strengthen links between the two countries, based on a greater understanding of the other nation. That colonialist ideas were of such limited importance in both British and New Zealand children's imaginative geographies is testament to the changing political relations between the countries. Nevertheless, children's imaginative geographies of each other were often still dependent upon 'suppositions, associations, and fictions' (Said 1985: 54) which were contested by their counterparts in the other country.

Indeed, in mapping children's imaginative geographies this article has shown that British and New Zealand children's perceptions of each other were a complex mix of highly stereotypical understandings of difference, as well as assumptions of sameness across boundaries. The understandings of difference were particularly clear in the context of place, where many children imagined the others' nation in terms of stereotypical difference to their own, for example in terms of hot weather in New Zealand, or inner-city landscapes in Britain. Such 'othering' of another nation is, according to Said, a universal part of the construction of imagined geography. However, understandings of sameness as well as difference were bound together in imaginative geographies of the other's people and culture. In thinking about what people in the other nations looked like, some children from both nations constructed Britain and New Zealand as racially homogeneous, emphasizing sameness in terms of race and difference only in terms of the presence or absence of suntans. Nevertheless, some New Zealand children avoided this 'whitewash' by imagining Britain to be a multiracial society, and by insisting upon the cultural diversity of their own nation. However, it was in thinking about daily life that children from both nations tended to emphasize similarity over difference (see Hengst 1997). Despite somewhat different cultural contexts, children from both nations imagined children from the other to have an essentially similar life to themselves. This emphasis on sameness rather than difference would seem to prove Hengst's hypothesis that children in advanced nations might imagine commonalities across boundaries, perhaps in this case because many children assumed a shared ethnicity between the nations (although methodological factors could also be important – see later).

When analysing these imaginative geographies, questions about the sources of information children draw upon inevitably begin to arise. Historical studies of late eighteenth- and early nineteenth-century England have clearly illustrated the role geographical education played in shaping children's understandings of sameness and difference (Maddrell 1996; Ploszajska 1996). This article also points to the considerable influence of the global entertainment media, and global cycles of consumption, in shaping the ways in which contemporary children envision the world (see Matthews 1992). New Zealand children's visions of Britain, for example, reflect the complex and sometimes contradictory stereotypes found in a range of television programmes and films. For example, their views of Scotland were quite clearly shaped by *Braveheart*, which was a very popular film in New Zealand when these exchanges took place. Similarly, many children's understandings of the built environment in Britain appear to be shaped by the British soap opera *Coronation Street*, which was watched by many of their mothers. Such media images of New Zealand are less available in Britain – with the possible exception of the soap *Shortland Street* – and consequently children rely on stereotypes of Australia, which are more accessible; for example, in films like *Crocodile Dundee*, soaps such as *Neighbours* and *Home and Away*, and even adverts, for example for Foster's Lager. Moreover, children rely upon their everyday experiences of consumption in Britain – in events as apparently banal as buying New Zealand lamb at the local supermarket – in constructing New Zealand as an agricultural nation, dependent on sheep farming.

In one way, the development of a global media, and increasing volumes of global trade, may be seen to provide children with yet more sources of stereotypical ideas about other people and places than would have been available to them in the earlier years of the twentieth century. However, the technological developments which underpin these changes should not be seen in entirely negative terms, as they also offer the potential to enhance children's learning about other people and places. The 'Interlink' project described in this article takes advantage of the development of new ICTs, in particular e-mail and the world wide web but also video-conferencing, to bring children together to learn from each other's knowledge of their own nation, and thus develop more nuanced understandings of the similarities and the differences between them.

The potential of this new technology is great, adding new and potentially enjoyable ways of learning about the globe to the curriculum. It also offers researchers a new medium through which to research children's views. On the one hand, analysing discussions between children about their images of elsewhere and experiences of their own nation opens up exciting possibilities for researching children's imaginative geographies, as we have shown in this article. On the other hand, learning from data produced through children's education exchanges also has a number of pitfalls which should not be overlooked. First, because these discussions were held between children (albeit in response to the co-ordinator's prompts), rather than between a researcher and a child, ambiguous or particularly interesting statements could not be followed up by the researchers. Second, some children e-mailed in groups rather than alone and the dynamics of these groups – who dominated, who was silent – are not as evident in the text of an e-mail as they would be in a transcript from focus-group research. Third, the fact that 'Interlink' was designed as an educational exchange rather than as a research tool encouraged the participation of schools (and thus ensured the compliance rather than the necessarily active consent of children within them; see Valentine 1999), but did not provide us with sufficient socio-economic data on the children in question to draw out fully the differences between them in this article. Finally, while use of ICT does allow some children to learn from other children's expertise, the potential is limited by the political economy of information technology which is much more readily available to some groups of children in some countries, and not even a distant dream of children in others. This not only means some children are excluded from the research process as they do not have access to the appropriate technology, but it might also lead to assumptions of sameness between children who do participate as they can assume that those with whom they communicate also live (relatively) privileged lives.

In summary, we have argued in this article that children's imaginative geographies of other people and places, including the ways children make assumptions of sameness and difference, and the manner in which these assumptions are endorsed or contested by the children to whom they refer, are an important area for future research in the new social studies of childhood. The article provides a tentative step in that direction, but further research which examines a wider range of nations, and explores in more depth the differences between children, is now required. Some of this research could take advantage of the possibilities offered by ICT, but lack of access to such technology in many parts of the world emphasizes the continued importance of more traditional research methods.

Notes

1 We use the term New Zealand rather than Aotearoa in this article as this was the language employed by 'The Link', one of whose projects forms our empirical focus.

2 The 'Interlink' initiative was commissioned by the British Council in New Zealand as part of their 50th year celebrations. 'Interlink' was developed and managed by Copeland Wilson and Associates (CWA) Ltd, New Zealand. CWA is a specialist producer of education learning materials across all media (www.cwa.co.nz). Our thanks go to the Economic and Social Research Council (ESRC) for funding (award no. L129 25 1055) our fieldwork with some of the children who took part in the 'Interlink' project, and to Nick Bingham, the research associate.

3 Questions suggested under, 'What are they like?' included: How big is the other country? Is it an island? More than one island? Is it attached to other countries? Whereabouts in the world is it? How many people live in the other country? What do the people who live there look like? What language do they speak? Is there a native culture? What do you know about it? What is their traditional costume like? How old is the country? (i.e. How long have people been living there?) What do you know about the history of the country? What does the countryside look like? What's the climate like? Questions suggested under the 'A day in the life' project included: What kind of house do they live in? What do they have for breakfast? What are their families like – what do they look like, how many are there in a typical family, etc.? What language might they be speaking? How do they get to school (think of as many different ways as you can)? How are they dressed at school? What is the school like, and their classrooms? What are the rest of the students in the school like? What subjects are being learned? What sports do they play at school? What sort of things might they do after school? What do they do for fun? Where do they go, what do they do, what do they eat? How are they dressed? How much does it cost?

4 The question about what members of the other nation look like was undoubtedly intended to lead into a discussion of cultural diversity and, in particular, native cultures in New Zealand. However, the focus on physical characteristics in no way challenged children's understandings of race as a biological construct. Indeed, challenges to some children's assumptions about the 'whiteness' of a nation were often made by other children who invoked ideas about other 'races'.

References

Ariès, P. (1962) *Centuries of Childhood*, New York: Vintage Press.

Bell, D. and Valentine, G. (1997) *Consuming Geographies: We Are Where We Eat*, London: Routledge.

Bonnett, A. (1992) 'Anti-racism in "white" areas: the example of Tyneside', *Antipode* 24: 1–15.

Brannen, J. and O'Brien, M. (eds) (1996) *Children in Families: Research and Policy*, London: Falmer Press.

Carrington, B. and Short, G. (1998) 'Adolescent discourse on national identity – voices of care and justice?, *Educational Studies* 24: 133–52.

Conrad, J. (1999) 'Lost innocent and sacrificial delegate: the JonBenet Ramsey murder', *Childhood* 6: 313–51.

Daniels, S. (1993) *Fields of Vision: Landscape Imagery and National Identity in England and the United States*, Cambridge: Polity Press.

Epstein, J.S. (1998) *Youth Culture: Identity in a Postmodern World*, Oxford: Basil Blackwell.

Frankenberg, R. (1993) 'Growing up white: feminism, racism and the social geography of childhood', *Feminist Review* 45: 51–84.

Gagen, E. (2000a) 'Playing the part: performing gender in American playgrounds', in S.L. Holloway and G. Valentine (eds) *Children's Geographies: Playing, Living, Learning*, London: Routledge.

—— (2000b) '"An Example to Us All": Child development and identity construction in early 20th century playgrounds', *Environment and Planning A* 32: 599–616.

Gullestad, M. (1997) 'A passion for boundaries: reflections on connections between the everyday lives of children and discourses on the nation in contemporary Norway', *Childhood* 4: 19–42.

Hengst, H. (1997) 'Negotiating "Us" and "Them": children's constructions of collective identity', *Childhood* 4: 43–62.

Holloway, S.L. and Valentine, G. (2000) *Children's Geographies: Playing, Living*, London: Routledge.

Jackson, P. (1998) 'Constructions of "Whiteness" in the geographical imagination', *Area* 30: 99–106.

—— (1999) 'Commodity cultures: the traffic in things', *Transactions of the Institute of British Geographers* 24: 95–108.

James, A. and Prout, A. (eds) (1990) *Constructing and Reconstructing Childhood: Contemporary Issues in the Sociological Study of Childhood*, Basingstoke: Falmer Press.

James, A., Jenks, C. and Prout, A. (1998) *Theorizing Childhood*, Cambridge: Polity Press.

Johnston, R.J. (1976) *The New Zealanders: How They Live and Work*, London: David and Charles.

Koester, D. (1997) 'Childhood in national consciousness and national consciousness in childhood', *Childhood* 4: 125–42.

Laurie, N., Dwyer, C., Holloway, S.L. and Smith, F.M. (1999) *Geographies of New Femininities*, Harlow: Longman.

Maddrell, A.M.C. (1996) 'Empire, emigration and school geography: changing discourses of imperial citizenship', *Journal of Historical Geography* 22: 373–87.

Mankekar, P. (1997) '"To whom does Ameena belong?" Towards a feminist analysis of childhood and nationhood in contemporary India', *Feminist Review* 56: 26–60.

Matthews, M.H. (1992) *Making Sense of Place: Children's Understanding Of Large-Scale Environments*, Hemel Hempstead: Harvester Wheatsheaf.

May, J. 1996) '"A little taste of something more exotic": the imaginative geographies of everyday life', *Geography* 81: 57–6

Mayall, B. (ed.) (1994) *Children's Childhoods: Observed and Experienced*, London: Falmer Press.

Okely, J. (1997) 'Non-territorial culture as the rationale for the assimilation of Gypsy children', *Childhood* 4: 63–80.

Ploszajska, T. (1996) 'Constructing the subject: geographical models in english schools, 1870–1944', *Journal of Historical Geography* 22: 388–98.

Povrzanovic, M. (1997) 'Children, war and nation: Croatia 1991–4', *Childhood* 4: 81–102.

Qvortrup, L., Bardy, M., Sgritta, G. and Wintersberger, H. (eds) (1994) *Childhood Matters: Social Theory, Practice and Politics*, Aldershot: Avebury.

Rose, G. (1993) *Feminism and Geography: The Limits of Geographical Knowledge*, Cambridge: Polity Press.

Rutherford, J. (ed.) (1990) *Identity: Community, Culture, Difference*, London: Lawrence and Wishart.

Said, E.W. (1985) *Orientalism*, London: Penguin.

Sibley, D. (1995) *Geographies of Exclusion*, London: Routledge.

Stephens, S. (1997a) 'Editorial introduction: children and nationalism', *Childhood* 4: 5–17.

—— (1997b) 'Nationalism, nuclear policy and children in Cold War America', *Childhood* 4: 103–23.

'The Link' (1998) *Britain and New Zealand: A Modern and Evolving Relationship*, Wellington: British Council.

Valentine, G. (1999) 'Being seen and heard? Ethical dilemmas of research with children and young people', *Journal of Ethics, Place and Environment* 2: 141–55.

Wood, D. with Fels, J. (1993) *The Power of Maps*, London: Routledge.

24 The worlds of girls and boys
Geographic experience and informal learning opportunities
Pamela Wridt

Children and youth learn about society and the environment through formal schooling and informal learning experiences in their everyday lives. The influence of formal schooling on shaping children's understanding of geography is generally the focus of academic research. However, informal learning experiences play a substantial role in understanding geography.

This article examines an alternative method for learning about the world advocated by Lucy Sprague Mitchell, a New York City geography teacher. Mitchell (1991 [1934]: 14) recognized that children learn geography through their own experiences in their everyday environments:

> Every environment is geographic. The kind of geography which we have found most natural to city children is human geography. The natural earth conditions are too overlaid with human modifications to make physical geography an easy field of exploration in the city. In the country, even in the suburbs, children discover relationships which concern soil, erosion, elevation and the growth of plants and animals at an earlier age than do city children.

Mitchell's analysis was largely anecdotal, driven by her experiences as a geography teacher in New York City. Unfortunately, scholars have generally not followed Mitchell's lead and have devoted little attention to understanding the everyday worlds of young people as a potential source of informal learning about peoples and places. There is, however, some concern among environmental psychologists that socio-cultural processes create variation in children's environmental experience which may facilitate or hinder their cognitive development. According to Hart (1997: 27), 'Children living in different cultures, environments, and social classes are exposed to different materials, experiences, and informal teaching by their families and neighbours, and this results in the appearance of different competencies at different times'.

Moore and Young (1978) suggest that children's everyday environmental interactions are shaped by three interdependent realms of experience: physical space or the landscape; social or cultural space; and inner, psychological space. These three realms of experience influence how children encounter geographic environments, and in turn mould children's images and conceptions of peoples and places. This suggests that variations in children's exposure to, and images of, environments are shaped by many variables including social relationships, a person's gender, his or her cultural background, personality traits, and the qualities of the physical landscape.

As geography educators, we should become more aware of how a child's exposure to environments relates to the formation of mental images and conceptions of places. In particular, geographic educators should become attuned to the variety of social, cultural and geographic backgrounds that shape a child's everyday perspectives. These backgrounds vary considerably from one child to another, and may vary between girls and boys. In an effort to stimulate such research, this chapter examines the degree to which environmental experiences vary among adolescent boys and girls. Highlighting these differences exposes the physical and social opportunities and constraints influencing an adolescent's use of geographic space proposed by Moore and Young (1978). In turn, educators can use their knowledge of adolescent geographies to link formal geography instruction with a student's everyday world. Given such, the purpose of this article is to present preliminary results from a case study which highlight differences in the everyday geographic experiences of adolescent males and females.

A case study was conducted in Eugene, Oregon, with 13-year-old adolescents. It was drawn from a larger action research project conducted with 'Finding A Way' teachers and one Texas Alliance for Geographic Education teacher in the autumn of 1997.[1] Preliminary results suggest that gender and social relationships influence the way in which adolescents interact with places in their communities. Specifically, the results highlight differences in how male and female adolescents get around in Eugene, the degree to which they travel from their immediate neighbourhoods, with whom they travel, the types of places to which they travel, and why they travel. The results suggest that educators should be attentive to the different kinds of informal learning opportunities boys and girls encounter in their daily environments that may complement the teaching of Geography in the formal classroom.

Gender, adolescence and geographic experience

During their development, children experience an expanding range of geographic settings. Generally speaking, children interact more closely with the spaces of their dwellings and the dwellings' immediate vicinity at younger stages of development, and by the time they reach adolescence they experience, on their own, more spatially distant places far from their dwelling (Harloff *et al.* 1998). During adolescence, the local neighbourhood and the greater metropolitan area constitute the main geographic settings within which young people experience different aspects of nature and society. However, the range in which they can travel from their homes and the nature of their experiences in place depend upon, among other variables, an adolescent's gender and social relationships.

Males and females are commonly thought to perceive and use space differently (Spain 1992). Studies suggest that female activities are associated more with private spaces such as homes and residential areas, whereas male activities are more visible in the public realm, creating gendered spaces within a community (Monk 1992; Spain 1992). Research by feminist geographers suggests that space is gendered; that is, the design and use of space is determined by ideological assumptions about gender roles (Seager 1992). However, this literature deals with adult populations and has not yet been adequately incorporated into studies on how boys and girls experience place and, in turn, acquire geographic expertise from their daily environments.

Only a few scholars have researched gender differences in a young person's exposure to geographic environments. These researchers hypothesize that differences in the socialization of males and females lead to varying degrees of environmental experiences for boys and girls (Hart 1979; Matthews 1987, 1992; Katz 1993). Hart's (1979) research suggested that boys cover larger geographic areas in their everyday play activities. Matthews (1992) documented differences in the degree to which males and females travel from home. He found that boys travel greater distances from home by themselves, and that these differences became greater with age.

Research by Katz (1993) in rural Sudan highlighted the relationship between children's daily chores and their spatial activities. Boys were allowed to roam unaccompanied far from home to gather wood, while girls were more restricted around the home area to help with domestic chores. However, these studies were conducted with very young children in small villages. Few authors have documented how male and female adolescents experience a range of geographic environments in larger, urban settings.

Understanding how males and females experience places can be explained by examining caretaker–child relationships and the social context of adolescent life in general. Adolescents negotiate their geographic experiences with their caretakers based on the opportunities and constraints presented by the physical and social landscape within which they live (Matthews 1992; Aitken 1994; Harloff et al. 1998). Adolescents are not passive recipients. Rather, they mould their everyday worlds under the guidance of their parents and other adults. Adolescents' experience of place also tends to be driven by social relationships with their peers (Medrich et al. 1982).

Experiencing the local neighbourhood is often guided by an adolescent's friendship networks and entails learning how to fit into larger groups, obey authority figures and keep distance from strangers. When adolescents are allowed to venture into the greater community with their peers, they make the transition from the private, seemingly protected world of the family to a more public, social life (Harloff et al. 1998). Typically, at the onset of her puberty, caretakers tend to be more restrictive of a female's direct interaction with a community, based on the perception that girls encounter greater opportunities to be harmed or injured in the public realm (Katz 1993).

Thus, research suggest that males and females may interact with different types of places in a city as a function of socially defined roles unique to girls and boys in a particular society (see, for example, Hart 1979). The primary hypothesis cited in the literature is that social relationships and gender-specific societal roles explain the private and restricted nature of environmental experiences for adolescent females (Katz 1993). Yet, this conjecture is not well studied from a spatial or geographic perspective with adolescent populations. Little is known about how, why, or where boys and girls roam in any given community, or whether the concept of gendered space can be applied to adolescent life.

According to Katz (1993: 88), 'The notions that access to and control of space are greater for males than females is so commonplace that they remain largely unexamined'. This research seeks to understand where boys and girls spend time, what types of places they travel to and why, how they get there, and with whom they travel. In this regard, the term *geographic experience* has multiple elements. First, geographic experience includes activity space (i.e. the spatial patterns created by a person's activities) (Porteous 1977). Second, geographic experience includes the notion of home range (i.e. the area beyond the home base which is habitually traversed) (Porteous 1977). Third, geographic experience includes an analysis of the characteristics of places visited. Finally, how adolescents get around and with whom complement the analysis of geographic experience. Studying the nature of a teenager's geographic experience helps expose the variety of environments boys and girls encounter in their daily lives, and such knowledge may facilitate the teaching of Geography.

Teachers and students as researchers

The methodology and data analysis techniques used in the study of students in Eugene, Oregon, derive from the research design of a larger 'Finding a Way' research project on adolescent life, 'Teens in Space: Mapping Everyday Geographies'.[2] The model employed in this larger study is based on a collaborative, participatory research design that invites both teachers and students to be researchers. The research model rests on the notion that the creation of knowledge pertaining to geographic education results from a dynamic collaboration among students, teachers and academic researchers. Using this approach, multiple aspects regarding the study of geographic education can be simultaneously researched, covering diverse geographic settings and student populations. The model facilitates a dialogue among teachers, students and researchers about geography teaching and learning.

In accordance with this model, and with the help of the teachers in the study, I created a learning activity that asked students to gather, map and analyse their everyday travel patterns.[3] The learning activity incorporates the national geography standards in *Geography for Life* (Geography Education Standards Project 1994) and exemplifies the philosophies of the 'Finding A Way' project by including gender in the discussion of traditional geography content and promoting gender-sensitive teaching strategies.

During the study, teachers were responsible for implementing the lesson plan in the classroom and monitoring its success in elevating the interest and achievement of students in Geography. This process created a dialogue between the teachers and me in regards to the effectiveness of geography teaching. Similarly the teachers were engaged in a dialogue with their students about how and what aspects of Geography they learned during the exercise. The students had a strong role in the research process, gathering data about their daily travels and providing explanations for the spatial distributions of their activities.

The teacher also served as liaison between me, as the researcher, and the students to help answer questions pertaining to the focus of this study. After producing summaries of student diaries and maps, I would send the information to the teacher and ask her to lead students in a discussion about questions I had regarding the results. I would then discuss the contents of student comments with the teacher via telephone or in person and take detailed notes.

The notion of an 'absent ethnographer' enabled the research to be conducted simultaneously in many locations. However, it also placed limitations on data inter-pretation and limited some of the analysis around a teacher's ability to relay the infor-mation to the researcher about the students' speculations and comments. Adequate funding would enable researchers to visit each site for follow-up visits and alleviate this shortcoming. None the less, this research model represents a more holistic picture of the dynamic interplay among teachers, students and academics concerning geographic education research. The model takes full advantage of the highly skilled, highly trained teachers from within 'Finding A Way' and state geographic alliance networks.

Adolescent life in Eugene, Oregon

The students participating in the study included 23 males and 23 females in an eighth-grade [Year 8] social studies class in an alternative school in Eugene, Oregon. Almost all the students in the sample are Anglo, were 13 years of age, and had lived in single-family homes in Eugene all their lives. The students resided in an economically depressed neighbourhood. Access to public transportation is via the city bus, which travels throughout the greater metropolitan area of Eugene and a number of outlying areas. During the study period no weather impediments, such as precipitation, occurred that could have limited students' travel.

For one week in October 1997, a 'Finding A Way'-trained teacher instructed students on how to keep a detailed diary of all the places they visited in Eugene.[4] The diary was presented in a chart-like format with these headings: entry number, date/time, who, what, where, when, why and how. On a daily basis, students gathered data about the types of places to which they travelled in the 'what' column (e.g. store, park, house), with whom they travelled in the 'who' column (e.g. mother, friends, alone), how they got there in the 'how' column (e.g. car, bus, walking), where exactly they travelled in the 'where' column (exact address or cross streets), and why they travelled to a particular place in the 'why' column (e.g. go shopping, visit a friend). They used the 'where' column to map the exact location of the places they visited using a detailed street map of Eugene taken from the local telephone directory.

On their maps, students were expected to correlate each location with their diary entry numbers so the researcher would be able to identify the nature of a student's travel behaviour to each place. The researcher could use the diary entry number to identify what type of place it represented; how the student got there; and with whom, when and why they travelled. The teacher mailed all student diaries and maps to the researcher. The researcher performed a content analysis of their diaries using the 'what', 'how', 'who' and 'why' columns to ascertain trends in the types of places males and females travelled to during the study period, how they got around, with whom they travelled, and why they travelled.[5]

Students' daily trips to school were excluded from the analysis. However, if a student participated in after-school programmes or special events, these locations and diary entries were included in the analysis. The content analysis revealed how many times a student travelled with their mothers or how often students travelled with their mothers or friends; and how often students travelled to places such as stores, friends' homes, or parks. These tallies are referred to as trips in the data analysis and maps, and reflect the total number of times students travelled in a particular way, with whom, and where.

Individual student maps were separated by gender group and layered on top of one another using GIS (Geographical Information Systems) software to create sets of maps differentiated by gender and land-use categories. Using the 'what' column in the diary, four land-use designations were developed that best represented the travel behaviour of adolescents in the larger study. These categories were commercial locations, residential areas, outdoor recreation/natural sites and other places (e.g. public places such as churches, public libraries and health-related facilities).

To protect the anonymity of each student, no residential locations are provided on the maps. The homes of all the students are located within the neighbourhood boundary. Sometimes a student would visit the same location more than once during the week or more than one student would visit the same location. These frequencies are illustrated on the maps as total numbers of trips and are represented by multiple dots on the maps.

In the final phase of the analysis, results were sent back to the teacher and students to seek explanations for variations in the geographic experience of males and females in Eugene. The teacher presented the maps to the students and led them through a classroom discussion in which they were asked several questions: What differences do you see in the maps? What explanations can you provide for the spatial patterns in the maps? Why do more girls/boys travel to these particular kinds of places? What do you do at these places? The researcher then discussed via telephone the contents of student comments with the teacher. These comments are woven into the analysis and complement the discussion of the themes derived from the 'why' column in student diaries.

Results

Table 24.1 presents an overview of the types of places males and females visited during the study period. The most dramatic observation was that female students travelled more frequently to commercial places than their male counterparts. On the other hand, male students travelled to a significantly greater proportion of outdoor recreation or natural sites.

Interestingly, females took a greater number of trips overall when compared to their male counterparts. At first glance, this finding is inconsistent with the idea that females spend more time in private residential places, but this seeming inconsistency may be explained in the more detailed comments below. No significant differences were seen between males and females in their travels to residential or private spaces. Males and females took relatively the same proportion of trips to more public places. Girls travelled to commercial establishments; boys travelled to outdoor recreation facilities. A discussion of student maps and diaries will help clarify why males and females travelled to particular places and will offer insight into how gender roles and social relationships play out in space in Eugene.

Figure 24.1 illustrates the spatial patterns created by differences in the number of commercial places girls and boys travelled to in Eugene. Those circles representing two or more trips generally reflect more than one student travelling to the same location. Although girls took a greater proportion of trips to commercial establishments, the spatial pattern of their activities tends to be clustered within their immediate neighbourhood. Boys took significantly fewer trips to commercial establishments and many of their spatial activities occurred outside of their immediate neighbourhood. The discrepancy between the activity patterns of boys and girls shown in Figure 24.1 can be explained by examining an adolescent's activities in commercial establishments.

The northern section of the neighbourhood is an area of multi-purpose strip malls including grocery and clothing stores and fast-food restaurants. Not surpris-

Table 24.1 Overview of places visited by adolescents in Eugene, Oregon, by gender and land-use category

Category	Females		Males		Difference of proportions
	Trips	%	Trips	%	
Commercial	88	39	27	16	23[a]
Residential	75	33	61	35	1
Outdoor recreation	28	12	54	31	19[a]
Other	36	16	31	18	2
Total	227	100	173	100	

Note
a   Significant at p <0.0125 adjusted for four comparisons.

ingly, girls cited shopping and eating as a major reason for going to these places. Other commercial establishments shown in Figure 24.1 represent several female students' attendance in structured after-school activities such as self-defence classes and ballet lessons. During the classroom discussion, girls stated that they generally use commercial places to 'hang out' and socialize with their friends. However, there was also some discussion among females that going on errands with their parents to commercial places was highly desirable. Some of the female students felt that travelling with their mothers enabled them to go places 'if their friends were busy'. According to some girls, parents would not allow them to go places without being accompanied by friends or adults. Running errands, usually with their mother, gave girls the opportunity to leave the house.

Running errands partially explains the cluster of trips within the immediate neighbourhood. As the literature suggests, parent–child negotiations may be influential in guiding the nature of a female's daily activities and, subsequently, her spatial experiences. Similarly, social networks or peer relationships were influential in guiding a girl's travel behaviour to commercial establishments.

The distribution of trips taken by males to commercial places was less clustered. This can be explained by the degree to which males frequented commercial establishments and by the type of activities motivating their travel behaviour. According to male students, the main reason for going to commercial establishments related to leisure activities such as bowling, seeing movies and playing video games. These types of activities are largely found outside of the students' immediate neighbourhood and help explain the higher number of circles in the greater metropolitan area.

Several of the boys stated that they go to the mall to 'flirt with girls', and others echoed the girls' statements about using commercial establishments as places to 'hang out' with their friends. In this regard, commercial establishments facilitated social interaction within and between gender groups. However, boys did not run errands to stores with their parents like the girls described in their travels. Male students confessed that 'going to the grocery store with your mom is not a cool thing to do'. Whereas girls viewed running errands with their mother as a positive

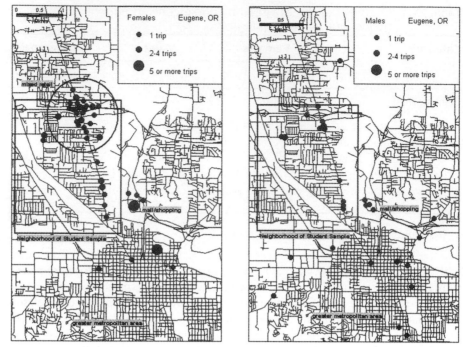

Figure 24.1 Commercial sites visited, by gender

geographic experience, males tended to 'get out of it' because of its socially unappealing consequences. Therefore, child–caretaker negotiations did not necessarily lead to travel restrictions for male students, but rather tended to enable boys to visit commercial establishments for their own reasons, which generally led them to engage in activities outside of their immediate neighbourhood.

As stated earlier, an almost equal proportion of males and females visited residential sites in Eugene during the period of the study. The distribution of residential sites visited by both groups remains clustered within the study-site neighbourhood. This pattern largely reflects where the students and their friends live. The middle school in Eugene is located within the neighbourhood boundary, and many of the students live in the immediate area. This enables students to form friendship networks within a small geographic area. Very few boys travelled to residential locations outside of their immediate neighbourhood when compared to the girls. Several girls travelled to the same residential places more than once, visiting friends on a regular basis. Only a handful of the boys travelled to residential locations more than once.

Female students travelled to a diversity of residential places, visiting friends, relatives, neighbours, and other homes to babysit. Visiting relatives and babysitting often took females outside of their immediate neighbourhood, particularly in the south-east portion of the city. In their diaries and in the classroom discussion, the girls cited vague reasons for visiting friends, relatives and neighbours, such as, 'I'm going to hang out' or 'I'm going there to go there'. However, a majority of females made clear that they used residential sites as places to socialize. Girls stated they went to residential locations to 'visit with friends', 'to spend the night', 'to play', 'to do homework', and 'to party'. Many of the girls lived next door to their friends, which enabled them to travel alone. In fact, several females were allowed unlimited opportunities to visit friends nearby. This type of unsupervised travel partially explains the number of trips females took to residential sites when compared to other geographic locations. As the literature suggests, it could also imply that the private nature of a residential location is perceived by caretakers to be safer for girls travelling alone.

In their diaries, males stated equally vague reasons for visiting friends like, 'I'm bored', 'I wanted to', or 'to do something'. Several boys stated more specific reasons, such as 'to play computer games', 'to play guitar', or 'to play'. Yet, an overwhelming majority of the males travelled most often to friends or neighbours on the way to someplace else 'to pick up a friend' or 'to drop off something on their way to school'. Therefore, it may be misleading to conclude that males travelled to residential sites for extended periods of time. Rather, their trips to residential places constitute brief encounters with friends or neighbours to fulfil specific tasks. Although males and females travelled to relatively the same proportion of residential sites, the nature of their geographic experiences varied with the intention of their trips, their access to residential locations and the extent of their social networks.

Opportunities for outdoor recreation are plentiful in Eugene. Many foot, biking and hiking trails are scattered throughout the city, and given the mild climate they can be used year-round. Male students engaged in outdoor activities to a greater degree than their female counterparts. Contrary to the girls, boys travelled to outdoor recreation or natural sites largely within their immediate neighbourhood, primarily because they visit these locations on bicycles. As the participating teacher described it, 'the boys have a clear mental map of all the new bike trails in the city'. Girls, on the other hand, visited nature trails or city parks outside of their immediate neighbourhood for family outings, and often were accompanied by their mother or father in an automobile.

The distribution of outdoor recreation sites visited by female students is largely explained by the location of city parks or nature paths along the Willamette River that cuts through the heart of Eugene. According to the girls, they visited these areas 'to exercise', 'to go for a run', or 'to walk the dogs'. The use of outdoor areas is therefore tied to the social concerns of females. In addition to 'getting fit', girls visited a neighbourhood park where they could 'party' and 'see boys on skateboards'.

Sporting activities, particularly skateboarding, were the primary reasons males travelled to outdoor locations. Skateboarding led boys to frequent more undifferentiated outdoor places such as streets and parking lots where they could find paved surfaces. Adolescents often appropriate spaces to engage in activities not intended in their original design (Harloff *et al*. 1998). Skateboarding, considered a sport among the male students, was also used to 'show off' to girls and other friends in neighbourhood parks. Other sporting activities such as soccer, [American] football and baseball took place in their intended recreational settings located on school grounds and area fields. Participating in sports underlies all activities occupying males in natural or outdoor recreational locations and can be viewed as an indication of social activities deemed appropriate for their age and gender.

Typically, adolescents do not experience the entire range of neighbourhoods within a metropolitan area. Rather, they experience islands of activity in the sea of

Table 24.2 Modes of transportation used by adolescents in Eugene, Oregon, by gender category

Category	Females		Males		Difference of proportions
	Trips	**%**	**Trips**	**%**	
Automobile	172	77	89	51	26[a]
Walking	33	14	29	17	3
Bicycle	19	8	32	18	10[a]
Other	3	1	23	14	13[a]
Total	227	100	173	100	

Note
a   Significant at p <0.0125 adjusted for four comparisons.

the city (Harloff *et al.* 1998). The types of activities that lead adolescents into the greater metropolitan area include attending youth clubs or organized activities, interacting with public places such as a library or church, or to see a medical specialist. There was little difference among the male and female sample in their travel to these types of places. Travel outside of the students' neighbourhood included trips to the doctor, music lessons and church. Travel to places such as these took students outside of their immediate neighbourhood. Although adolescents can typically negotiate travel on their own in the local neighbourhood via bicycling or walking, venturing into the greater metropolitan area usually depends upon driving by parents. An overwhelming majority of students relied heavily upon their parents for travel to many of the public, commercial, residential and recreation sites described previously.

Even though most of the students' daily travels occurred within their neighbourhood in the range of places they visited, the major method of transportation used by both groups was the automobile (Table 24.2). The primary difference among gender groups was the degree to which males and females negotiated their travel themselves, rather than being a passenger in a vehicle. A significantly greater proportion of females took trips in an automobile. On the other hand, males took a significantly greater proportion of trips by bicycle or by using other modes of transportation such as a skateboard. There were no significant differences in adolescents' travels with their peers.

Female students were often accompanied by an adult in their daily travels, whether running errands, visiting relatives, or attending family outings (Table 24.3). Male students tended to engage in activities that reflected more of their own desires, such as skateboarding and bicycling to a friend's home. Although boys often relied on a parent to take them to commercial establishments outside of their immediate area, girls took a significantly greater proportion of their trips accompanied by an adult, while boys travelled significantly more often by themselves. This discrepancy, along with the large number of travels with the mother, highlights the gendered nature of caretaker–child negotiations that are likely influencing the spatial patterns found ….

Table 24.3 Adolescent travel companions in Eugene, Oregon, by gender category

Companions	Females		Males		Difference of proportions
	Trips	%	Trips	%	
Alone	19	8	40	23	15[a]
Adults	157	70	89	52	18[a]
Peers	51	22	44	25	3
Total	227	100	173	100	

Note
a   Significant at p <0.0167 adjusted for three comparisons.

Summary

The results of this study indicate that male and female adolescents frequented different types of places in Eugene, travelled in different ways and travelled with different companions, as a function of their gender and social relationships. Adolescent girls and boys had different motivations for visiting places and were placed under varying degrees of restrictions in their geographic experiences. As Katz (1993) and Hart (1979) suggest, the socialization of males and females creates variations in their daily activities and, ultimately, their activity patterns. However, boys and girls alike travelled beyond their immediate neighbourhood quite frequently. Overall, girls travelled to a greater number of places in Eugene, although they did so largely under the guidance of their parents.

As the literature claims, male adolescents were able to travel more often alone or with their peers (Hart 1979). In addition, male travel behaviour sometimes took on a quality of being in motion, rather than visiting places for an extended period of time. This observation was evident in the degree to which boys travelled to residential places on their way someplace else. Boys tended to have more freedom than girls to get to places on their own via biking, walking and skateboarding. Girls used trips with their parents to travel places, often covering great distances. The manner in which girls and boys travelled to different types of places adds further insight into our understanding of gendered space. Contrary to the literature on adults (Spain 1992), both girls and boys frequented both private residential spaces in the community and public places such as commercial establishments and outdoor recreation facilities. This does not necessarily negate the concept of gendered space as it applies to adolescents. Rather, an adolescent's daily activities, social networks and caretaker–child negotiations create distinct spatial patterns that vary by gender.

How can such knowledge of the different worlds of girls and boys be used to tap into particular strengths students acquire from transactions in their local communities? Although Moore and Young (1978) suggest a link between daily use of geographical space and images of place, students may not be consciously aware of the types of geographic knowledge they gain in their daily lives. While not the focus of this article, it is important to discuss the characteristics of an adolescent's place behaviour in Eugene as a potential source of geography learning that could be linked to classroom activities.

Given their degree of travel to commercial locations, teachers could engage girls in a discussion of economic geography to highlight their understanding of the distribution of goods and services in their community. Similarly, boys may be able to describe personal experiences with the topography or physical geography of Eugene from their travels on bicycles and skateboards to outdoor recreational sites. Our research suggests that adolescents understand the geography of 'cool places' or social hangouts, which could be linked to topics in human geography. Future research should seek to understand the specific geography content children acquire from informal learning opportunities presented in their immediate environment. For example, how do the experiences of the students in Eugene relate to the concepts in the national geography standards? What links can be made between environmental experience and a student's ability to produce mental maps or models of their own community? And finally, how does variation in the environmental exposure boys and girls receive shape their geographic expertise?

Asking students to construct and analyse their own personal geographies made them aware of factors, such as gender, influencing their exposure to places in their community. Anecdotal evidence from our classroom research project suggests that adolescents appreciate a more personal approach to learning Geography. In this regard, geographic educators should develop ways to connect the set of skills and knowledge children acquire through their personal environmental experiences to teach the more global geography curriculum within a formal classroom environment.

As our study suggests, adolescents spend most of their time interacting with the immediate neighbourhood; surrounding local areas; and, to a lesser extent, the greater metropolitan area. On the other hand, the typical geography curriculum for middle-school students asks them to analyse more distant regions and foreign lands. Therefore, while our students are more intimate with the geography of their own backyards, the formal geography curriculum demands that they move beyond this experiential domain of understanding to thinking about geographic relationships in faraway places. This in no way is meant to suggest that adolescents are unable to handle abstract knowledge or learning materials. It simply implies a pedagogical argument in favour of a geography curriculum that links a student's personal geographic experience with the study of Geography. In particular, educators and researchers should be concerned with the diverse environmental biographies shaping a student's view of the world.

Acknowledgements

I would like to thank Ginny Berkey and her students for their participation in this study. Their valuable insights and comments about the research design, process, and results were invaluable in the production of this article. In addition, this research would not have been possible without the support of Rickie Sanders and the 'Finding A Way' project staff and teachers. I salute their efforts to impact educational reform at the local and national levels.

Notes

1   'Finding A Way: Encouraging Under-represented Groups in Geography' is a three-year grant awarded by the National Science Foundation to the National Council for Geographic Education. The project trained middle-school teachers in feminist geography content and gender-sensitive teaching strategies designed to elevate the interest

and achievements of girls of all racial and ethnic backgrounds in Geography. See Monk (1997) … for more detailed information about the 'Finding a Way' project.

2   Study sites include Eugene, Oregon; Barstow, California; Iola, Kansas; Sapulpa, Oklahoma; New Braunfels, Texas; Hastings, Minnesota; and Toronto, Ontario, Canada.

3   This learning activity – The Gendered Geographies of Adolescent Life – can be obtained from the National Council for Geographic Education as part of a 'Finding A Way' module on Gendered Spaces/Gendered Places.

4   The diaries used in the overall project are an adapted version of those used in Hart's (1979) research on children and their experience of place.

5   Since the initial research project in 1997, 'Finding A Way' teachers have continued to use an updated version of the learning activity that requires students themselves to perform the content analysis of the diaries and to create maps by gender and land-use categories.

References

Aitken, S.C. (1994) *Putting Children in Their Place*, Washington DC: Association of American Geographers.

Geography Education Standards Project (1994) *Geography for Life: National Geography Standards 1994*, Washington DC: National Geographic Research and Exploration.

Harloff, H.J., Lehnert, S. and Eybisch, C. (1998) 'Children's life worlds in urban environments', in D. Gorlitz, H.J. Harloff, M. Bunter and J. Valsiner (eds) *Children, Cities, and Psychological Theories*, Berlin: Walter de Bruyter.

Hart, R. (1979) *Children's Experience of Place*, New York: Irvington Publishers.

—— (1997) *Children's Participation: The Theory and Practice of Involving Young Citizens in Community Development and Environmental Care*, New York: United Nations Children's Fund.

Katz, C. (1993) 'Growing girls/closing circles', in C. Katz and J. Monk (eds) *Full Circles: Geographies of Women over the Lifecourse*, London: Routledge.

Matthews, M.H. (1987) 'Gender, home range and environmental cognition', *Transactions of the Institute of British Geographers* (new series) 12: 43–56.

—— (1992) *Making Sense of Place: Children's Understanding of Large-Scale Environments* Maryland: Barnes and Noble Books.

Medrich, E.A., Roizen, J.A., Rubin, V. and Buckley, S. (1982) *The Serious Business of Growing Up*, Berkeley: University of California Press.

Mitchell, L.S. (1991) *Young Geographers*, New York: Bank Street College.

Monk, J. (1992) 'Gender in the landscape: Expressions of power and meaning', in K. Anderson and F. Gale (eds) *Inventing Places: Studies in Cultural Geography*, Melbourne: Longman Cheshire.

—— (1997) 'Finding a Way', *New Zealand Journal of Geography* 104: 7–11.

Moore, R.C. and Young, D. (1978) 'Childhood outdoors: Toward a social ecology of the landscape', in I. Altman and J.F. Wohlwill (eds) *Children and the Environment*, New York: Plenum.

Porteous, J.D. (1977) *Environment and Behaviour*, Reading MA: Addison-Wesley Publishing Company.

Seager, J. (1992) 'Women deserve spatial consideration (or geography like no one ever learned in school)', in C. Kramarae and D. Spender (eds) *The Explosion: Generations of Feminist Scholarship*, New York: Teachers' College Press, Columbia University.

Spain, D. (1992) *Gendered Spaces*, Chapel Hill: University of North Carolina Press.

25 Facilitating research in geographical and environmental education

Ashley Kent

Increasing numbers of teachers are nowadays engaging in educational research as a part of higher degree work. MA, MEd, MPhil and PhD qualifications have become an accepted route for professional development and advancement. Degrees in curriculum studies and educational management have, of late, proved particularly popular, but a number of others concern specific subject areas such as geography education.

In spite of these greater numbers, achievement of such qualifications is a considerable burden on teachers. Increasingly, as local education authority financial support has declined, teachers have had to pay their own fees, at the same time as finding that their profession has become ever more demanding, not least for middle managers who have been faced with greater administrative workloads. Successful completion of such degrees requires considerable commitment and efficient time management. This is the *raison d'être* of this chapter: that is, the identification of clear working principles to support teachers in conducting educational research. From now on, when the word 'student' is used it refers to teachers engaged in higher-degree research work.

The most common higher degree undertaken by teachers is at the MA/MEd level, and that is why this is the focus here. Since 1968, there has been an MA Geography in Education at the University of London Institute of Education. Established by Norman Graves, it continues to offer a unique qualification and professional development for geography teachers. For part-timers it is a two-year course, and nowadays requires a 25,000-word dissertation, two pieces of coursework and one examination paper. Most teachers take it part-time, but over the years full-timers, especially from overseas, have completed it within one year. The themes focused upon have varied with the concerns of different times, but most take on an action research approach: that is, the issues and concerns of teachers working in their own or similar establishments. The time available to complete such research is limited to a year, since it is usually in the second year that teachers focus on their dissertation research. This naturally restricts the scale of any such research, but none the less important insights are gained, often from case studies.

A flavour of the dissertation topics and approaches is given in the book by Graves *et al.* (1989). Interestingly, the demographic profile of students has changed over the last few years. Originally it was a course dominated by experienced teachers, often heads of department. Increasingly it tends now to be for the younger teacher recently having completed a degree and PGCE, who sees it as a way of furthering his or her professional development and a necessary qualification for advancement. Teachers consciously wish to complete the degree before they are engaged in burdensome head-of-department duties.

To write this chapter, I have relied on the experience and insights of my geography tutor colleagues, Norman Graves, David Lambert, Michael Naish and Frances Slater, who between them have supervised a considerable number of such MA-level research students. To frame our conversations, I put forward the headings listed below and these provide the structure for the rest of this chapter. I am most grateful to my colleagues for agreeing to be interviewed, thereby allowing me to communicate their often shared insights, which I feel are most valuable for tutors and tutees alike engaged in MA/MEd-level geography education research.

- Identifying an area of interest/finding a research question
- Choice of methodology and appropriate data collection techniques
- Literature search/reading around
- Time schedule/deadlines
- Starting to write/draft chapters
- Meetings/tutorials – role of the tutor
- Pitfalls/mistakes to avoid
- 'Doing it' successfully – tips/strategies.

A relatively recent development at the Institute of Education has been the provision of research training/techniques sessions for students up to PhD level. In this respect we in the UK have been well behind research training offered in the USA. In the MA Geography in Education course, in particular, there is now a 'Research and Research Methods' module over a ten-week period in the spring term, which addresses some of the methodological issues facing students and leans heavily on examples from dissertation research already completed. Panels of past students and homework tasks on earlier dissertations have been popular and are seen to be valuable.

A growing literature is now at the disposal of such researchers. These vary from the short, manageable and accessible, such as Bell (1987) and the Rediguide series from Nottingham University School of Education (now sadly out of print), to the more demanding and complex, such as Burgess (1985, 1986), Cohen and Manion (1994) and Tesch (1990).

It is my intention that this brief chapter will offer practical guidelines and help to those tutors and tutees struggling with the challenge of conducting or supporting research into geography education. Clearly the scale and level of originality of an MPhil or PhD is greater, but all the working principles mentioned here are, it could be argued, just as appropriate for that level of research.

Finding a focus

Educational research has an unfortunate and somewhat misleading image, not least with teachers. It is felt to be something esoteric and 'out there', whereas in reality most MA-level research is highly focused, practical and based upon school realities. However, such research is a new way of working, and something of a culture shock, for those intimately involved in schools. It requires a critical, more distant look at the education system, and it is therefore helpful for a student to be well engaged on a higher degree course before making decisions about research focus. Lectures generate possible avenues for exploration, as do conversations with tutors and fellow students. These early experiences broaden a student's conceptual understanding of education and build confidence, which are vital. Indeed one colleague spoke of the necessity to get over the 'confidence hump', not least so that the 'level' of writing will be seen to be of the requisite standard!

Most vital in determining a research focus is to identify a real interest, or a 'burning interest', as it was described to me. Very often that is likely to be concerned with students' professional lives and the problems and challenges associated with them. Tutors may in some cases feel the need to 'steer' this decision-making process heavily. For instance, they may well be aware of a current issue or concern that merits inquiry or on which previous research has been undertaken but further work is still needed. On the other hand, some students may not need or may even resent such a 'heavy steer'.

Particularly practical advice from my colleagues included the importance of not making a decision on focus too early, indeed considering at the start of the process a range of broad research avenues and keeping these going as long as necessary. Also important was to look at previous dissertations to get a 'feel' for style, organization, methodology and the like.

Similarly important is seen to be the opportunity of meeting with earlier researchers and discussing their approach and ways of coping. This can be immensely reassuring for students. Equally, fellow students and tutors are important sounding boards for research ideas, particularly when a brief written statement of a research focus can form the basis for discussion.

The approach to take

The choice of methodology and related data-collection techniques is an important one for any researcher. An unfortunate and inaccurate assumption made by many students is that the only approach possible is the 'hard', quantitative, scientific one. They are often pleasantly surprised that 'softer', more qualitative approaches have become both accepted and more common. The challenge for the latter, however, is the way of analysing the data collected. This is often not straightforward and needs to be the basis for tutorial discussions. Overall, as far as choice of methodology is concerned, the tutor's job is to widen the student's knowledge of possible approaches and methods of collecting data.

The choice of approach is made easier if a precise and focused research question is posed. Too many questions can be diverting and make the research unmanageable. Often students have over-ambitious research proposals, and these need considerable reduction through tutorial advice.

Pragmatism and manageability have to be the guiding principles in shaping the research design, since most researchers have little more than a year to complete such research part-time. As one colleague put it, 'You can't get perfection in data collection and it must be modest according to what can be achieved.' This practical reality determines the scale of survey or experiment, and a case study therefore has important advantages. Time available, the statistical and other expertise of the researcher, and access to resources at school will all determine the research approaches possible.

Perhaps the most important advice of all is that the research focus comes first and will determine the methodology adopted.

Written guidance on research approaches and data-collection techniques exists in an expanding literature, but previous dissertations can be studied profitably for the methodological debates written in some of them. Research approaches are new concepts to students, which is why some sort of formal research training is needed. A particularly helpful model for structuring curriculum-oriented research used by two colleagues is Bastiani and Tolley (n.d.).

Reading round

Time is the greatest single bugbear for students engaged in geography education research, particularly for those who are fully employed elsewhere. Reading is a particular problem and some advocate attempting to ask for time from employers to undertake it. Most critical is the reading undertaken at the start of the research process, since that will strongly influence the form the research eventually takes. Here a tutor's role as guide is important; in addition, many of my colleagues advocate a computer search as the first step to take. Although there is the danger of throwing up too much literature, and a good deal of it inappropriately American, the choice of a few key words can generate vital early reading and influence thinking about research designs. Equally, the very act of devising the key-word search is an important element of the research process and a useful discipline to get students to focus on the essences of the work.

Apart from tutors' advice on reading, there is often a need to consult specialists. Those in curriculum studies, media studies and educational psychology are the colleagues most used by Institute of Education students. They can point out readings from quite different disciplines and perspectives.

When undertaking relevant reading, my colleagues suggest that the 'bread and butter' skills of literature searching (in other words tracing back references, developing a systematic card index and writing everything down, including quotations) are vital if the writing stage is to go well.

So important is this reading-round stage of the research process, according to one colleague, that it can be the cause of borderline or failed dissertations. All the more reason therefore to build in reading time to the research schedule, remembering that books are rarely available in multiple copies nowadays in higher education, faced as it is by greater student numbers and pegged-back budgets. There is an important case here for ordering books and checking their availability ahead of time.

Making and meeting deadlines

Making out a firm time schedule and sticking to it as far as possible are advocated by all my colleagues. The schedule provides an important stimulus through an agreed set of time deadlines to make sure the work is completed. Working back in time from the bound and finished dissertation is one approach, and insisting on an early timetable as the basis for seminars is another. Some students need much less structure and 'heavy steering' and more encouragement than anything else. Given the time constraints on such research, the problem is that, as one colleague put it,

'Creativity doesn't work to time schedules'. One tutor's tactic is to organize tutorials only when the next phase of a schedule is completed and, in particular, a piece of writing has been produced. Seminars on a personal basis are profitably based on written work prepared for them. 'Keeping to deadlines is vital,' argued one colleague, whereas another felt that it was those students who started to write early who tended to complete, and not to fail to finish, the research.

Starting to write

The act of beginning to write is clearly critical. Sometimes tutors ask for an early draft on the research topic and why it interests the student, so as to give an early indication of the level and style of writing. An outline of the research and a part of a chapter are regarded as important early objectives, since 'Writing at an early stage is absolutely crucial', as a colleague remarked. Students possibly find this first putting of pen to paper the most demanding of all tasks. They lack confidence and struggle at first over the 'refining, recreating, revisiting' process. Usually students devise their own chapter headings, but in some cases tutors need to help by providing these.

Early, detailed constructive feedback on written work is much appreciated by students, although some expect every word to be read, sometimes more than once, which is often impossible. Others only proffer a selection of their work for tutors to comment upon. It is sensible for at least an early chapter to be looked at by a tutor to ensure that points are being communicated effectively. 'I haven't written anything like this since college' is a regularly heard remark and hides considerable anxiety – often unjustified.

Meetings

Regular meetings with a research supervisor are sources of encouragement and motivation and can also act as helpful deadlines. The personal relationship that often develops between tutor and tutee can be an important support for the student. If there is a mutual expectation for written work to form the basis of the meetings, and particularly if the work is submitted in advance of the meeting, then there is a clear stimulus for the student to produce work of quality, to be scrutinized and on time. 'To be critical yet supportive with this writing' was how one tutor put the tutor's role. Often the early meetings are organized and instigated by the tutor, and further dates are decided at those meetings. Equally, at each meeting the agenda for the next meeting needs to be discussed, and in particular the progress to be made by then. A letter is usually sent by a tutor to a student about whose progress little has been heard.

Interestingly, no formal training in the skills of tutoring are provided for tutors and most have to 'learn on the job', so to speak. Tutoring courses are run, however: for instance, by R.G. Burgess at Coventry.

Clearly, tutors see meetings as part supportive and part goading. As one tutor remarked, one 'needs to harass students a bit, particularly with part-timers, to produce something regardless of quality … since there is a fear of putting pen to paper … once that starts it tends to get easier.'

Pitfalls

The overriding problems seem to be:

- over-ambitious research objectives;
- too many research questions;
- too much and diverse data; and
- a lack of clarity in the statement of research question.

One tutor argued that students need to go through the painful and relatively lengthy business of devising a research methodology, since short cuts by the tutor can foreclose various options too quickly, so that the student fails to have a full grasp of the research exercise. This can be related to the small minority of students who are over-keen to finish it all too quickly, and thereby do not give sufficient reflection to the research and critical awareness to the proposals.

Overall anxiety can be a serious pitfall. It can cause students to worry about 'negative' results – research findings just as vital as those which confirm one's expectations! It can cause a felt need for constant reassurance and, from the tutor's perspective, near-harassment.

Strategies

Most strategies have been encapsulated in the previous pages, but additional suggestions include the advice to be methodical throughout: for instance, systematically keeping records of the progress of the research and reading undertaken. Furthermore, students are advised to speak to tutors and to past and present students about their research. This can lead to helpful short cuts and the realization that one is not alone in facing the challenge. Such conversations offer considerable reassurance. Another specific suggestion is formally to set aside a time in the week for research and stick to it! However, probably the most recurring theme in my conversations with fellow tutors was the need for research to be, on the one hand, both tightly focused and circumscribed and, on the other hand, not over-ambitious.

References

Bastiani, J. and Tolley, H. (n.d. but printed 1981/82) *Research into the Curriculum*, Rediguide 16, Nottingham: Nottingham University School of Education.

Bell, J. (1987) *Doing Your Research Project*, Milton Keynes: Open University Press.

Burgess, R.G. (1985) *Issues in Educational Research*, London: Falmer.

—— (1986) *Strategies of Educational Research: Qualitative Methods*, London: Falmer.

Cohen, L. and Manion, L. (1994) *Research Methods in Education*, London: Croom Helm.

Graves, N.J., Kent, W.A., Lambert, D.M., Naish, M.C. and Slater, F.A. (1989) *Research in Geography Education MA Dissertations 1968–1988*, London: University of London Institute of Education.

Tesch, R. (1990) *Qualitative Research*, London: Falmer.

Index